MW00850327

Choctaw Resurgence in Mississippi

Indians of the Southeast

SERIES EDITORS

Michael D. Green
University of North Carolina

Theda Perdue
University of North Carolina

ADVISORY EDITORS

Leland Ferguson
University of South Carolina

Mary Young
University of Rochester

Choctaw Resurgence in Mississippi

Race, Class, and Nation Building in the
Jim Crow South, 1830–1977

KATHERINE M. B. OSBURN

University of Nebraska Press
Lincoln & London

© 2014 by the Board of Regents of the University of Nebraska

Acknowledgments for the use of copyrighted material appear on pages xi–xiv, which constitute an extension of the copyright page.

Publication of this volume was assisted by the Virginia Faulkner Fund, established in memory of Virginia Faulkner, editor in chief of the University of Nebraska Press.

All rights reserved

Manufactured in the United States of America

Library of Congress Cataloging-in-Publication Data

Osburn, Katherine M. B.

Choctaw resurgence in Mississippi : race, class, and nation building in the Jim Crow South, 1830–1977 / Katherine M. B. Osburn.

pages   cm — (Indians of the Southeast)

Includes bibliographical references and index.

ISBN 978-0-8032-4044-5 (cloth: alk. paper)
ISBN 978-0-8032-7387-0 (pbk: alk. paper)
ISBN 978-0-8032-7389-4 (ePub)
ISBN 978-0-8032-7390-0 (mobi)
ISBN 978-0-8032-7388-7 (pdf)

1. Choctaw Indians—Mississippi—History. 2. Choctaw Indians—Mississippi—Goverment relations. 3. Choctaw Indians—Civil rights—Mississippi. 4. Self-determination, National—Mississippi. 5. Mississippi—Race relations. 6. Mississippi—Politics and government. 7. Mississippi—Social conditions. I. Title.

E99.C8O74 2014

976.004'97387—dc23

2013049977

Set in Adobe Garamond by L. Auten.

To Charlie, love of my life since 1973

Grow old along with me,
The best is yet to be,
The last of life, for which the first was made.

—ROBERT BROWNING, "Rabbi Ben Ezra"

Contents

Illustrations

Series Preface

At the beginning of the twenty-first century, we often use the word "miracle" to describe the Mississippi Choctaws. Examining their history before the "miracle," Katherine M. B. Osburn reveals that the achievements of these people do not really constitute a miracle. Refusing to remove when the United States forced the Choctaw Nation west in the 1830s, the Mississippi Choctaws struggled tirelessly for their right to remain in Mississippi, for their economic survival, for the preservation of their identity as Choctaws, for education, for land, for federal recognition and services, and, most importantly, for their right to manage their own affairs. They did so by skillfully manipulating Mississippi politicians and using white supremacy to their own advantage. By focusing on how Mississippi Choctaws negotiated race, Osburn tells a quintessential story of Indians in the American South. At the same time, it is a story of unparalleled success. When they finally were able to exercise tribal sovereignty, largely free of meddling by federal bureaucrats and local politicians, Mississippi Choctaws created an economic system that has sustained their people and their culture. Osburn has written an enormously important book about a tribe whose accomplishments are often noted but whose history is barely understood. We welcome it in the series Indians of the Southeast.

Theda Perdue
Michael D. Green

Acknowledgments

My interest in the Mississippi Choctaws began about a decade ago when Theda Perdue asked me about my second book. I told her that I did not yet have a project and she suggested this one. "But Theda," I replied, "I'll have to learn the entire field of southern history in order to do that." "Yes, you will," she replied. "You'd better get started." So I did. Writing a book in a field for which I had only minimal preparation while carrying a four-four load in a service department seemed overwhelming. Fortunately, the scholars of Southeastern Indians are exceedingly helpful and generous with their time and expertise. For their guidance in the very early stages of this project (while I was still just trying to piece together the story) I thank Greg O'Brien, Jamey Carson, John Finger, and Dan Usner. Dan's assistance was especially beneficial and is most deeply appreciated. Claudio Saunt also read very early drafts of this work, and his astute feedback afforded many "aha!" moments in my thinking on race. Rose Stremlau offered help in conceptualization of southern history and, more importantly, in supportive friendship as I ventured into this field.

I was privileged to attend three seminars that shaped my thinking in significant ways. One was the 2004 Newberry Library's Lannan Summer Institute at the D'Arcy McNickle Center for American Indian History. In addition to the participants in the seminar, Newberry archivist John Aubry, and Brian Hosmer and Rob Galler, director and assistant director, respectively, of the D'Arcy McNickle Center, assisted me immensely. Thanks to Lannan participant Mike Tsosie for his kind help in dealing with some challenging issues in writing Indian history. Fred Hoxie directed the seminar, read my work conscientiously, and challenged me to think about Indian history in a much more sophisticated way. His continued assistance since then has been an inspiration and a joy. The participants in the *Beyond Red Power Seminar* at Miami University in Miami, Ohio, in 2005 shared insightful comments on my chapter on the Indian New Deal. Thanks to Jessica Cattelino, Daniel M. Cobb, Tony Clark, Loretta Fowler, Don Fixico, Clara Sue Kidwell, Larry Nesper, Helen Tanner, John Troutman, and Sherry L. Smith. Special thanks to John Troutman and Dan Cobb for making music a delightful part of the seminar and of subsequent professional conferences. The National Endowment for the Humanities Summer Institute on Indians in the American South was perhaps the most collegial and productive academic seminar I have ever attended. While all the participants at that seminar enriched my thinking, Clara Sue Kidwell, David Nichols, Clyde Ellis, Susanna Michele Lee, and Malinda Maynor Lowery read drafts of chapters and provided incisive analyses along with delightful fellowship. I am especially appreciative of Larry Nesper for his insights into academia, Malinda for her fun-loving friendship, Clyde for his folksy humor and tall tales, and David for his razor-sharp wit and wry insights into life, which continue to make me laugh out loud, as does the pink cowboy hat with the silvery feather boa trim and flashing rhinestone crown that he bought me on our kitsch quest in Branson, Missouri.

Series editors Michael Green and Theda Perdue have provided beneficial criticisms and care, not only for this project but during the difficult, painful years that my father's health declined and the project languished. For walking through that dark vale with me and facilitating my slow assent out of it, I owe them, along with my dear friend Don Fixico, my eternal gratitude.

I gratefully acknowledge the financial backing of the Phillips Fund of the American Philosophical Society, the National Endowment for the Humanities, the Newberry Library Summer Institute, and the Faculty Development Fund of Tennessee Technological University.

I was proud to be a member of a group of steadfastly professional scholars that made up the Tennessee Tech history department, and am especially thankful for the man who was my department chair during this project, Jeff Roberts. Jeff was enormously encouraging of my research and scheduled my teaching to make sure I had the maximum time to write. Interlibrary loan librarian Sonya Bowman provided me with numerous sources critical to this work, and I thank her for all her hard work. At Tennessee Tech I was also privileged to work under administrators of unfailing integrity—former dean of arts and sciences Jack Armistead, current dean of arts and sciences Paul Semmes, and associate dean of arts and sciences Kurt Eisen, all of whom put the faculty first in university governance and supported this research project. Singular thanks to the former president of Tennessee Tech, Robert Bell, for his unflinching defense of academic freedom even when it cost him.

I also thank Rita Barnes, Carolynn Johnston, Nancy Shoemaker, Donna Martin, Pippa Holloway, Kathryn Abbott, Kris Lindenemyer, and Jeff Corntassle for their comments on various portions of the manuscript. The graduate students in my 2012 American Indian Identity Seminar at Arizona State University—Aaron Bae, Alysa Broughton, John Goodwin, Grace Hunt Watkinson, Laura Keller, Farina King, William Kiser, and Seth Koury—all sharpened my thinking about issues of identity through our most stimulating dialogues about the construction of knowledge. Thanks to Justin Weiss for all the help with my illustrations. The two scholars that read my book for the University of Nebraska Press provided effective critiques, as did my intrepid editor, Matt Bokovoy, who attacked my gerunds ferociously and gave me the extensions I needed to deal with all the upheavals that life threw at me. I am also beholden to editorial assistant Heather Stauffer for her guidance on formatting and pictures and to the sharp copyeditor, Lona Dearmont, who saw the errors and typos that I missed and corrected them.

I appreciatively acknowledge permission to reprint revised portions of this manuscript that have appeared in the *Journal of the Gilded Age and Progressive Era* (Cambridge University Press), *Ethnohistory* (Duke

University Press), *Southern Cultures* (Center for the Study of the American South, University of North Carolina, Chapel Hill), and *Beyond Red Power: Indian Activism in the Twentieth Century* (School for Advanced Research Press).

It was a joy and an honor to work with Choctaw archivists Amanda Bell and Sonja Monk and with my Indian friends of all nations, including Choctaw, on the Advisory Council on Tennessee Indian Affairs. I learned so much from all of you and am grateful for your patience, your kindness, and the insights into Indian activism and identity that you provided.

Finally, I offer my deepest heartfelt appreciation to my family—to my daughter, Jennie, who always encouraged my work, even when it meant moving far away from her, and to my brilliant grandson, Jacob, who has brought tremendous joy to my life. Most of all, however, I would like to express my thankfulness to my loving husband and partner in life and in the production of this book. Over several years, Charlie drove me many miles to archives, stood at numerous copiers while I tagged documents, read reels of microfilm searching old newspapers for me, and helped me clarify and refine my thinking by asking me insightful questions about my work. He read numerous drafts of these chapters, proofed it for errors, and was willing to upend his life and move to Arizona State University for my job. This study is very much a result of his efforts, and it is to him I lovingly dedicate this book.

Choctaw Resurgence in Mississippi

Introduction

In the summer of 2004, my husband, Charlie, and I visited the reservation of the Mississippi Band of Choctaw Indians in Philadelphia, Mississippi, to meet with the director of research, Creda Stewart. Ms. Stewart graciously suggested several sources for research and then remembered that the Choctaws' Indian agent might be of assistance. She could not recall his name, however, and it took several inquiries to come up with it. This striking moment illustrated how tangential the Bureau of Indian Affairs (BIA) had become in Choctaw life. The Mississippi Choctaws manage their own affairs with little interference from the BIA. Self-determination has sparked the political and economic revitalization known as the "Choctaw Miracle," when, beginning in 1979, the Mississippi Band of Choctaw Indians built a thriving reservation economy and became a leading employer in east-central Mississippi.[1]

Choctaws credit Phillip Martin, who entered tribal government in 1957, with lifting them out of poverty with his resolute vision for economic development.[2] Martin's accomplishments were undeniably remarkable, but he was building on a century-long tradition of savvy political activism. This study locates the Choctaws' tribal resurgence in that long struggle by analyzing the ways in which Choctaws proclaimed and performed their Indian identity for their political allies amid the class and racial conflict in rural Mississippi.

The Mississippi Band of Choctaws descends from Choctaws who remained in Mississippi following the removal of the Choctaw Nation to Indian Territory (later Oklahoma). Their survival as a distinct community of Choctaws living apart from the Choctaw Nation began with Article 14 of the 1830 removal treaty, the Treaty of Dancing Rabbit Creek. This provision had promised that Choctaws who wished to remain in Mississippi could apply for allotments of land and live as citizens of the state. Several thousand Choctaws had attempted to claim these lands, but the government failed to follow through, leaving the Choctaws landless and impoverished.

Nevertheless, over a century and a half, the Mississippi Choctaws slowly rebuilt their lives. They maintained their identity as a third racial group in a biracial legal system. They also persuaded the federal government to supply them with services and lands, created a functioning tribal government, and established a prosperous reservation economy, all in defiance of the overwhelming poverty and racial prejudice of the rural South. The success of this tribal resurgence was contingent upon federal recognition of the Choctaws as a lawful Indian tribe with a government-to-government relationship with the United States.

Between removal and rebirth, officials at all levels of government debated the Choctaws' tribal status, focusing on race, culture, Mississippi citizenship, and connection to the removed Choctaw Nation. These deliberations produced conflicting rulings. Sometimes government bureaucrats conceded the Choctaws' racial and cultural Indianness while denying their political and legal legitimacy as an Indian polity because they were a "remnant" of the officially recognized Choctaw Nation in the West. Other times officials declared the Choctaws to be assimilated citizens of Mississippi with no Indian identity. The U.S. Supreme Court finally settled these questions in *United States v. John* (1977). The justices held that regardless of their degree of assimilation and despite their separation from the Choctaw Nation of Oklahoma, Choctaws in Mississippi were an Indian tribe.[3]

The Supreme Court ruling finally acknowledged what Choctaws had always said: *Chahta Hapia Hoke* (We are Choctaw), meaning "we are members of a distinctive community sharing a unique culture and history; we are an Indian nation." Irrespective of how policy makers and politicians regarded them over the centuries, Choctaws remaining in Mississippi held a sense of their collective identity as an Indian nation holding treaty rights.

Although the idea of nationalism is a European construct, many indigenous peoples have embraced it as a way to distinguish themselves from other minority groups. The U.S. Supreme Court ruling that Indian tribes were domestic dependent nations in *Cherokee Nation v. Georgia* (1831) afforded the legal sanction for Indian nationalism.[4] Until the mid-twentieth century, Choctaws who continued to live in Mississippi after removal did not have the institutions of governance that characterize domestic dependent nations. They did, however, retain a shared sense of themselves as set apart from their neighbors by kinship, language, ancestry, a deep connection to their sacred homelands, and unique customs and world views.[5] Politically, they were Indians holding treaty rights and therefore entitled to as much self-determination as any other Indian nation. Choctaw activism over the nineteenth and twentieth centuries was ultimately about rebuilding an Indian nation from a so-called remnant.[6]

Estimates of the number of Choctaws in Mississippi at the end of removal in 1833 ranged from four thousand to seven thousand, but by the twentieth century only a few thousand Choctaws remained.[7] The majority of Indians lived in the east-central portion of the state in ethnically distinct closed communities that marked their boundaries by Choctaw language and customs, networks of kinship, and a political identity as Indians holding treaty promises.[8] Each of these communities has its own history, and some observers have noted that they are only loosely connected into a central polity.[9] Yet they are all members of a federally recognized Indian nation that has recently achieved a notable level of self-determination.

The Choctaws accomplished this impressive renewal by skillfully lobbying Mississippi's civic leaders and politicians to pressure the federal government to fulfill their treaty promises. Choctaws gained these allies by carrying Choctaw identity into public and political spaces where they leveraged it in service of their cultural distinctiveness, assertions of their treaty rights, and protection from the worst abuses of racism. Choctaw leaders mediated the boundaries between their communities and politicians at all levels of government, reinforcing, recreating, and reifying Choctaw identity over time.[10]

Understanding this process requires investigation of how Choctaw activists engaged their supporters. How did the Choctaws negotiate the political landscape of rural Mississippi? What was their political, economic, and social standing in the biracial South? How did they construct their Indian identity around the challenges of segregation, poverty, and racism? How did their survival strategies adapt to changing conditions in rural Mississippi and the vagaries of shifting federal policies? Furthermore, why did Mississippians passionately committed to white supremacy help the Choctaws? How did the Choctaws' presence in rural Mississippi serve their political, economic, or cultural interests?

Answers to these questions reside in a close interrogation of Choctaw activism. Choctaws asserted an Indian identity in a range of venues. They affirmed their ethnicity through crafts, stickball games, dances, and tribal fairs. They acted as anthropological informants and subjects of anthropometric study, spoke with journalists, lobbied for legislation, testified before congressional committees, filed lawsuits, and instituted claims with the Indian Claims Commission. These activities acknowledged their Indianness, challenged biracial legal systems, and eventually brought about their tribal recovery. In each of these interactions, the Choctaws deployed a set of narratives of Indian history and identity that resonated with white Mississippians.

The first narrative concerned the Choctaws' military service, starting with the actions of the legendary Choctaw leader Pushmataha, who fought with Andrew Jackson in the War of 1812. Choctaw leaders proudly declared themselves descendants of this great warrior, and Mississippians likewise noted Pushmataha's heroics to remind federal officials what the entire nation owed the Choctaws. Choctaws' service to the Confederacy reinforced their standing as military heroes and reflected the martial tradition and Lost Cause—both dear to southern hearts.[11] Choctaw participation in World War I was instrumental in winning the congressional appropriation that opened the Choctaw Agency in 1918 in Philadelphia,

Mississippi, and their contribution in World War II shaped the leadership of the postwar tribal council that finally attained self-determination.

The second theme that linked the Choctaws and their white supporters was the account of Choctaw dispossession. Choctaws invoked this story to shame the federal government into action. For Mississippians, this tale supported the popular mythos of Indians as vanishing noble savages, which generated Christian compassion—a posture important to southern cultural identity. Pinning this saga of decline on the federal government and ignoring the role Mississippi settlers had played proved a bonus for politicians asserting states' rights as a marker of southern identity. Following the Civil War, Mississippians reinterpreted the Choctaws' refusal to remove (once seen as an impediment to progress) as representative of regional pride and defense of homelands against invasion. Resonance with the Lost Cause fortified Mississippi politicians' determination to support Choctaw claims.

The third topic concerned the Choctaws' racial identity, the framing of which shifted in response to historical circumstances. In order to protect their standing as Indians, Choctaws infrequently interacted with either whites or blacks, and intermarriage was rare. Because they were sensitive to the brutality of racial hierarchy, they were especially careful to distinguish themselves from African Americans.[12] When Jim Crow laws took effect late in the nineteenth century, Choctaws adopted the language of Indian blood, proclaiming themselves to be full-blooded. For their white supporters, the Choctaws' self-proclaimed racial purity and separatism were symbolic of their own racial attitudes. In addition, federally operated segregated Indian schools provided propaganda for white supremacists following the Supreme Court decision in *Brown v. Board of Education of Topeka*. Even though Choctaws called for integration into public schools in the 1960s, their traditional racial separatism and declarations of full blood were significant indicators of Indian identity at several stages during the drive for tribal rebirth.

These three narratives, interwoven into a storyline of the tragic demise of a heroic and noble people, appear in nearly every account of Choctaw activism for more than a century. Choctaws and Mississippians reiterated these themes as they navigated intersecting systems of power and influence at the local, state, and federal levels. My analysis of these interactions adds to a growing body of literature that complicates interpretations of race and class in southern history.[13]

As Indians asserted a third racial identity, white southerners were forced to grapple with a people who did not fit their biracial model. That many white supremacists held positive (albeit condescending) attitudes toward Indians demonstrated a degree of elasticity in the racial binary that characterized the Jim Crow South.[14] Issues of class also affected Choctaws' relationships with their neighbors, for federal funds created a patronage economy in a deeply impoverished region. This economic arrangement exacerbated existing class tensions, the study of which has only recently become part of tribal histories.[15] Generally, the Choctaws were able to work these rivalries to their advantage.

Analysis of how Mississippians interacted with Choctaws also elucidates another broad theme that characterizes southern history: states' rights. The willingness of Mississippians to feed at the trough of federal patronage underscores how commitment to states' rights and vilification of the federal government were sometimes more slogans of political expediency than deeply held principles.[16] By focusing on the relationships between Choctaws and southern politicians, this book also highlights the importance of Indian political activism at the state and local levels.

As Indian policy is the province of the federal government, scholars have traditionally paid scant attention to Indian activism at the state level.[17] The Mississippi Choctaws' case establishes how power and influence in Indian affairs can flow from the state to the federal level, and that support for Indians can sometimes come from the most unlikely sources. It also locates Choctaws in the context of poor communities in the rural South and reveals how both Indians and the federal government shaped local political and economic relationships in the region.

Apart from their relationship to policy makers, the Choctaws emerge from the historical records as a people with complex layers of political identity.[18] Choctaws who remained in Mississippi traded their indigenous polity for the right to stay in the land of their ancestors, which represented the spiritual foundation for being Choctaw. Choctaw creation stories articulate their deep connection to an earthen mound called Nanih Waiya, which contains the bones of their revered ancestors.[19] The promise that they could remain in these consecrated lands lay at the heart of their political organizing. Although the Choctaw nation had been removed, Choctaws believed that claims to their homelands (supported by the Treaty of Dancing Rabbit Creek) gave them a collective juridical identity in the absence of institutions of governance. They fought for these claims for over a century.

As they engaged this battle, Choctaws had to negotiate varying political identities with politicians and policy makers. Both the 1832 Mississippi Constitution and Article 14 had decreed them to be citizens of Mississippi. It is impossible to know for certain how Choctaws interpreted state citizenship, but some of them occasionally embraced this status for political purposes. Choctaws exercised their rights as Mississippi citizens when they hired attorneys to sue for their land claims. In petitions to Congress immediately following removal, Choctaws also presented themselves as citizens of Mississippi, perhaps to indicate compliance with Article 14. As Choctaws lobbied their elected officials for land and self-determination, they behaved as though they were constituents despite their disfranchisement under Jim Crow laws. Choctaws thus utilized certain rights and privileges of state citizenship to reinforce their Indian identity.

Likewise, Choctaws manipulated notions of race to their political advantage. As a people who owned slaves before removal, Choctaws had adopted racial hierarchy early in the nineteenth century. Although Choctaw petitions to Congress in the years immediately following removal did not reference their degrees of Indian blood, by the late nineteenth century, Choctaws proclaimed themselves to be "full-blooded Choctaw Indians." This monograph explores how Choctaw racial identity evolved, both in response to Jim Crow and federal requirements for blood quantum, and as a strategy to distinguish themselves from throngs of pretenders attempting to traffic in Choctaw identity.[20]

Choctaws again modified the presentation of their public identity following World War II. By the end of the 1950s, Choctaw leaders had embraced pan-Indianism, which was a new way of expressing their political identity. They worked with the Association on American Indian Affairs and joined the National Congress of American Indians. Choctaws also recognized an affinity of interests with other Indians of the Southeast and helped to found United Southeastern Tribes (USET).[21] Simultaneously, they began to convey their demands by reference to their American citizenship, granted in 1924. As citizen Indians, they could seek the benefits of American democracy while also positioning themselves as an Indian nation entitled to self-determination. Broader changes in civil rights legislation and in federal poverty programs assisted Choctaw nationalism in the postwar period.

In the early 1960s, the economic, social, and political landscape of America began to shift in ways that allowed Choctaws to achieve their goals of economic development and self-rule. The 1964 Civil Rights Act set the stage for greater inclusion of Choctaws in the economies near their communities. More importantly, the Great Society provided resources necessary for Choctaws to build a truly independent government and economy on Choctaw lands.[22] This movement toward autonomy unsettled some state and local officials.

State courts challenged Choctaw authority over their reservation in the 1970s and put their tribal renaissance at risk. As they had since the 1830s, Choctaws mounted legal rebuttals, which ultimately secured solid federal recognition. When the U.S. Supreme Court ruled that the Mississippi Band of Choctaw Indians were a legitimate Indian tribe in 1977, they sanctioned over a century of nation building.

In the early nineteenth century, the citizens of Mississippi removed the majority of Choctaws because they regarded them as impediments to economic development and white nationalism. In the mid-twentieth century, the descendants of those "impediments" transformed a failed rural economy into a far more successful one. The story of how this came to be begins at a treaty ground on a stream which the Choctaws called the "Creek Where Rabbits Dance."

CHAPTER ONE

From the First Removal to the Second, 1830–1898

In 1830 agents of the United States government convinced the Choctaw Nation to sign a removal treaty by inserting a provision, Article 14, allowing some Choctaws to stay behind on allotments of land as citizens of Mississippi. The federal government failed to follow through, however, and the Choctaws who remained lost their lands. As they resisted dispossession, the Choctaws asserted a composite legal identity as both citizens of the state and Indians with a unique relationship to the federal government. They publicly leveraged their ethnicity to uphold their Article 14 claims and defend themselves against racism. In the mid-nineteenth century, they laid the foundations of the political rhetoric and strategies that they would employ over their century-long struggle for tribal rebirth.

The Choctaws' neighbors and Mississippi officials constructed a narrative about the Choctaws that suited their purposes. Settlers, speculators, and Choctaws fought over the Choctaw cession. Mississippi citizens initially gave lip service to Choctaw claims but nonetheless dispossessed the Choctaws. Over the next few decades, they came to scorn the Indians as the remnant of a once-powerful race and sought the Choctaws' complete removal. After the Civil War, however, the Choctaws became symbols of many cherished southern values connected to race and regional identity. Interpretations of the Choctaws' dispossession, devised by white Mississippians in the late nineteenth century, resonated well into the twentieth. These two intertwining tales began with the Treaty of Dancing Rabbit Creek.

Dispossession and Juridical Status

On September 15, 1830, Major John H. Eaton and Colonel John Coffee arrived at the council grounds near Dancing Rabbit Creek hoping to persuade the leaders of the Choctaw Nation to exchange their territory in Mississippi for lands in Indian Territory.[1] The Mississippi legislature had set the stage for removal earlier in the year by abolishing all tribal governments in the state, revoking all tribal laws and customs (excluding marriage), and establishing a fine of one thousand dollars and one year's imprisonment for anyone exercising the office of "chief." To complete their extension of state sovereignty over the Choctaws, the legislature granted them "all the rights, privileges, immunities, and franchises . . . enjoyed by free white persons." Although this provision may appear enlightened, its ultimate purpose was to subject Choctaws to Mississippi laws and drive them out of the state.[2] Choctaw leaders passionately denounced this act in their national council, and some members suggested moving to avoid being subsumed under state law. Most Choctaw leaders did not want to move, however, and the council could not act without a majority.[3]

The Choctaw polity had historically consisted of three autonomous geographic regions, the Eastern, the Western, and the Southern. A head mingo (Choctaw for chief) and his council of captains governed each division. Although their people were related through matrilineal kinship and shared a common world view, the Choctaws were only loosely affiliated politically until 1826, when the leaders of the Eastern and Western divisions, David Folsom and Greenwood LeFlore, united their regions under a constitution. The Southern division, led by John Garland, joined the alliance a few months later.[4] These men had hoped that adopting a constitutional government would help them resist the expanding American state, but they were mistaken.

Many Choctaw mingoes gradually realized that their best option was to accept removal and try to set their own terms, but there was little agreement on what those might be. When Eaton and Coffee arrived at Dancing Rabbit Creek, they faced three principal chiefs at odds with each other: Greenwood LeFlore, mingo of the Western towns, Mushulatubbee, an important leader in the Eastern division, and Nittakaichee, mingo of the Southern division, all of whom endorsed removal but none of whom could speak for the entire Choctaw Nation.[5]

Whatever treaty the Choctaw leadership negotiated would have to be approved by their captains, who eschewed removal, as did the roughly six thousand Choctaws attending the deliberations. Reminding the commissioners of their military service to the United States, many Choctaws denounced removal, and the council rejected the treaty. Major Eaton replied by threatening forcible relocation, and the majority of Choctaws left the treaty grounds indignantly.[6]

Several Choctaw headmen remained, however, and signed the Treaty of Dancing Rabbit Creek.[7] Their motives were varied, but the inclusion of Article 14 was the principal reason they capitulated. This provision allowed individual Choctaws to continue living in Mississippi on allotments of land. The head of a family could receive 640 acres, an additional 320 acres for every unmarried child over age ten, and 160 acres for children under ten. Families who resided on these lands for five years acquired title in fee simple and became Mississippi citizens. Article 14 also promised that claimants "shall not lose the privilege of a Choctaw citizen, but if they ever remove are not entitled to any portion of the Choctaw annuity."[8] For Choctaws who wished to remain in Mississippi, this appeared to be a good compromise.

Racial ideology made this provision acceptable to government policy makers. They believed that the majority of Choctaws, who were ostensibly full-blood, had been deceived into resisting removal by a minority of prosperous "half-bloods," leaders of mixed Choctaw and Euro-American descent who sought to remain in Mississippi on their plantations. When full-blood leader Mushulatubbee expressed a desire to emigrate (providing that the government would appoint him chief with a substantial salary), Choctaw agent William Ward predicted that he would lead the other full-bloods to the West, and "the half-breeds could be made full citizens."[9] Policy makers believed that mixed-descent Indians could be assimilated because the presence of "white blood" made them more amenable to civilization.[10]

Racial heritage, however, meant little to the Choctaws. To the extent that they owned slaves, Choctaws embraced racial hierarchy. Yet kinship, not race, determined membership in the Choctaw polity.[11] On the eve of removal, an estimated 20 percent of the Choctaw Nation was of mixed descent, having been incorporated into the tribe through marriage, adoption, or captivity. Because the Choctaws were matrilineal, these individuals were full members of the tribe if their mothers were Choctaw. Choctaws also sometimes adopted people who chose to live among them.[12]

Ancestry did not affect either the decision to emigrate or to remain, for Choctaws of all degrees of blood followed both courses of action. Culture, not ancestry, inspired Article 14 claimants. They resisted removal because of their reverence for their homelands. Although some of these men and women held plantations and may have been partially motivated by economics, they also had spiritual connections to their property. Both well-to-do Choctaws and those of more modest means refused to leave the territory containing the bones of their ancestors and their venerated Mother Mound, Nanih Waiya.[13] Some Choctaw creation stories told of a primordial migration in which the *fabussa*, a sacred pole carried by their spiritual leader, led them to the site of a large earthen mound, Nanih Waiya. There they buried the bones of their ancestors that they had carried with them. Another version describes the Choctaws' emergence from the underworld at this Great Mother Mound. Either way, their Great Father Aba (the divine incarnation of the sun) established the Choctaws on this land and promised them a prosperous life if they remained on the bright path of his purposes.[14] For Choctaws who filed for allotments, the specter of living under Mississippi law was far less terrible than leaving this sacred site.

Estimates of the number of Choctaws remaining at the end of removal in 1833 ranged from four thousand to seven thousand people. These men and women had six months to apply to federal agent William Ward for their lands.[15] The enrollment process, however, immediately became a bureaucratic fiasco and a moral tragedy. Ward and his brother Stephen (who helped with enrollment) were frequently too drunk to function, and settlers periodically stole and altered the enrollment ledgers. Ward refused to accept most Choctaw requests for enrollment as well.[16] His final roll of allottees contained only sixty-nine families, thirty-nine of which were the children of Choctaw women and white men.[17] Several thousand Choctaws were still in need of allotments, and a political and legal conflict ensued over the Choctaw cession.

Many settlers ignored the allotment process and drove Choctaws out of their homes, claiming the land by right of preemption. Wealthy land speculators also snatched up huge tracts of Choctaw land at government auctions.[18] Most of the remaining Choctaws then withdrew to isolated areas or gathered around the homes of the few Choctaws who had retained their property. Some Choctaw leaders held their lands as payment for military service—such as Colonels Samuel Cobb, James Pickens, and Little Leader—while others had simply been lucky enough to be allotted lands. Dispossessed Choctaws pressed their claims. Examination of their activism reveals their complex interpretations of their political position in Mississippi.

Choctaws quickly filed suit for their allotments, operating under laws making them citizens.[19] Sixty-six men and women placed their marks upon documents declaring that "we, the subscribing Choctaws now being citizens of the state of Mississippi," had retained attorneys in return for one-half of their lands.[20] How these Choctaws understood state citizenship is unclear. Nevertheless, by filing court documents, Choctaws took advantage of rights granted to Mississippi citizens.

The standard narrative of Choctaws' relationship with the American legal system is that the majority of them were duped by unscrupulous lawyers who speculated in Choctaw lands.[21] Many attorneys were indeed unprincipled and cheated the Choctaws, yet filing suit for their claims also signified Choctaws' using their new status as citizens to fight back against dispossession. The Choctaws' exercise of their right to sue did not mean, however, that they adopted the ideologies that underlay state citizenship—individualism, private property, and allegiance to the Mississippi legislature.

Choctaws instead instructed their attorneys to exchange their scattered allotments for more communal ones.[22] Although he knew that Mississippi had outlawed the office of chief, Choctaw mingo Colonel Samuel Cobb claimed that a white friend had promised that "me and my people should stay in the country and that I should be their principal chief."[23] Choctaws who accepted land under the Treaty of Dancing Rabbit Creek had implicitly agreed to live under the rubric "citizen of Mississippi." By disregarding legislation that banned their culture and continuing to live under the authority of their mingoes, however, Choctaws demonstrated that they interpreted citizenship selectively, regarding it as one possible tool for self-determination.

In the early 1830s, agent Ward visited these communities to demand they disband. He threatened their members with imprisonment.[24] There is no evidence that he followed through, and local authorities generally ignored the 1830 law unless it suited a specific goal. Henry S. Halbert, who worked as an educator among the Choctaws in the late nineteenth century, documented the inconsistent ways that state citizenship operated in the years following removal. In his unpublished manuscript, "History of the Choctaw Indians East of the Mississippi," he wrote that "as soon as the state got rid of the bulk of her Indian population, the legislative act of 1830 became a dead letter. Indians could live under their tribal laws, could practice polygamy, one member of the tribe could kill another, and no action was taken by the civil authorities of the counties where these crimes were committed."[25] Halbert also noted, however, that the authorities would invoke the 1830 law when it served their purposes.[26] He illustrated this by chronicling Little Leader's scrapes with the law in another unpublished manuscript, "Life of Little Leader or Hopaii Iskitimi."

Little Leader, a successful warrior who had served with Andrew Jackson in the Redstick War, was the head mingo of Choctaws living on Sukanatcha Creek in Kemper County.[27] As payment for his military service, he had kept his property and secured adjoining lands for fourteen families under his leadership. Little Leader actively recruited followers, promising protection from removal and abuse. His growing following made some people nervous, and he was arrested twice in 1835 for allegedly planning uprisings. The charges in both cases were dismissed for lack of evidence.[28] When Little Leader's enemies finally succeeded in bringing him to trial, they discovered the limitations of their authority over the Choctaws.

In 1836 the state of Mississippi charged Little Leader with murder. Little Leader frequently bragged of his military prowess, and his peers challenged his boasting. Little Leader always assaulted his critics, and he killed at least two of them. In one of these instances there was insufficient evidence to charge him, but in the other authorities brought him to trial.[29] His court case illustrates how considerations of class and race shaped settler views of Indian citizenship.

According to Reuben Davis, the district attorney for Kemper County who prosecuted the case, Little Leader had able counsel who defended him as a "high mingo" of the Choctaws subject only to the laws of the Choctaw Nation, not those of Mississippi. It is unclear from the historical record whether Little Leader or his attorneys proposed this line of defense, but Little Leader had previously resisted arrest by citing his mingo status and his military service alongside General Andrew Jackson.[30] His continued role as chief in defiance of the law also suggested that he believed himself beyond Mississippi law.

Incongruously, Davis found this line of reasoning compelling. In his autobiography, *Recollections of Mississippi and Mississippians*, Davis argued that the Treaty of Dancing Rabbit Creek had merely transferred land: "The political status of neither [the United States nor the Choctaw Nation] was involved," he wrote, "nor did the chiefs of the nation pretend to give up their jurisdiction." He believed that Choctaw tribal laws "were still in force, and [Little Leader's] sovereign power unquestioned by the wild people who willingly submitted to his rule." Davis disregarded the 1830 law, the 1832 state constitution, and the Treaty of Dancing Rabbit Creek because he viewed the Choctaws as a separate group of people still living under their own "peculiar system of government."[31]

Davis lamented that if he "could have controlled the matter" he would not have brought charges, and he recommended a pardon as soon as he won the conviction.[32] Similarly, despite their verdict of guilty, jurors immediately petitioned the governor for a pardon. They argued that Little Leader had a right to exercise "a species of authority and power over one of his subjects," and noted his military service. One hundred and twenty-four citizens signed this document, including two sheriffs, one probate judge, and two county clerks.[33] After President Andrew Jackson added his signature, the governor pardoned Little Leader.[34] Little Leader continued to act as mingo but avoided further confrontations with the law.

The civil authorities' response to the case reflected class tensions as well as racial ideology. Davis recognized Little Leader's real offense: "He had in some way incurred the hatred of the land companies organized to purchase reservations," who had brought in a battery of attorneys to assist Davis.[35] Resentment of these speculators probably affected the outcome. The Mississippi legislature had sent a memorial to Congress in 1832 complaining indignantly that the Choctaws were "rapidly selling off [Article 14 lands] to wealthy capitalists," depriving "the poor pioneers of the wilderness . . . a fixed and permanent home," and demanding that the federal government reserve lands for these yeomen.[36] Whether these memorialists represented actual yeoman farmers is open to question. The memorial nevertheless accurately captured economic tensions behind the discord over Indian lands. Such attitudes may have prejudiced the jurors against the prosecution.

The petition for Little Leader's pardon also highlighted nuanced practices of citizenship in the early nineteenth century. Citizenship was generally subsumed under common law traditions that defined individuals' legal standing according to categories of personal status, such as master-slave, husband-wife, parent-child, and guardian-ward.[37] In this hierarchy, Indians held the personal status of racial dependents. Cultural considerations also dictated the rights and privileges of citizenship, and states restricted the full benefits of citizenship to those who met the standards of civilization as defined by the Anglo middle and upper classes.[38] Even though the Choctaws' legal status was equal to that of free whites, Little Leader's continued Indian identity signaled his neighbors to regard him as someone living outside state laws. Ideologies of Indian blood undergirded this view.

Little Leader was a full-blood Indian and thus lacked the white blood that would make him acceptable as an equal fellow citizen. His style of living highlighted his racial identity. Although he owned a fine home and slaves, he dressed in traditional Choctaw clothing, wearing leggings and a turban, and he adorned himself with "silver gorgets to the belt and silver bracelets and earrings." He sponsored Indian dances, held stickball games, and generously distributed goods to his followers, in keeping with the redistributive roles of headmen.[39] Little Leader lived as a Choctaw mingo, a status he clearly believed was neither impeded by Mississippi laws nor contingent upon legal recognition of a Choctaw Nation in Mississippi.

Yet Little Leader also did not seem to view his position as a Choctaw headman and his Mississippi citizenship as mutually exclusive. Demonstrating his fluid political identity, he joined other Choctaw mingoes who petitioned Congress in 1836 as "citizens of the States, and late members of the tribe of the Choctaw nation" for redress of their Article 14 claims.[40] These references to citizenship may have been meant to indicate that the mingoes were in compliance with the Treaty of Dancing Rabbit Creek and therefore deserved settlement of their treaty claims. Or perhaps these Choctaws genuinely believed themselves to be citizens. Choctaws did not divide the world into binary opposites, but rather held alleged incongruities in creative tension.[41] Congress considered the Choctaws' pleas along with those from white Mississippi citizens.

In January of 1836 the Mississippi legislature informed Congress that land speculators were bringing Choctaws back from Indian Territory to file false claims.[42] The Indian Office appointed Publius Pray, P. D. Vroom, and James R. Murray to investigate.[43] Their commission dismissed the charge of fraudulent claims and countered the class card with paternalism, arguing that Choctaws were unsophisticated in the ways of the law and needed the protection of wise officials. If some Choctaws engaged unscrupulous speculator lawyers, they wrote, it was only because they were easily duped. Indian naïveté was no excuse for denying the Choctaws' just claims.[44]

Mississippi settlers agreed in principle. They informed Congress in 1837 that they stood "both against and in favor of the Indians' rights to reservations" under Article 14. They praised the Choctaws "whose valor saved us from the murderous Creeks," and co-opted the rhetoric of paternalism by castigating those who impeded Choctaw removal to the West where they "could enjoy with less restraint the chase." Mississippians thus portrayed themselves as the Choctaws' defenders against greedy land barons.[45]

The petitioners viewed Choctaws as noble savages—a patronizing position evident in their references to Choctaws enjoying "the chase." This was a common reading of Indian livelihood, for white Americans in the nineteenth century frequently cast Indians as hunters and gatherers, ignoring their agricultural activities. As historian Daniel H. Usner Jr. has persuasively argued, this interpretation of Indian subsistence strategies sanctioned dispossession by relegating Indians to a primitive past.[46] Clearly, relics of the past had no place on the booming Mississippi frontier.

Even though the Murray-Vroom Commission found in favor of 194 Choctaw claims, concerns over speculators prevented allotment, and settlers continued to seize Choctaw lands under rights of preemption.[47] The government of the Choctaw Nation in Indian Territory, seeking payment for lands ceded under the Treaty of Dancing Rabbit Creek, rose to the defense of their Mississippi kinsmen. In 1842 the War Department formed a second Choctaw Claims Commission chaired by Mississippi congressman Colonel J. F. H. Claiborne.[48]

Claiborne seemed a good choice to chair the commission because he was friends with Choctaw headman Colonel Samuel Cobb, whose father had adopted Claiborne as his son.[49] Yet Claiborne sought to dispossess the Choctaws. As most of the good public land in Mississippi was gone, the government now offered payments for Article 14 claims in scrip, which were certificates redeemable for public lands in Mississippi, Alabama, and Louisiana.[50] Claiborne viewed the Choctaws as "incapable of managing their affairs" and thought it best that they remove.[51]

In 1843 Claiborne convinced Choctaw mingoes to meet with the emigration agent John McRae. The men listened to McRae and then retired to deliberate. A few days later they called a council.[52] The Indians' behavior at that meeting suggests that although the Choctaw Nation had been removed and the remaining Choctaws were citizens of the state, Choctaws in Mississippi believed that they still held a government-to-government relationship with the United States.

Colonel Claiborne described the encounter. "A circle of council fires was lit up," he wrote. "The pipe was passed around with great solemnity, and everything was conducted with due form and stateliness."[53] These were rituals of diplomacy between sovereign nations, and Cobb employed a form of oration known as treaty language, also common to diplomatic protocol. Native American treaty language sought to build understanding by reference to a common humanity and by employing kinship terms. Cobb repeatedly used the term "brother"—suggesting a more equal relationship than had he called the Americans "father"— and spoke in the paradigm of familial demands of reciprocity.[54]

Cobb cited the Choctaws' military service: "When you were young we were strong; we fought by your side."[55] Numerous Choctaws were military allies of the United States, but one chief had especially distinguished himself—Pushmataha, the Choctaw leader who had urged his people not to join Tecumseh's uprising in 1812. Pushmataha had fought with Andrew Jackson in the Redstick War and accompanied him to the Battle of New Orleans following the War of 1812.[56] As the descendants of military allies, the Choctaws distinguished themselves from Indians who had taken up arms against the United States. By reminding his audience of these interactions, Cobb again invoked ties of reciprocity.[57]

Cobb's broad themes echoed the Choctaws' 1836 memorial. Both protests disputed whether the United States was a just nation because of its treatment of the Choctaws. In assuming this rhetorical position, Choctaws engaged in what historian Frederick E. Hoxie has called "an anti-colonial critique of the American settler state." The words may appear obsequious, but they were a direct challenge to the legitimacy of the United States' self-identification as a just democracy. The subtext suggested that a just nation kept its word.[58]

The intent of the speech was clearly to persuade the federal government to act as an appropriate treaty partner and was indicative of a sense of Indian juridical identity. Whatever the ultimate accuracy of these words (which may have been embellished in translation), they resonated with the Choctaws. Over the next century, Choctaw headmen would quote this speech in numerous challenges to the federal government. Despite Cobb's eloquence, his words had little effect.

The growing white population eventually forced more Choctaws to emigrate.[59] In September 1843 the Leake County justice of the peace invoked Mississippi law against Cobb and threatened him with imprisonment on various charges including bigamy and Sabbath breaking. His alleged white ally, Colonel John B. Forrester, told him that there was no way to avoid this punishment. "Thus alarmed for liberty and property," Cobb informed the Choctaw Commission, "I consented to hold a council and stated to my people my situation; and we all agreed to go."[60] Cobb signed his land over to Forrester and, along with Choctaw mingo Colonel James Pickens, accepted a government contract to move his people to Indian Territory.[61] In this case, the Choctaws' state citizenship proved an effective tool of removal.

By 1845 the federal government appeared weary of Choctaw claims. They decided to issue only half the scrip owed to the Choctaws and to give them the value of the other half in a fund, bearing 5 percent interest, to be paid annually.[62] Discouraged, over three thousand more Choctaws moved to Indian Territory by 1849, and those left behind abandoned pursuit of their treaty rights.[63]

Even though the Choctaws held the legal status of whites under Mississippi law, their racial identity meant that they did not hold white social status. As both free and enslaved African Americans were subjected to extreme oppression, Choctaws were careful to avoid association with African Americans. Choctaws were proud of their status as indigenous people who had never been enslaved and who had lived in Mississippi long before either whites or blacks.[64] In this racialized atmosphere, Choctaws began squatting on unoccupied lands in closed endogamous communities that allowed them to support a social identity as a third racial group.

Choctaws continued to maintain distinct cultural boundaries around their communities by holding to Choctaw language, dress, and customs. These communities further underscored their Choctaw identity by competing in stickball games.[65] Choctaws primarily played for their own enjoyment, but these occasions also affirmed their ethnicity before their white neighbors, who enjoyed attending the contests.[66] Thus stickball games fulfilled the traditional function of inter-group mediation in a new context. They confirmed for Mississippi settlers that Indian communities still existed in Mississippi.

Although Choctaws were scattered across Mississippi, the 1853 census of Special Indian Agent Douglas Cooper documented that the majority lived in the east-central portion of the state. The Cooper census identified 2,262 Choctaws living in clans numbering from perhaps fifty to one hundred individuals. They resided in Neshoba, Newton, Jasper, Lauderdale, Leake, Carroll, Scott, and Kemper Counties. There were also Choctaw communities along the Gulf Coast in Mobile, Alabama, and in St. Tammany Parish and the Parish of Orleans in Louisiana.[67] In identifying these settlements, the federal government acknowledged the Choctaws as Indians culturally even if it did not consider their communities to be polities. This lack of political recognition meant that the federal government did not provide economic support, which contributed to Choctaws' severe poverty.

Choctaws lived as subsistence farmers or sharecroppers on marginal lands and supplemented their crops with hunting and gathering in seasonal circuits. Most cotton production in this part of Mississippi occurred on relatively small farms cultivated by yeomen or tenant farmers who were overwhelmingly white. These small holdings had relatively few slaves, which provided a labor market for Choctaws who picked cotton or cut firewood for low wages. They may have worked alongside African Americans even as they held themselves apart from them.[68]

Fig. 1. Jim Tubby, with stickball sticks, 1908. Photographer: Mark Raymond Harrington. Source: National Museum of the American Indian, Smithsonian Institution (P12169). Photo by Photo Services.

Choctaws also marketed crafts, both to bolster their ethnicity and to supplement their paltry incomes. Women sold cane baskets and herbs and men produced small crafts such as blowguns, rabbit sticks, and tool handles.[69] Choctaws would later leverage this ethnicity in pursuit of treaty rights, but with the fear of removal ever present they no longer pressed their land claims. Their brethren in Indian Territory, however, did.

Officials of the Choctaw Nation requested payment in 1853 for territory relinquished during removal, including Article 14 claims. Conflict over the proposed payments landed the matter in the Supreme Court in 1886.[70] In *Choctaw Nation v. United States*, the court awarded the Choctaw Nation $417,656 for Article 14 descendants.[71] The Choctaw Nation did not distribute these funds in Mississippi. Instead, they gave them to people who had moved to Indian Territory between 1842 and 1852.[72] For the Mississippi Choctaws, living in the land of their ancestors was once again a component of their identity for which they paid a very high price.

Pushed to the margins of society, the Choctaws endured both scorn and pity from many of their neighbors. By the mid-1840s, references to them as noble savages had vanished from the public record, and Mississippi citizens simply demanded that "the State of Mississippi may be rid of this most annoying population."[73] The few scattered accounts of settlers interacting with Choctaws were equally unflattering. In *Mississippi Scenes*, published in 1851, a planter named Joseph Beckham Cobb (no relation to Samuel Cobb) wrote that the Choctaws were cowardly, duplicitous, filthy, and mean, "hardly above the animals." The planters with whom Frederick Law Olmsted interacted in 1854 professed similar judgments about the Indians who picked cotton for them.[74]

This disparagement had several sources. In the 1840s and 1850s most of Mississippi was still a frontier, and settlers viewed themselves as taming a savage wilderness. Indians symbolized that savagery.[75] Moreover, as removal had taken their churches, the Choctaws were "heathens" in a region where religion was becoming increasingly important. In the 1840s, Baptist minister N. L. Clarke pleaded with the Mount Pisgah Baptist Association to evangelize the Choctaws, but was rebuffed. The American Baptist Home Mission Society supposedly sent a missionary in 1845, but there is no record of his success.[76]

Ideologies concerning class may also have shaped settlers' attitudes. Upper- and middle-class Americans differentiated between whites who were merely poor and those who were "poor white trash," disdaining the

Fig. 2. Choctaw ethnicity, 1908. Group of Choctaw men, a young woman, and a young girl posed outdoors, probably at a stickball game. Photographer: Mark Raymond Harrington. Source: National Museum of the American Indian, Smithsonian Institution (N02667). Photo by Photo Services.

latter because they did not produce surplus crops for markets. "Respectable" observers believed this behavior demonstrated laziness and lack of moral fiber.[77] As the Choctaws eked out a subsistence economy on marginal lands, it is possible that settlers extended these views to them.

The Choctaws' position in the racial hierarchy of antebellum Mississippi is more difficult to ascertain. Some settlers regarded Indians as lower than blacks: "Although slaves for life, and begetting slaves, I do not know a negro that would countenance an exchange of situations with a Choctaw or Chickasaw Indian," planter Joseph Cobb wrote in 1851.[78] Cobb was in no position to speak for his slaves, many of whom may have gladly traded slavery for even the most deprived existence as free. Judging how representative Cobb's remarks were of general racial attitudes is problematic.

It is possible that other settlers consigned Choctaws to the bottom of the racial order because of ideologies underlying slavery. The majority of African Americans were under the strict control of slave codes. As free people of color, Choctaws held more potential to upset social stability should they attempt to exercise their rights. Increasing criticism from abolitionists in the 1840s and 1850s had also pushed southern slaveholders to depict slavery as a benevolent institution that uplifted African Americans. Relegating Indians to the lowest position in society would have supported this view.[79] However white Mississippians ranked Indians and blacks, postremoval Choctaws appeared pitiful in contrast with the once-powerful Choctaw Nation. The popular author William Gilmore Simms made this case in an 1845 story.[80]

Simms's narrative "Oakatibbe, or the Choctaw Sampson" depicted the majority of "remnant Choctaws" as lazy, sullen, and backward, and contrasted them with one character whose nobility embodied the romanticized memory of the vanished Choctaw Nation—a Choctaw man named Oakatibbe. Simms called him "one of the most noble specimens of physical manhood that my eyes had ever beheld."[81]

In the tale, Oakatibbe killed another Choctaw named Loblolly Jack. Choctaw jurisprudence required that Oakatibbe's clan owed Loblolly Jack's clan one life in recompense. Even though several white people urged him to flee, Oakatibbe laid down his life. As Simms gazed down into Oakatibbe's grave, he grieved the loss of this gallant man.[82] Simms made it clear that Oakatibbe's courage and integrity symbolized the once mighty Choctaw Nation, which he contrasted harshly with the "degraded condition" of the "remnant." Within slightly more than a decade, however, white Mississippians would view the Choctaws by the former paradigm instead of the latter.

Civil War, Reconstruction, and Segregation

The Choctaws' service to the Confederacy rehabilitated their standing in Mississippi. Major General J. W. Pearce organized the First Battalion of Choctaw Indians, Confederate army, in 1862. The Union army captured these soldiers while they were training in Tangipahoa, Louisiana. Some of them escaped and returned to Newton County, but the fate of the rest is uncertain.[83] After this misfortune, other Choctaw soldiers joined Major S. G. Spann's Battalion of Mounted Scouts, where they served honorably for the remainder of the war.[84]

The Confederacy assigned Choctaws to combat rather than to labor, suggesting that the Confederacy respected the Choctaws' historical reputation as warriors. Major Spann praised the "proud-hearted young braves" of his company. He selected a man named Eahantatubbee, also known as Jack Amos, to interpret because he was allegedly "the grand-nephew of the great Chief Pushmataha."[85] In the fires of war, the Choctaws were once again noble savages whose warrior prowess proved valuable.

The Choctaws' eligibility for conscription raised questions about their legal standing. Early in the war, Percy Walker, an attorney from Mobile, informed some Choctaws that they were exempt from service and offered to procure papers to that effect. The Choctaws' senior officer, General Dabney H. Maury, silenced Walker, and Choctaw recruitment continued.[86] The historical record does not explain how Maury accomplished this, but he may have invoked the Choctaws' obligations to the state as citizens.

Choctaw soldiers distinguished themselves in 1863 during the Battle of Vicksburg when severe rains washed out a bridge over the Chunky River and swept a train carrying Confederate soldiers into the waters. Jack Amos and Elder Williams led the Choctaws in the rescue efforts, saving twenty-two men and burying the bodies of the ninety-six who perished in the accident.[87] These heroics won the Choctaws praise and improved their image among their neighbors.

Even as class and racial conflict intensified during the Reconstruction era, Choctaw communities stabilized, and white Mississippians became more charitable toward them. Railroads arrived in Choctaw country in the 1870s, encouraging the timber industry.[88] Property taxes went up to pay for the lines, freight and passenger rates were high, and elite merchants were the primary beneficiaries of the railroad in rural Mississippi.[89] Merchants charged high prices and held many small

Fig. 3. Jack Amos (Eahantatubbee), 1906. Photographer unknown.
Published in "Paths to the Past." Courtesy of the Lauderdale County
Department of Archives and History, Meridian, Mississippi.

farmers' mortgages in exchange for credit. Falling cotton prices in the 1880s increased foreclosures and resulted in antilandlord violence.[90] Aside from the railroad, east-central Mississippi lacked infrastructure and capital.[91] The politics of Reconstruction further complicated economic hardships.

The Ku Klux Klan conducted campaigns of terror against former slaves, who, along with their Republican allies, became the scapegoat for the state's postwar troubles. One of the most infamous race riots occurred in 1871 in Meridian, not far from several Choctaw communities. Racial violence had sparked African American protest rallies that provoked white counter-rallies. One evening in 1871, conflicting assemblies erupted into several days of rioting and lynchings that killed thirty African Americans. The federal government eventually suppressed the Klan, but race relations remained tense.[92] This atmosphere gave new urgency to Choctaw separatism, a strategy soon to be in sync with Mississippi laws.

Democrats retook control of the Mississippi legislature in 1875 and began passing statutes prohibiting interracial education and segregating railroad cars.[93] Beginning in 1880, the legislature approved a series of miscegenation laws, but they did not include Indians.[94] Mississippi politicians may have excluded Choctaws from Jim Crow legislation because, technically, Choctaws still held the legal status of whites. More likely, however, they did not regard the Choctaws as a threat to the racial order. Their relatively small numbers, their geographical and social isolation, and their lack of political or economic power probably influenced the decision not to segregate them by statute. Choctaws faced customary discrimination, however, and the 1890 Constitution officially disfranchised them through poll taxes and literacy requirements.[95]

Segregation statutes institutionalized the separatism by which Choctaws marked their ethnicity and inadvertently offered opportunities to reinforce their racial identity through segregated churches. Prior to the Civil War, whites and blacks worshiped together, blacks sitting in the back of the church. Racial etiquette would have forced Choctaws to join them. To avoid the sting of discrimination, Choctaws would have refused.[96] In the Jim Crow South, however, African Americans established their own churches. Some of these congregations, such as the Tribulation Baptist Church near Carthage, Mississippi, held separate services for Indians. Some Choctaws began to worship there around 1878.[97] In the late nineteenth century, the appearance of missionaries to the Choctaws (part of a larger outpouring of piety nationwide) also afforded additional resources to strengthen Choctaw separatism.

Choctaws embraced the missionaries because they supplied schools around which to strengthen their communities. Some churches also offered farmland.[98] In 1882 Peter Folsom, a descendent of Choctaws Israel and McKee Folsom, who had been ministers before removal, came from Indian Territory to establish a Baptist church.[99] Catholics built a mission and school near Tucker in Neshoba County in 1883–84 and offered Choctaws land.[100] Methodists moved in by 1891 and ordained Choctaw minister Jim Johnson, who established a mission school at Tallachulok in 1896. By 1900 nine Baptist churches had approximately three hundred members, nearly seven hundred Choctaws were Catholics, and four Methodist churches served roughly 157 members.[101]

These churches reinforced Choctaw ethnicity. Choctaw preachers conducted services in Choctaw, and Christian hymns alternated with Choctaw songs about their daily lives. Church grounds furnished meeting places for stickball games and picnics. Worship was segregated by sex, and Choctaw men shared pipes of tobacco during services. Choctaws' customary courtship practices and wedding ceremonies continued in the Christian context, as did funeral rituals.[102] Choctaws also marked their ethnicity in their Sunday clothing and adornment, wearing brightly colored clothes trimmed in ribbons and rickrack. Women wore beaded combs in their hair, and many men wore bright handkerchiefs around their necks to complement their suit coats or vests.[103]

Churches also imparted a new organizational model for community politics. Baptist churches functioned according to parliamentary procedure, which Choctaws eventually adopted for community meetings.[104] Baptist and Methodist missionaries trained Choctaws to be church leaders, which translated into political leadership. Many Choctaw preachers would lead the ongoing struggle over Choctaw claims.[105] Methodist minister Simpson Tubby (born in 1864 or 1867) also recounted that mingoes of separate communities sometimes gathered for political deliberations on matters affecting the Choctaws as a whole.

Tubby shared stories of postremoval Choctaw politics with anthropologist John Swanton in the 1920s. He informed Swanton that Choctaws lived along the five creeks that flowed into the Pearl River near the Nanih Waiya, whose site also contained a small mound. Tubby recalled that mingoes met at the small mound to decide local matters, "which they afterwards carried to the chief on the big mound for approval, but the laws for the nation as a whole were made at the big mound."[106] The degree to which this council actually governed is open to question, but the stories suggest that representatives of the scattered settlements may have worked together for common goals. Unlike in the early nineteenth century, however, the growing Choctaw communities drew favorable attention from their neighbors.

In the 1890s a series of sentimental works about the Choctaws written by people who had known them before removal began to appear in print. In 1894 Horatio Bardwell Cushman characterized the Choctaws as quintessentially noble savages in *History of the Choctaw, Chickasaw, and Natchez Indians.* In the 1898 *American Antiquarian and Oriental Journal,* John A. Watkins declared them, "a moral people" who had never deceived anyone.[107] Newton County resident A. J. Brown published a county history in 1895 which proclaimed that "in their primeval state," the Choctaws were "the most honest, virtuous people of which we have account."[108] Each of these authors lauded Choctaw military skills, which naturally brought Pushmataha back into the public eye.

In 1906 the *Publications of the Mississippi Historical Society* posthumously published Gideon Lincecum's "Life of Apushmataha." This hagiography outlined Pushmataha's amazing feats as a warrior and praised his superior oratory skills. Even though Lincecum exaggerated Pushmataha's exploits, the article was an important reminder of what the United States owed the Choctaws.[109] This sudden remembrance of Choctaw heroism was most likely part of a broader trend in

Mississippi in which sectionalism following Reconstruction influenced Indian-white relations.

The glorification of the Civil War as the Lost Cause colored the memory of removal, portraying Choctaw resistance in a more positive light. In his 1880 work *Mississippi as a Province, Territory, and State*, former removal advocate Colonel J. F. H. Claiborne called the Choctaws "those noble natives of our soil" and mourned their demise.[110] Claiborne now regarded the Choctaws' ardent affection for their homelands to be noble: "This is the foundation of all patriotism. The most heroic actions in history spring from this source. In the South, it should be cultivated and impressed on our children; the first lesson in every household should be 'God and our native soil.'"[111] Henry S. Halbert and Belle Scott, teachers who worked among the Choctaws, also equated the Indian's love of their ancestral lands with true patriotism.[112] Following Reconstruction, Mississippians reenvisioned the Choctaws' refusal to emigrate as a tragically doomed defense of their homelands from incursions by a stronger power. This implicitly paralleled the southern experience with invasion and brought the Choctaws into the cult of the citizen-soldier that was part of the Lost Cause.

At the turn of the century, an outpouring of sentiment for all things Confederate animated the state. In 1888 the state legislature provided pensions for injured veterans and erected a memorial to the Confederate dead on the state capitol grounds. The death of former Confederate president Jefferson Davis near Biloxi the following year produced an outburst of grief that reinforced glorification of the Lost Cause.[113]

These events led southerners to herald Choctaws in Mississippi and Indian Territory for their military service to the Confederacy. Celebrations of Choctaw warriors appeared in Confederate veterans' publications. A group of Confederate veterans organized Camp Dabney H. Maury no. 1312 in 1901. Eighteen Choctaw veterans joined and began collecting pensions. Confederate soldier reunions featured Choctaw veterans, who were "feasted by the ladies and lauded by the press."[114] In 1903 the *New Orleans Times-Democrat* remarked that Choctaw veteran Jack Amos was "being praised and pampered by the old soldiers whose cause he espoused in the sixties with so much fervor."[115] Major Spann campaigned in 1905 to place a memorial commemorating "the patriotic devotion exhibited by the Choctaw Indian braves" at the Chunky River, where they had buried the Confederates they had pulled from the water in 1863.[116]

White men identified with the Choctaws' masculine heroics and thus established their claims on their state's first citizens as brothers in arms in upholding the racial hierarchy of the Confederacy. Confederate veterans praised the Choctaws, but they nonetheless made it clear that Choctaws were not entirely their equals.

In his article on the Choctaws in *Confederate Magazine*, Spann cautioned that Indians did not fare well with the tactics of modern war, which presented "too many surprises for his manner of savage warfare."[117] The Indian was best utilized as a scout, for "his instinct for courses and geographic precision is equal to the bee and surpasses the horse or other animals."[118] Spann attributed Choctaw success to innate animalistic qualities held by savages. Still, as defenders of the South, the Choctaws were now the noblest of noble savages, and as such, they were also disappearing.

The notion of the vanishing Indian was popular nationwide in the late nineteenth century despite evidence to the contrary. Although there were Choctaws still living in his neighborhood, county historian A. J. Brown wrote, "They have gone from our midst, a peculiar people has passed away" leaving only a remnant declining from pulmonary disease.[119] The Choctaws' poverty prompted legitimate concerns about their survival, but their population was roughly two thousand at the time Brown wrote. The perception that the Choctaws were disappearing reflected nostalgia for a once populous and powerful nation. Seeing them reduced to a few thousand people struggling with poverty, Mississippians concluded that Choctaws were fading from history.

Educators who worked among the Choctaws in the late nineteenth century complicated this idea, simultaneously noting the Choctaws' continued Indian identity (their use of Choctaw language, their closed communities, their attachment to their ancestral lands, and their Choctaw worldview) and their progress toward assimilation evidenced by their acceptance of Christianity and their willingness to educate their children. This tension between the "vanishing" and the "progressing" Indians propelled publication of works documenting Choctaw traditions.[120] This new concern for the Choctaws, however patronizing, translated into increased support for public services. The Choctaws now had allies in state government.

Everyone concerned with the Choctaws saw education as the answer to their plight, which raised the issue of segregated schools. Despite their legal equality with whites, Choctaws were barred from white schools. Because of their racial separatism, Choctaw parents refused to send their children to African American schools. The Mississippi legislature affirmed this approach in 1882 by creating state-sponsored Indian schools, funded and administered at the county level. The legislature appointed amateur anthropologist Henry S. Halbert as state superintendent for Indian education in 1888.[121] His reports to the State Board of Education revealed how the Choctaws used education both for economic advancement and to reinforce their Indian identity.

Choctaw schools met in churches from four to six months a year and taught reading, math, English, history, and geography. Classes were bilingual. By 1892–93, eight Choctaw schools operated in five counties—Kemper, Newton, Neshoba, Leake, and Jasper—but attendance was often sporadic because Choctaw children had to work or lacked proper clothing.[122] Most Choctaws wanted to educate their children, who were "bright attentive pupils."[123] Adults also used school facilities. The Conehatta community formed a debating society "in which all practical, economic and business questions are discussed," as were more philosophical matters. Similarly, schools served as community centers in other locations.[124]

The Bogue Chitto Community of Neshoba County was the exception to this pattern. Noting that the establishment of schools had preceded the first removal, Bogue Chitto elders predicted that a second removal would likewise follow these schools, and refused all contact with school officials.[125] In 1893 Superintendent Halbert derided this prophecy of the "old fogy mingoes": "an absurd argument it is true, yet it still has its weight with the ignorant Tubbee element."[126] Yet the prophecy of these "old fogy mingoes" proved prescient. The same year that Halbert scoffed at fears of a second removal, the federal government's actions in Indian Territory set the stage for fulfillment of the prophecy.[127]

Conclusion

The Choctaws used several strategies to resist their dispossession. As citizens of Mississippi, they exercised their right to sue for their land claims. As Indians holding treaty promises, they pressed the federal government to fulfill Article 14, using treaty language and diplomatic protocols even though the legal context for these highly stylized interactions between sovereign nations no longer existed in Mississippi. These tactics did not win many claims, but they created a legal paper trail the Choctaws could later use to document their identity as descendants of Article 14 claimants. Choctaw memorials and speeches also supplied rhetorical tools that the Indians and their allies brandished well into the next century.

Defying Mississippi law, Choctaws resided in ethnic enclaves under the authority of their headmen. These communities provided economic support and bolstered Choctaw ethnicity. Growing racial tensions during the nineteenth century further reinforced the need for Choctaw separatism from African Americans, and Choctaws deployed their unique culture to distinguish themselves as a third racial group in the biracial South—a status whites were willing to accept.

Mississippians viewed the Choctaws through the lenses of race and class, and their perceptions changed significantly over time. Racial ideology persuaded them to imagine that only easily assimilated mixed-bloods would stay behind after removal. When thousands of Choctaws remained and refused assimilation, settlers were faced with communities of Indians whom they regarded with ambivalence. The legislature had granted Choctaws state citizenship, but racism and class conflict shaped how Mississippians viewed the Choctaws' legal position. Local governments inconsistently interpreted Choctaw citizenship, at times protecting them as racial dependents and at other times using Mississippi law to remove them. Settlers initially expressed appreciation for Choctaw treaty rights and military service and defined the Choctaws as victims of speculators. Then, invoking the injustice of speculation, they used the rhetoric of yeoman farmer republicanism to complete the process of dispossession.

Once the Choctaws had been driven to marginal lands, Mississippi settlers employed them as low-paid wage laborers. Their poverty generally brought disparagement until after the Civil War. Choctaw heroics during the war and their value as symbols of the Lost Cause following Reconstruction upgraded their status in their neighbors' eyes. Notions of vanishing Indians further elicited sympathy for the Choctaws. This new paradigm encouraged outreach to Choctaw communities, which resulted in state-funded Indian schools and support for missionaries. By the end of the nineteenth century, Mississippi citizens were once again attempting to assimilate the Choctaws. The Choctaws, of course, had other ideas.

CHAPTER TWO

From the Second Removal to Recognition, 1898–1918

Having only recently rebuilt their communities, the Mississippi Choctaws again faced removal in 1898 when the federal government moved to allot the Choctaw Nation in Indian Territory. Because of Article 14, Choctaws remaining in Mississippi were also entitled to land, but deciding who should appear on the Choctaw tribal rolls proved difficult because Mississippi Choctaws lacked appropriate documentation of their eligibility. Policy makers' ubiquitous concern with race at the turn of the twentieth century meant that enrollment turned on the issue of Indian blood.

As they pursued allotments, the Mississippi Choctaws again encountered incompetent officials and broken promises, and again they protested with memorials and petitions. In this new context, they employed the language of Indian blood, identifying themselves as the full-blood Mississippi Choctaws—a definition that included language and culture in addition to ancestry. The Choctaws' declaration of a full-blood identity echoed the federal government's requirements for renewed Article 14 claims under allotment policy—requirements that represented changing perceptions of how Indian blood had affected the historical outcome of Article 14. As they sought to sort out competing claims, Mississippi Choctaws, ersatz claimants, lawyers, and federal officials sparred over the meanings of Choctaw ancestry, history, and culture.

The Mississippi congressional delegation sought enrollment with the Choctaw Nation for Choctaws in Mississippi. They did so for a variety of motives, many of which echoed their beliefs about tragic, vanishing, noble savages expressed following the Civil War. So powerful were these preconceived notions of Indianness that elected officials initially battled not on behalf of the actual Choctaw communities, but for pretend claimants along the Gulf Coast. Mississippi politicians' engagement in the campaign for enrollment reflected the distance between actual Indians and ideas about Indians that complicated the Choctaws' struggle for recognition.[1]

Although the efforts of both Indians and politicians failed to win enrollment with the Choctaw Nation, the campaign drew attention to the predicament of Choctaws in Mississippi and finally prompted a congressional appropriation for them. The Choctaws' hard-won recognition as Indians deserving federal aid was the first victory in their campaign for tribal resurgence.

The Second Removal: Rights, Race, and Identity

In 1893 Congress created the Dawes Commission to persuade Native governments in Indian Territory to accept the allotment of their lands and the dissolution of their tribal status. The Office of Indian Affairs (OIA) had already begun allotting other Indian lands under the General Allotment Act of 1887 (also known as the Dawes Act, after its chief sponsor Massachusetts senator Henry Dawes). The Dawes Act had divided Indian reservations into individual allotments, throwing open the remaining communal lands to white settlers and dissolving the Indians' institutions of government. This policy had excluded the nations of Indian Territory until 1898 when the government passed the Curtis Act, which allotted the nations of Indian Territory. After a bitter political battle, the Choctaw Nation had accepted allotment under the Atoka Agreement in 1897. This agreement was added to the Curtis Act and passed the following year.

Mississippi representative John Sharp Williams, who represented the fifth district containing most of the Choctaw communities, joined with the Choctaw Nation seeking allotments in Indian Territory for Choctaws in Mississippi.[2] The Curtis Act authorized the Dawes Commission to enroll Mississippi Choctaws who could prove descent from persons entitled to land under Article 14. Qualified Choctaws then had six months to move to Indian Territory to retain their land.[3] This opportunity prompted a flood of applicants, which raised questions of how to identify legitimate enrollees. In the hyper-racial atmosphere of the late nineteenth and early twentieth centuries, race became a crucial component of enrollment.

The text of the General Allotment Act made no specific mention of race as a criterion for allotment, but references to Indian blood abounded in administrative documents and practices. The pervasive preoccupation with racial purity in the late nineteenth and early twentieth centuries strongly influenced both Indian policy and tribal constructions of identity. For example, the Dawes Commission held segregated hearings in Indian Territory and drafted three separate rolls—one for intermarried whites, one for freedmen (former slaves), and one for Indians by blood, where enrollees were listed by blood quantum. The operative measurement for inclusion on the latter roll was "one-half Indian blood," provided that the racial mixture was Indian and white. Any portion of African American blood meant enrollment with the freedmen.[4] Enrollment procedures thus placed racial considerations in the forefront of tribal membership.

For federal policy makers, blood quantum requirements served several purposes. Assuming that intermarriage would eventually diminish a group's bloodline, these regulations could ultimately reduce membership rolls and end treaty obligations.[5] The definitive objective of Indian policy was assimilation, and policy makers believed that race affected this goal. They viewed Indians of mixed ancestry as farther along the road to civilization than full-blood Indians.[6] This taxonomy reflected a broader racial ideology with which governments at all levels restricted access to status and resources by race.[7] Accordingly, both federal policymakers and tribal officials sought to safeguard resources reserved for Indians from the claims of usurpers.[8] The multitudes of people who filed for enrollment as Mississippi Choctaws fueled this concern.

Since blood was a matter of descent, family genealogies were a logical starting place for enrollment. Yet few people had documented genealogies, and since family names changed over time, Mississippi Choctaws could not always identify their ancestors on earlier rolls.[9] This ambiguity opened a wide door for fraud. Commissioner Archibald McKennon, who oversaw the enrollment hearings for the Choctaws in Mississippi, finally decided that persons who showed a "predominance of Choctaw blood and characteristics" did not have to produce evidence of descent from an Article 14 claimant, but those who "displayed . . . a half or anything less" did.[10]

McKennon did not explain how one discerned these degrees of blood, but many commissioners believed that phenotypes were significant markers.[11] Early in the enrollment process Congressman Williams had complained to Dawes commissioner Tams Bixby that "ordinary eyesight is the very best testimony possible. A man must be a fool who cannot tell a full blood, a half blood, or even a quarter blood Indian."[12] Attorneys for the Department of the Interior objected that "eyeballing" was insufficient to prove race but failed to stipulate an alternative. Consequently, the Dawes Commission decided on a procedure called the full-blood rule of evidence.[13]

The full-blood rule of evidence began with racial phenotypes but did not end there—it also included cultural indicators, such as clothing, language, and body decoration. Reversing previous assumptions, the full-blood rule presumed that most full-blood Choctaws who had remained in Mississippi were successors of Article 14 claimants because the "more progressive mixed-blood Indians" had supposedly removed.[14]

McKennon also insisted that authentic aspirants could be distinguished by their demeanor. He wrote: "Negro applicants, always insistent and voluble, are in striking contrast with the stolid full-bloods who could be induced to testify only after the most persistent questioning."[15] McKennon believed that fear of removal motivated this reticence. Under the full-blood rule of evidence, if a candidate for enrollment in Mississippi spoke the Choctaw language (albeit reluctantly) and "appeared" to be a full-blood Choctaw, he or she would be enrolled as the rightful progeny of an Article 14 claimant.[16]

With these criteria, the Dawes Commission created the McKennon Roll of Identified Mississippi Choctaws in 1899. The list included 1,961 full-bloods and 279 mixed-bloods.[17] It is not clear if Choctaws coming before McKennon openly articulated their blood quantum, for the records of testimony rarely recorded the claimants' full affidavits. These documents suggest that Commissioner McKennon issued verdicts on peoples' blood quantums according to their appearance and use of the Choctaw language.[18]

The McKennon census was incomplete, for roughly five hundred Choctaws never came before the commission. Others were prevented from doing so by poor weather, lack of transportation, or intimidation by employers. An elderly Choctaw man, John Johnson, later recounted that his white neighbors had invoked powerful racialized images to dissuade him from migrating, warning that "he would be ku-kluxed and driven out" of the West.[19] Attorneys seeking half the allotment in return for registering claimants also discouraged Choctaws from coming forward on their own.[20] Because of these omissions, lawyers for rejected applicants persuaded the OIA to shelve the roll and rehear claims from 1900 to 1902.[21] This left the McKennon enrollees in limbo. They had been identified as Mississippi Choctaws but not officially enrolled with the Choctaw Nation.

Choctaw leaders challenged the enrollment process in Congress, and, unlike their ancestors, engaged the issue of Indian blood. In 1900 Congressman Williams introduced a "Petition of the Mississippi Choctaws" calling for citizenship rights in the Choctaw Nation. This document began, "Your humble petitioners are full-blood Choctaw Indians, speaking the Choctaw language, citizens of the Choctaw Nation, residing in Mississippi. We are entitled to every privilege of a Choctaw citizen, except the Choctaw annuity, under the treaty of 1830."[22] Was the convergence of the Choctaws' definition of their political identity with the requirements of the full-blood rule of evidence coincidental? Probably not.

This terminology likely meant that the Choctaws understood the legal importance of race in enrollment.[23] That Choctaw leaders had ignored racial references in earlier petitions, even though they were speaking to men who certainly thought in such terms, supports this idea.

It may also have been that they were simply more sensitive to racism after living under Jim Crow laws.[24] Observing the racial violence in Mississippi, Choctaws knew the significance of establishing that they were not black. As intermarriage with African Americans meant enrollment with the freedmen (which meant second-class citizenship in the Choctaw Nation), they had special incentives to emphasize their racial purity. Identifying themselves as the "full-blood Choctaws speaking the Choctaw language" was a way of carving out a niche in the broader racial hierarchy—one that had the potential for benefits due to Indians.

Mississippi Choctaws believed that these benefits included citizenship rights in the Choctaw Nation while they remained in Mississippi. They based this on the provision in Article 14, which stated that "persons who claim [allotments in Mississippi] under this article shall not lose the privilege of a Choctaw citizen." In a petition to Congress filed in 1900, Mississippi Choctaw leaders argued that this stipulation entitled them to share in the profits of the Choctaw Nation's coal and asphalt leases.[25] This represented a modification of their earlier petitions in which they forfeited claims to resources held collectively in Indian Territory.

In 1901 the "full-blood Mississippi Choctaws, speaking the Choctaw language," filed a bill to allow them to make their case in the Court of Claims. The House Committee on Indian Affairs agreed that they should be allowed to do so: "The Mississippi Choctaws contend that citizenship in the Choctaw Nation exists by virtue of blood, and not because of locality of residence."[26] The U.S. Court of the Central District of Indian Territory had already ruled (in *Jack Amos et al. vs. Choctaw Nation*) that the citizenship provision of Article 14 was intended to assure equality for Choctaws who relocated to Indian Territory after removal, not to bestow resources in Mississippi.[27] Congress agreed with the court, and the bill failed.

Shortly thereafter, Congress drafted the 1902 Choctaw-Chickasaw Supplemental Agreement to settle conflicts that had arisen during the enrollment proceedings. Section 41 of the Supplemental Agreement did not contain the full-blood rule of evidence, which prompted another deluge of applicants.[28] The number of Choctaw claimants—some 24,634 people nationwide —threatened to overwhelm the Choctaw Nation's assets and usurp the Mississippi Choctaws' requests.[29]

In response, the "full-blood Mississippi Choctaws, speaking the Choctaw language," again memorialized Congress, requesting reinstatement of the term "full-blood" in the eligibility requirements. The memorialists complained that "many thousand[s of] persons have set up claims pretending they were Mississippi Choctaws and have put in jeopardy the rights of the real Mississippi Choctaws . . . who have been identified."[30] Because the Choctaws' status as full-bloods distinguished them from ersatz claimants, ancestry became a form of political capital in their bid to fulfill their treaty rights.

The government heeded this memorial and reinstated the full-blood rule of evidence, continuing enrollment hearings into 1902.[31] These later hearings were disorganized, and some people who had been enrolled failed to resubmit their names and were dropped from the final rolls. Many enrolled Choctaws could not get to Indian Territory within six months to claim their allotments, either because they lacked transportation or because they had waited in vain for the government to move them.[32] Sharecroppers' contracts prevented other Choctaws from leaving.[33]

Baptist missionary and rejected claimant James Arnold Jr. of Meridian, Mississippi, led the Choctaws' resistance to this treatment. From 1905 to 1907 he collected the memorials of Choctaw leaders documenting their difficulties with enrollment and forwarded them to Congress and the president. He also filed petitions from other failed claimants across Oklahoma, Texas, and Mississippi.[34] Bowing to this pressure, Congress held the enrollment hearings open until 1907. When the process finally concluded, 1,634 Choctaws had moved to Oklahoma.[35] Many churches closed following the migration, and Mississippi shuttered its Indian schools. These actions proved to be premature, for census data indicates that roughly 40 percent of those who left in this second removal had returned by 1910.[36]

Again the Choctaws had to rebuild their communities, and again they turned to their few remaining churches. To facilitate this process, representatives from the Choctaw churches in Leake, Newton, and Neshoba Counties formed the New Choctaw Baptist Association in 1911 and elected Choctaw minister Ed Willis as their leader. Though the Catholic mission school at Tucker in Neshoba County had closed, the church had continued. These institutions helped Choctaws reconstruct their communities.[37]

The Struggle for Recognition: The Harrison Bill and Contested Identities

Meanwhile, rejected enrollees and their lawyers attempted to reopen the enrollment processes.[38] In 1912 attorney Harry J. Cantwell persuaded Congressman Pat Harrison—whose district included persons claiming to be Choctaws—to introduce a bill to re-open the Choctaw rolls.[39] This prompted lobbying from two organizations in Mississippi. The Mississippi, Alabama, and Louisiana Choctaw Council, which hailed from the eastern-central counties, represented the "full-blood identified Choctaws," and the Society of Mississippi Choctaws, which spoke for people alleging Choctaw descent along the Gulf Coast and elsewhere.

The Society of Mississippi Choctaws was an example of marginalized citizens seeking the benefits of Indian identity.[40] Members claimed Indian ancestry, no doubt to escape poverty and discrimination, but they did not have the currency to purchase those benefits. They could not meet the government's criteria for legitimacy either by language, for none spoke Choctaw, or by ancestry.[41] The society submitted a membership roll to the OIA in 1914, but it did not record blood quantum, perhaps because, as founding member Luke Connerly said, "There are no full-bloods where I live."[42] Membership in the society was based on one's ability to prove lineal descent from "the Choctaw Tribe of Indians as it existed" in 1830, but there were no standards for establishing this lineage.[43]

Addressing charges that many in this group were African Americans appropriating Indian identity, the society's constitution noted, "No per-

Fig. 4. Mississippi representative Pat Harrison, 1924. Photographer: National Photo Company. Source: LC-F81-31073, Library of Congress, Prints and Photographs Division, Washington DC.

son tainted with Negro blood shall be received into membership of this Society."[44] The Gulfport, Mississippi, newspaper, the *Gulf Coast Progress*, had editorialized that the society represented "all shades and colors, running from the real Indians to the coal-black, thick-lipped, flat-nosed, kinky-headed Negro."[45] These were not the individuals whom the Dawes commissioners had identified as acceptable enrollees. Rather, they appeared to be the type of people whom Choctaw leaders, in their 1902 memorial, condemned as pretenders.[46]

The OIA had similar concerns. Testimony during the hearings for the Harrison bill exposed Connerly's links to a firm called the Texas-Oklahoma Investment Company, which funded lobbying efforts to reopen the Choctaw rolls. The firm had paid expenses for the Society of Mississippi Choctaws, although Connerly insisted that the money had come out of his salary.[47] An investigation by OIA Inspector John Reeves in 1916 reported that the majority of the society had no Choctaw blood. He based this on visual cues and on the 1910 census of Harrison County (on the Gulf Coast), which had listed only two Indians. Fifty-five people from that area were now claiming to be Choctaws. Other skeptics included the sheriff at Gulfport, who scoffed, "I don't believe there is a real Indian in the county." He offered no evidence for this claim but implied that these "Choctaws" simply did not look like Indians.[48]

There was a community of Choctaws living along the Gulf Coast in Bay Saint Louis in Hancock County, but no Indians from that area appeared on the rolls of the Society of Mississippi Choctaws. Rather, those registered with the society lived in Gulfport or Biloxi in Harrison County.[49] The majority of Choctaws in Mississippi lived farther north, and they rejected Harrison's bill and introduced a competing one.[50]

In May of 1913, with the Harrison bill still pending, the full-blood identified Choctaws gathered in council, first in Carthage and then in Meridian—each Choctaw community sent delegates. In defiance of Mississippi law forbidding tribal councils, the assembled Choctaws established the Mississippi, Alabama, and Louisiana Choctaw Council.[51] Choctaw Methodist minister Simpson Tubby chaired the meetings and became assistant secretary and treasurer. Wesley Johnson was elected chief, Peter Ben assistant chief, and William Morris secretary.[52] James E. Arnold acted as "attorney-in-fact."[53] Testifying to the House Committee on Indian Affairs, Arnold explained that "in view of the fact that these claims called for the rendition of services to them as a class," they were resurrecting the Choctaw tribe in Mississippi.[54] Their bill, "Proposed Legislation for the Full-Blood and Identified Choctaws of Mississippi, Louisiana, and Alabama," called for the reestablishment of full tribal status for Choctaws in Mississippi independent of the Choctaw Nation in Oklahoma.

This legislation mandated a supplemental roll of Mississippi Choctaws that included everyone listed on the McKennon roll of 1899 and "all full-blood Mississippi Choctaw Indians who may claim identification" under the Curtis Act. It also urged the creation of a trust fund, taken from the Choctaw and Chickasaw Nations, to pay for an Indian agent, an agency, and a school in Carthage, Mississippi. They requested trust lands in Mississippi, stock, household items, farming implements, and per capita payments.[55]

The council justified these requests because they were heirs to the promises of Article 14 and were "full-blood Choctaws, for the most part speaking only the Choctaw language, living in their own communities in the state of Mississippi, and following the habits and customs of Indian life [as] shown by the records of the Interior Department."[56] By insisting on the same treatment as other Indian tribes, the council had upped the ante. No longer content to be members of the Choctaw Nation in absentia, the Mississippi Choctaws asked for their own agency and trust lands, the first steps toward tribal rebirth.

In January 1914 the council drafted a "Memorial—The Mississippi Choctaw Claim" in support of their bill, and delegates took it to Congress. This document reiterated that despite their separation from the Choctaw Nation and state citizenship, they were still treaty partners affirming "the continuing force" of Article 14, and "to the termination of which they have never assented."[57] The memorialists admitted that some of them were not on any rolls but were nonetheless legitimate claimants. The Choctaws thus professed their right to decide who was a Choctaw—a right that is fundamental to a sovereign Indian nation.[58]

The memorial sought to authenticate the identity of the "full-blood Choctaws" in opposition to other claimants. Noting several other Choctaw claims bills before Congress, the memorial contrasted the "identified full-bloods" with people "seeking a forum for the determination of their identity" through the Harrison bill.[59] Unlike this other legislation, their bill embodied the desires of legitimate Choctaws. The memorial requested that the government recognize the council's attorneys as the only lawful representatives of the "identified full-blood Choctaws."[60]

The government considered the legal standing of the council and their "attorney-in-fact" James Arnold and concluded that "there is no tribal organization existing among the Choctaws of Mississippi, Louisiana, or Alabama, recognized by the government."[61] First assistant secretary of the interior A. A. Jones informed the council of the Supreme Court's ruling in *Jack Amos v. Choctaw Nation* that any Choctaws desiring rights of Choctaw citizenship had to move to Oklahoma.[62] The Mississippi Choctaws were again reminded that the only recognized Choctaw polity was in the West.

Nonetheless, Arnold continued to agitate, soliciting support from white community leaders. Prominent officials and businessmen of Newton County signed notarized statements decrying the Choctaws' poverty and emphasizing their potential to become productive citizens.[63] These pleas invoked the myth of the vanishing Indian, with one Union businessman imploring, "For the benefit of this fast-disappearing and downtrodden race, we make an earnest appeal and the affidavit of facts."[64] Arnold submitted these letters to the 1914 congressional hearings on enrollment. He also summarized the Choctaws' case for the *Indian's Friend*, a publication of the advocacy group the National Indian Association.[65]

Ironically, these appeals rallied the Mississippi congressional delegation to try and move the Harrison bill—not the "Proposed Legislation."[66] Despite their commitment to white supremacy, Representatives Percy E. Quin of the seventh district (which included the western

Gulf Coast), William Webb Venable (who now represented the fifth district), and Senators James Kimble Vardaman and John Sharp Williams all lobbied to help the Indians. Representative Harrison and Senator Williams were polite bigots who shunned racial invectives.[67] Vardaman was widely known for his diatribes against "the Negro," whom he characterized as "a lazy, lying, lustful animal which no conceivable amount of training can transform into a tolerable citizen."[68] Yet he also worked hard to move a bill that benefited people of color.

The willingness of so many of Mississippi's civic leaders to lobby for people of color raises significant questions. Why did these men bother with the Choctaws (real or alleged), who, disenfranchised and impoverished, could neither vote nor contribute to their campaign chests? Why this interest in a nonwhite minority from men passionately committed to white supremacy? What did this crusade reveal about racial attitudes in twentieth-century Mississippi?

These questions are even more puzzling considering that Representative William Venable, who represented the region where most Choctaw communities were located, did not carry the council's bill. Venable introduced the full-blood Choctaws' memorials to Congress, but he joined the rest of the Mississippi congressional delegation in support of Harrison's legislation filed on behalf of the Society of Mississippi Choctaws. Caleb Powers of Kentucky filed the council's "Proposed Legislation."[69] Why did Mississippi politicians support the claims of alleged Choctaws living on the coast rather than those of the "full-blood identified" Choctaws whose separate ethnic communities were clearly Indian?

Like so many non-Indians in the early twentieth century, Mississippi politicians appeared more committed to the Choctaws as historical artifacts than as living human beings. This view coincided with widespread attitudes about Indians that they were exotic symbols of a romanticized culture that served as a critique of the modern industrial state. For many Americans, "authentic" Indians were those whose culture was frozen in some alleged traditional past untouched by modernity. Actual Indians who modified their traditions to adapt to the

Fig. 5. Mississippi senator James K. Vardaman. Date and photographer unknown.
Source: LC-F81-3781, Library of Congress, Prints and Photographs Division,
Washington DC.

twentieth century were often invisible to many Americans.[70] Mississippi's elected officials overlooked what Choctaws in clearly defined Indian communities wanted and concentrated on the economic and symbolic benefits that Choctaw enrollment provided. Analysis of their remarks before Congress supports this interpretation.

The Choctaws' supporters had economic motives. Harrison's bill called for allotments, or payments that were double the value of a 320-acre allotment, and for compensation equal to whatever Choctaw Nation citizens had received from the federal government since allotment.[71] Harrison was notoriously fond of "pork," and any influx of federal funds would find its way into the pockets of white landowners and merchants who were his constituents.[72] The proprietor of the Williams-Brooke Mercantile in Union commented bluntly: "We, their merchants, are assuming great risks in furnishing them the actual necessities of life."[73] Federal cash was a godsend to seriously poor counties cut over by timber companies and beginning to suffer boll weevil infestations that decimated southern cotton crops at the turn of the twentieth century.[74]

The Choctaws continued to symbolize the southerner's love for and defense of one's homeland. When opponents of Harrison's bill remarked that the Mississippi Choctaws could have prevented their dispossession by moving to Indian Territory, an exasperated Senator Williams countered that "they very properly said, 'we prefer to stay here.'" Williams proclaimed that "the Senator from Oklahoma surely never ate a Youghiogheny [River region] squirrel" or a Mississippi catfish, or he would know that the Choctaws could not have gone to Indian Territory. (In response to this gustatory challenge Senator Owen replied, "I am willing to.") Likewise, in a 1916 speech, Harrison praised the Choctaws' love of their "ancient territories" and their "accustomed hunting grounds." Senator Williams called Mississippi "the happiest hunting ground in the Union," and Senator Vardaman asked that the Choctaws not be penalized because "they did not want to leave the land of their fathers."[75]

Vardaman also invoked the noble vanishing Indian: "these long-suffering stoics of the woods" were "dying out very rapidly, and it will only be a few years before there will not be any of these Indians left." This would be a tragic outcome, given the delegation's general consensus that the Choctaws were honorable people.[76] Williams, in particular, asserted that Choctaws lived "an honest and simple life" and "never possessed a white man's love of money."[77] Harrison agreed: "these Mississippi Choctaws are good people."[78]

Much historical testimony indicates that Mississippi Choctaws were hard working and good hearted, but the politicians' invocation of these traits was framed in the language of pity and paternalism. Such oratory distanced these men from living Choctaws through supercilious melancholic rhetoric and displayed their own integrity as Christian southerners attempting to help these virtuous helpless Indians.[79] The Choctaw crusade was indeed meant to signal the delegation's commitment to charity, a significant component of their Christian identity.

Senator Williams expressed this notion when he hoped for sufficient funds "to take care of the rightful claims of, I started to say of my constituents—but they are not my constituents; they are nobody's constituents on the surface of the earth unless they are God's."[80] Virtually every speech lamented the Choctaws' terrible poverty and pleaded for their relief as a moral duty.[81] Representing a region of deep religious piety, the Mississippi congressional delegation paraded their Christian credentials before their colleagues.

Nevertheless, it would be too cynical to assume that these words were only pious posturing. Mississippi's civic leaders may have genuinely cared for these impoverished neighbors. The editor of the *Neshoba County Democrat*, Clayton Rand, observed that local citizens were deeply charitable. "The county had never operated a poor farm, a home for its aged, nor an orphanage," he wrote. "To care for old and feeble parents was a child's natural responsibility. Orphans were taken under the parental care of relatives in the spirit of man's eternal brotherhood, and to help one's needy neighbors was a Christian duty."[82]

Racial contexts constrain concepts of charity, however. No one suggested that this "Christian duty" included granting Choctaws access to white schools and good employment. Indians were wards of the federal government, and calling on that body to care for them had the dual benefit of relieving Mississippians of their charitable obligations while also upholding racial segregation. Since the Choctaws requested resources to sustain their separate communities, their appeals complemented the southern social order.

The Choctaws' racial purity was another common theme in congressional speeches. Harrison frequently quoted the Dawes Commission's affirmation of the Mississippi Choctaws' full blood. "Do not be misled by men saying that they are half breeds and Negroes and all that," he expounded, "They are full-blood Choctaw Indians."[83] Likewise, Senator Williams declared that only full-blood and half-blood Indians should be aided, an argument Senator Vardaman took further when he protested that Choctaws in Oklahoma—"many of whom are more white than Indian"—should not be allowed to "rob the full-bloods."[84]

The Indians whose bill these politicians fought to move, of course, were not actual "full-bloods," but that mattered little. The crusade to open the Choctaw rolls revealed how white politicians engaged notions of Indianness for their own political ends. It also reflected a more nuanced view of the federal government than state's rights rhetoric would assume.

On one hand, Harrison's speeches recounted the federal government's mishandling of Article 14 claims, and Senator Williams proclaimed that there was no more "shameful" incident in the history of Indian-white relations than the way the federal government treated the Choctaws. Congressman Quin also blamed dispossession on federal irresponsibility, and Senator Vardaman further lamented that the U.S. government's neglect had reduced the Choctaws to the status of "simply flotsams and jetsams on the sea of life."[85]

Even as they decried the U.S. government, the delegation also laid claim to intense nationalism. Historian Philip Deloria has argued that Indians have served as symbols of American identity at numerous historical moments.[86] In this particular instance, Mississippi politicians invoked the Choctaws' military service to the United States in the War of 1812. This reminded their colleagues that without the Choctaws there might not have been an America. In claiming the Choctaws as "their Indians," this rhetoric also linked southerners with patriotism.[87]

This topic delivered some of the most colorful rhetoric of the campaign. Representative Percy E. Quin informed his colleagues in the U.S. House that the Choctaws "went out with old Andrew Jackson and waded through mud and blood up to their navals [*sic*] and fought for the American flag."[88] Harrison invoked the spirit of Pushmataha with florid oratory: "And today, even though Pushmataha has long since gone to the happy hunting ground, his spirit still lives and animates the breasts of the scattered remnant of his race in the land of his nativity, and, methinks, if he were present today he would appeal to his white father in yonder White House, to his brethren in Oklahoma, to his white friends in this Chamber, and say, 'Give to the Mississippi Choctaws the rights guaranteed to them under the fourteenth article of the treaty of 1830.'"[89] For Harrison and his colleagues rescuing the Choctaws may have represented catharsis and redemption for the sins the nation's forefathers had committed in Indian Removal.[90]

Despite these efforts, Choctaw Nation lawyer Patrick J. Hurley successfully blocked legislation to reopen the rolls.[91] Hurley admitted that the Mississippi Choctaws' condition was deplorable but contended that Article 14 claims had been extinguished by offering the Mississippi Choctaws allotments in Indian Territory.[92] The Mississippi congressional delegation then shifted strategies. At the same time they changed constituents, probably without even noticing.

Discredited in congressional hearings, the Society of Mississippi Choctaws faded out of the historical record after the defeat of the Harrison bill. Congressman Venable then began working on behalf of the Choctaw communities in his district.[93] Nothing in the historical record indicates that he even noticed this shift. Perhaps Venable had supported the Harrison bill out of collegiality, figuring that Choctaws in his district would share in the spoils. Or perhaps he now helped the Choctaw Council because the Society of Mississippi Choctaws had been discredited. Whatever his motives, transferring his focus from one group to another so seamlessly supports the idea that Mississippi politicians were primarily focused on Indians in the generic sense.

In response to Venable's request, the government sent Special Superintendent of the Indian Service John T. Reeves to Mississippi in 1916 and scheduled hearings in Union and Philadelphia for the following year. Mississippians rallied to the cause. On March 15, 1917, Venable placed an advertisement in the *Neshoba County Democrat* announcing: "Get every Indian you can to come to Philadelphia."[94] On the appointed day, three hundred Choctaws assembled at the Philadelphia courthouse. The Reverend Pat Chitto, who probably helped organize the meeting, addressed them in Choctaw. The congressional committee failed to reach Philadelphia because of a railroad strike. Venable, however, arrived and explained that the meetings in Union had gone well, and that he would get the Choctaws the aid they so desperately needed.[95]

Congressional hearings highlighted the Choctaws' unwavering sense of Indian identity. When asked what the government owed them, the general reply was that, since they were Indians, they should get schools, land, and help with farming.[96] Simpson Tubby reiterated a collective identity: "as a tribe, we see what the government has done for all the tribes, the different tribes of Indians, but the Mississippi Choctaw has not had anything at all, as I notice, since the Treaty of Dancing Rabbit Creek."[97] Despite lacking a tribal government, the Mississippi Choctaws still believed that they were entitled to government services because they were Indians. Eventually, this persistence paid off. In 1916 the OIA requested an appropriation for the Mississippi Choctaws.

Conclusion

The Choctaws' campaign for government recognition highlighted how federal policy makers reified the Choctaws' survival strategy of ethnically distinct closed communities through the full-blood rule of evidence. Choctaws were quick to take advantage of this convergence of blood quantum policies and their own racial practices. Similarities of credentialing do not imply analogous goals, however. Policy makers hoped to assign allotments to Indians as an instrument of assimilation. The Mississippi Choctaws demanded land to claim their treaty rights and reassert a tribal identity.

As race was not an indigenous concept, blood quantum policies could represent another example of federal interference in tribal affairs.[98] Yet perhaps a more nuanced interpretation is in order. As historian Alexandra Harmon has argued, the politics of blood quantum enrollment represented an attempt by both sides to affirm their own conceptions of race and belonging. Indians across the United States engaged notions of race in complex ways consistent with indigenous cultural symbols, conceptions of ancestry, and categories of inclusion.[99] They used the terms full-blood and mixed-blood literally or as metaphors for cultural or behavioral attributes.[100] The Mississippi Choctaw example tells a similar complicated story.

Although the Choctaws wielded racial terminology, understanding how they internalized race is problematic.[101] Analysis of the Choctaws' campaign reveals multifaceted meanings of their full-blood identity. References to full-blood reflected commitment to racial separatism and politically strategic thinking to comply with government requirements. Choctaws also used the language of blood to distinguish themselves from pretenders who attempted to usurp their Article 14 claims. Finally, their appropriation of the language of full-blood was also a reflection of Choctaw identity rooted in the culture that had sustained them since removal.

Choctaws obscured the boundaries between racial and cultural delineations of ethnic identity.[102] Their characterizations of themselves as full-blood Choctaws were not linked to race as whites generally understood it. These texts do not contain allusions to phenotypes, nor is there evidence of conflict between factions identified by blood quantum.[103] Choctaws articulated their historical and cultural identity in terms intimating a lack of race-mixing to establish themselves as the only lawful claimants of Article 14 lands.

The Mississippi Choctaws also used the ideology of full-blood to reconcile two sometimes competing conceptions of Indian identity—

ethnicity and tribal citizenship. Preserving their bloodlines through endogamy, Choctaws in Mississippi had maintained an "unadulterated" ancestry, which entitled them to tribal membership. Officials of the Choctaw Nation recognized their Mississippi kinsmen as Choctaws by blood, but the two groups diverged as to how that affected tribal citizenship. Choctaws in Indian Territory regarded citizenship as contingent upon residence in the Choctaw Nation.[104] Choctaws in Mississippi, however, held that their ancestry guaranteed them access to the resources of the Choctaw Nation regardless of where they lived.[105]

When the Mississippi Choctaws failed to make the case for absentee citizenship in the Choctaw Nation, their identification as the full-blood Mississippi Choctaws prompted the OIA to supply them with their own government services. Over the next few decades, the Choctaws used these federal resources to begin building better lives.

CHAPTER THREE

Establishment of the Agency, 1918–1930

Finally winning the 1918 appropriation was a triumph of political organizing, but it was only the first step toward tribal rebirth. Congress had recognized the Choctaws as Indians who deserved government land and services. Within two years, however, the U.S. Supreme Court proclaimed that they were not Indians but assimilated citizens of Mississippi because they had no reservation or tribal councils and they "had adopted the manner of living of the white citizens of the state."[1] Historian Paige Raibmon has deemed this the "one drop rule of civilization," an ideology by which government officials can decide that any evidence of assimilation obliterates Indian identity.[2] For Choctaw leaders, their manner of earning a living and lack of tribal government was irrelevant to their continuing collective identity as treaty partners with promises that the appropriation had only begun to fulfill. Thus, Article 14 lands remained at the center of Choctaw nationalism. Politicians and policy makers at the federal level were sympathetic to Choctaws' desires for land, but conflict over convoluted land claims made resolution of their claims difficult.

Nevertheless, government funds delivered much-needed support for destitute Choctaw communities. During the first several decades of the twentieth century, the federal government purchased farms for Choctaws. Unlike in most jurisdictions, the government did not regard these lands as allotments held in trust, but rather expected the Choctaws to reimburse them for these purchases. The OIA also constructed schools, which they hoped would promote middle-class norms, not only for Choctaws but for the region's poor whites. Choctaws, on the other hand, used these schools to fortify their communities and bolster their status as a third racial group. All of these efforts played out against a backdrop of rural poverty and racism—a setting that presented constant roadblocks to Choctaw success. As always, Choctaws negotiated these obstacles as best they could, and their communities saw slow improvements.

Securing the Appropriation:
Disease, War, and Paternalism

The 1916 Choctaw appropriation remained unfunded until a series of events in 1918.[3] The 1918 influenza pandemic devastated the Choctaws. The government estimated that several hundred Choctaws died, and 1920 census data suggests a possible twenty percent loss. The Choctaws and their allies used this grave situation to move the appropriations bill.[4] The flu pandemic was important in drawing attention to the Choctaws, but Indian oral histories attribute the government's interest to the need for manpower in the First World War. Former Choctaw Council member Baxter York believed that the federal government only "rediscovered" the Mississippi Choctaws because they were "looking for good men to fight the Germans."[5]

Military conscription sparked mixed emotions and raised questions about the Choctaws' legal standing. Several Choctaws wrote to Monsignor William Henry Ketcham, director of the Bureau of Catholic Indian Missions, requesting aid in resisting the draft.[6] J. A. Charley, a Choctaw man from the Conehatta community in Newton County, informed the monsignor that since the Choctaws "had nothing," they should not be obligated to go to war. Other Choctaws emphasized that Indians were not United States citizens and had no quarrel with anyone. A few of these letters explained that some white men had threatened Choctaws with arrest if they refused to register, while others had told them that they need not enlist. These Choctaws requested that Monsignor Ketcham ask the president what he wanted them to do.[7]

Both Monsignor Ketcham and Father A. J. Ahern, the priest at the Tucker mission, sought exemptions for the Choctaws because both men believed that state citizenship did not equate with U.S. citizenship. They soon discovered that such actions were futile. "I will let the authorities know what you say about the Choctaws of Mississippi being taken into the army," Ahern wrote to Choctaw leader Culbertson Davis. "I am afraid they will do as they please no matter what we say."[8] Some Choctaws raised enough money to send Willie Jim to Jackson, Mississippi, to inform the draft board they would not serve. Choctaws' failure to register for the draft prompted at least one complaint to the War Department, but no prosecutions for draft evasion followed.[9]

Choctaws' resistance to conscription echoed that of their poor black and white neighbors, for lower-class southerners generally did not support the war. Mississippi was the center of defiance. Most opposition condemned the war as a "rich man's war and a poor man's fight."[10] For Choctaw draft resisters, however, the issue was their lack of U.S. citizenship—a point of view held by other Native Americans. Despite protests, numerous Indians did serve in the war; fifty-nine Mississippi Choctaws were among them.[11]

A lack of documentary evidence makes it difficult to determine why some Choctaws served and others resisted. The geography of military service may be instructive, however. J. A. Charley noted that no Choctaws in Newton County had registered, but in Neshoba County "where there are so many bad white men they registered nearly all of the Indians."[12] Actually, one man, Anderson John, served from Newton County. Thomas Teach Roberson was the sole recruit from Kemper County, and John Hollan Charley was the lone soldier from Scott County.[13] Most Choctaw doughboys came from Neshoba and Leake Counties. This may simply reflect the denser population of Indians— Neshoba having 484 Choctaws and Leake having 249. Still, Kemper County had 102 Choctaws, 127 lived in Newton, and 124 resided in Scott. These counties could have contributed more men to the war effort.[14]

Historian Jeanette Keith's insightful work on draft resistance has demonstrated that draft officials in the less developed areas of the rural South often failed to fill their recruitment quotas, for resisters could easily avoid federal agents. Perhaps the Choctaw data reflect greater isolation of communities in Kemper, Newton, and Scott Counties.[15] Keith also documented, however, that avoidance of military service was not unheard of in Neshoba County.[16] Why, then, did so many Choctaws from Neshoba enlist?

Some may have been forced into service, as Charley suggested, but many probably went voluntarily. As with other Indians, Mississippi Choctaws enlisted to seek adventure and economic opportunity, to honor their traditional roles as warriors, or to demonstrate their patriotism and fitness for U.S. citizenship. As the list of World War I veterans included men from many families who had been active in the struggle for land claims, this latter motive was probably strongly at work in some communities.[17] Men who were petitioning the federal government for help probably did not want to explain why their people were not in uniform.

In maintaining good relations with their allies in Congress, Choctaws could have gone either way, for, signaling their divergent class backgrounds, Mississippi's senators were divided on the war. The champion of the "rednecks," James K. Vardaman, opposed the war, while the Delta patrician John Sharp Williams favored it.[18] Whatever the Choctaws' supporters thought of the war, Choctaw enlistment supplied them with an heroic image to manipulate in support of the appropriation. The use of the Choctaw language as a code during World War I further engendered respect for Choctaw military service. The visit of the commissioner of Indian affairs Cato Sells (an avid supporter of Indian enlistment) to Mississippi may have also contributed to Choctaw enrollment.[19]

In 1918 Commissioner Sells toured the South to visit Indians "which have been overlooked and neglected," and he promised them his "earnest attention."[20] This endorsement finally moved the Choctaw appropriation, which mandated salaries for "one special agent, who shall be a physician, one farmer, and one field matron," and furnished funds to establish schools and farming programs and purchase land for Indian farms on a reimbursable basis.[21]

As Indian settlements were dispersed across forty-seven thousand square miles in eight counties it was difficult to decide the best location for the agency.[22] After his tour, Sells recommended that it be erected in Philadelphia, which was the seat of Neshoba County, had a railroad, and appeared to be close to the center of the Indian population. He appointed Dr. Frank McKinley, a physician with ties to the Choctaws, as agent.[23] McKinley opened the agency in October of 1918, using the living room at his boarding house in Philadelphia.[24] The federal government was now prepared to give the Choctaws their "earnest attention."

"Uplifting" the Choctaws: Agency Programs, Rural Poverty, and Choctaw Communities

Government officials soon discovered, however, that regional poverty hindered their plans. The labor market in rural Mississippi in the early twentieth century was primarily confined to agricultural and extractive industries. Boll weevil infestations struck the area's small-scale subsistence farms and depressed the economy.[25] This downturn hit the Choctaws hard. In 1916 less than 10 percent of Choctaws owned their lands, and most of these farms were "heavily encumbered." The remaining Choctaws were sharecroppers or hired hands living on white men's farms, exchanging labor for room and board. Low-paid wage labor supplemented subsistence-level farming for most families. Choctaw families picked cotton (some migrating to the Delta), and men cut firewood and labored in lumber mills and camps.[26] Choctaw men could earn fifty cents per day clearing and splitting rails but generally avoided more skilled work in the sawmills, which they viewed as dangerous. Olmon Comby testified before the 1916 congressional hearings that he could earn seventy-five cents per day building bridges.[27]

Opportunities for Choctaw women were equally limited. With one exception—Molly Jim, who resided in the Bogue Homa community ninety miles south of Philadelphia—Choctaw women shunned domestic work, regarding it as an African American job.[28] Indian women worked in the fields, took in wash, or made and sold baskets. Women sold their crafts directly to their customers or marketed them through

Baptist minister James E. Arnold. After the agency opened, McKinley sold baskets and split-bottom oak chairs made by Choctaw men in his office, and persuaded the Municipal Art Gallery in Jackson to carry Choctaw baskets. As always, income from these sales was negligible, but production of these crafts underscored the Choctaws' unique ethnicity.[29]

Manufacturing, retail, and professional employment was available near Choctaw settlements, but Indians rarely held nonagricultural jobs, teaching and preaching excepted.[30] Choctaws could teach in segregated county and religious schools. Willie Solomon, Frank Johnson, Maggie Gibson Briscoe, Cornelia Stephens Ben, W. W. Jimmy, and Simpson Tubby were teachers between 1900 and 1928.[31] Simpson Tubby was also a sharecropper (until the government bought him a farm in 1928) and a Methodist minister.[32] Ed Willis and Willie Jimmie were part-time preachers who earned their primary livings by farming.[33]

Choctaws lacked education and language skills for retail jobs, and it was highly unlikely that a white-owned establishment would hire a person of color to interact with the public. The Philadelphia Bottling Company, an ice plant, and a mattress and upholstering business were nearby manufacturing facilities, but OIA officials never sought employment for Choctaws at those places.[34] This decision may have reflected policy makers' preference for making yeomen farmers out of Indians, or it may have signaled a realistic appraisal of the racial environment. Agent McKinley did, however, increase the number of Choctaw men who worked for the Molphus Lumber Company, one of the primary employers of skilled labor.[35]

Inadequate employment opportunities underscored the Choctaws' privation. Choctaw farms contained "a few heads of stock and one or two farming implements," and homes were generally "decrepit shacks and cabins."[36] Their main diet was cornbread supplemented with fish— meat was a rarity. Lacking kitchens, Choctaws cooked over outdoor fires. Choctaw women made all of their families' clothes—mostly by hand, as few women owned sewing machines—and most families did not have sufficient clothing. Few Choctaws were literate.[37] Poverty produced unsanitary conditions and diseases such as tuberculosis. The death rate exceeded the birth rate in all of the Choctaw communities. By 1916 scarcely one thousand Choctaws remained.[38]

Under these circumstances, extended families were crucial to survival, as they were for other poor rural people. Choctaws often shifted their residences between family and friends as they sought work. Extended families usually ate together even if they lived apart, and younger Choctaws cared for their elders.[39] Communities afforded support networks for extended families.

Choctaw communities had been slowly rebuilding after the Second Removal, and by 1916 several churches were reestablished. The Methodist church in Kemper County, the Catholic mission in Neshoba County, and James and Gena Arnold's Baptist mission in Newton County supplied farmland for Choctaws, but other Indian churches did not. Most of these congregations did not even have church buildings—they worshipped in schoolhouses.[40]

The Mississippi legislature supported segregated common schools for Indians in the early twentieth century.[41] Neshoba County had three and Leake County had two. Despite having eighty-eight school-age children, Kemper County had not resumed educating Indians after the Second Removal, nor had Scott County, with eighteen children.[42] Lacking educational opportunities, the Choctaw appropriation was a godsend.

The Mississippi Choctaws came under the administration of the Indian Office during a time in which government agents sought the incorporation of all Americans into a homogenous nation based on the cultural norms of the white middle class.[43] The 1887 General Allotment Act had mandated Indian assimilation. Under this legislation, the federal government allotted Indian reservations and established boarding schools to inculcate Indian children in Anglo-American culture. OIA officials assumed that most Indians resided west of the Mississippi and held collective lands where they could be effectively administered. This model had limited application for the Mississippi Choctaws, who did not have a reservation and whose children attended county schools. Nonetheless, OIA personnel attempted their broader goal of "uplift," beginning with education.[44]

The OIA hoped to use education to eradicate Indian culture, but they also sought to educate Indians for material improvement, a goal shared by Choctaw leaders. To shore up county-run Indian schools, McKinley persuaded the OIA to pay half of the teachers' salaries.[45] Federal inspectors reacted to these schools with revulsion, however, as their slovenly conditions offended their middle-class standards. OIA Inspector Peyton Carter, visiting in 1922, was appalled at the dirty, rundown, ill-equipped schools, the poorly trained teachers, and the low level of student achievement. He recommended that the OIA "cease any involvement with them."[46]

Government inspectors feared that poor county institutions would retard rather than encourage progress. This critique was part of their larger concern over the "hillbilly" environs of the Choctaw communities, which encouraged the OIA to promote the agency as an "edifying force" in rural Mississippi. For example, in 1921, when McKinley asked to move the agency to Jackson (for ease in travel to all communities), chief medical supervisor Robert R. Newberne recommended against it on the grounds that the agency could exert a "moral influence" on the community of Philadelphia, which he dubbed a "more degrading environment" than Jackson.[47]

Newberne's comments were typical of federal officials' reaction to rural Mississippi, where they reinterpreted their mission as one in which Indians were not raised to the economic level of their neighbors, but rather elevated above them. Policy makers hoped to improve the lives of poor whites by showcasing industrious Choctaw communities. Using Indians as examples of industry contradicted notions of Indian indolence held by many Americans, and revealed complicated attitudes toward race and class in the Indian Service.[48] Indians were part of a racialized minority requiring uplift, yet they ranked higher than poor whites in this OIA taxonomy. The Indian Service emphasis on promoting a middle-class lifestyle among poor whites resonated with other government bureaucrats, such as county extension agents and school administrators.[49]

Mississippi's boosters appreciated these efforts. At the time the agency opened, the editor of the *Neshoba County Democrat*, Clayton Rand, described Philadelphia, which had a population of 1,669, as "a village of squalor." The town was "without pavement or concrete walks, or electric lights, and possessed an antiquated and uncertain water system and limited plumbing facilities"; piles of rubbish cluttered the unpaved streets.[50] Neshoba County was also a violent place—the site of twenty-six murders between 1918 and 1922. Inspector Carter characterized these murders "typical of the feud histories of our mountain districts."[51]

The Philadelphia, Mississippi, judicial system did little to deliver justice. Rand remarked that, on the sporadic occasions when murder cases actually went to trial, juries rarely convicted murderers.[52] Florence Mars, a daughter of the prominent Mars family, remarked that an unwritten law in Neshoba County entitled a white man "to kill anyone he suspected of threatening his home." African Americans did not have the same leeway.[53] Observers agreed that despite prohibition, liquor motivated much crime, and nearby Leake County produced more moonshine than any other Mississippi location.[54] In short, the personnel of the Choctaw Agency had a Herculean task to reform the hill country.

To isolate the Choctaws from the "degrading influence" of poor whites, the OIA immediately opened three government day schools near Indian settlements. Pearl River (near Philadelphia in Neshoba County) and Standing Pine (in Leake County) opened in 1920, and Tucker (adjoining the Catholic mission in Neshoba County) began classes in 1921. Appropriations were slow in coming, however, and it took ten years to build government schools in each of the seven main Choctaw communities. The Bogue Homo School, ninety miles from the agency in Jones County, opened in 1922. The OIA launched Red Water Day School in Leake County in 1925, the Conehatta School in Newton County in 1928, and the Bogue Chitto School in Neshoba County in 1930.[55]

By operating schools solely populated by Indians, the federal government found itself in the awkward position of upholding racial segregation. Completely missing the irony, government inspectors criticized Mississippi's racial laws, but only one man proposed challenging them.[56] Jess Ballard, a U.S. probate attorney, recommended that the

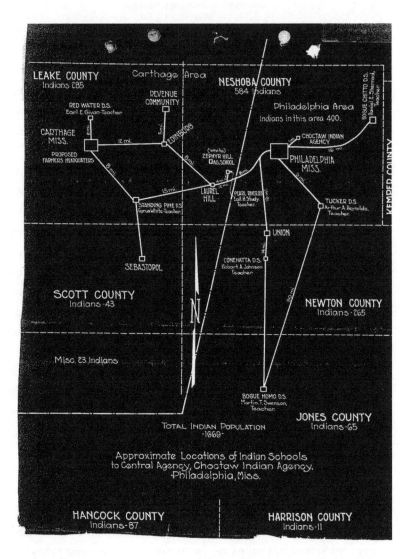

Fig. 6. Choctaw communities in Mississippi. Map from the Henry Roe Cloud Report, September 22, 1931. Source: CCF 150-29352-1931, NARA, Washington DC.

oia take action to save the Choctaws the "humiliation" of riding in segregated railroad cars. Rather than suggesting integration, however, he suggested that Indians be given their own coaches to prevent their association with poor people who might be in the white coaches.[57] The Choctaws, however, did not trouble themselves with the government's contradictions.

Some Choctaws eschewed oia schools—especially in the more conservative community of Bogue Chitto—but most Choctaw parents saw education as the solution to poverty. This was part of a long-standing tradition of embracing education for pragmatic reasons. Yet these schools also served broader purposes, and many parents viewed Indian schools from multiple perspectives.

In 1923 "the full-blood Choctaw Indians of Leake County" (location of the proposed Red Water School) petitioned the commissioner of Indian affairs to request that their school be constructed "on or near what is known as the Pioneer Public Highway" near Carthage because it was a more convenient location for accessing the railroad and would keep them "in touch with the outside world."[58] Local attorney William Weir forwarded the document, explaining that the agent was considering a more isolated spot and the Choctaws feared that "the owners of the land which are white people will be the only beneficiaries."[59] The tract the Choctaws wanted was unavailable, but McKinley honored the Indians' request for a location convenient to markets and purchased land on the Kosciusko federal highway.[60]

Generally, Indian Service school curriculum emphasized suppression of Indian identity. oia schools in Mississippi, however, inadvertently bolstered Choctaw ethnicity.[61] They allowed Choctaw parents to shun African American schools, which reinforced their status as a third racial group. School buildings became community centers for adult education and social gatherings. At the Standing Pine School ten to fifteen adults attended evening classes. Women held sewing circles where they discussed community matters; Dixie Johnson and Callie Chitto, wives of community headmen, organized one of these groups.[62] Likewise, wives of political leaders at the Red Water School had a sewing circle, led by Alice Billy and Katie Joshua, and a cooking club, led by Katie Joshua, Eva Sockey, and Maggie Anderson.[63] These women had their own standing in their communities apart from their husbands, and their gatherings served important community functions of solidarity and problem solving. OIA schools thus proved central to Choctaw communities.

Land and Choctaw Identity

Despite the Choctaws' enthusiasm for education, school enrollments were sometimes low and attendance sporadic because families needed their children's labor or landlords demanded that children work.[64] Agent McKinley lamented that he faced "the same responsibilities encountered on the reservations" but lacked "authority over citizen Indians who live for the most part on the lands of the white man."[65] McKinley's use of the term "citizen Indians" recognized that Choctaws were legally bound by state laws governing sharecroppers. He could not give farming help to Choctaw sharecroppers nor could he compel their children to attend school. The Indian appropriation did not negate state power over Choctaw lives, which landlords used to thwart attempts to escape peonage.

McKinley observed that many landlords did not want Indians educated for fear that Choctaws could no longer be tricked. He requested an investigation of landlord fraud, and the OIA sent United States probate attorney Jess L. Ballard to Mississippi in 1919.[66] Ballard's report concluded that most landlords did not pay Choctaw sharecroppers their promised wages. OIA Inspector Robert L. Newberne confirmed this in 1921 but also observed some exceptions, writing that "there are many that would extend a helping hand."[67] McKinley initially supposed that the presence of the agency would deter fraud, assuring Commissioner Sells in 1919 that "robbery of the Indians was sharply on the decline. Your visit and my watching has put the fear of God and the Law into many a crook."[68] McKinley's bravado did not last long.

The next year a nationwide agricultural depression following World War I collapsed the cotton market, and numerous landlords seized the corn Choctaws had saved for food. Even previously self-supporting families were now in danger of starvation, and McKinley pleaded for relief funds.[69] This was the first of many letters that Choctaw agents would write, venting frustration with debt peonage. Requests for an attorney to fight landlords went unheeded, and federal officials concluded that the only hope to escape peonage was to buy Choctaws their own farms.[70]

The agency had a fund to grant reimbursable loans for this purpose, and some Choctaws sold property they had inherited in Oklahoma and bought farms in Mississippi.[71] Because legal affairs in rural Mississippi were so disorganized, however, obtaining deeds for land was difficult.[72] In most cases, the territory stolen from the Choctaws lacked patents. One attorney estimated that roughly seventy thousand acres of land in Mississippi had no titles. Farmers claimed ownership by squatter's rights, living on the property and making improvements, or by paying property taxes. Families passed this land down through generations or sold it with no legal documents.[73]

Such actions were generally accepted by state and local officials, but the federal government demanded titles, and transactions often took years to complete. Some people refused any further dealings with the agency after these discouraging experiences. Missing the irony that their ancestors' theft of Choctaw lands was now hindering them, some Mississippians complained bitterly to the Office of Indian Affairs.[74] Not surprisingly, Article 14 moved to the center of this controversy.

As soon as the agency opened, Choctaw leaders requested an investigation into Article 14 claims.[75] In 1924 McKinley requested legal descriptions of all Article 14 lands granted to Choctaws whose fee patents had never been issued. Commissioner Charles Burke complained that sorting out patents would be too time-consuming, but McKinley countered that the federal government could save thousands of dollars budgeted annually for land purchases. "From my investigations," he wrote, "there are a hundred thousand acres or more of land reserved for these Indians the title of which is still vested in the United States; all of this land is in possession of whites."[76]

McKinley made little headway on the land issue, but his successor, Dr. Robert J. Enochs, and agency clerk Harry M. Carter examined tract books in fifty-five counties and uncovered unissued Choctaw patents for twenty-three thousand to twenty-five thousand acres. Enochs asked for assistance in reclaiming these lands, but assistant commissioner E. B. Merritt instructed him to pursue the matter in the state courts, which Enochs declined to do.[77]

A Senate subcommittee hearing in Philadelphia in 1929 discussed Article 14 claims at length. Enochs and Carter recounted how they located Indian patents and instructed the heirs to claim the land. They recognized, however, that anyone who attempted to redeem these patents would probably be shot.[78] The entire subcommittee also concluded that it would be "calamitous" to displace the white squatters. North Dakota senator Lynn Joseph Frazier and Mississippi representative Ross Collins opined that because of the unredeemed patents, the federal government should cease requesting reimbursement on Indian farms.[79] The rest of the subcommittee concluded that the OIA should abandon these unredeemed patents and continue to require Choctaws to purchase farms. Choctaws challenged this conclusion.[80]

Eleven Indians testified before the subcommittee and all expressed frustration with the government's efforts to help them; land issues were at the center of most complaints. Olmon Comby (spelled Cumby in some records), agency policeman, was one of the first to testify. Asked if the Choctaws believed that the government had given them a "square deal" by opening the agency, Comby was evasive. He finally answered that feelings were mixed and that the failure to expedite Article 14 claims was their "principal complaint." Willie Jimmie supported this conclusion, expressing his fears that he would never be able to repay his farm loans. Willie Solomon, Simpson Tubby, and Tom Jackson asked for more help with farming to avoid that same fate. Ike Jimmie pleaded for protection from men who were breaking into his house and trying "to get my land."[81]

Pat Chitto returned to the matter of unredeemed patents. "Lots of land could be recovered," he remarked, "but the Government never

sent out a lawyer." When Senator Frazier asked if they would be satisfied with other lands, Chitto replied, "We would be more satisfied if
we could get our ancestors' allotment."[82] Over the next four decades,
the Choctaws filed repeated suits and congressional bills seeking payment of Article 14 claims. Meanwhile, the Indian Service continued
to purchase reimbursable farms.

The agency slowly acquired lands, yet the overall impact of these
purchases fell far short of the government's aspirations. By 1927 the
number of Choctaws who were sharecroppers had been reduced from
90 percent to 75 percent of the population.[83] Land purchases accelerated in 1937, under the Indian Reorganization Act. By the 1950s only
half the Choctaws lived as tenants.[84]

Yet procuring farms did not always promote prosperity. Like most
of their poor neighbors, Choctaws lacked modern farming equipment.
Planting seeds by hand and using a single mule for plowing, hill country
farmers could not compete with large-scale mechanized cotton grow-
ers.[85] Choctaw farms, averaging less than forty acres, were too small to
supply sufficient income.[86] Finally, the primary cash crop, cotton, was
subject to price fluctuations, vulnerable to boll weevil infestations, and
dependent on weather patterns that were often either too wet or too dry.[87]

Rather than see Choctaw communities collapse due to farm foreclosures, in 1939 the government decided to hold lands procured with
reimbursable funds in trust for families who defaulted on their loans.[88]
By 1946, 80 percent of farm loans were in default, and the lands reverted to trust status. Many Choctaws, however, did not worry about the
failure of their loans. They believed that these farms were justly theirs
as descendants of the Article 14 claimants.[89]

Evaluation of the reimbursable farm program over the first four decades of the twentieth century suggests mixed results. It certainly did
not create the flourishing Choctaw communities that policy makers
had envisioned. Some observers thought that the Choctaws had ex-
changed dependency on one landlord for dependency on another—
the federal government. Yet government farms allowed some Choctaws
to break away from disreputable landlords and educate their children.

The agency provided better services to Choctaw farmers than those of landlords.[90] Agency schools had gardens and dairy cows, providing Choctaw children a hot meal at noon and plenty of milk, commodities that were rare in sharecropper homes. Choctaw families could occasionally sell wood and supplementary produce and dairy products to the schools.[91] Agent Enochs said in 1929 that families on reimbursable farms were "easily brought into the general activities of the agency for hospital and general health care."[92]

A few Choctaws on government farms commented that they had enjoyed more freedom farming for landlords, but more expressed gratitude for the government.[93] Landownership was the bedrock of respectability in rural Mississippi, and obtaining a farm was the goal of most poor people. Agency-procured farms improved the Choctaws' social status with their neighbors and stimulated Choctaw tribalism.

Land purchases strengthened communities and promoted political leadership. As the Mississippi, Alabama, and Louisiana Choctaw Council had ceased operating once the Choctaws won their appropriation, the agency was now the organization officially empowered to make collective decisions for the Indians. Yet it lacked formal mechanisms of governance. Though there was an agency policeman, Olmon Comby, there were no tribal courts, no tribal councils, and no jail. Comby's work consisted of doing odd jobs around the agency and taking intoxicated Indians to the Philadelphia jail.[94] Even though there was no tribal council, Choctaw community leaders continued to behave politically, pressing their land claims with numerous government officials. They also sought autonomy over their communities through farm chapters.[95]

Disdaining the segregated Farm Bureau, Choctaws organized their own farm chapters, which set community goals for crop production and stock ownership. At Standing Pine the "best organized and most enthusiastic" farm chapter functioned under the leadership of Olmon Comby, Johnson Billy, and Bennett York. A Parent Teacher Association, directed by Comby, Ben York, and Bennett York, also offered input into educational matters.[96] Agent Enochs proclaimed the Red Water School to be the second most "progressive" community. Ollie

Anderson, Will Wilson, and Pat Chitto led this farm chapter.[97] At the Pearl River School, Simpson Tubby and Byrd Issac ran the farm chapter, which operated by a committee comprised of John Simpson, Will Jimmie, Jack John, Albert Lewis, and Bill Willis.[98] Even the Conehatta community (which had no school) organized a farm chapter, headed by John W. King, Jim Lewis, and W. M. Solomon. Superintendent Enochs praised this chapter as an example of industriousness "most deserving of a Government School."[99]

Ironically, the Choctaws' limited success rebuilding their communities had unintended negative consequences for federal recognition. Some observers regarded functioning Choctaw communities as evidence that they were no longer Indians, as if Indians did not live near churches and schools. This came to light in a 1920 U.S. Supreme Court case, *Winton v. Amos*. In 1906 Wirt K. Winton, one of the heirs of an attorney who had sought to reopen the Choctaw Nation rolls, petitioned the U.S. Court of Claims regarding outstanding payment for his relative's services; several others who had aided in the effort later joined the suit. The Court of Claims ruled against them, declaring that they had no right to payment, and their appeal landed in the U.S. Supreme Court in 1920.[100]

During the trial, the federal government argued against the appellants' right to contract with the Mississippi Choctaws as a tribal group because the only legitimate Choctaw polity was in Oklahoma. The High Court agreed, holding that the State of Mississippi had declared the Choctaws' tribal government illegal and had made them citizens of the state. U.S. assistant attorney general Davis further submitted that "Choctaws who remained in Mississippi under that article adopted the dress, habits, customs, and manner of living of the white citizens of the state. They had no tribal or band organization or laws of their own, but were subject to the laws of the state. They did not live upon any reservation, nor did the government exercise supervision or control over them."[101]

The decision ignored the agency and schools the OIA had recently built. More importantly, it discounted the Choctaws' fierce preservation of their culture in crafts, ball play, dance, and language. Even though it was true that Choctaw men dressed like their white and black counterparts, Choctaw women and girls continued to favor the long calico dresses of the last century and to wear their hair long rather than bobbing it. Although this may have been due more to poverty than choice, it still marked Choctaw women as ethnically distinct from their neighbors.[102]

The true significance of the ruling was its disregard for the decisions of the Executive Branch to recognize the Choctaws as a discrete group of Indians. Thus, one branch of the federal government was busily administering the Choctaws as Indians while another declared that they were not Indians at all. The Supreme Court had therefore established a precedent that the allegedly assimilated Mississippi Choctaws had no legal standing as a tribe. Rather, they were solely citizens of Mississippi.

Conversely, some state officials denied that the Choctaws were Mississippi citizens because they had *not* assimilated. At the 1929 congressional hearings, newspaper editor and self-proclaimed Indian expert E. T. Winston, speaking as a representative of Governor Theodore Bilbo, asserted that "under our state law the Indian is not a citizen."[103] Although he admitted that the state had extended its jurisdiction over the Choctaws, he argued that this was meaningless because Choctaws had not assimilated enough to become citizens. Rather, they kept to themselves and lived like Indians, and Indians were wards of the federal government, not citizens of the state.[104]

Unfortunately, ran Winston's convoluted argument, the federal government had refused to "claim" the Choctaws, meaning that they did "not belong to anybody." He urged federal officials to step up and fulfill their treaty responsibilities.[105] Resurrecting the rhetoric used in the enrollment hearings, Winston remarked that "we owe these Indians our civilization today" because of the actions of Pushmataha. He promised that the state would cooperate with federal programs because the Choctaws had many prominent friends, including Representative Ross Collins.[106]

Senator Frazier countered that the United States had granted all Indians U.S. citizenship in 1924, which meant they were Mississippi citizens as well. Asserting states' rights, Winston replied that the Indians were "out of our Constitution" because they were disenfranchised by poverty. U.S. citizenship therefore mattered little.[107] The Choctaws' allies encouraged federal appropriations for the Choctaws because they were Indians while denying them full legal standing in the state of Mississippi for the same reason. These issues of jurisdiction would resurface repeatedly over the next forty years.

Conclusion

Neither the Supreme Court ruling nor the pronouncements of Mississippi officials had an immediate effect on Choctaw communities. Although government officials debated the role of assimilation in Choctaw citizenship and tribal standing, Choctaws ignored these issues. They continued to mark their ethnicity through dress, adornment, and crafts, and to affirm their treaty rights even as they embraced selected aspects of government programs. Choctaws viewed agency resources as a means to develop community leadership, fight poverty, and escape peonage. Indian schools helped them avoid African American faculties and provided an education that was roughly equivalent to that given poor white children. All these things supported Choctaw tribalism, which remained embedded in Article 14 claims.

Yet the presence of a federal organization in rural Mississippi proved complicated. As soon as the agency opened, class conflicts, sectarian strife, and regional hostility toward federal power sparked resentments among some of the Choctaws' neighbors.

CHAPTER FOUR

The Choctaw Agency and the Patronage Economy, 1918–1930

Evaluation of the role the Choctaw Agency played in rural Mississippi sheds light on the context in which the Choctaws negotiated their survival and reveals the multiple perspectives of class, race, and power Choctaws engaged as they sought autonomy. The Choctaw Agency was a contested ground. It created a patronage economy that was both a source of community pride and a cause of envy and resentment. White politicians and community leaders leveraged the presence of the agency to promote civic improvements. Indian Service schools accentuated class divisions over the role of government in education, and the agency's connections to the Catholic Church exacerbated sectarian strife that fed into the 1920s revival of the Ku Klux Klan. Klan-generated conflict further emphasized the gulf between Philadelphia's business leaders and their middle- and lower-class neighbors. All this occurred at a time when the penetration of the modern consumer economy into rural America had destabilized class relations.

Additionally, racial ideologies strengthened links between the agency and Philadelphia elites. Segregated Indian Service schools reinforced Jim Crow laws, and the need for the Office of Indian Affairs (OIA) to maintain the support of Mississippi's civic leaders facilitated the entanglement of agency personnel in racial politics. Analyzing these conflicts highlights how Choctaw alliances operated.

For the Choctaws the agency was a place to interact with community leaders who could further their goals. Agency resources enhanced the Choctaws' position in the economic hierarchy, but, like their poor black and white neighbors, their struggles with poverty remained the most salient feature of their daily lives. At agency ceremonial functions, Choctaws performed a blended identity for their neighbors. They stressed their "quaint and colorful" ethnicity, which played to their neighbors' imperialist nostalgia. Yet they also showcased their desire for economic progress and self-determination—actions that distinguished them from "poor white trash" in the racial triangulation of the rural South. At the height of the 1920s Klan revival, Choctaws cooperated with anthropologists John Swanton and Henry Bascom Collins in their studies of Choctaw culture and racial characteristics designed to prove that the Choctaws were not black. As they long had done, Choctaws traversed the convoluted tangle of race, class, regionalism, and ethnicity that characterized rural Mississippi by attempting to work their allies to their advantage. Their allies worked the Choctaw Agency as well.

The Agency and the Patronage Economy

The opening of the Choctaw Agency created both opportunities and challenges for rural Mississippians. When the OIA began planning schools, agent Frank McKinley warned of possible conflicts with potentially violent poor whites: "I shall have to exercise considerable tact in dealing with this feature [schools] as there is bitter opposition among the lower type of whites to educational help for Indians. They grudge every penny so expended and object to the economic emancipation of the Indian."[1] The editor of the *Neshoba County Democrat*, Clayton Rand, echoed this sentiment: "Neshoba citizens envied the Choctaw their new schools which were much better than those provided for white children."[2]

In response, Philadelphia's civic leaders instituted "Better School Week," holding rallies where luminaries such as Chief Justice Sidney Smith of the state supreme court urged educational progress. Yet low cotton prices and years of short crops had hurt tax revenues. Philadelphia elites proposed tapping the Smith-Hughes Federal Aid Act of 1917, which offered funding for local schools. This prompted some lower-class citizens to protest on the grounds of states' rights. Mississippi politicians also proclaimed commitment to states' rights but were nonetheless happy to embrace federal funding for their pet causes. Eventually, Philadelphia's boosters won the argument and began constructing better schools.[3] This did not, however, quell the controversy over Indian schools.

The presence of outsiders representing several reviled institutions incited conflict. A 1921 editorial in the *Union Appeal*, a newspaper in Newton County, sniffed: "We believe in education, but cannot see the justice of Congress appropriating vast sums of money to erect elegant schools in neighborhoods already provided with county schools, which money must be paid by the overly burdened tax payers who send their children to the county schools no better than the ones . . . for the Indians."[4]

Outraged citizens wrote to Congressman Ross Collins echoing this assessment and expressing fears of outside interference in schooling. Several people recommended that Collins channel all federal funding through the state so that local officials could make all spending decisions. One man grumbled, "Don't you know there are more than a thousand white voters in this District who are just as poor as these Indians and who have no better way of making a living than the Indians have?"[5] Despite these occasional expressions of petulance, however, there were no recorded incidents of violence, and some people encouraged the building of government schools.

Philadelphia's boosters recognized the potential of Indian Service facilities to motivate civic improvements and sought government subsidies for building projects, including an Indian hospital.[6] McKinley endorsed the idea but warned that using taxpayer money to construct a hospital available only to Indians when there was no hospital in Neshoba County would provoke resentment.[7] Clayton Rand used this possible antipathy to editorialize in the *Neshoba County Democrat* for a town hospital to match the proposed federal facility.[8]

By the time the project began, McKinley had been transferred and Dr. Robert J. Enochs had taken over.[9] Enochs judiciously marketed the hospital as a civic benefit and eventually convinced Philadelphia's elites to purchase and donate the land for it.[10] Articles in the *Democrat* proclaimed benefits for the entire community, such as a new road and water line in the neighborhood. The *Democrat* praised Enochs for preserving "the beautiful grove [of trees] around the buildings . . . in their natural beauty" and gushed that, "visitors to the grounds are pronouncing the site the most beautiful spot in Philadelphia."[11]

The Choctaw hospital opened in 1928 with a public reception. Father Philippe of the Tucker mission blessed the building, and Enochs, state representative T. B. Williams, and Philadelphia mayor A. B. McCraw gave speeches.[12] The hospital was an asset to the community, for although its services were not open to all, the infrastructure and aesthetic improvements it had brought were.

As with schools, the Indian hospital had encouraged development from the private sector. Dr. Claude Yates, an illustrious community leader, constructed a twenty-bed hospital in April 1927.[13] The success of these ventures prompted the *Neshoba County Democrat* to promote an Indian boarding school.[14] The Neshoba County chamber of commerce wrote the commissioner of Indian affairs and offered land for the school, enclosing a marketing brochure with pictures of county attractions. The chamber documented the need for this facility because Choctaw schools stopped at the sixth grade.[15]

The Choctaws desired a local boarding school as well.[16] Emmett York had contacted the commissioner in 1928 requesting such a school for grades 7 through 12. "This fall we sent 19 boys and girls to [boarding schools in] Oklahoma and Kansas," he wrote, and it was painful to part with these children. Emmett knew this personally, as he had sent his sons Baxter and Berkeley to Chilocco Boarding School in Oklahoma. Indian Service officials replied that there was no funding for this venture.[17] The chamber dropped the issue, but the town's most prominent citizens continued regular interaction with the agency, allowing Choctaws to reinforce relationships with their allies.

The Choctaw Agency played a significant role in the rhythm of small-town life, and Clayton Rand featured it prominently in the

Democrat. Everything that happened there was news: federal appropriations, ceremonial events, personnel changes, OIA inspections, and Indian activities received glowing coverage in the press.[18] According to Rand, OIA inspectors praised the outstanding work done by the dedicated staff, and one had concluded that "none in the Indian Service excel the Mississippi Schools."[19] In 1931 the "Twentieth Century Edition" of the paper, created by the members of the women's club of the same name, featured several laudatory articles on the Choctaws.[20] These stories recounted the familiar narrative of federal betrayal and the Choctaws' heroic efforts at self-help, aided, of course, by the "best citizens" of the county.

Highlighting the importance of the agency to Philadelphia, its employees were active in the town's social scene. Throughout 1932 the *Democrat* reported on monthly meetings of the Federal Employees Union—a social organization that performed programs of interest to the general public. Agent Enochs's wife frequently addressed their meetings as an authority on Indian history and lore.[21] Mrs. Enochs was a pillar of the community and appeared in the paper's "Society Notes" on a regular basis. When the OIA transferred Enochs to Kayenta, Arizona, in 1932, there were two receptions honoring him and his wife, and the paper ran a front-page story that made the role of the Indian Service in rural Mississippi most explicit: the paper praised Enochs for all the money he had brought to the city.[22]

The paper also covered other well-to-do matrons' Indian work. Mrs. H. L. King, whose husband ran a grocery in Philadelphia, was elected state chair of the Indian Welfare Committee by the General Federation of Women's Clubs (GFWC). She won national recognition for her "Tribal History of the Mississippi Choctaw," published in the state GFWC magazine. Mrs. J. M. Lofton, another doyenne of Philadelphia society, served as the state chair of the Indian Welfare Committee in the 1930s to congratulatory press reports.[23] The agency was an institution of the federal government, but Philadelphia's elites embraced it in part because the first superintendents were highly respected in the community.

In addition to reporting on the agency, Rand ran stories about the Choctaws, mostly emphasizing their gratitude to their benefactors. A classic example was Rand's account of the gathering at the Pearl River School to thank the U.S. government "for all it has done for the Choctaws since the agency was established at Philadelphia."[24] Rand's hyperbolic story about the opening of the school year at Tucker in 1920 described the distribution of school supplies and remarked that "one little buck was so overcome with joy" about his corduroy suit that he "lost all consciousness of the presence of others" and immediately began changing his clothes.[25]

Chatty items about Indians appeared in the same format used to note the activities of white people. Echoing the status hierarchy of the town, Rand generally focused on the families of Indian leaders: "The United States government has purchased 40 acres each for Simpson Tubby and Ed Lewis"; "Lena Pearl York spent last week nursing her ill mother"; "Mrs. Nancy York and Celia Simpson are recovering from illness"; "Mack Jimmy and Gassler York went to Carthage on business"; "a wedding of unusual interest among the Choctaw Indians took place at the new home of Simpson Tubby."[26] These stories reminded readers that despite their unique ethnicity, Choctaws led lives similar to theirs. Although use of such terms as "buck" and "squaw" were racist stereotypes, much of Rand's press coverage of the people he called "Original Americans" nonetheless normalized Indian lives for his readers.[27]

Not all of Rand's reporting was positive, for a small-town newspaper had important social control functions. Intermittent references to Choctaw misbehavior usually focused on drinking and fighting, but these were no more numerous than stories of other drunken brawls, nor were they sensationalized. These stories sometimes mentioned that Choctaws caught with liquor were found in the "Negro quarters," perhaps to remind them what happened when one keeps "bad company," and to reinforce the color line. Such reports served the same social shaming purpose as all tales of dysfunction in a small community—they publicly humiliated the wayward in hopes of provoking repentance.[28]

These accounts were the exception, however, for Rand generally presented the Choctaws in a favorable if condescending light.

Emphasizing the patronizing nature of this reporting, only one newspaper account presented a Choctaw viewpoint. In 1931 the *Democrat* ran a well-written piece by Bamen York, a sixth-grade student at the Pearl River School and son of Choctaw leader Emmett York. In Rand's estimation, this proved the "success of the Government schools."[29] Even when Choctaws claimed their own stories of success, Rand spun them to showcase the accomplishments of white elites.

The paper celebrated the Indians' progress toward assimilation, but notices inviting the public to Choctaw stickball games also appeared regularly. For Choctaws, these announcements served to remind their neighbors that Indians lived among them. For Rand's readers, they highlighted the entertainment value of Choctaw ethnicity.[30] The juxtaposition of progress and primitivism indicates that Mississippians still had bifurcated beliefs regarding their Indian neighbors.

The citizens of Neshoba County held Indian tradition and progress in tension by compartmentalizing Indian behavior and ignoring the context of rural poverty. Even though they urged material improvements, they also appreciated the Choctaws' colorful artistic traditions, their "euphonious and epigrammatic" language, and their exotic ritual funeral weeping.[31] There were no stories about Choctaws' suffering and poverty. Like those who had earlier lobbied for the ersatz Indians of the Gulf Coast rather than for Choctaw communities, many Philadelphia citizens seemed to prefer their ideas of Indians to actual Indians. This permitted them to control public discussion concerning the Choctaws.

The *Neshoba County Democrat* also used Choctaws to shore up regional pride. Rand reported that OIA inspectors viewed the Choctaws as more "advanced" than the "depraved" and "nomadic" western tribes. Mississippi's Indians were law-abiding, teetotaling, and chaste.[32] Some inspectors did indeed favorably compare Choctaws to other tribes: Choctaw women were excellent homemakers, "doing many things that your northern Indians have not yet learned to do," and Choctaw men were "generally good workers and have not the roving habit so common among the Indians." Choctaw children were superior to other Indian children in their chaste relationships: "The Indians of Mississippi in their primitive way with their native customs have brought about a condition which our schools in the north and west . . . have failed to accomplish entirely."[33] The newspaper spun Choctaw lives for the booster agenda, but it also presented positive public relations for the Choctaws, who found ways to capitalize on it.

Choctaw leaders actively promoted their own interests in the *Democrat* by participating enthusiastically in agency ceremonies marking their accomplishments. This publicly reinforced ties with their supporters. For example, in 1921 Simpson Tubby asked Rand to speak at the dedication of the Indian school at a Methodist mission in Blackjack, Neshoba County.[34] The field day at the Pearl River School in April 1927 drew Congressman Ross Collins, state representative T. Weber Wilson, and T. Brown Williams, president of the Cotton States Merchants Association, all of whom made pompous speeches extolling the virtues of hard work. Cooking and sewing displays made by women in the adult education classes prompted much praise, the children's choir performed "My Country, 'Tis of Thee," and Choctaw leaders Scott York and Simpson Tubby encouraged the crowd to continue their hard work.[35] In the fall of 1927, the Choctaws held a fair at the Pearl River School. The *Democrat* reported that the Indians had an excellent display of produce, poultry, and beautiful crafts.[36]

Unlike in other contexts where Euro-Americans divided Indians into a binary of assimilated "progressives" or conservative "blanket Indians," the Choctaws' supporters encouraged "their" Indians to be a little of both, and Choctaws took advantage of that dichotomy.[37] By featuring Indian crafts and promoting stickball games in the *Democrat*, Choctaws used the press to assert their ethnicity. By also celebrating their agricultural and educational accomplishments, the Choctaws promoted an image of themselves as progressive. Given the politics of race and class in rural Mississippi in the early twentieth century, however, the triumphalist stories told by leaders of each group masked a complicated reality.

The Agency in Rural Mississippi: The Politics of Race and Class

Many prominent individuals supported the Choctaws, and those who publically resented expenditures for them tended to be lower-class whites. Yet interactions with the Indians were shaped by a variety of self-interests, and no single class was either entirely supportive or tyrannical. Rather, the Choctaws' position in the economic, social, and political hierarchy of rural Mississippi in the early twentieth century was influenced by a range of variables. It could be argued that the primary issue in Choctaw lives was poverty, which subjugated whites, African Americans, and Choctaws alike. There is conflicting evidence regarding the degree to which race affected this oppression. Were all sharecroppers equally miserable regardless of their race or were people of color more downtrodden than poor whites? If so, where were Choctaws located in this taxonomy? The answers to these queries depend on specific categories of analysis at particular moments in history.

Beginning with politics, Mississippi's Democratic Party was a white man's party beset with class tensions that stretched back into the nineteenth century. Following Reconstruction, planters and business leaders from the Delta dominated state government. Power briefly shifted away from this group in 1903, when escalating agrarian discontent brought about an era of "redneck rule" in Mississippi. This period ushered in Progressive reforms helpful to the middle and lower classes, such as changes in banking practices that had favored the wealthy and laws restricting the power of corporations. By the time the agency opened in 1919, planters and business interests had regained control of Mississippi's political machinery, instituting "business progressivism" more amenable to their objectives.[38]

The agrarian interests that had led the so-called revolt of the rednecks, however, were numerous in the hill country, and their champions, such as James K. Vardaman and Theodore Bilbo, both of whom had served in the state legislature and the U.S. Senate, remained very popular in Neshoba County. These men spoke to cheering crowds at the county fair every year. Philadelphia's business elites, however, disapproved of

Vardaman and Bilbo, and Rand complained that the Neshoba County Democratic Party was bitterly divided between the two camps.[39]

With regard to race, white supremacy was the political bedrock doctrine, holding all whites to be superior to all nonwhites regardless of class, but lived experience in Mississippi was more convoluted than this model suggests.[40] The upper and lower classes of Mississippi differed sharply on how to frame alleged black inferiority. Middle-class politicians courted the lower classes by racial invectives that reinforced white solidarity across class. Mississippi's wealthier leaders considered this approach vulgar, and planters feared that race-baiting would drive away their black laborers.[41]

Despite the racial rhetoric, class sometimes trumped race in state politics. Poll taxes and literacy requirements could disfranchise the poor and uneducated regardless of race. The "understanding clause" that regulated voting allowed poll officials to disenfranchise anyone who could not answer questions about the state constitution. Depending on the circumstances, Mississippi's ruling elites were as likely to use this clause to withhold the vote from poor whites as they were to send away people of color from the polls.[42]

In the hill country, however, political participation was sharply constrained by race. All classes of whites were politically active, and all people of color were excluded from politics. Commenting on the "understanding clause" of the Mississippi Constitution, Rand remarked that while African Americans were asked to define such obscure political terms as "an *ex post facto* law . . . no white man was ever subjected to this severe test."[43]

The Choctaws did not appear to concern themselves with disfranchisement. Choctaws sought aid from their elected officials, but they remained aloof from electoral politics.[44] This may have been a means of highlighting their separate juridical identity. Choctaws had their own community politics, and as long as Choctaw leaders had the support of elected officials, they may not have felt the need to help select them.

Beyond politics, landownership conferred respectability regardless of race. Philadelphia's elites often held Choctaw and African American yeoman farmers in higher regard than landless poor whites. The majority of African Americans in the hill country were tenant farmers or domestic workers, but there was a small community of relatively comfortable black yeomen farmers in the Mount Zion community on the outskirts of Philadelphia. Founded in 1879 by two former slaves, Mount Zion had several schools. Florence Mars, granddaughter of one of the town founders, remarked that Mount Zion residents were "treated with a respect not ordinarily afforded Negroes or even some whites; they could borrow money on their names and reputations." Poor blacks received no such consideration, but "poor white trash" seemed to have been most scorned.[45]

As was true a century earlier, Neshoba County elites such as Mars and Rand drew distinctions between poor whites and "white trash." The issue was, in Mars's view, "their manner of living . . . they did not live like decent white folks were expected to." Mars characterized them as transient, drunken, violent, slovenly, and "sullen and standoffish"— meaning not sufficiently deferential to their "betters." They neither attended church nor sent their children to school.[46] In his writing, Rand's portrayal of the "hillbillies" was only somewhat kinder, expressing sympathy for their poverty but also indulging stereotypes of lower-class incest.[47] Evidence of these attitudes supports recent studies that demonstrate how a generalized commitment to white supremacy among white southerners was strongly influenced by class concerns.[48] Choctaws, of course, were also quite poor, but their behavior was more in line with expectations of propriety.

Both Mars and Rand regarded the Choctaws affectionately, noting that even the poorest Choctaws attended church and attempted to educate their children. Choctaws were perfect examples of the "deserving poor" because of their sobriety, industry, and integrity.[49] The degree to which these attributes helped the Choctaws economically was a matter of debate. Over the first four decades of the twentieth century, several government inspectors concluded that Choctaws lived somewhat better than African Americans, and some observers viewed the Choctaws as superior to African Americans in the social hierarchy.[50] Several Choctaws, however, did not share this interpretation.

Choctaws who commented on race relations in the 1917 Senate subcommittee hearings in Union believed that their African American neighbors generally lived better than they did because blacks were more employable. As Simpson Tubby observed, African Americans knew "when to move when the white man speaks to him" because he had learned to work "under the lash of the whip."[51] The remark drew a boundary between Choctaws and African Americans that implied pride in the Indians' historical status as free people, and intimates that some Choctaws believed that African Americans' status was forever linked to slavery. This was an idea widely debated among Indian intellectuals in the early twentieth century.[52]

Some Indians believed that this history had condemned black people to a lower rung on the socioeconomic ladder, but Tubby seemed to believe it conferred an advantage. One OIA inspector contradicted Tubby's assessment, writing that Indians were the more employable because they were "more docile and more tractable, and would work for a cheaper wage." He concluded, however, that this meant little, for Choctaw homes reflected the lowest standard of living in the region.[53]

Whatever group was more employable, relations between the Choctaws and their African American neighbors appeared to be either amiable or nonexistent.[54] In 1922 OIA inspector Robert L. Newberne wrote: "I am glad to say that the colored people treat the Indians kindly. The two races do not mingle—nor does one seek to pauperize the other through indirection—but maintain a live-and-let-live policy in their relation to each other."[55] Over the years, other OIA personnel echoed this sentiment, and Choctaw oral histories confirm it. Faced with severe racism, Choctaws' primary concern in race relations was protection of their own ethnic status.[56]

It is difficult to measure the subjective suffering of each group accurately, for their relative situations depended on specific contexts.[57] For all sharecroppers in rural Mississippi, life was brutal, and some government officials perceived no differences between the manner in which sharecroppers of diverse races lived.[58] Escape from peonage was rare, and farm ownership was out of reach for most sharecroppers regardless of race. Before the arrival of federal funds, however, African Americans were more likely, as a percentage of their total population, to own their farms than were Choctaws. This may have been because African American communities valued individual landownership while the Choctaws tended toward a more collective model.[59]

Yet once the agency opened, the Choctaws had access to resources unavailable to both poor whites and blacks—including access to capital. Choctaw families' day-to-day existence might have differed little from their poor neighbors, but Choctaw ethnicity conferred tangible material benefits. Ultimately, however, segregation (whether legally prescribed or customary) meant that individuals achieved their financial and social status in very separate contexts.

Though county residents of all races filled Philadelphia's town square on Saturdays, shopping and mingling, they otherwise lived in distinct worlds.[60] During the 1920s the population of Neshoba County was overwhelmingly white and Protestant. The total white population in 1920 was 15,872. African Americans numbered 2,949, and there were roughly 477 Indians. There was one Chinese man and a handful of Catholics at the Tucker mission or the Holy Cross Catholic Church in Philadelphia.[61]

Florence Mars believed the races got along, and that most whites "did not approve of violence towards Negroes so long as the Negroes stayed in their place." Violence against blacks was only socially acceptable "if they stepped out of line by disputing a white man's word or looking at a white woman."[62] As long as nobody challenged the hierarchy, racial accord appeared to be the norm. Therefore, many people could not fathom why the Ku Klux Klan would suddenly revive. The Klan campaign suggests insights into the convoluted maze of race, ethnicity, and class that characterized the Mississippi hill country and reveals places where the Choctaws and their agency intersected with the local politics of race and class.

The 1920s Klan Revival: Race, Class,
and Ethnicity in Neshoba County

According to several reports, controversy over the Klan "split the town wide open."[63] The Klan was, Rand wrote, "a strange conglomeration of religious bigots, decent citizens, visionaries, and bootleggers."[64] Rand surmised that frustration with lawlessness had driven the "decent citizens" to the Klan, and this drew politicians courting votes. An agricultural depression from 1919 to 1922 also fueled Klan membership. As farms failed, Neshoba County's lumber mills, the primary industry in the area, struggled to stay solvent. Simultaneously, county taxes rose, and a scandal involving the engineer who oversaw drainage districts for county farms raised the cost of drainage work 30 percent. According to Rand, a speaker at one taxpayers' meeting "advocated the rebirth of the Ku Klux Klan" as a solution to these woes.[65]

Rand surmised that economic resentments underlay Klan attacks on African Americans in the sawmill community of Deemer near Philadelphia.[66] Founded in 1907, the Deemer Manufacturing Company rapidly became one of Neshoba County's premier employers. The sawmill had shut down during the agricultural depression following World War I, but reopened about 1923 as cotton prices rebounded.[67] When the mill hired African American workers, Klansmen visited Deemer at night, setting off dynamite and firing guns into the workers' homes. On several occasions, Klansmen fired into trains on which black men worked, once killing a black brakeman.[68] The African American victims of this violence left no public records, and their ultimate fate is unclear. The Klan did not target Choctaw sawmill workers at the Molphus Lumber Company, however, perhaps because of their relatively small numbers, their perceived inability to compete economically, or their close relationship with one of the Klan's most notorious organizers.

Agency farmer T. J. Scott, one of the Choctaws' most beloved allies, was also one of the most vocal proponents of the Klan.[69] The Neshoba Klan drew support from across economic lines, but, as in other southern locations, it was directed by reputable people—including Baptist

Fig. 7. Agency farmer and Klan organizer T. J. Scott with a group of Choctaws, 1925. Photographer: Henry Bascom Collins. Source: National Anthropological Archives, Smithsonian Institution (01778500).

ministers, physicians, and other professionals—who organized through the Masons.[70] Scott certainly fit this model of respectability. He was a self-made man—a Mason who held a civil service appointment earning an annual salary of eighteen hundred dollars, a Sunday school teacher, and a member of the school board.[71] Scott's long-standing good relationship with the Choctaws may have deflected Klan violence. His facilitation of an anthropometric study of the Choctaws' racial purity by anthropologist Henry Bascom Collins—arranging the interviews at a home where the Klan held meetings—may have reinforced the Choctaws' unique racial standing.

Henry Bascom Collins was an archeologist and curator for the Smithsonian's Bureau of American Ethnology and Department of Anthropology. He began a study of Mississippian mounds in 1925, at which time he contacted Scott and asked to measure Choctaws' racial characteristics to evaluate their degrees of Indian blood.[72] This activity fell under the discipline of anthropometric science, which was popular at the turn of the twentieth century. Anthropometric science measured skin tone, hair texture, and head and facial characteristics to determine degrees of blood, which government officials regarded as a gauge of competence.[73] The OIA sometimes hired academic anthropologists to determine blood quantum, as they did on the Anishinaabe reservation at White Earth in 1916. As historian Melissa Meyer noted, this action meant that "outright racism received the imprimatur of academia."[74] Collins was not interested in policy, however, but in furthering anthropological taxonomies of racial types.

The Choctaws' reputation for full blood was well known among anthropologists, and Collins believed that they represented one of the "purest" strains of Indians in America—the "brachycephalic type of the lower Gulf Coast." Collins measured fifty-eight Choctaws, including Joe Chitto, Scott York, Ed Willis, and Willie Solomon, and made meticulous notes about their bodies, faces, skin tone, and hair.[75] The resulting 1925 and 1926 papers in the *American Journal of Physical Anthropology* were inconclusive and called for further research.[76]

As it is doubtful that the citizens of rural Mississippi read and debated Collins's work, his conclusions were less important for the Choctaws' purposes than was the study itself. The Choctaws' willingness to participate implies that they wanted to buttress their racial credentials in the face of Klan tensions—Scott's facilitation supports this notion. As both a Choctaw ally and an organizer for the Klan, he wanted to protect his friends from violence. Ironically, then, both Scott and the Choctaws used the methods of scientific racism to fight against racism. Choctaw reactions to Collins's study are lost to history, but their participation in this intrusive exercise underscores their continued emphasis on their pure Indian blood. This may have shielded them from accusations of race mixing that led to violence elsewhere in the South.

To further stress Choctaw ethnicity, Simpson Tubby and Olmon Comby gave interviews to ethnographer John R. Swanton in the early 1920s. Also a member of the Bureau of American Ethnology, Swanton documented Choctaw culture for his work *Source Material for the Social and Ceremonial Life of the Choctaw Indians*, published in 1931. Acting as a salvage anthropologist, Swanton's goal was to collect historical accounts of Choctaw life into a synthesis that would portray a vanished Choctaw culture.

Swanton conducted interviews but did not accept the notion of continuing Choctaw ethnicity, writing that "on account of the rapid disappearance of the ancient customs, little can be gathered at the present day that has not already been recorded in a much more complete form."[77] Like other anthropologists working in the early twentieth century, Swanton believed that accepting elements of mainstream culture meant that Indians had assimilated. This prevented him from seeing how Choctaws had adapted to modern circumstances while preserving their culture.

Comby and Tubby supplied Swanton with stories of the Choctaw migration legend, subsistence practices, political and social structures, stickball games, warfare, ceremonies, and medicinal practices.[78] Neither man explained why they cooperated with this endeavor, but these public assertions of Indianness reinforced their "non-colored" identity. As subjects of two anthropological studies in the 1920s, the Choctaws were now more firmly categorized as Indians, which may have helped to deflect Klan violence.[79] Some Choctaws, however, suffered indirect harassment because of their Catholicism.

Religion figured prominently in the Neshoba County Klan. Ministers preached pro-Klan sermons and led attacks against its critics—Clayton Rand being the most vocal.[80] Rand's anti-Klan editorials made him the subject of vitriolic sermons, but his real offense was his regular visits to the Choctaw Catholic mission. Rand went to discuss literature and the arts with Father Philippe, but Klansmen spread rumors that he was taking instruction for conversion. One evening as he was returning home, they fired guns into the air and lit a cross beside the road. Rand slept with a gun underneath his pillow for a time, but there were no further confrontations.[81] Aside from rancorous rhetoric and the single incident of the cross burning there is no evidence that the Neshoba County Klan directly attacked any Catholic property or personnel.[82] Nonetheless, the majority of Catholics in the county were Choctaws, who were undoubtedly frightened by ugly sectarian language and the burning cross near their mission.

The agency's connection with Catholicism might have encouraged Klan harassment of agent McKinley. Former Choctaw Tribal Council member Baxter York recounted that McKinley endured "a little rough time too [*sic*] himself, because he got into some of the worst K.K. nest in this country."[83] McKinley purportedly confronted Klan aggravation by threatening that if anyone hurt him, numerous federal marshals would retaliate, but "if I shoot you down, it won't be nothing said."[84] Remarkably, McKinley's clash with the Klan did not affect his relationship with Scott. Indeed, he praised Scott precisely because of his "redneck" credentials, informing Commissioner Sells that "I need experienced mature men who know the laws and customs of the hill country as well as its agriculture. Men who can and will beard a hill billy in his den and make him come clean. Callow timid youths fresh from college simply get in our way."[85] It is unclear exactly what conflicts McKinley had with the KKK, but his harassment may have reflected cultural tensions triggered by the agency's support of the Catholic mission.

Before the agency opened, Commissioner Sells had to dispel rumors that the Choctaw appropriation placed Indian Service schools under Catholic control.[86] Priests at the Tucker mission encountered so much hostility that they decided against building chapels in isolated areas for fear they would be burned down. Instead, they held mass on farms in Stratton, Pearl River, and Standing Pine where Catholic Choctaws sharecropped.[87] In 1919 one landlord in Stratton warned Father A. J. Ahern that he could no longer hold mass on his farm, for "he could not risk drawing down on himself the anger of his neighbors."[88] Choctaw catechist Culbertson Davis warned Ahern that a mob had threatened "to take him into the woods" if he returned to Stratton.[89]

Ahern traced the ill feelings to Baptist missionary James E. Arnold, who spread rumors that Catholics were arming the Choctaws to fight for the Germans.[90] Sectarian frictions continued in 1921 when someone informed Congressman Ross Collins that the majority of Protestants were offended by Catholic school appropriations.[91] Thus, even though Indian schools never became direct targets of Klan violence, they nonetheless contributed to the sort of anxieties that motivated many people to join the Klan.

A backlash organized by Philadelphia's wealthiest leaders eventually drove the Klan out of town.[92] Adam Mars, the region's largest landholder, frequently expressed his disdain for the Klan.[93] J. H. Hester, president of the Bank of Philadelphia and general manager of Anderson Molphus Mercantile Company, and J. C. Garrett, office manager of Hendersonville Mercantile Company, also led efforts to discredit the Klan.[94] Abner DeWeese, owner of a profitable lumber company and dry goods establishment, stood up at a Klan presentation and objected to scurrilous remarks about Clayton Rand. After his scandalized neighbors chastised him for this public display of rudeness, he sent a long letter to the paper defending himself and Rand.[95] Why did these prominent men despise the Klan?

Like other southern community leaders, these men did not condemn Klan racism, for they generally shared it. Rather, there is a resounding note of outraged paternalism in their letters to the *Neshoba County Democrat*. DeWeese asserted that no one could "handle the negro as diplomatically and successfully as our Southern citizenship." Likewise, businessman Andrew Gibson stressed, "We don't need [the Klan] to tell us we are superior to the negro [*sic*]."[96] Gibson questioned whether the Klan really sought to protect white women from rapist black beasts allegedly stalking the South: "Do we have to hide behind masks to uphold and fight for the purity of our womanhood? No, rest assured that if that was the Klan's real purpose there would be no masks, they would only be proud to show their faces."[97] The Klan's patrician critics angrily rejected the notion that they did not have race relations under control. They viewed this suggestion as evidence that their class hegemony was under assault, and indeed it was.

Conflicts between wealthy merchants and less affluent farmers tore the social fabric of the community in the years following World War I. Neshoba County's farmers were beginning to form cooperatives with the Farm Bureau, allowing them to buy supplies in bulk and to market their produce directly to the public. Both these actions sidestepped the town merchants.[98] Despite Philadelphia's isolation and poverty, elements of modern consumerism began filtering into the rural economy. When electricity came to Philadelphia in 1911, people began filling their households with electric appliances and radios.[99] Mail order catalogs were the cheapest source of these consumer goods, and this further undercut the merchants. Rand conducted a fierce editorial crusade against the catalogs in 1923, accusing them of creating a "false economy" in which business profits left the community, hurting infrastructure and civic projects.

To illustrate his point, Rand informed his readers indignantly that a well-known catalog company had refused to donate to Philadelphia's Boy Scouts. Rand had chosen this example carefully, because scouting had allegedly halted a growing problem with drug addiction among young men. Philadelphia's business elites had raised seven thousand dollars for a Boy Scout lodge and camp. For these community scions, then, perhaps the worst insult of catalog shopping was that it smacked of ungratefulness. As Rand reminded his readers, when hard times befell the community, local merchants granted credit but mail order houses did not. The social order in which Philadelphia's business elites had received deference was under assault.[100] Besides, bigotry was bad for business.

Philadelphia's business community denounced Protestant chauvinism in the *Democrat*.[101] Whatever Philadelphia's Protestant elites thought of Catholicism privately, publicly they were tolerant. The Neshoba County chamber of commerce created a flyer for business investors in the 1920s that featured thirteen of the town's most beautiful buildings. The handbill displayed "The Holy Cross Church (Catholic)" along with the First Baptist Church and other public buildings.[102] Philadelphia's boosters probably included the picture of the Catholic church to showcase Philadelphia as tolerant and progressive. The presence of the Ku Klux Klan upset this bucolic image and discouraged business investment.[103]

Apprehension over economic stability also motivated Klan detractors in the Mississippi congressional delegation. Senator John Sharp

Williams and Congressman Pat Harrison joined patricians from across Mississippi in resisting the Klan. Senator LeRoy Percy, a Delta planter, became a national anti-Klan crusader, publishing his criticisms in the *Atlantic Monthly*. He eventually drove the Klan from his county.[104] By 1924 the KKK was fading from the state.[105] About that time, a Philadelphia bank foreclosed on the building that had been Klan headquarters, and the *Neshoba County Democrat* bid the Klan good riddance.[106]

Highlighting the multifariousness of racial attitudes in Mississippi, Choctaws drew support from both advocates and opponents of the Klan.[107] The same combination of noblesse oblige and economic interest that motivated Philadelphia's elites to help the Choctaws also encouraged them to reject the Klan. As historian Barbara J. Fields has argued, racial ideology exists within patterns of social relations that often necessitated holding in tension contradictory views.[108] Thus Klansman T. J. Scott's affection for the Choctaws—even those who were Catholic— shows how racial compartmentalization operated at the level of individual relationships.[109] Choctaws' embrace of segregation and their use of scientific racism to promote their full-blood status encouraged many white supremacists to view them positively. Though the Choctaws were not white, for Klan purposes they were also not "colored." Nevertheless, they were still denied access to public accommodations reserved for whites. In public spaces, individual feelings for the Choctaws were subordinated to the dictates of segregation.

The most egregious example of this occurred when Indians who lived far from the agency came to transact business and needed overnight lodgings. Because no white hotels or rooming houses would take them and they refused to sleep in black facilities, the Choctaws were compelled "to sleep out[side] even in the most inclement weather."[110] Agent McKinley reported that visiting Choctaws were sometimes forced into livery stables, "where they are thrown in with the most vicious elements of the population."[111] McKinley rented a building for these Indians but it was "hardly more than a shed."[112] The need to preserve the operational relationship between the Choctaw Agency and Mississippi politicians meant that the federal government did not insist that

Choctaws be accommodated in white lodgings. This dilemma crystallized when, in the midst of the Klan controversy, the agency was dragged into a political scandal involving the allegedly Choctaw Baptist minister J. E. Arnold.

The Agency in Mississippi's Racial Politics

J. E. Arnold had been first in line to tap the 1918 appropriation, lobbying to locate the agency near his home in Union and seeking funding for his mission school. Assistant commissioner E. B. Merritt initially rejected his requests.[113] His wife, Gena, however, persuaded one of the most distinguished men in Meridian, William McLemore—a descendant of the town's founder Richard McLemore—to lobby Congressman Webb Venable on their behalf. Merritt relented, allowing tuition payments for Indians in the Arnolds' school.[114]

This move incited controversy. Agent McKinley cautioned against funding the Arnolds, noting that they falsely portrayed themselves as working for the OIA and questioning their claims to Indian blood.[115] OIA inspector Peyton Carter investigated the situation in 1923 and raised similar questions about Arnold's alleged Choctaw identity: "A considerable number [of whites] believe him to be colored. I am certain we will find that it would be unfortunate for us to put our school in any place where it might be dominated to any extent by a person of this sort. You will understand I am not now referring to the fact that this man is part colored, but to the fact that many people believe him to be so."[116] Carter was sensitive to the racial politics of small communities, and given the Klan agitation, he wanted to protect the agency. Circumstances, however, had already thrust the agency into the eye of a racial storm in Philadelphia, one that swirled around the 1922 Democratic primary.

In this primary, Gena Arnold challenged Congressman Ross Collins for his seat representing Mississippi's Fifth Congressional District. Collins was a renowned politician who had served as state attorney general before assuming his congressional seat.[117] When Arnold announced her candidacy, McKinley took out an ad in the *Meridian Star*—a newspaper from Collins's hometown—proclaiming that J. E. Arnold was the descendant of a Negro woman. Agency farmer Scott sent letters repeating these charges to the board of the Southern Baptist Convention.[118]

Mrs. Arnold lost the primary, and she and her husband filed a libel suit in the District Court of Washington DC against Collins, commissioner of Indian affairs Charles R. Burke, assistant commissioner E. B. Merritt, McKinley, and Scott. The Arnolds asserted that James was of Choctaw descent and demanded twenty-five thousand dollars in damages.[119] Collins countered that his pronouncements were a public service, fulfilling his "duty" to inform his constituents that Mrs. Arnold had violated Mississippi's miscegenation laws. Collins emphasized that none of his constituency was Negro (a technically accurate statement as the thousands of African Americans in his district were disfranchised) nor would any of them ever vote for a Negro or a white woman who "consorted" with Negroes.[120]

The case highlighted the political complications of appointing Mississippians to agency jobs. Ignoring his responsibility to the Indian Service, McKinley had given Collins damaging information on Arnold from OIA files. The Arnold family had sued for enrollment with the Choctaw Nation, and the case had been heard in the Choctaw Citizenship Court.[121] Even though the court had not conclusively proven Arnold's ancestry, strategically leaked documents from the agency alleging his Negro blood had sunk Mrs. Arnold's campaign.[122] The Arnolds had little choice but to claim a Choctaw identity in their defense.

For a second time, James E. Arnold defended his alleged Indianness in court, but this time his defeat was decisive. Collins's lawyers produced a copy of a will, dated May 11, 1870, wherein James Arnold Sr. proclaimed: "I formerly owned as a slave a woman by the name of Martha. She is now free and known by the name of Martha Arnold." He then acknowledged his "mulatto children who bear my name," listing James E. Arnold among them.[123] Having substantiated the charges of "Negro blood," everyone named in the suit was cleared of libel.

The trial brought to light the close connections between Congressman Collins and employees of the Indian Service—links that raised concerns in Washington. The Civil Service Commission investigated McKinley for disclosing confidential information from agency records. McKinley defended his actions as necessary to democracy, and Collins backed him up. In April 1923 Collins wrote McKinley that he had spoken with assistant commissioner Merritt on his behalf. "My parting words," he wrote, "were, 'don't let anything happen to McKinley, because any injury to him is likewise and [*sic*] injury to me, and I know you don't want to injure me.' He told me he would take care of you."[124] Collins's political power protected McKinley, who was not fired despite the gravity of his offense. Collins gained political capital with this episode, for the case had generated many letters of support.[125]

After he lost the lawsuit, Arnold appealed unsuccessfully for a new trial on procedural grounds, and resigned his church at Union.[126] He unapologetically continued to make his living off the Choctaws, remaining in the area and trading in baskets.[127] Arnold's final correspondence with the federal government came in 1940, when he wrote to the secretary of the interior from the Washington Home of Incurables requesting relief. He began his letter: "My mother was a full-blood Mississippi Choctaw Indian. I have, under written contract with the Mississippi Choctaws in the state of Mississippi, kept their needs and conditions before you, the department, and the Committees of Congress for 44 years and have not received one cent from the Indians or anyone for my services and expenses."[128] He took credit for every appropriation the Choctaws had received over the years and asked for relief. D. E. Murphy replied for the secretary, requesting more information, but there is no further mention of Arnold in the public record.[129]

Arnold was clearly a liar and an opportunist, but he had proven helpful to the Mississippi Choctaws. Even though they probably heard the rumors of his African American ancestry, it did not hinder his relations with them. The Choctaws left no records of their feelings for Arnold, but their continued association with him suggests that his service to them outweighed his ersatz Indianness. On the other hand, given the Choctaws' long-standing segregation from most African Americans, they may have accepted him as Choctaw. Whatever his racial heritage,

J. E. Arnold was useful to some Choctaws as they struggled to build their communities.

By the end of the 1920s, the Choctaws had begun to see small improvements in their lives. Although the majority of them still lived in poverty, the government had built twenty-one new homes for Indians near OIA schools, which were filled to capacity.[130] Between 1926 and 1929, the OIA purchased property for Choctaw farms and sold $4,775 worth of timber from the lands to the Henderson-Molphus Lumber Company, setting aside the proceeds to pay Choctaws to clear their lands and build irrigation ditches.[131]

The irrigation work began in 1928 under the supervision of T. J. Scott and the teacher at the Red Water Day School, Earl E. Givens. Annoyed by cumbersome government accounting procedures, Scott consigned the funds to a "special deposit" account in the Bank of Carthage and began administering the program apart from the agency. He also took over dispensation of loans made for drought relief and began purchasing seeds and implements for fifty-three Indians.[132] His actions would soon erupt into controversy, but at the end of the 1920s, the Choctaw Agency and its programs were functioning relatively smoothly.

Conclusion

The Choctaw Agency was a microcosm of social, political, and economic relations in rural eastern Mississippi, and as such, it reflected the stresses of an era when the modern consumer economy was beginning to intrude into rural America. The agency created a patronage economy that proved both beneficial and contentious. County elites— planters, merchants, bankers, business owners, and legal and medical professionals—used the agency to advance civic improvements, and federal patronage probably helped replace some of the merchants' revenues lost to catalog sales.

The agency also afforded a stage to showcase Neshoba County elites' civic accomplishments and good works, reminding their neighbors, who appeared to be questioning the social order, that they were still "the best people." Similarly, the Democratic Party appropriated agency resources to uphold Congressman Collins's credentials as a defender of white supremacy. The presence of Indian Service schools and the Choctaw Catholic mission exacerbated sectarian conflicts when the Ku Klux Klan resurfaced, but both the Choctaws and their agency escaped Klan violence.

Choctaws likewise used the agency for its economic resources and as a place to build their political alliances. They made use of local elites' interest in them and effectively interacted with the press to highlight both their ethnicity and their progress. Choctaw leaders met the Klan challenge by cultivating their long-term relationship with Klan organizer T. J. Scott and participating in anthropometric studies as examples of pure Indian blood. These actions may have helped them evade the aggression visited on their African American neighbors.

Choctaw activism had created a space where Mississippi's racial and class conflicts could play out against the backdrop of federal patronage crucial to a faltering economy. The stock market collapse and Great Depression would bring new conflicts that revealed continuing fault lines of class and the limits of the patronage economy.

CHAPTER FIVE

The Depression and the
Indian New Deal, 1929–1945

The Great Depression and the New Deal brought significant challenges to the Choctaws. Economic collapse accentuated the importance of
federal funds for all Mississippians. Yet discord over administration
of those resources aggravated long-standing class conflicts in Neshoba
County. In the 1930s, merchants and farmers vied for control of federal
patronage, and both sides sought Choctaw support. Demonstrating the
fluid nature of Choctaw political alliances, Choctaws joined the efforts
to contest elite Mississippians' domination of the patronage economy.

The Indian New Deal opened additional avenues for Choctaw tribal resurgence. The implementation of the Wheeler-Howard Act, also
known as the Indian Reorganization Act (IRA), in 1934 incited a dispute over who had the right to construct the Choctaws' tribal government. Choctaw leaders and their allies opposed commissioner of Indian affairs John Collier and Choctaw superintendent Archie Hector
(who had replaced agent Robert Enochs in 1932) for control of the IRA
process. The resulting clash pitted federal paternalism against Choctaw
autonomy and again raised questions of the Choctaws' tribal standing.
As in the allotment period, the Choctaws' racial identity was central
to federal recognition of their rights.

As they struggled with federal officials over the creation of their tribal government, Choctaws employed attorneys and Mississippi politicians to press their Article 14 claims based on their shared narratives of
Choctaw history and identity. Again they contended with ersatz claim-

ants trafficking in Indianness and with governmental indifference to the injustices they had suffered. As always, Choctaws responded with flexibility and attempted to maximize their self-determination.

The Depression in Choctaw Country:
The Patronage Economy in Hard Times

Mississippi was already suffering from fluctuating cotton prices when the depression hit in 1930, and by 1931 cotton had fallen to five cents per pound. Eighty-five banks in Mississippi had failed by 1932, and nearly forty thousand farms went into foreclosure. In response, the legislature instituted a program to expand the state's manufacturing base, allowing cities to issue bonds to recruit industry and construct factories. Combined with efforts to pave the state's appalling roads, the city bond program drew industry to rural Mississippi.[1]

The only industrial project to help the Choctaws, however, was the Sweet Potato Starch Plant in Laurel, founded in 1934 under the Federal Emergency Relief Act. The factory provided four Choctaw families from the nearby Bogue Homa Community with a market for yams.[2] The depression closed some Philadelphia sawmills, but the Molphus Lumber Company, which employed Choctaws, remained open by paying workers in scrip for the company store.[3] Other business closures cost Choctaws their day labor jobs, however, and some merchants stopped extending credit. Under these trying circumstances, the federal government supplied essential support.

The agency employed Indian men to build homes and barns and to dig wells and toilets for fifteen Indian families.[4] Choctaw women did not have similar opportunities for agency work, but some women at the Bogue Homa community began doing laundry for white women.[5] Choctaw men also signed up for public works at New Deal agencies.[6]

Under the leadership of Emmett York, several Choctaw men labored for the Public Works Administration building the Pearl River Road.[7] Choctaws also constructed roads for the Indian Division of the Civilian Conservation Corps (CCC-ID). Between 1934 and 1936, the CCC employed an average of twenty-four Choctaws for twenty days a month at a wage of one dollar and fifty cents per day. Choctaws did not live in CCC camps, and the agency compensated them with an extra fifty cents per day.[8] The CCC-ID operated as late as 1941, when agent Mc-Mullen bragged that he had employed 249 men for infrastructure work on Choctaw lands.[9]

In addition, a handful of Choctaws participated in vocational training run by the CCC-ID from 1939 to 1941. The program educated men in truck and tractor driving, blacksmithing, first aid, soil conservation, and farm terracing operations.[10] It appears that the only employment that resulted from this training involved Choctaw land conservation, which engaged 364 farmers by 1942.[11] Choctaw self-sufficiency remained elusive, and many Choctaws lived precariously close to the edge of serious malnourishment and illness. Government employment barely held them back from this precipice.

The Indian Service partnered with state and county extension workers to bolster subsistence production and the barter economy. Home economists helped Choctaw women can foods, garden, raise poultry, and make clothing and bedding.[12] In 1932 agency farmer T. J. Scott complained that the high cost of equipment limited canning, prompting McMullen to allow Choctaw women to trade produce to agency schools in return for canning supplies.[13] Families on reimbursable farms produced and canned a lot of food, but most Choctaw sharecroppers did not. A few landlords encouraged gardening to save expenses, but others forbade it. Speakers at a Home Economics Conference at agency schools in 1939 advocated telling Choctaws' landlords "that better work is done by a person who is adequately nourished."[14] Scott intervened with several landlords on this issue with mixed results.[15]

By 1943 home production for tenant farmers had risen. While this was primarily due to the campaign for "victory gardens" in support of World War II, the intervention of agency workers may have encouraged this trend.[16] Home economics instructors also procured cast-off bedding and mattresses from CCC camps for women to launder and refashion as linens. One home economist helped some Choctaw women take lint cotton to the cotton gin for reprocessing into material for blankets and quilts.[17]

Choctaws' home production helped alleviate hunger and cold, but it also called attention to Choctaw ethnicity. Choctaw women displayed canned goods, sewing projects, and baskets and beadwork at county fairs in community booths marked with distinctive Choctaw decorations.[18] The Conehatta and Bogue Chitto Schools held Indian fairs with stickball, dancing, and handiwork exhibits. Women and girls at the Pearl River School made 250 baskets (which sold at an average of twenty cents each) for the Business and Professional Women's Convention in Jackson.[19] The low prices paid for Choctaw crafts meant that reinforcing Choctaw ethnicity proved a more realistic objective than making a living by craftwork.

Basket production had declined between 1935 and 1945, and home economics instructors lamented how few girls wanted training in basketry.[20] Superintendent Archie McMullen used CCC funds to send a Choctaw woman and a home economics instructor to North Carolina to study the preparation of native dyes with the Cherokees because greater "authenticity" would create a more marketable product.[21] This venture dovetailed with the Mississippi legislature's vision for increased tourism.

The Choctaws could potentially draw visitors, but Mississippi's abysmal roads hindered tourism. The state legislature created the Mississippi Advertising Commission in 1936 to market the state to investors and tourists and began an ambitious road paving program. By 1940 four thousand miles of asphalt had been laid down.[22]

The legislature also promoted tourism in partnership with the Works Progress Administration (WPA), which, in 1938, published *Mississippi: A Guide to the Magnolia State*, in which the Choctaws were a "point of interest." The book featured pictures of a Choctaw basket and basket weaving and noted where visitors could obtain crafts.[23] The guidebook devoted a chapter to "archeology and Indians," which described the Choctaws' exotic customs and emphasized racial phenotypes, calling the Choctaws "broad headed people with light mahogany complexion." The chapter ended with the ubiquitous reference to the Choctaws' bloodline: "The descendants of the 3,000 Choctaw of pure blood who refused to leave Mississippi still till the soil of their ancestors (*see Tour 12*)."[24] Tour 12 included Choctaw communities, the agency, and Na-nih Waiya, and encouraged readers to attend "tribal games and dances" at the Neshoba County Fair.[25]

The Federal Writers' Project also documented Choctaw history and culture. Oddly, there were no Choctaw interviews in the WPA Folklore Project, which had been charged with capturing ethnic groups in the process of assimilation. Instead, folklore researchers produced one folder called "Folk Customs: Choctaws," which contained stories of Indians by elderly pioneers, ethnographic accounts by John Swanton, or stories by agency officials.[26] Nonetheless, Choctaw leaders appeared in interviews for several county histories.

Interviewers in Neshoba County gathered picturesque details of Choctaw ceremonies, crafts, and customs from Simpson Tubby, J. W. Issac, and Mary Charley. WPA employees from Newton County constructed a similar amateur ethnography by consulting the "Indians of the Conehatta," without providing informant's names. In Jones County, the interviewers described how the "simple Choctaws" at Bogue Homa held dances every Friday night, stickball games every Sunday afternoon, and sporadic funeral rituals, and how the "more industrious among them" wove baskets. Interviewers reinforced their informants' accounts with quotations from Swanton, as though they were checking the Choctaws' stories against the "real" authority on Indian culture.[27]

A triumphalist vision of colorful Choctaws overcoming poverty through hard work and agency services dominated these narratives. WPA worker Prentiss Barnett, of Leake County, invoked tragic noble savage imagery by quoting nearly the entire speech of Samuel Cobb at the 1843 council. He then redeemed this saga of declension by interviewing Pat Chitto, Scott York, and J. C. Allen as representatives of the "progressive Indians" who were "uplifting their people." WPA employees in Winston County also accentuated Choctaw advancement by interviewing Simpson Tubby about his conversion to Christianity.[28] Interviewers may have stressed this trajectory because they hoped that Choctaw stories of declension and uplift could draw positive attention to the state.

The Choctaws' sacred mound, Nanih Waiya, was one possible tourist destination. In 1935 Dunbar Rowland, director of the Mississippi Department of Archives and History, learned that Mr. Munch Luke, who owned the mound, was planning to level it. Rowland urged Luke to instead consider the prospects for tourism.[29] Agent Hector brought the OIA and the Smithsonian into the discussion.[30] The curator of the state archives, Moreau Chambers, reported that the Choctaws were intensely interested in preserving their sacred mound and predicted their collaboration in excavation.[31] Senator Pat Harrison won WPA approval for excavation, but uncertain congressional funding for the WPA derailed the project.[32]

Within a few months, the funding had stabilized, but the regional director of the Meridian WPA office, T. J. Bolster, held up the plan.[33] Chambers warned Bolster that citizens desperate for work had threatened to blow up the mound if the project failed.[34] These ominous predictions did no good, and by January 1937 Chambers declared the Nanih Waiya dig a "closed issue." Fortunately for the Choctaws, no one dynamited the mound in retaliation.[35]

Public works and tourism fell short of meeting Choctaw needs, and Choctaw communities sought direct public aid. Sharecroppers were eligible for county support, and Indians near the agency got assistance from the Indian Office. Within the first six months of 1931, over six hundred Indians (out of a population of roughly sixteen hundred) received federal relief funds. Both Enochs and his successor Hector pleaded for relief money but rarely procured sufficient funds.[36] Other federal officials were critical of Choctaws' need for "the dole."

Despite his empathy for destitute families, agency farmer Earl Givens nonetheless stigmatized those on relief. In 1932 he attached pictures of ten Choctaw men to his annual report with the caption "A few of the boys awaiting the issue of rations. I hope this will never have to be repeated." Givens had never used the term "boys" in his previous correspondence.[37] As a matter of policy, the OIA reserved relief funds for the elderly, orphaned, infirmed, or widowed. In practice, however, they sometimes aided the able-bodied as well.[38] In the early 1930s Enochs's attempt to siphon work-relief funds into a dole caused upheaval that touched on deep class animosities and highlighted the importance of patronage to the regional economy.

Red Water Land Improvement Project:
Class Conflict and the Patronage Economy

The Red Water Land Improvement Project, authorized in 1930, was a drainage ditch funded by timber sales on Choctaw lands. The agency hired forty Choctaws to dig the ditch and assigned Pat Chitto of the Standing Pine community as manager. The workers deposited their earnings in the Leake County bank, subject to the countersign of either T. J. Scott or Earl Givens, teacher at the Red Water School (and later agency farmer).

After the project began, Enochs requested authority to use some of the timber funds for direct assistance. When the OIA refused, he ordered the ditch reduced in size, and diverted several hundred dollars into relief payments. Not only did the ditch remain unfinished, but completed sections collapsed.[39] The ditch would have been merely an unfortunate waste of money had not a local farmer, W. H. Hodge, sent an angry letter to Senator Pat Harrison protesting it as an example of misuse of government funds.[40] Harrison contacted the OIA, who sent Inspector C. R. Trowbridge to investigate in the spring of 1931.

Hodge's grievances were quickly dispatched, but Enochs used the visit to accuse agency farmer T. J. Scott of "political activity," and a full-scale investigation of agency affairs began.[41] Field representative Henry Roe Cloud opened a second enquiry in the fall of 1931. The government's study uncovered bitter rivalries for control of agency resources, with all sides claiming to represent the Choctaws' best interests. T. J. Scott was the most vociferous advocate for the Choctaws. "I was born with the Mississippi Choctaws," Scott told Roe Cloud. "The first playmates I had were all Indians."[42] Scott explained how he mediated disputes with landlords and merchants, coordinated the construction of Indian homes, and lobbied his personal friend Congressman Ross Collins on behalf of Choctaws' welfare.[43]

Circumventing agency regulations, Scott had supervised Choctaws' timber sales and deposited the profits in the Leake County Bank. He handled farm loan checks issued by the federal government for drought relief in a similar manner, consigning them to the Citizens' Bank of Philadelphia. All accounts were subject to his countersignature.[44]

Trowbridge and Roe Cloud were most concerned with the impropriety of assuming business relationships with Indians, but they also noticed the awkward situation it created for the agency. Scott's bank and the Bank of Philadelphia, where Enochs banked, competed for agency accounts. Roe Cloud remarked: "This is a valuable consideration as where in a small town sums of money comparatively small are greatly sought after." He feared that "having appealed to outside political influence," the agency could not continue to function with both men present.[45] Yet the problem went beyond banking to the heart of social, economic, and political power relationships within the agency and between the factions of citizens aligned with it.

According to Roe Cloud, both Scott and Enochs sincerely desired to help the Choctaws but clashed over what that meant. Enochs was a "fine gentleman," but he was a poor administrator bullied by Scott, who had little patience for government regulations. Though Scott was insubordinate, it was, in Roe Cloud's judgment, "only because of his failure to find leadership worthy of the name" in Enochs.[46] Roe Cloud interpreted their disagreement as symptomatic of a more philosophical matter—the contradiction between official power and genuine status in the Indian community. "Both [men] desire conflicting measures of control," he wrote. "One has a sense of proprietary right from long knowledge, intimate association, strong native following, and having influenced beneficent legislation for the Choctaw while the other claims it by right of executive position."[47] Although the agent was formally in charge, Choctaws often bypassed him in favor of their longtime ally T. J. Scott.

Using his friendships with county agents, Scott had helped some Choctaw farmers obtain loans for drought relief. "I secured sixty-five of these for the Indians" he bragged, and "the Choctaws produced the greatest crop in all history." This monumental harvest was not universally celebrated, for Scott had also used his membership in the Farm Bureau to procure seed and fertilizer at very low prices.[48]

Not only did this action bypass regulations for competitive bidding but it spurned the local merchants in direct defiance of Enochs's order to turn the loan checks over to them.[49] Roe Cloud was unaware of earlier clashes between merchants and farmers, but he recognized economic rivalries when he wrote, "All the letters of endorsement of these two men are inspired by their innate integrity and their power to yield financial patronage."[50]

Enochs acknowledged the role of patronage when he defended his administration by reference to "the growth and accomplishments of this Agency" since his arrival. True to Roe Cloud's analysis of Enochs as a man with official status, he focused on his administrative achievements: the construction of ten government buildings and sixty-eight Indian houses, doubling the staff, and tripling the number of children in school.[51]

Scott also acted according to Roe Cloud's assessment as a man with status chafing under the restraints of authority. Scott framed his disagreements with Enochs as a clash between a "man-of-the-soil" who had enhanced the Indians' collective economic power through the Farm Bureau, and wealthy merchants who sought to profit from the patronage economy without regard to the Choctaws. The citizens of Philadelphia also acknowledged these two contradictory positions.

Enochs's most wholehearted advocates were merchants. J. H. Hester, president of the Bank of Philadelphia and general manager of the Anderson-Molphus Mercantile, stated, "Leading citizens regard Dr. Enochs as a leading citizen." J. C. Garrett, office manager for Henderson Mercantile, concurred that Enoch was "a high toned gentleman in whom I have explicit confidence." George Mars, president of the Citizens' Bank and manager of the Mars Brothers Clothing Company, praised Enochs for getting the "best prices" on agency merchandise from local merchants. All these men regarded Scott as insubordinate, and many still held a grudge over Scott's Klan organizing.[52] Economic interests were not entirely about money, of course; they were also about deference. Scott's affiliation with the Farm Bureau, which undercut the merchants, rankled these men because it defied their control of the patronage economy.

Farmer Scott's white defenders were not quite as prestigious as Enochs's, but they were respectable citizens who enthusiastically praised him. The state and county farming establishment was in his corner, including county extension agents, administrators from the Farmers' Seed Loan Offices in Tennessee and Mississippi, and members of the Philadelphia Drought Relief Committee. Scott's former boss, Frank McKinley, weighed in, calling Scott, "a man of Lincolnian simplicity; ruggedly honest."[53] Scott's Baptist pastor reported that Scott led bible studies.[54] All these men agreed that Scott's good relationship with the Choctaws was his best quality.

Scott's allies argued that hurting Scott would, in one man's words, "work a very serious injustice upon the Indians he has served so faithfully and so well." The mayor of Carthage also remarked that "the Indians have confidence in him and are deeply appreciative of the interest he has taken in them."[55] These men were correct, for Scott's strongest support came from the Choctaws.

Even though two Choctaws claimed to like both men equally and two aligned with Enochs against Scott, eleven others favored Scott over Enochs, and everyone agreed that the majority of Choctaws preferred Scott. Choctaws contrasted Enochs's stinginess with Scott's direct support. Others criticized the dismissive way Enochs treated them. When word spread that Enochs wanted Scott relocated, Bennett and Scott York and Joe Chitto circulated a petition for Enochs's removal. Agency policeman Olmon Comby summarized the Indians' relationship with Scott: "Mr. Scott is a friend of the Choctaw ever since he was a little fellow."[56]

Outraged, Enochs blamed Scott and Cyrus White, teacher at the Standing Pine School, for the petition and demanded Scott's immediate dismissal.[57] Government officials were inclined to agree that Scott was a problem, but they also believed that Enochs should step down. Roe Cloud brushed off the petition but nonetheless concluded that "antagonisms . . . on the part of business interests, merchants and bankers" would hinder Enochs's future effectiveness. Both he and Trowbridge recommended that Enochs be transferred "without prejudice."[58] Roe Cloud urged that Scott be moved to Carthage, because of "the universal respect and friendship Choctaws entertain for him." Trowbridge also advised Scott's reassignment, but Scott stayed and the OIA reassigned Enochs to Kayenta, Arizona.[59]

In this dispute between the agent and his merchant supporters and the Choctaws and farmer Scott, the Choctaws won. Although the OIA claimed that "antagonisms" between business interests rendered Enochs ineffective, virtually all Philadelphia's business leaders wanted him retained. Enochs could have worked with Philadelphia's elites. What he could not do was manage Scott, who was more valuable to the Choctaw Agency because of his knowledge of farming.[60] By removing Enochs instead of Scott, the OIA sent the message that Philadelphia's farmers were more important to the agency's mission than were its merchants.

On a more abstract level, however, retaining Scott instead of Enochs intimates something about how the federal government was negotiating power relationships in rural Mississippi. Although Scott's friendship with Congressman Collins may have influenced the decision to keep him, most likely Scott, "by reason of his strategic position holding the universal esteem of the Indians," had successfully outmaneuvered Enochs.[61] Enochs's supporters were the most economically and politically dominant people in the county, but he held only "official power" among the Choctaws.

Roe Cloud's discussion of real versus ersatz power acknowledged the Choctaws' desire to guide their own lives. Although Choctaws worked with elites when it served their interests, they used this controversy to align themselves with the middle- and working-class people who challenged elites' control of the patronage economy. Their victory in this particular contest reveals the limits of entrenched class privilege in rural Mississippi. The Choctaws' champion, T. J. Scott, would continue to clash with authorities. The Indian New Deal would afford a fresh context for this quarrel.

The Choctaws and the Indian Reorganization Act

The appointment of Indian activist John Collier as commissioner of Indian affairs in 1933 instituted a new era in Indian policy. The Indian New Deal abandoned forced assimilation and sought the revitalization of Indian tribes by restoring tribal land bases and government, providing funds for economic development (in a revolving credit fund), and encouraging Native crafts and culture.[62] The centerpiece of the policy was the Wheeler-Howard Act, also known as the Indian Reorganization Act (IRA), passed in 1934.[63] This legislation offered the Mississippi Choctaws a chance to reestablish their tribal government. After a century of holding a collective Indian identity with no institutional structures, they quickly embraced this opportunity.

In February 1934 Superintendent Hector formed a Tribal Business Committee (TBC) of seventeen Choctaws to consider adopting the IRA. This was the committee's sole responsibility, and they met only when Hector convened them. Three representatives came from Conehatta (Bart Gibson, Paul Farve, and Frank Johnson), Tucker (John Charley, Elie Willis, Will Davis—aka Anthony McMillan), and Pearl River (Simpson Tubby, Byrd Issac, and Necie Starr York), and two hailed from the smaller districts of Red Water (Pat Chitto and Ollie Anderson), Standing Pine (Joe Chitto and Charley Ben), Bogue Chitto (Dempsey Morris and Robert Henry), and Bogue Homa (Billy Nickey and Henry Jim). The delegates held office until Hector or one of his supervisors decided to replace them.[64]

In March 1934 Hector put the IRA before the TBC, which approved of the legislation in principle but also raised pragmatic concerns. Most of the TBC wanted to wait until their children had more education before organizing a government, and two TBC members stated that "there were a considerable number of Indians who had received practically no help and that they believed that such Indians should be helped first."[65]

In April Joe Chitto, a TBC representative from the Standing Pine community, wrote to Collier informing him that agency policeman Olmon Comby and Choctaw Baptist minister Ed Willis of Philadelphia had aligned themselves with some white people who had told them that Collier wanted them to design a tribal government.[66] Collier replied that Chitto should organize a council or a committee and "proceed to adopt a constitution" so as to be ready for self-governance when the bill passed.[67] Taking Collier at his word, the Choctaws and their allies met to create the framework of tribal governance.

On May 12, 1934, representatives from each of the seven communities and their white allies held an organizational meeting in Union, Mississippi, which several observers called "the largest assemblage of Indians that had gathered in Mississippi since 1895." Citing their approval of the Wheeler-Howard Act, the Choctaws constructed the Mississippi Choctaw Indian Federation (MCIF) and approved a constitution drafted by state senator Earl Richardson. Chitto was elected secretary-treasurer, and the Reverend Willis became chief.[68]

Simultaneously, Senator Richardson—a Philadelphia attorney and friend of the Choctaws—and E. T. Winston—newspaper editor, self-proclaimed expert on Indian lore, and close associate of newly elected Senator Theodore Bilbo—founded the Mississippi Choctaw Welfare Association (MCWA) to "assist the Indians in their very laudable undertaking toward self-government and self-expression."[69] Chief Willis wrote Superintendent Hector informing him of these actions and enclosing a copy of their constitution. Two-thirds of the TBC had attended the Union meeting and voted in favor of the MCIF.[70]

Hector immediately denigrated the organization as an example of Scott's insubordination. He requested Collier's backing for the TBC, and Collier dutifully scolded Scott.[71] Collier also wrote to the TBC, explaining that "the drafting of a constitution" would require "careful guidance" that policy makers were still considering. Collier repudiated his earlier instructions to Chitto, noting that the previous letter had been written by a staff member who was unaware of the proper procedures. Collier claimed to support the rights of all Indians "to meet as and when they please without reference to a Superintendent," but he could not endorse the MCIF because he had already approved the TBC as the legitimate government.[72]

The same day, Collier wrote Chitto regarding a petition calling for Hector's removal that the MCIF had sent him. Two hundred fifty-two Choctaws had petitioned Collier to remove Hector because he was "fighting our organization known as the Mississippi Choctaw Indian Federation . . . trying to make us believe that our organization is not legal unless whatever business we do [is] done through him. . . . In a name of justice and fairness we ask that you remove him at once." The TBC members in attendance endorsed this document, as did leaders of community farm chapters and ladies' sewing circles from Red Water, Standing Pine, and Conehatta. Additionally, the petition requested that Collier transfer another agency farmer, the head nurse, and the field nurse.[73]

Collier assumed full blame for the mistake that had allowed the two groups to emerge but declined to act on the petition. He then sanctioned the MCIF as an organization of salvage anthropology, encouraging their involvement with the Mississippi Choctaw Welfare Association to promote "historical research and endeavor to keep alive the traditions of the inhabitants," and reiterated that "only one body or organization can be recognized as officially representing the tribe"—the TBC.[74]

Chitto responded with a sharp assertion of Choctaw autonomy. He informed Hector that they had not organized the MCIF to fight the TBC, but Federation members would boycott the upcoming TBC meeting because the majority of Choctaws endorsed the MCIF.[75] "It is over one hundred years since we lost our right of organization," he wrote, "but we are making up [for it]."[76] Chitto also noted that the organizing procedures had not been "carried out as the[y] should [be]" because they did not allow the Choctaws to elect their own council.[77] Although the petition for Hector's removal directly confronted the OIA, Chitto seemed to view it as a means to gain recognition of the Federation, not necessarily as a way to replace the TBC, in which he retained membership.

Given that the majority of the TBC leaders were members of both organizations, it is reasonable to conclude that they viewed the two not as mutually exclusive but as complementary. If one political organization did not meet all their needs, they could create another.[78] When Chitto insisted that he was not fighting the agency, he most likely meant that the focus of the campaign was elsewhere—it was on reestablishing the Choctaw polity on their own terms.

Chitto also wrote to Collier criticizing the IRA process as undemocratic. He complained that the TBC was not "approve[d] by vote or otherwise, just named." In an apparent irony, Chitto then claimed legitimacy for the MCIF by appealing to the authority of the TBC, noting that all but one member of that body had attended the meeting in Union and all but three had voted for the MCIF.[79]

Chitto also addressed Collier's charge that the MCIF was a "faction," which was a common way for federal bureaucrats to devalue their Indian critics. He argued that instead, the MCIF carried out grassroots political actions. The petition for Hector's removal was written on MCIF letterhead, but Chitto claimed that it "was started and signed by the Indians [as] individuals [*sic*] citizens" not by the MCIF.[80] He stressed that the Choctaws sought to devise their own solutions to their problems, which was the true purpose of a tribal government.

The MCIF's allies echoed Chitto's charge of faux democracy in the IRA procedure. Senator Earl Richardson, president of MCWA, confirmed that the Choctaws believed that they were "carrying out the personal wishes of the Commissioner in this matter." He explained to Collier how he had come to draft their constitution: "The head men of the Choctaw tribe came to me several months ago with a view of organizing a federation."[81] He acknowledged the TBC, stressing that the Choctaws did not intend to interfere with that body because several men served on both committees.

Nonetheless, he wrote, the TBC "did not partake of any of the ancient customs, rules, and regulations. They wanted a more democratic and larger organization, one that . . . all the Indians would have an opportunity to have a voice in." In Hector's plan, Indians living outside the seven "official" communities had no representation on the TBC.[82] The Choctaws wanted a more inclusive body modeled on their historical councils.

Indigenous Choctaw politics were ranked, but all Choctaws had input into council decisions.[83] Unlike the TBC, the MCIF bestowed membership on "any Mississippi Choctaw Indian of twenty-one years of age or more, or who is the head of a family as husband, wife, or guardian, and whose degree of blood is more than one-half."[84] The provision for blood quantum was not part of the aboriginal government, of course, but signaled changing notions of Choctaw identity.

The legislative body, the Grand Council, consisted of representatives of community councils or committees, who chose a chief and secretary-treasurer from among the grand councilors. The MCIF allowed any Choctaw community to join if 20 percent of its members endorsed the constitution and elected members to the Grand Council. The document did not specifically define a "Choctaw community," but it did restrict membership to those groups with twenty-five eligible members, who got two delegates; communities with forty or more got three.[85] This structure was similar to the one Choctaws used in the eighteenth century, as was the loosely defined function of this body.[86]

The Grand Council existed to "do any and all things to promote the social, physical, economic, and moral well-being of the Mississippi Choctaw Indian, not herein prohibited nor forbidden by the laws of the State of Mississippi, and of the United States of America."[87] This clause suggests a multifaceted Choctaw political identity. Just as their ancestors had accepted that they were Mississippi citizens and also treaty partners with the United States, MCIF members likewise acknowledged all three levels of political authority. Yet because Choctaws had created it, the MCIF would not be a tool of either federal or state officials. Rather, it would embody the resurrected Choctaw Nation in Mississippi.

MCIF leaders interpreted the IRA as a means of reestablishing their lost political standing stolen from them by a duplicitous government. In his next letter to Collier, Chitto cited at length Samuel Cobb's speech to the Choctaw Commission in 1843. Chitto's choice of passages from this speech stressed the Choctaws' military service to the United States and Cobb's scolding of Commissioner McRae for failure to honor diplomatic reciprocity between allies: "When you took our country, you promised us land. There is your promise in the book. Twelve times the trees have dropped their leaves, and yet we have received no land."[88]

Chitto concluded by drawing the obvious parallels: "You see how the government treated our fathers, and now after more than one hundred years, the remnant of the once powerful Choctaws took Mr. Collier at his word" and created the MCIF, only "to be told by you that you would not recognize our federation. It makes us Choctaws wonder if the government ever makes its promises good to the Indians."[89] Chitto hoped both to shame Collier into accepting the MCIF and to declare the Choctaws' identity as people still holding unredeemed treaty promises.

As a member of the MCWA, newspaper editor E. T. Winston also lobbied Collier on behalf of the Mississippi Choctaw Indian Federation.[90] "Present economic conditions create a new order," he wrote, and both Indians and whites needed federal aid to "stay the impending calamity that threatens both civilizations." Thus they had created the MCIF and the MCWA. He asked Collier for "your sanction, advice, and council" and instructed him to send all correspondence about the Choctaws to the MCWA.[91] In reply, Collier commended "the citizens of Mississippi for taking an interest in these Indians" and reiterated that the TBC was the only legitimate council.[92] Both the MCIF and the MCWA rejected this.

Ignoring Collier, the two groups organized a ceremony to install MCIF officials. They chose September 27—the 104th anniversary of the signing of the Treaty of Dancing Rabbit Creek—and held it at Winston's home in Pontotoc, Mississippi. After playing a stickball game, George H. Ethridge, assistant justice of the state supreme court, was to swear in the new government.

The Choctaws and their allies made good use of this ceremony and other symbols of Choctaw history and culture in the press. One newspaper picture featured the MCIF leadership with a drum that had allegedly been used during the signing ceremony at Dancing Rabbit Creek.

The Mississippi congressional delegation was invited, and the new representative from Pontotoc attended.[93] Analysis of the press clippings and correspondence around this ritual illuminates the Choctaws' strategies for political renaissance.

When first faced with the prospect of forming a tribal government, members of the TBC had raised several concerns. They had feared their lack of education. Aligning themselves with Senator Richardson and newspaper editor Winston, "the best read student of Indian history and lore in the state," solved that problem.[94] Some had wanted greater financial assistance first—the MCWA also addressed that anxiety. Winston knew of the IRA's revolving credit fund, which granted low-cost loans to Indians for economic development, and the land purchase program. No doubt he promised that he would deliver these things.

Winston's press releases broadcast that the MCWA planned to press the Choctaws' Article 14 claims.[95] The Choctaws had filed a claim with the Indian Claims Commission in 1933, but no ruling had been issued. Presumably, the MCWA would help win the settlement. Winston also suggested that the MCIF could advance the stalled plans to create a national park at Nanih Waiya.[96] The Choctaws clearly felt these allies could help them achieve self-determination, but beyond access to government appropriations, what was in it for their allies?

The Choctaws' supporters in the IRA battle sounded many of the same notes heard over the years. Continuing the narrative established in the late nineteenth century, Choctaws were portrayed as tragic romantic primitives, and Mississippi's Indians had played a central role in American history as military allies. Winston appealed to his readers to restore to the Choctaws "at least a semblance of their ancient glory" by supporting the MCIF and MCWA.[97]

Predictably, the legendary story of Pushmataha surfaced. Winston upped the regionalist ante of this tale by recalling that "New England was passing resolutions of secession" when Pushmataha had deflected an all-out Indian uprising by giving a speech that was "in a class with Patrick Henry's appeal to the Virginia Assembly, or Demosthenes' Oration on the Crown."[98]

In Winston's narrative, the tragic trajectory of Indian Removal also played out in the usual manner as the federal government (not Mississippi settlers) failed the Choctaws.[99] Winston emphasized that Choctaws had served this country despite their shabby treatment, informing his readers that "today there hangs in the Sorbonne, the great French art gallery, the portrait of a young Choctaw Indian, who was selected as the model for the typical American soldier in the World War."[100]

Winston also used race to position the Choctaws in a national narrative. They were genuine Americans because they were indigenous: "100 percent, simon-pure 18-karat native-born Americans."[101] Winston praised the Choctaws' commitment to racial separatism, calling them "the purest blood of any Indians on our continent."[102] The reference was clear: do not fear the Choctaws' dark skin, Winston assured his neighbors, they were not black, they were Indian, and Indians were acceptable, particularly in their current impoverished state.

Winston believed that poverty had degraded all races. He explained to Collier that Indians were not inherently inferior because of race. Rather, they "were contaminated" by association with the lower classes because they were tenant farmers.[103] Naturally, this condition would be rectified by association with the "right" people, such as members of the MCWA, which limited membership to those with "moral and civil reputations."[104] These upstanding citizens would guide the Choctaws to a higher standard of living—aided by government funds, of course.

As the TBC was the federally recognized organization, and thus the only one with access to the revolving credit funds, the MCWA's overwhelming preference for the MCIF seems counterintuitive. Yet Winston believed that the supreme authority regarding Choctaw sovereignty derived from the 1830 state law that had abolished all tribal governments.[105] In his view, the Choctaws were not subject to the authority of the Indian Service "until their tribal government is first reinstated by the state of Mississippi."[106] The installation ceremony would reestablish federally recognized Choctaw political institutions under state authority.[107] Winston summed up this position succinctly in a letter to Collier: "Now, getting down to cases—your Bureau doesn't recognize the Mississippi Choctaw Indian Federation. The Mississippi Choctaw Indian Federation likewise does not recognize your Bureau."[108]

This pursuit of federal funding while asserting local authority in administration reflected larger patterns of southerners' interactions with the New Deal.[109] Mississippians embraced New Deal funding but resisted federal authority. For example, despite provisions designed to protect tenants when landlords downsized their farms under the Agricultural Adjustment Act, southern landlords often evicted their tenants and frequently failed to distribute parity funds designated to lessen these hardships. These actions threw former tenants onto federal relief roles, shifting landlords' paternalistic duties to their tenants to the federal government.[110]

Similarly, IRA funds relieved the Choctaws' neighbors of their charitable obligations to the Indians.[111] Creating a tribal government in partnership with the MCWA would also strengthen states' rights because it would link state officials with the new Choctaw government in development projects. The Choctaws exhibited similar attitudes about the Indian New Deal, embracing public works employment and skillfully using their allies to advance their agenda of self-government. This effort paid off, but indirectly.

The Choctaw campaign may have affected OIA decisions on agency matters. In August an anonymous memo assessed the discord at the agency and stated that agent Hector should be reassigned because his problems with Scott had been "accentuated by local politics and politicians. He has not the support of the local congressmen."[112] Around the same time, the farmer named for transfer on the MCIF petition was reassigned. Hector warned against this, fearing that "certain Indians will feel that they had something to do with this and that they can tell the Agency what to do."[113] It is plausible to conclude from this that the OIA considered the opinions of Mississippi political leaders in these matters. The Choctaws counted on that in their campaign.

Over the late summer and early fall of 1934, MCIF leaders maintained their push for recognition. In a TBC meeting of August 10, Chitto stalled a vote for council officers and demanded recognition for the

MCIF. A two-hour argument "part in English and part in Choctaw" ensued, and the TBC delayed the vote pending further discussion.[114] When Hector called for another meeting on August 16, Chitto announced a boycott, which left the meeting shy of a quorum. The TBC again adjourned without electing officers.[115]

In response, Hector sent letters to government officials complaining about the MCIF and blaming their activities on farmer Scott and "the local politicians."[116] Still, he continued preparations for an election to vote on the IRA. Even as Joe Chitto organized a strike at Standing Pine School to protest Hector's refusal to acknowledge the MCIF, Hector claimed that support for the IRA was building.[117]

The Choctaws voted on the IRA on March 19, 1935. The Conehatta, Tucker, Pearl River, Red Water, and Bogue Homa communities accepted the IRA.[118] Bogue Chitto only turned in three votes, and Standing Pine cast a majority negative vote. Hector rejoiced that Chitto was only able to sway his own community.[119] At first glance, the vote appears to support Hector's contention that he had triumphed over the MCIF, but a close analysis of this election suggests a more nuanced interpretation.

A minority of Choctaws apparently followed Chitto's idea that they had already formed a government and did not need to vote in this election. Other Choctaws claimed that members of the MCIF had voted for the IRA because it was the only way to get land and access to the revolving credit funds.[120] Yet those who voted in favor of the IRA did not view this action as a repudiation of the MCIF. Instead, MCIF activism may well have shaped the vote.

Superintendent Hector now addressed criticisms of his heavy-handed leadership that Chitto had raised in his letters to Collier. In this election he arranged for the "scattered Indians to vote in the school districts with which they should be affiliated."[121] Perhaps his willingness to include these Indians made the election process more acceptable to MCIF members. Secondly, instead of appointing a new Tribal Business Committee, Hector called for elections.[122] Hector assumed that this newly elected TBC would put an end to the Mississippi Choctaw Indian Federation, but it did not.

The Choctaws' actions following the election suggest that they coun-
tenanced two governments, for the MCIF continued to function and
the new council took no actions to stop it.[123] The TBC discussed the
strike at Standing Pine in their first meeting and "someone" suggested closing the school. The new TBC, however, voted unanimously to
keep the school open until the "parents of the district could discuss the
matter."[124] Over several months, parents at the Standing Pine School
gradually returned their children to the classroom.[125] Perhaps Chitto's presence on the TBC alleviated tensions between the community
and the agency.

Opposition persisted with other MCIF members, however. In June
the Bogue Homa community went on strike, led by Henry Jim, who sat
on both the TBC and the MCIF. Using MCIF letterhead, he petitioned
the Mississippi congressional delegation to transfer the teacher at Bogue
Homa and close the school.[126] Congressmen Bill Colmer and Albert
Dunn contacted Collier asking that he look into Jim's grievances.[127]

These complaints led to an investigation that resulted in the teacher's transfer.[128] Thus, even though the majority of Choctaws had come
to embrace the new TBC, the MCIF continued to serve as a vehicle to
protest the agency establishment and lobby Mississippi's elected officials. The Tribal Business Committee's refusal to disband their allegedly rival government suggested that they viewed this organization,
which clearly got results, as another way to protect Choctaw interests.

In June 1936 Joe Jennings, field administrator in charge of organization, visited the Choctaws to formally establish an IRA government.
He observed that "it should be comparatively easy to bring both groups
together in a new constitution and bylaws." He instructed Hector to
include delegates of the MCIF in all meetings of the TBC, which was
not difficult since many MCIF members were also on the TBC. Hector claimed to comply, and his complaints about the MCIF fade out of
OIA records about this time.[129]

A few months later, however, Jennings decided that the Choctaws
were ineligible for the IRA because they were not a documented tribe
and did not live on trust lands.[130] Once again, the Choctaws were told

that they had no legal standing as Indians despite receiving OIA services and funds. As with earlier recognition campaigns, the Choctaws' racial identity was relevant to the outcome of this conundrum.

Section 19 of the IRA stated that Indians who were members of a tribe acknowledged by the federal government, were living on a reservation, or were one-half or more Indian blood could participate in the IRA. Collier considered so-called remnant tribes in the East to be unqualified for acknowledgment on political grounds, but admitted that some of them could be included for racial reasons. Indians who met the blood quantum requirements could apply for lands and organize a governing body, but they were not an officially recognized tribe and could not access the revolving credit fund.[131] Ultimately, then, neither the MCIF nor the TBC prevailed, and the Choctaws had to begin the organizing process anew.

Searching for solutions to the Choctaws' organizational quandary, the OIA debated various proposals. One plan, citing section 4 of the act organizing Indians in Oklahoma, allowed the Choctaws to construct local councils. Another suggested that the OIA reclassify the Choctaws' reimbursable lands as a reservation so they could organize a single council. Both propositions proposed purchasing lands for racially defined Indians.[132] Choctaw leaders embraced both plans, voting to form local councils and keep the central business committee to address "matters of general concern" and negotiate with federal officials. This council could operate under a constitution, but not as an IRA government. How the two groups would function together was unclear.[133]

Again the Choctaws opted for flexibility and for dual governing bodies. Furthermore, the MCIF persisted. A letter from Ed Willis dated May 3, 1940, invited Senator Theodore Bilbo to their annual gathering to discuss the status of the Choctaws' claims bill before Congress.[134] No other records of these annual meetings exist, and it is not clear when the MCIF ceased to function. Still, continuing their centuries-old patterns of activism, the Choctaws operated politically in Mississippi outside official federal channels.

The matter of a tribal government lay dormant over the next few years, but in 1936 the OIA began procuring lands under the "half-blood or more" provision. This further confirmed the value of the Choctaws' racial identity. Their political position, however, remained indeterminate. Unlike in the allotment hearings, the OIA decoupled race and tribal standing. Although the interior department solicitor authorized land purchases because of the Choctaws' blood, he also held that the Choctaws were still not a legally recognized tribe.[135]

By 1939 economic depression and inadequate farming programs had driven most families to default on their loans, and the OIA declared these farms to be trust lands.[136] At this point, the government could have designated the Choctaws a tribe, yet they did not. Even so, these landholdings eventually afforded the Choctaws a means to political recognition.

In 1944 the Shell Oil Company requested an oil lease on Choctaw lands, but there was no governing body authorized to approve it. J. M. Stewart, director of lands, announced that the Choctaws' trust lands would be reclassified as a reservation and the Choctaws would now be a tribe so that an IRA council could negotiate the leases.[137]

The second TBC disbanded and the communities elected representatives to a temporary tribal council that would draft an IRA constitution. Following the example of the MCIF, these representatives called meetings in all Choctaw communities to gather input. On April 20, 1945, the Choctaws approved this council and constitution 346 to 71. They called themselves the Mississippi Band of Choctaw Indians, differentiating their polity from the larger Choctaw Nation.[138] They defined themselves by reference to their race and their homelands.

Reflecting IRA recognition requirements, the constitution required one-half blood quantum for tribal membership. It also stipulated that tribal members had to reside in one of the seven "recognized communities."[139] The new council consisted of four members of the original TBC and five men who had not previously held leadership positions.[140] The new council would continue to spar with their superintendents and push for greater self-determination. As always, Article 14 was central to Choctaw political activism.

Land Claims

Not content to wait for the OIA to decide who represented them, the Choctaws had been seeking settlement of their treaty claims throughout the IRA skirmish.[141] They hired Philadelphia, Mississippi, attorneys Thomas Rhodes and Odie Moore, whose legal brief reiterated the Choctaws' full-blood status and their history of military service. More significantly, the brief disputed the idea that the payments given in Indian Territory in 1886 had settled Article 14 claims. It cited statutory requirements that had expressly mandated these payments to be "issued or delivered in the west."[142] The Choctaws demanded the same amount of money that had been appropriated in 1852—$893,800—plus interest.[143]

Ignoring the government's failure to follow the conditions specified by the legislation authorizing the funds, Collier rejected the claim in 1932. He said that the Choctaws had "no valid group claim" because they were not a tribe, and he urged them to resubmit individual claims.[144] Surprisingly, neither Collier nor attorneys for the Department of the Interior cited *Winton v. Amos*; perhaps they had not discovered it.

Again the question of Indian tribal standing hung on the vagaries of personal interpretations. Collier was willing to recognize the Choctaws racially and offer them land under the IRA, but he was unwilling to recognize them politically and grant redress of their treaty claims. Since the Treaty of Dancing Rabbit Creek had extinguished the government-to-government relationship with the Choctaws in Mississippi, he argued, there was no recognized political entity to hold the federal government accountable.

Believing that they were indeed a tribe, the Choctaws turned to Senator Theodore Bilbo, who filed legislation in 1935 allowing the Choctaws to sue in the U.S. Court of Claims.[145] Standing on his role as chairman of the TBC, Pat Chitto wrote Collier requesting support for the bill and pointing out that the Court of Claims had heard the grievances of the Oklahoma Choctaws in 1924. Chitto emphasized that all Choctaws everywhere had the same rights, "growing out of the same treaties between the government and our people."[146]

Collier's reply stressed that this issue had already been conclusively decided "by competent authority."[147] He further hoped that the Indian Reorganization Act could supply the Choctaws with the "material benefit[s]" they needed to improve their lives. The Interior Department also recommended against the bill because the Mississippi Choctaws were not a tribe, and it died in the Senate Indian Affairs Committee.[148]

Bilbo filed a similar bill in 1937, but he shifted the argument slightly. Instead of demanding compensation for their lost lands, the new bill asked that the Choctaws be allowed to recover damages for breach of contract in regard to the 1852 appropriation.[149] This modification reframed the question of broken treaty promises by reference to a more generic legal principle—the right to hold organizations accountable for contractual obligations. The Choctaws' allies pressed the second bill with vigor.

As had his predecessors, Bilbo made a flowery speech in the Senate, invoking the usual beatification of Pushmataha, and closing with an appeal to the greatness of the United States as a haven of justice for all oppressed peoples.[150] Similarly, Representative Ross Collins testified in favor of the companion bill that he filed in the House.[151] When the hearings concluded, the subcommittee recommended the bill as a matter of "equity and justice."[152]

The Department of Justice issued a long memorandum against the bill. Their objections were entirely dismissive—the dispossession happened a long time ago; recompense would be costly; identifying the appropriate beneficiaries would be burdensome; revisiting the decisions of the Dawes Commission would be disrespectful; the legislation would hold the federal government responsible for the Oklahoma Choctaws' failures. In short, justice for the Mississippi Choctaws was inconvenient.[153] President Franklin Roosevelt vetoed the bills in 1938, stating that the Mississippi Choctaws were not a tribe and the federal government was not responsible for the failures of the Choctaw Nation.[154]

Over the next four years, Bilbo introduced the same bill repeatedly, amending it to address objections that arose. The Choctaws lobbied hard for these bills, even co-opting government propaganda during World War II. In 1942 Cameron Wesley sent a resolution to Congress and the president affirming the Choctaws' support for "the present war effort against the Axis powers that are undertaking to persecute and oppress the free and loving peoples of the world" and comparing the Choctaws with peoples the United States was defending.[155] The attorney general of Mississippi contributed a brief in support of the bill, and numerous citizens of Mississippi weighed in as well.[156]

Bilbo got his bills past the Committee on Indian Affairs in the Senate, but they stalled in the House Committee. Finally, in 1942 Bilbo managed to get a bill through both committees but failed to move it on the Senate floor.[157] The Choctaws' treaty claims would have to wait until after the passage of the Indian Claims Commission in 1946. They would file suit again in 1949.

As usual, Choctaw claims were complicated by persons claiming Choctaw blood. In the 1930s, the Choctaws' own attorney, Odie Moore, founded the Dancing Rabbit Creek Club. He charged annual dues to those who thought they might be entitled to claims monies and sold stock with promises of a large settlement. Councilman Ed Willis requested that Bilbo try to shut down the club, but Bilbo's reply was evasive.[158] In a 1943 letter to one of his cronies, Bilbo baldly declared: "I do not want to introduce any legislation that will involve any direct 'monkey business,' so write me fully just what you want done and how the spoils are to be divided in case this legislation ever gets through."[159]

The failure of the bills made the question of spoils moot, but Indian identity remained a commodity that even the Choctaws' allies sought to exploit. In fact, some observers assumed that the Indians themselves were also motivated to political action by profits.

Conclusion

In May 1944 assistant secretary of the interior Oscar Chapman wrote that the Mississippi Choctaws had organized politically not because of "tribal feeling and a desire to reconstitute tribal life" but rather to access revolving credit funds.[160] Chapman's dismissal of Choctaw nation-

Fig. 8. Mississippi senator Theodore Bilbo in Indian garb, 1937. Photographer
unknown. Source: Special Collections, McCain Library and Archives,
University of Southern Mississippi.

building revealed the ignorance of Indian Service personnel. Choctaw "tribal feeling" had echoed across the years, from 1830 until the Choctaws created the IRA Constitution in 1945. After a century of testifying before indifferent congressional committees, filing petitions and claims, hiring attorneys, and beseeching their elected officials, the Mississippi Choctaws finally had institutions of tribal government again.

The Tribal Council's attempts to create a functioning government and economy constitute the next chapters in this story. Although it is unclear what happened to the Mississippi Choctaw Welfare Association, the Choctaws would continue to work with their elected officials over the next decades to bring federal funds into Mississippi.[161] True to their promises to help mitigate the Choctaws' poverty, their political allies continued to support their efforts at self-determination—efforts that now centered in the postwar tribal council.[162]

CHAPTER SIX

The Choctaw Tribal Council, 1945–1965

The creation of the Tribal Council in 1945 marked the Mississippi Choctaws' official political rebirth, but it did not create an autonomous government. Bureau of Indian Affairs (BIA) paternalism frustrated the council's attempts to administer their shared resources in ways congruent with Choctaw values.[1] This led many council members to blame the Indian Reorganization Act and to search for ways to circumvent its limitations. When Choctaw assertions of sovereignty brought them into conflict with agency personnel, they continued to appeal to their congressional representatives, but they also began to work with Indian advocacy groups. They strengthened their communities by partnering with state and county agencies, and they continued to broker relations with outsiders through fairs, stickball games, and crafts. The council's unrelenting pursuit of Article 14 claims suggests that land and treaty promises still undergirded Choctaw nation building.

The Mississippi Choctaws' experiences from 1945 to 1965 confirm other studies demonstrating that American Indians worked steadily toward self-determination despite the looming threat of a new policy called termination.[2] This policy called for the dissolution of the trust relationship between Indian tribes and the federal government and will be discussed in detail in the next chapter.[3] This chapter focuses on the tribal council's attempts to create a government that upheld Choctaw values while promoting development and self-determination. The council began functioning at the end of World

War II, but Choctaws had begun working towards self-sufficiency during the war.

Choctaws in World War II

World War II brought significant changes to Indian Country. Indians served in the armed forces, worked in defense industries, and supplied food and raw materials for the war effort. These actions brought greater prosperity and new perspectives to many American Indians.[4] Estimates of Mississippi Choctaws who served in the war range from 102 to 150.[5] On the home front, the war depleted the Choctaws' labor force, and women stepped up to run farms and meet sharecropping obligations.[6] Choctaws who remained in Mississippi supported the war and worked toward self-sufficiency through two programs designed to encourage agricultural production.

Choctaws embraced the federal government's Live At Home (LAH) and Food for Victory (FFV) programs. In the LAH program, federal and county agricultural agencies joined the Choctaw Agency to promote self-sufficient farming as part of the war effort.[7] By 1944 agent Archie H. McMullen, who had replaced Hector in 1938, proudly proclaimed widespread Choctaw participation, for landlords who had opposed gardening now encouraged it to offset rationing. By 1946 these small truck gardens supplied enough crops for most Choctaw families to live at subsistence levels.[8]

The Food for Victory Program was less successful. The government encouraged growing oil-producing seeds, and the Choctaws chose peanuts. They produced over one thousand bushels in 1941, but production declined over the next four years because the necessary harvesting machines went to "other farmers" (the implication being white farmers). By 1945 most Choctaws were too discouraged to continue.[9]

Although subsistence farming helped stave off hunger and malnutrition, the war brought limited prosperity to Choctaw communities. From 1939 to 1945, 252 Indian families on tribal lands earned an average of $307 annually from farming and $53 from wage work. The 163 sharecropper families earned more, taking in from $600 to $1,000, because wartime labor shortages drove up wages and some landlords offered jobs in their sawmills. Choctaw women and schoolgirls produced crafts to supplement their family incomes.[10]

Money sent home from relatives in the armed services, which McMullen estimated at roughly $70,000 over the course of the war, also aided Choctaw families. Most of these funds went into farming, but some Choctaws used the extra cash for consumer goods, purchasing radios, vehicles, and sewing machines.[11] These changes enhanced the quality of life for some families, but many Choctaws hoped for more widespread prosperity through collective action.

Now that they had a council, the Choctaws could develop their joint resources. Beginning in 1944, a ten-year lease with the Shell Oil company delivered a tribal income of $21,105.25 for the first year and $5,225.75 annually thereafter. A ten-year farm lease in the Bogue Homa Community also generated funds.[12] What did this economic data mean in relative terms for the Choctaws?

BIA inspectors compiled statistics in 1945 suggesting that each family needed an annual minimum income of $1,000, including the value of producing 75 percent of their own food.[13] By these standards, the seven Choctaw communities were impoverished, but profits from tribal leases had allowed for modest improvements in reservation housing. By 1945 the agency had either built or refurbished 202 homes on tribal lands. Sharecroppers, however, still lived in decrepit shacks. Most Choctaw families had no furniture or adequate housewares. Only three reservation families had running water and four had electricity—two of these were agency employees.[14] In planning the postwar Choctaw economy, government officials and Indian leaders also hoped to reduce appalling mortality rates.

By almost any indication, Mississippi Choctaws suffered from poor health. Between 1937 and 1944, infant mortality rates were nearly twice that of their white neighbors and roughly a third higher than African Americans. Tuberculosis, hookworm, and malaria were the primary killers, for Indian homes lacked screens and access to clean water. Nearly all tribal houses had sanitary privies, but sanitation conditions among sharecroppers were dreadful. Tuberculosis spread rapidly, and the hospital was not equipped to treat it. Choctaws' use of the agency hospital had grown steadily over the 1930s and 1940s, but many people lived too far from the facilities to come in for treatment.[15]

To combat these grim statistics, agency officials and the tribal council prioritized economic development. The BIA stressed Indian leadership in meeting development objectives, and Choctaws were eager to comply. The tribal council furnished a forum to debate economic and political progress.

Establishing the Tribal Council

Firsthand investigations of the Mississippi Choctaws in the postwar years emphasized their poverty, and reflecting the research paradigms of the times, such studies concentrated on levels of Choctaw assimilation. They determined that religious leadership at the community level was most significant, and dismissed the tribal council as inefficient and powerless relative to the agency. Even agent Paul Vance reported little participation in tribal elections.[16] Likewise, John Peterson's 1970 anthropological research on the Choctaws skims over the 1950s tribal council, noting that they met in the kitchen of the agency and had little authority.[17]

Yet the actions of the tribal council in the postwar period should not be dismissed. With the threat of termination hanging over their heads, with leaders mostly uneducated beyond grammar school, in a stagnant economic environment, with racial unrest simmering around them, and facing agency personnel who held racist attitudes toward them, the tribal council nonetheless labored for political and economic self-determination in the decades following World War II.[18]

An overview of the council reveals that although communities competed for resources and sharp disagreements sometimes arose, the council generally functioned relatively smoothly.[19] There appear to be no clear lines of factionalism based on communities or generations, and no clashes between "mixed" and "full" bloods such as characterized other tribal councils of the 1940s and 1950s.[20] This comparative harmony reflected Choctaws' interpersonal ethos, which emphasized politeness and discouraged expressing strong opinions.[21] Council records indicate that disagreements were often expressed by withholding votes rather than casting negative ones. Only on matters absolutely central to Choctaw identity did the council openly split. It is probable that the Choctaws' centuries-long struggle to win settlement of their Article 14 claims had imparted a political model for community leaders that stressed cohesion. The lingering fear of removal, personified in the discussions of termination, also served as a unifying force. Leaders who encountered dissent sometimes played the "removal card" to build consensus.

Not surprisingly, Choctaws elected community leaders such as Joe Chitto and Nicholas and Cleddie Bell (who ran a general merchandise store in Pearl River) to the council. Religious leaders, such as the Reverend J. C. Allen of Red Water, were also prominent. World War II veterans comprised from one-third to one-half of the postwar council.[22] The same families tended to win elections, and following patterns of kinship obligations, they were inclined to grant tribal resources to their kin. Yet representatives also consulted with their communities and sought the good of all Choctaws.[23]

During the postwar decades (1945–65) the chairmanship of the band alternated between three formidable men: Joe Chitto (1945–49; 1951–55) of Standing Pine, Emmett York (1949–51; 1955–59) of Pearl River, and Philip Martin (1959–65) of Tucker. J. C. Allen, of Red Water, was usually appointed vice chair.[24] Keeping with his previous activism, Chitto was the most contentious with respect to the agency. But men were not the only leaders.

Four women sat on the council: Pearl River's Cleddie Bell (1950–63) and Nettie Jimmie (1961–63), Mary Lou Farmer of Conehatta (1955–63), and Ina Thomson from Bogue Chitto (1963–65). Both Bell and Jimmie were wives who succeeded their husbands on the council. Bell proffered the most vocal leadership, challenging her colleagues at every juncture where she feared for Choctaw values, asserting Choctaw autonomy against the Indian Service, and leading the campaign for a Choctaw high school. Her death of a heart attack in 1963 ended her devoted service to her people.

Women formed the Women's Council Club to serve meals at council meetings, to raise funds for council activities, and to lobby for improvements in education. Even though serving meals is a role that is often devalued in American culture, for Native peoples political business has traditionally begun with women cooking. Women who want to protest a course of action sometimes simply refuse to cook, which can derail actions.[25] Women also worked for Choctaw self-determination at the community level, serving on election committees and lobbying for local improvements.[26] Both women and men, therefore, wrestled with how best to govern the band.

Because the Choctaw reservation consisted of seven separate and autonomous communities, governance proved challenging. How were the Choctaws to integrate these divergent communities into a unified polity?[27] The Choctaw constitution provided for the election by secret ballot of sixteen members who served for two years. Bogue Chitto, Conehatta, and Pearl River had three representatives, Red Water, Standing Pine, and Tucker each had two, and Bogue Homa had only one. The council selected the chairman, vice chairman, and secretary-treasurer. All tribal members over the age of twenty-one could vote, and each community was authorized to form their own governing bodies and "adopt rules and regulations in harmony" with the tribal constitution.[28]

Council members were uncertain how to coordinate the two levels of governance. The temporary tribal council, which met in early 1945, decided that "most questions should be settled on a community basis," perhaps using separate committees for each community.[29] Yet further discussion revealed problems common to all Choctaws, and the council created four committees to serve the band as a whole: Credit; Natural Resources; Agriculture, Rehabilitation, and Other Enterprises; and Land Rehabilitation and Assignments.[30]

Tribal council minutes for the late 1940s are sporadic and indicate that much business was standard: approving road right-of-ways, hearing reports on agency programs, authorizing oil leases negotiated by the agent, and discussing community problems.[31] These deliberations usually returned to the Choctaws' poverty, pushing the council to stress economic development.

As farming was the preferred occupation, one of the council's first initiatives was a program to improve agriculture. They instituted Public Law 16 and Public Law 346, which established a partnership between the Veterans Administration, state and county educators, and the agency to educate and train returning veterans for civilian jobs. By 1948, agency schools enrolled two classes of twenty-four men.[32] The Pet Milk Company purchased milk from three families of Choctaw veterans, while other veterans established a poultry farm and orchards. The council also provided agricultural loans from the revolving credit fund (established under the IRA) to veterans and other Choctaw farmers. The BIA insisted on leases for these improved tribal farms, and the council agreed to charge an annual rent of twelve dollars.[33]

Extension agents were pleased with the Indians' efforts but lamented that poor weather, shortages of fertilizers and equipment, and boll weevils hurt their returns. The annual income from one year's crops rarely covered the cost of materials, let alone rents and loan repayments.[34] Consequently, by 1949 the tribe had collected only four hundred dollars of the nearly ten thousand dollars owed for rents from 1939 to 1949, and the revolving credit fund was similarly short. Only seventy-two of the 310 loans made between 1945 and 1947 had been repaid, and the tribe was forced to write off some $72,390.71, leaving $9,228.88 still due.[35] Persistent poverty meant that failed loans and unpaid rents would be a problem throughout the postwar decades.

Inspections of the agency in late 1951 and early 1952 revealed that racist and incompetent administrators also hindered progress. After her 1951 visit, Mrs. Ada C. Burdeau, a Cherokee woman who was finance specialist for the Area Credit Office, wrote, "I was appalled by the weakness of the Indian Service's own efforts to improve the condition of Indians. There is obvious lack of planning, of cooperation, of effort, even of sympathy."[36] She deplored the bigoted attitudes of many agency employees, reporting that the director of the veterans education program referred to the Choctaws as "worthless Indians."[37] The following year, special inspectors Evan L. Flory and T. W. Taylor concurred, blaming officials' desire to maintain the status quo.[38]

Nearly everyone agreed that the primary problem was Superintendent Archie McMullen, who was outspoken in his prejudice. Chairman Chitto had requested his transfer in 1949, and then contacted the Association on American Indian Affairs (AAIA), an Indian advocacy organization in New York, for support.[39] In his reply to AAIA queries, BIA commissioner John Province explained that policy makers had feared that the presence of "Yankees" would alienate the white community. "It is my feeling that we had allowed the agency to become too completely staffed with Mississippians, some of whom retained a southern prejudice against people of dark skin—whether Indian or Negroes. Apparently," he admitted, "we erred too much in the opposite direction."[40] Heeding the complaints of the council and the AAIA, the BIA reassigned McMullen.[41] Chairman Chitto thanked W. O. Roberts, the director of the Muskogee Area Office that administered the Choctaws, for moving McMullen and requested a superintendent from another region. Instead, the BIA picked another Mississippian, agency soil conservationist Paul Vance, as acting superintendent.[42] Chairman Chitto protested that despite "a lot of good people" in the state, the council "would like to go on record saying that we are opposed to any definite appointment of any Superintendent that should be selected from the state of Mississippi." They had resolved that "Indian Affairs should be out of politics."[43] The Choctaws' coolness to Vance was rooted in local racial politics, but it also reflected new attitudes toward race relations stemming from veterans' participation in World War II. Charlie Ben, a community leader from Standing Pine, wrote the commissioner of Indian affairs explaining that veterans had "mingled with people of other races. They know what they are being deprived of." He requested an agency staff "free from prejudice."[44] Yet it was difficult to find BIA employees willing to go to Mississippi, because, as area director Roberts remarked, they understood the "legacy of 'carpetbaggers'" and Southerners' fear of "outside interference in race relations."[45]

The full impact of civil rights agitation was years away, but white citizens were already defensive over changing race relations. During the war, some northern African American soldiers posted to Mississippi had resented segregation, and there had been two serious incidents of racial violence, one at Camp Van Dorn near Centerville and the other at Camp Shelby at Hattiesburg.[46] Neshoba County had also been under some strain. Some African Americans had earned enough money in the military to buy the lands they had sharecropped, prompting white resentment. The decline of the cotton economy had also triggered outmigration of roughly four-thousand people, causing landlords to fear for their profits.[47]

Politically, white Mississippians were closing ranks around segregation. Following President Harry Truman's support of the civil rights planks in the Democratic Party platform of 1948, Mississippi joined Louisiana, Alabama, and South Carolina in abandoning the Democrats for the States' Rights Party, also known as the Dixiecrats. Mississippi governor Fielding L. Wright was the party's candidate for vice president.[48]

In the hill country these national tensions surfaced in new anxieties over the Choctaw Agency. McMullen had stoked racial apprehension by spreading rumors throughout Philadelphia that the BIA was planning to replace Mississippians with agents who would force Choctaws into white schools and communities.[49] Thus, local whites were in no mood for Yankees to come to the Choctaw Agency, and unfortunately for the Choctaws, Yankees were reluctant to come. Agency personnel reacted to these criticisms somewhat cynically.

For example, when the new dental assistant, a Cherokee woman named Ethelyn Saloli, protested her difficulty renting a room in Philadelphia in 1951, agency staff told her to accept segregation. When Roberts confronted him, agent Vance told the Muskogee Office that Saloli knew of the situation before she came and should have declined the posting.[50] Vance also accepted segregated county extension services and voiced skepticism about integrating Choctaw children into white schools.[51] Reports of Vance's prejudiced behavior continued throughout his tenure, reaching a crisis later in the decade as interracial conflict escalated following the *Brown v. Board of Education* decision. Meanwhile, the Choctaws attempted to work with him.

Under the Vance administration (1952–62), the council strived to manage their collective resources, which were held in trust by the federal government under the Indian Reorganization Act.[52] Oil and gas leases were the original reason for the council's existence, but they required little Council involvement. Generally, Vance negotiated the leases and council members approved them without debate.[53]

There was much debate, however, over what to do with those profits. Some people wanted to use the money for whatever needs arose, but Vance explained that no one could touch it without a specific development plan approved by the BIA.[54] This paternalism brought criticism of government red tape, but no one ever challenged the leases. Choctaw timber resources and agricultural leases, however, generated discord between the council and the agency, for the two organizations had very divergent notions of Choctaw self-determination.

Managing Choctaw Timber: Autonomy and Employment

Timber was the first tribal commodity the council developed. It was a crucial resource—homes needed constant repair, wood was important for heat and cooking fuel, and trees were a marketable product. Choctaws had always used timber freely, and in January 1945 the temporary tribal council had allowed farmers to sell timber on their lands if they deposited 10 percent of their profits in the tribal treasury.[55] Following the Choctaws' reorganization under the IRA, however, the BIA forbade the cutting of timber on Choctaw lands without an approved forestry plan.[56] In December 1952 the Natural Resources Committee, chaired by Woodrow Billie of Standing Pine, unveiled the forestry program.[57]

Agricultural extension agent H. C. Kinnard and W. H. Heritage of the U.S. Forestry Service had drafted the program with no input from the Choctaws. The U.S. Forestry Service contracted to manage the program, and the most contentious issue was the provision restricting harvesting of trees for home repairs. Rather, timber was to be sold and the proceeds used to benefit all Choctaws.[58] The council wanted lumber for home repairs, but Vance explained that this excluded the sharecroppers. Jimmie Allen, of the Red Water Community, protested that the profits from his community's forests should remain with those who had cared for the trees. Kinnard countered that the United States government held the timber in trust for the entire band, but he promised that only community residents would be employed to harvest in their vicinity. Because they needed the money and jobs, the council approved the plan unanimously.[59] Within a year, however, agency paternalism had provoked more dissent over the program.

In January 1956 Woodrow Billie introduced a routine resolution authorizing a timber sale at Pearl River and set off a vehement debate. Cleddie Bell, Tom Ben (of Standing Pine), and J. C. Allen were angry that Vance had advertised the sale in the newspaper before the council had approved it. Allen worried about the effects of excessive cutting on Choctaw subsistence: "The white folks have cattle, chickens, hogs, and things like that to store in freezers and iceboxes," he said, "but us poor Choctaws hunt wild game for our meat and they are destroying the homes of these wild games that we live on." Despite these misgivings, the resolution finally passed, again because the band needed the money. Conflict quickly resurfaced again over a lack of Choctaw labor in harvesting the timber.[60]

The council was angry that their white neighbors profited from Choctaw resources. Pressed on the question, Vance told the council that Choctaws were not hired because they refused to follow instructions. Cleddie Bell rebutted that timber companies gave the easy assignments to white workers and stuck Choctaws with cuts where there were no roads. Vance shrugged off this criticism.[61] Six months later, the DeWeese Lumber Company bid on Choctaw trees, and Bell suggested that, since lumber companies sold them back their own timber at three times what they had paid to cut it, the Choctaws should establish their own lumber business. Ellis Sam, of Tucker, and Bobbie Hickman, of Bogue Chitto, concurred.[62]

Speaking "as a representative of the property," Vance rebuked Bell sharply, but Joe Chitto, who had returned to the chairmanship in 1951, slapped back. He quoted the Choctaw Constitution, which granted the council the right to regulate all tribal assets.[63] Bell added that the Choctaws had often felt "bribed" into accepting agency actions, implying that they were now resisting such manipulation.[64] The council had acted as a unified body and asserted their right to profit from tribal forests.

When the council met again in October, the Natural Resources Committee again complained that IRA red tape obstructed the committee's goals of providing employment, shelter, and fuel with their timber.[65] Hudson Tubby, of Pearl River, recalled that Choctaws had once controlled their timber, but that "changed when we entered the Reorganization Act."[66] Bobby Hickman likened the timber program to another oppressive relationship: "Sharecroppers do all the work and landlord[s] ride by and get the money." Hickman blamed racism and demanded "all Indian labor" on timber cuts.[67]

He also remarked that "at the last meeting there was so much communist activity," that he had concluded the Choctaws were "behind the Iron Curtain." Rather than accusing the Indian Service of holding to the doctrines of Karl Marx, this Cold War rhetoric probably meant to conflate the IRA with totalitarianism and shame government officials into loosening their grip.[68] Vance offered to invite Tom DeWeese to the afternoon meeting, and the council concurred.

Chitto opened the afternoon session by acknowledging DeWeese as a longtime ally and inferring that the council was delaying this sale to force the agency to listen to them. Tom DeWeese then spoke briefly about his plans to cut timber.[69] Everyone listened politely and then voted six to five to approve the lease. Sensitive to the closely divided vote, Chitto asked if his colleagues wanted to continue selling timber providing that they formulated a plan for home improvements. There was a consensus, and he appointed a committee to draft the plans.[70]

The Choctaws had resisted BIA paternalism even though it risked alienating a longtime supporter. By delaying the sale, they communicated that their relationship with Tom DeWeese was not merely one of patronage—that they wanted any tribal program to produce more benefits for the Choctaws than for the whites with whom they did business. As many other Indians in the postwar era had also done, they had expressed this vision with the language of democracy.[71]

In early 1958 the timber management contract with the U.S. Forest Service came up for renewal, and the chair of the Natural Resources Committee, Edmond Martin from Tucker, complained that the agency had drafted the new contract without Choctaw feedback. The contract employed few Choctaws for cutting, and Indians still could not compete effectively for their own contracts to cut timber. Chairman Emmett York suggested that they approve the plan and then adopt a resolution to employ more Indians. This mollified the critics, and the new contract passed unanimously as amended. The council then took steps to level the playing field so that Choctaws could effectively bid on harvests.[72]

In 1960 the council reduced the acreage of the bids, which improved the Indians' chances to compete, and hired a full-time forester.[73] The new tribal timber program ran smoothly, filling the revolving credit fund, and the council devised plans to tap the fund for home repairs. They passed a resolution in 1962 to allow Choctaws to harvest timber on their own lands and took over full administration of timbering from the Forest Service. By that time, timber sales were the primary source of tribal income, producing 40,000 to 50,000 dollars annually.[74] Over the course of the decade, the council had engaged in "self-termination" of the BIA's trust control of their forests.[75]

Managing Tribal Farms: The Political Economy of Tribal Values

Running parallel to the forestry debate was a dispute over land assignments and rent payments. This topic touched on fundamental issues of Choctaw identity—land, sovereignty, and notions of interdependence. Management of tribal farms underscored Choctaws' sharp divergence from the mainstream economic order that valued money above community. Persistent poverty had driven most Choctaws to default on their farm loans, and these lands had reverted to trust status in 1946. The BIA had insisted that the council charge fees to use trust lands.[76] Most Choctaws, however, resisted paying leases, regarding their farms as payment for their Article 14 claims. Choctaws' farms were at the center of their identity, for being Choctaw meant a right to lands that the federal government had owed them for over one hundred years. Numerous Choctaws believed that the purpose of paying rent was not to pay off their reimbursable loans but rather to fill a pool of money for home repairs.

By the late 1950s the majority of the 227 Choctaw houses on tribal lands were in disrepair, and all but three of them lacked access to clean water. A 1957–58 sanitation survey estimated that bringing these homes up to minimum standards would require roughly $98,500—money the tribe did not have. Nonetheless, some Choctaws were angry that these improvements were not forthcoming and felt justified in withholding rents.[77] Other Choctaws could not have paid even if they had wanted to.[78]

Choctaw farms were too small to make an adequate living. Inspectors Flory and Taylor had written in 1951 that each farm had "15 acres of open land" and working capital of five hundred to one thousand dollars. Yet the *Journal of Mississippi Farm Research* estimated that a decent standard of living required fifty or sixty acres of cropland, with supplemental woodlands totaling about 160 acres and working capital of ten thousand dollars. Even if Choctaw lands had been administered perfectly, they concluded, Choctaws "could not have succeeded with this sort of land base."[79] Yet agency superintendents still demanded farm lease payments.

The fundamental issue behind the debate over rents was who had sovereignty over Choctaw territory. The Choctaw Constitution gave the authority to lease tribal lands to the agency, with the approval of the council, which held veto power.[80] This created insecurities, for some families feared that federal agents might reassign their farms at any time. If the Choctaws owned their lands, argued Councilman Woodrow Billie, they would be happy to pay for them. Joe Chitto and Comeal Polk agreed, with Polk adding, "Since the land status has changed in 1944 [with the IRA] everything has just clashed and stopped."[81]

Whether these men were arguing for private property in the Euro-American sense of the term is unclear. It is likely that they were speaking of owning Choctaw lands as a tribe free from BIA control. Underlying this discussion was the fear of removal fueled by talk of termination. Inspector Flory met with the council and explained that termination was not designed to take away Choctaw lands, but to eventually issue fee patents so that everyone would own their property. With this assurance, the council then agreed to consider a land management plan.[82]

In 1952 Thomas J. Hatch, head of the Department of Extension and Credit, presented the plan to the council and incited a yearlong battle over its provisions. The proposal proclaimed that all lands were tribal property and should be leased so that rents helped the entire tribe, including sharecroppers. It acknowledged desires for land security, for leases could be made permanent if the tenant lived on the land faithfully for three years.[83]

Yet administrative control of leasing remained with the superintendent, who could evict any tenant who failed to pay. Leases were subject to the approval of the council, who could also hear appeals from evictees. After amending the plan so that the council also had to approve evictions and rejecting the standard lease form (for unspecified reasons), eight people voted in favor, six voted no, and two abstained. Despite the close vote, Vance urged everyone to admonish their communities to follow the council's will.[84]

The question of who should control Choctaw leases triggered vigorous deliberation at the next council meeting. Some people expressed fears that Vance would evict anyone he "did not like," while others pointed to the appeals process and the council's veto rights. Finally, Emmett York stressed that the government might take their lands if they did not resolve this problem. Playing the removal card worked, and everyone but Allen (who asked why the Choctaws should even have a tribal council when the federal government had all of the power) approved these regulations.[85]

Conversely, area director Roberts, who had to approve the plan, held a different view of tribal sovereignty. In his view, the federal government had the sole authority to administer tribal lands. He argued that council members, who depended on voters for reelection, would never evict anyone. Roberts also dismissed tribal leaders as incapable of effective management and recommended the BIA reject the plan.[86] The Choctaws' behavior over the next several months would prove that Roberts's assessment of their leadership savvy was erroneous.

Despite Roberts's counsel, the BIA approved the plan. The first step in implementation was for the council to accept all responsibilities for tribal lands held in trust; they voted unanimously to do so. Vance explained that the council now had an "unquestioned documented authority in the management of Tribe [sic] assets."[87] The next step was to cancel all existing leases so that they could be renegotiated under the new rules.

In a tempestuous meeting, the council voted seven to six to revoke and renegotiate all land leases. This action canceled any legal rights Choctaws had to their lands, inciting fears of removal; in the words of Emmett York, "The lands of the Mississippi Band of Choctaws are wide open."[88] The council insisted on reworking the lease forms, both to assert self-governance and to defend against the ever-present fear of removal. This action caused a two-year delay in implementing the program, which left the Choctaws more vulnerable to losing their lands.[89]

Once again the legitimacy of the IRA was at the center of the controversy. Choctaw leaders uneasy with the leasing program aimed their criticism at the IRA, claiming it gave ultimate authority over Choctaw territory to the BIA and that the majority of Choctaws did not support it. Others defended the IRA in principle but called for greater Choctaw autonomy in practice. Joe Chitto argued that the council should devise their lease forms so that the lessee would pay the Choctaw tribe and superintendent rather than the agency, and the council should designate the rent money for home improvements.[90]

Yet these actions still skirted the fundamental problem of charging rent for tribal lands. As council members debated the issue, Chitto refused to allow a final vote on the program until they had reached consensus. "People are the law," he proclaimed. "It should be government by the people and that is why I am holding this thing." Extension agent Hatch then threatened that the Choctaws would be "forced to use a regular government-approved lease that is worse than this," but Chitto still refused to budge until everyone was satisfied. The council adjourned without drafting new lease forms.[91]

Discussing these maneuverings with Roberts, Vance wrote that he could have gotten five men on the council to insist on a special called meeting, but the controversial nature of the issue gave him pause. "There are already various rumors among the Indians," he wrote, "some of them to the effect that this is a move to force them to leave this area," and compelling a meeting would confirm that.[92]

True to their threat, the BIA went forward with the program in January 1954, using a standard lease form.[93] In February, Chitto, Cleddie Bell, J. C. Allan, Woodrow Billie, Tom Ben, and Dolphus Henry traveled to Muskogee, Oklahoma, to raise their objections with Roberts. The notes of the meeting are vague, but the Choctaws apparently intimated that the government's leasing program was a continued violation of Article 14. Roberts disagreed, and nothing was resolved.[94] The imposition of the government lease form lit a fire under the appropriate committees, however, because two months later Bobbie Hickman introduced a document that the Choctaws had designed.

The language of the form was much easier to understand, and it gave more control over the leasing process to the Choctaws. The renter signed the lease with the tribal chairman, who acted as the lessor on behalf of the tribe and the administrative officer. At the end of the lease period, the lessee agreed to vacate the premises "peacefully and without legal process" if he or she did not want to renew. The lease was transferable to heirs, and the council could revoke it and remove the lessee with the agent's approval. The council approved the new form unanimously.[95] The problem of the lease forms had been solved, but the Choctaws' inability to pay their leases remained.

In 1956 Vance sent out letters of eviction, and once again many blamed the IRA for this action. Councilman Allen reminded his colleagues that they had been elected under the IRA to serve their communities, "not to step over our own people and go the white man way."[96] Employing a tactic of passive resistance, Cleddie Bell addressed her colleagues in Choctaw despite Vance's demand that she stop. No one would translate her words for Vance, but the minutes recorded her assertion that the IRA did not grant the agent the power "to scare the Choctaws." She demanded a congressional investigation of the IRA, urged resistance to Vance, and, invoking Article 14, called on the government to give the Choctaws their lands as allotments unencumbered by leases.[97] Woodrow Billie agreed, noting that the council should have abolished the IRA long ago.[98] At the following meeting, Bell introduced her own resolution. It stated that the Choctaws were too poor to pay leases, and it ended with "we earnestly plead for the abolishing of the Land Lease." The council voted unanimously to kill the program.[99]

The area director's office refused to allow this action without a new leasing program, so the Agriculture Committee proposed one in 1957. The new arrangement charged everyone a nominal fee for land and use of wood, but only wage earners and widows (who got a monthly pension) owed rent. There were no provisions for dealing with delinquents. After much debate, the council could not agree on these provisions and voted thirteen to zero to return to the old program, with two members abstaining.[100] Most Choctaws still could not pay their leases, but the council did not evict them.

After two years, Vance took matters into his own hands and began charging delinquent renters with trespassing.[101] Commissioner of Indian affairs Glenn Emmons recommended suing these lessees for back rents in state courts and initiating eviction proceedings in federal courts. After his election as chair later that year, Phillip Martin assured everyone that he did not want to prosecute Choctaws, especially since Choctaw farms were not sufficient to earn a living. Nonetheless, he argued, the council needed to devise a working program.[102] The Agriculture Committee began working on a resolution to deal with delinquent rents.

Six months later, the council debated the committee's document. It noted that Choctaws were too poor to pay the back rent they owed and forgave delinquents who paid "the full amount on the last lease statement." The tenants would then sign a new lease in January 1961, and the council would evict those who refused to maintain their new leases. The resolution passed with ten votes. Cleddie Bell and Tom Ben, still believing that Choctaws should not have to pay for lands the government owed them, abstained.[103]

This compromise apparently worked, because by 1962 most renters had kept up with their payments. Martin then introduced a resolution to begin removing the few remaining offenders. He encountered universal opposition. Nettie Jimmie and Cleddie Bell insisted that this was not a "Choctaw solution." The council voted unanimously to table the matter and to go home and talk with the delinquents "in a nice way" about how they could pay.[104]

The following month, Martin reintroduced the eviction resolution and again met a backlash. Council members had heard bitter words from many of their constituents who were angry that the council was not providing public works projects. They castigated council members for condemning those without jobs while they were on the white man's payroll. Nettie Jimmie announced that she now refused to pay her rent in solidarity with her poor neighbors. Cleddie Bell made a motion to reject Martin's resolution and it carried thirteen to two.[105]

The problem of unpaid rents remained unsolved, in part because of poverty and in part because of continued frustration with what some Choctaws viewed as the council's refusal to help their constituents. In turn, the council denied repair funds to delinquents, making them more determined to withhold their rents.[106] Evictions, however, were simply not an option for most council members.

There were political reasons to oppose evictions, yet Choctaw identity played the larger role. Many council members regarded the notion of charging Choctaws to live on Choctaw land and ejecting them if they failed to pay as an alien system forced on them by the Indian Reorganization Act. Even those like Emmett York, who emphasized the importance of establishing regulations for good government, found themselves unable to evict people.

Because the council could not collect the rents needed to improve tribal housing, Chairman Martin sought funds from the Great Society, filing papers with the Public Housing Administration in 1964.[107] Choctaw leaders then formed the Choctaw Community Action Agency to address housing needs.[108] The U.S. Public Housing Authority (PHA), however, ruled that the council was not authorized to create this organization and needed to call a general meeting to approve it. Annoyed, Martin wrote Senator James O. Eastland, noting that "the negro and white housing programs in our area did not require all of them to assemble for such a council. The Mississippi Band of Choctaw Indians is a legally organized and constituted organization authorized by the Indian Reorganization Act." He urged Senator Eastland to expedite this process.[109]

Again, the Choctaws' plans had collided with the limitations of the government created by the IRA. The Public Housing Authority responded rapidly to Senator Eastland's inquiry, explaining that Indian tribes were eligible to participate if they had "the legislative power to promote peace, health, safety, and morals on the reservation." PHA officials said that the band's constitution did not grant the council these enumerated powers.[110] Unable to proceed with their plans, the band jumped through the government's hoops.

On June 11, 1965, 151 people attended a meeting of the Choctaw General Council and elected Martin chair of the gathering. He explained Tribal Ordinance No. 1, authorizing the Choctaw Housing Authority (CHA). Under this plan, Choctaws who made less than three thousand dollars annually would qualify for a house, provided they helped build, insure, and maintain it, and pay a low rent based on their annual incomes. At the end of eighteen years, they would own their house and lands. The council held sole power over leases and could make construction loans. The General Council approved the CHA.[111] The CHA then obtained a grant of fifteen thousand dollars from the Economic Opportunity Act, and began work.[112]

Using the resources of the Great Society, the council had finally resolved the myriad dilemmas created by BIA paternalism. The band would hold the land collectively and the council—not the BIA—would administer it. Choctaw leaders had dodged BIA bureaucracy and avoided being forced into evicting their constituents. Holding to the idea that they were entitled to lands in Mississippi by virtue of Article 14, Choctaws could not accept either the government's control of their territory or their vulnerability to removal.

As land was central to Choctaw identity, the council also continued to pursue treaty claims. This action highlighted continuing tensions and contradictions between the Choctaws' racial and ethnic identity and their legal status as an Indian tribe organized under the IRA.

Choctaw Claims Revisited

In 1949 the Choctaws filed a claim with the Indian Claims Commission (ICC), which had been created in 1946 to settle outstanding land claims as a prelude to termination.[113] The process went awry in predictable ways as numerous citizens besieged the Mississippi congressional delegation claiming Choctaw ancestry.[114] The BIA discovered in 1950 that the Choctaws' attorneys, W. T. Weir and J. A. Riddell, had sought out people who claimed Indian ancestry, charging them one hundred dollars to join the suit.[115] The Dancing Rabbit Creek Clubs of Philadelphia and Kosciusko resurfaced and put up several thousand dollars to help pay attorney's fees.[116] Concerned over these actions, McMullen investigated but could not uncover any illegal activity. The BIA took no action, and the case proceeded.[117]

In March 1953 the ICC began hearings at the federal courtroom in Meridian, Mississippi. Joe Chitto, Baxter York, Emmett York, Nicholas Bell, Will Jimmie, and others told of their dispossession, their hardships, and their Choctaw identity in Mississippi. They filed documents tracing the history of the federal government's recognition of them as "the Mississippi Choctaws," a group distinct from "Oklahoma Choctaws," declaring this as grounds for their application. Their brief recalled how the Choctaw Nation had paid Article 14 settlements to Choctaws in Indian Territory, and argued that government was still liable for this award.[118]

Attorneys for the federal government rejected the political existence of the Mississippi Band of Choctaw Indians, claiming that they "are neither jointly nor severally a *presently existing* tribe, band or other identifiable group of Indians or successors" (emphasis added). The defendants acknowledged the Choctaws' racial status and IRA government but denied that these conferred legitimacy to sue under the ICC.[119] Although legislation creating the ICC empowered the commission to hear the claims of any "identifiable group" of Indians, the federal government had found a loophole through which they believed the band fell.[120]

In 1948 the solicitor of the Interior Department, Mastin G. White, had defined an "identifiable group" of Indians as groups recognized by either Congress or the Executive Branch. This excluded many communities in the eastern United States who had state recognition as opposed to federal.[121] Technically, this provision should not have disqualified the Choctaws, who were recognized through the BIA and not the state. The federal government, however, had discovered *Winton v. Amos*—the 1921 Supreme Court case that had declared the Choctaws to be assimilated citizens of Mississippi, not an Indian tribe—and officials asserted that this ruling negated any other federal recognition.

Government lawyers further argued that Article 14 claims had been settled in 1886. They contended that the Choctaw Nation had been the proper authority to dispense Article 14 payments because it held a government-to-government relationship with the United States, unlike the Mississippi Choctaws. The Choctaw Nation had no obligation to distribute funds in Mississippi because the refusal of the Mississippi Choctaws to move to Indian Territory canceled their citizenship in the Nation.[122]

The Indian Claims Commission rejected this argument. They held that the Mississippi Choctaws did "constitute an identifiable group by reason of recognition." Citing numerous federal documents, the ICC demonstrated that the federal government had consistently referred to them after 1845 as "the Mississippi Choctaws." The provision of Article 14 preserving their citizenship rights in the Choctaw Nation permitted them to participate in any monetary settlements from the U.S.

government. The government still owed the Mississippi Choctaws the $417,656 awarded in 1886. They instructed that the funds be taken from the resources of the Choctaw Nation and given directly to the Mississippi Choctaws.[123]

Even though the Choctaw Nation in Indian Territory had technically been dissolved by the Atoka Agreement of 1897, Choctaws still held trust monies and timber, coal, and asphalt resources in common. They retained a chief, appointed by the president, and a general council responsible for administering these assets.[124] Because the government proposed to siphon money from them to pay this settlement, Choctaws in Oklahoma filed a motion to intervene, which the ICC denied. The Choctaw Nation appealed to the U.S. Court of Claims, which overturned the ICC ruling and allowed them to interpose as the only officially recognized Choctaw polity.[125]

The Choctaw Nation's lawyers argued that because Congress had authorized them to file suit for payments promised by the Treaty of Dancing Rabbit Creek, it also sanctioned them to distribute the settlement. Attorney William F. Semple chided the Mississippi Choctaws for not seeking these funds at the time of their distribution. He produced the statements of witnesses who had testified that Indians from Mississippi came to hearings on the claims.[126] As to the Choctaws in Mississippi, they had produced no credible evidence that they were the direct descendants of anyone dispossessed in 1830.[127]

The Court of Claims accepted this argument in 1956 and dismissed the case. The petitioners, whom they referred to as "the Chitto group," had not established their rights to Article 14 claims. The court also decided that it would not rule on "whether or not the Chitto group is an identifiable group entitled to sue under the Indian Claims Commission."[128] Thus, bewilderingly, they let stand both the *Winton* decision that the Mississippi Choctaws were not an officially recognized group, and the Indian Claims Commission assertion that they were. Attorney Weir and his colleagues appealed to the Supreme Court, which refused the case.[129] Still, the Mississippi Choctaws pressed on with their claims, but not with the same legal team.

Unbelievably, Weir appeared before the council in 1958 and explained that he was still working on the case. Reflecting their disregard for Choctaw self-determination, neither he nor anyone in the BIA had informed the Choctaws that their suit had been dismissed.[130] In 1959 Emmett York, who was chair of the council, asked the commissioner of Indian affairs about the case and learned of its fate.

The council revoked Weir's contract and attempted to route their claims through an act of Congress.[131] They turned to another ally, Representative Arthur Winstead, who told them he could probably not move such legislation.[132] In response, Martin located another law firm—Wilkinson, Cragun, and Baker—to investigate if there were any cases pending in which they could intervene. In April 1963, the lawyers informed the council that there were not. Choctaw leaders then decided that their case was hopeless and the matter finally ended.[133]

The Choctaws' 133-year fight for the lands promised them in the Treaty of Dancing Rabbit Creek reflected their powerful sense of justice. Only when they were absolutely forced to did they give up their legal fight. By then they had a small land base that they administered as a corporate legal entity. Being Choctaw was still deeply embedded in the lands of their ancestors. Yet those lands remained mired in poverty that threatened the Choctaws' ability to remain in Mississippi. Council members turned to their communities to change that.

Fighting Poverty: Community Development Clubs

The council sponsored and promoted Community Development Clubs, which trained leaders to set development and home improvement goals.[134] The Conehatta community organized the first club in 1952 at the urging of Marie Hayes, tribal relations officer of the Muskogee Area Office. The tribal council took over its sponsorship in 1953 and created a Tribal Community Club Committee to encourage each community to establish development projects.[135]

Additionally, Pearl River, Standing Pine, and Conehatta organized Women's Clubs and coordinated their activities through a Home Extension Club Council, for which Cleddie Bell served as secretary-treasurer. These associations, which met weekly, provided leadership training for women. By 1959 Bogue Chitto had also organized a Women's Club; sixty-eight women were active in these organizations across the communities.[136]

The Branch of Land Operations oversaw all the clubs, and each community competed for prizes according to a point system designed by the Tribal Club Committee.[137] Over the years, the Indian Service staff marveled at how much these communities sought to outdo each other in competition for improvement.[138]

The broader impact of these clubs is difficult to evaluate. In the late 1960s, anthropologist John Peterson wrote that the clubs were mostly filled with Choctaw employees of the agency and that they served "as an extension of the schools and Agency."[139] Peterson's evaluation was no doubt accurate for the purposes of his study, which focused on degrees of assimilation. Reports from the meetings, however, paint a somewhat different picture.

Some Choctaw families appear to have participated enthusiastically in the monthly meetings and club projects. In an area with very limited opportunities for recreation, clubs served a social function, providing meals and organizing leisure activities. Clubs at Bogue Chitto, Tucker, and Conehatta built ballparks, and Red Water sponsored a baseball team. The Pearl River club held a talent show, and Standing Pine's club organized a cakewalk. Some clubs sponsored Boy Scouts and all of them coordinated exhibits for the Choctaw tribal fairs.[140] Development clubs also afforded a venue for activities promoting political cohesion.

Choctaws used the clubs as a forum for discussion of community problems and a support system for addressing them. These were not organizations designed for political activism and governance but rather for self-help and leadership training. Their goals were modest—encouraging students to attend school, promoting soil conservation, and furnishing help with home canning and sewing projects.[141] Not surprisingly, past and present members of the council and their families often led these groups.[142]

Annual school reports from 1955 to 1965 discuss the clubs as center-pieces of community efforts for training in self-determination.[143] For example, though retention of the Choctaw language was a crucial part of Choctaw identity, each club conducted business in English so that Choctaws could learn to speak with their white neighbors.[144] In her annual report of 1958, Marie Hayes praised the clubs as the council's most effective method of adult education.[145] Vance wrote a similar assessment in his annual reports of 1957 and 1958.[146]

The council regarded the Community Development Clubs as an important conduit into the scattered communities. Other than local churches, council members had no formal mechanism to consult with their constituents until the clubs were formed. Council members used club meetings to discuss tribal matters. In 1957 Chairman York requested that the agency send minutes of the council meetings to each club. The agency also used these forums to inform Choctaws about the State Employment Services.[147] Chairman Martin distributed copies of the tribal constitution and bylaws at club meetings in 1963.[148]

As with other attempts to improve the Choctaws' standard of living, poverty impeded progress and results were moderate. Vance recorded that the Community Development Clubs produced "very good early gardens," and home extension reports featured cheery discussions of training women in the domestic arts and men in soil conservation and farm improvements.[149] Yet extension agents remarked that home production often slumped because "most of the women are helping in the crops." The Superintendent's Annual Report for 1958 drew similar conclusions. Vance regretted that the need for labor was "the reason that the house is not clean, the dishes are not washed, the beds are not made, the children are not clean—the women have to work right by their husbands."[150]

Home improvement programs were completely useless for women sharecroppers, who comprised roughly half the population. The 1952 extension report observed, "Housing is bad for the Choctaw who hunt labor. As many as twenty to twenty-five live in one or two small rooms."[151] Damus Z. Rhodes, home management supervisor, lamented that entire families hired out at locations far from their residences. Because of this, their homes were merely places "to return to for meals and sleep."[152] By 1959 the Superintendent's Annual Report concluded that the Home Extension Development Clubs had "made more progress in the intangibles than in the tangible. The pleasant smile and greeting as you call at the home, the clean sheet on the bed in the 'front room,' the timid mother who waits until the Agent is leaving to show her jars of canned beans, and the middle-aged couple who sowed the front yard in mixed flower seed as their yard improvement project— it seems like nothing, but to those of us who remember when this was not true, we say progress."[153] Community Development Clubs helped with basic subsistence tasks, but poverty overshadowed their efforts, just as it did for other poor people in the rural South.[154] Ultimately, their most important function became coordinating crafts production and participation in the Choctaw Fair—activities that aided public presentations of Choctaw ethnicity.

Conclusion

From 1945 to 1965 the tribal council sought control of their lands and natural resources and encouraged the economic revitalization of their communities in ways consistent with Choctaw values. Government trust regulations over Choctaw resources prompted pointed criticisms of the alien and imposed nature of the IRA. Council members debated both its efficacy and its legitimacy, particularly when the demands of designing a functioning economy clashed with Choctaw culture in painful ways. Choctaw leaders desired progress, but they also insisted that economic advancement be driven by Choctaw ideals. Their attempts to balance these two necessities often frustrated the superintendent and the area director, and development proceeded slowly.

Eventually, the Choctaws found ways around BIA bureaucracy, rallying allies to move recalcitrant officials, devising new techniques to manage their resources, obtaining funds from the Great Society's War on Poverty to solve their housing problems, and partnering with state and county officials in community improvements. Yet fear of removal also haunted the Choctaws and motivated many of their actions. Land remained central to Choctaw identity, and the council pursued Article 14 claims until they ran out of legal options. The council accomplished all this under the threat of two onerous BIA policies known as termination and relocation, which are the subjects of the next two chapters.

CHAPTER SEVEN

Termination, Segregation, and Choctaw Nation Building, 1951–1964

Paradoxically, the Mississippi Choctaws constructed a tribal government just as federal Indian policy had shifted toward a program called termination. World War II had drained funds from the Indian Service, and Cold War ideology condemned Indian reservations as enclaves of socialism. In 1953 Congress passed House Concurrent Resolution 108, calling for the termination of the Indian Service and the dissolution of the trust relationship between the federal government and Indian tribes. Policy makers hoped to turn Bureau of Indian Affairs (BIA) health, education, and welfare services over to state and local governments.[1] In Mississippi, racism and poverty hindered these goals, and the BIA pursued a contradictory course that both contested and upheld the Choctaws' recent political rebirth.

The BIA's termination strategies emphasized both relocation to urban areas (the subject of the next chapter) and assimilation into local economies and institutions. Government administrators recognized that Mississippi's segregation statutes would be problematic. Although the Indian Service had done nothing to counter discrimination in the early twentieth century, attitudes had shifted by the 1950s. Officials of the Muskogee Area Office now refused to allow state officials to place Indians in segregated health care facilities and sought to integrate Choctaws into the white labor force. These men and women believed they could make Choctaws acceptable to whites through selective assimilation.[2] They encouraged Choctaws to modify their ethnicity for the labor market and celebrate it for the tourist industry, and they focused much of this effort on women.

Choctaws' reaction to termination was mixed. Like most other Indians in the postwar period, they were critical of federal paternalism and wanted an autonomous reservation economy. Therefore, the tribal council embraced elements of the termination program that promoted economic independence. Choctaws marketed their ethnicity for tourists, but they did not treat it as an anachronism. Rather, Choctaw crafts and public performances of their ethnicity reinforced their political status as Indians who were not subject to segregation statues. They resisted the loss of BIA services for fear of segregation in public accommodations. This chapter highlights the lived experience of termination policies in the unique context of the segregated South.

Termination: Economic Opportunity and Choctaw Identity

Termination of the Choctaws officially began in 1951 with the "Management Improvement Schedule for the Five Civilized Tribes," a document that caused consternation on the council. Commissioner of Indian affairs Dillon Myer met with them in 1952 and explained that termination and relocation presented opportunities for nonagricultural employment and self-sufficiency. Council members responded that racism would impede their ability to find work or obtain health and education services outside the BIA.[3]

Plans to close the Choctaws' hospital in 1953 drove this point home.[4] In a council meeting in 1954, Cleddie Bell read a letter from the Pearl River community protesting the closure and introduced a resolution to stop it. Both documents stressed the hospital's importance in reducing mortality rates. The resolution explained that segregation and "the natural timidity of the Indian people" prevented them from obtaining health care in other venues.[5] It passed unanimously and went out to Choctaw political allies.

The prospect of closing the hospital concerned the Choctaws' supporters, who recognized the crucial need for such a facility. Senators James O. Eastland and John Stennis and Representative Arthur Winstead wrote to commissioner of Indian affairs Glenn L. Emmons, asking that it be kept open. Emmons replied that no definite decision had yet been made.[6] Meanwhile, keeping with their determination that the Choctaws would receive medical care "without segregation or discrimination," federal officials sought integrated health care in medical facilities near Choctaw communities.[7]

These administrators had underestimated the power of segregation. County health care administrators made it clear that hospitals would place Choctaws in wards reserved for African Americans. Against recommendations from Washington to demand integration, agent Paul Vance persuaded county medical personnel to segregate Indians from both white and black patients and worked out a schedule of fees for Indian patients.[8] The next year, however, Congress transferred BIA health services to the U.S. Public Health Service (PHS), which saved the Choctaw hospital but altered its operation.[9]

The hospital became more restrictive under the PHS. Veterans were shunted to the VA hospital and free care was limited to those who were unemployed. Anyone with a job had to pay a portion of their bill or use other public facilities. The PHS further constrained access according to race and marital status. As the PHS administrator Dr. Comerford explained to the council, a "non-Indian wife of an eligible Indian" would receive care "since her husband is legally required to provide for her," but the families of a non-Indian man "who will be assumed to have lost their identity with the Indian community will not be eligible."[10]

The autocratic manner in which the government decided who had "lost their identity with the Indian community" reveals how gender was used to reduce BIA services. The council did not immediately protest these new rules (perhaps because of the Choctaws' low rates of intermarriage), but Choctaws believed that "health is the basic foundation for all human potential," and when Phillip Martin was elected tribal chairman in 1960, he began pushing for expanded health care services.[11]

In 1960 Martin, Emmett York, and J. C. Allen traveled to Washington DC to ask for a full-time surgeon for the PHS hospital and medical care for Choctaws sharecropping in the Delta. The BIA agreed to consider these requests but failed to follow through.[12] In 1963 Martin and York again met with PHS officials, calling for a new hospital and an end to regulations that limited who could use the facilities.[13] Over the next year, Martin and York worked with Senators Stennis and Eastland to secure the new hospital, but it took a decade of lobbying before the project broke ground in 1974.[14] Choctaws' persistent assertions of autonomy resisted termination and eventually brought about "culture-specific efficient health care" in their own facility.[15]

The BIA's other major termination initiative was to find employment for Choctaws, which the council embraced enthusiastically. Tribal leaders and policy makers agreed that economic advancement was crucial to self-determination, and together they sought solutions to the problems that racial prejudice and a severely limited labor market posed for these goals.

Although they ultimately advocated relocating most Choctaws, BIA placement and relocation officer Robert Cullum and Vance nonetheless sought employment for them in Mississippi. Cullum found a few jobs as sawmill operators for Choctaw men, and Vance placed five men in "industrial training" in Philadelphia businesses.[16] Preaching and the practice of Choctaw medicine also bestowed modest incomes on several men, while others continued to hold day labor jobs in construction, truck and bus driving, and the lumber and paper industries.[17]

Farming was the preferred occupation for Choctaws, but small farms in rural Mississippi were disappearing.[18] Neshoba County, for example, lost 65 percent of its agricultural jobs in the 1950s, triggering layoffs of Choctaw sharecroppers.[19] In response, Cullum, council chairman Emmett York, and Superintendent Paul Vance visited state employment offices. The men convinced state officials to advocate hiring Choctaws to chop cotton in the Delta and to harvest snap beans and tomatoes in Florida.[20]

Yet Choctaws were reluctant to risk their carefully guarded racial identity by traveling anywhere where they had to "seek lodging among the Negroes." They also wanted control over the terms of this employment.[21] The council finally agreed to promote migrant farm work if

Choctaws could create separate worker camps, establish their own crews, and make their own contracts through a Choctaw labor boss.[22] The employment office agreed, and by the end of 1951, over three hundred Choctaws had reported to the Delta. Choctaws continued to perform itinerant labor throughout the 1950s.[23] Entire families migrated to the Delta, but single men went to Florida in 1952 and 1953. Emmett York and Councilman Anthon Johnson traveled with them as crew bosses. In Florida, Choctaws worked alongside ethnic Mexicans but stayed in their own camp.[24] Everyone hoped that peripatetic farm labor would be short-term. Although the BIA preferred that Choctaws seek private-sector employment, Choctaws saw no reason why the patronage economy should not also apply to them.

The Women's Council Club wrote the commissioner of Indian affairs in 1955 (copying the Mississippi congressional delegation) to request that the agency hire more Choctaws in professional jobs to "inspire a greater degree of incentive for education."[25] Congressman Winstead and Senator Eastland then contacted Commissioner Emmons, who informed them that the agency employed thirty-six Choctaws in service jobs and that he could do little more, as managerial and professional agency jobs were limited. By the end of the decade, only two Choctaws taught in reservation schools.[26] Nicholas and Cleddie Bell operated the Indian General Store in Pearl River, which was the only Indian-owned business in the area.[27] Serving on the council also constituted participation in the labor force, as members earned a modest part-time income. The BIA increased per diem payments for members from six dollars to ten dollars in 1957. These few white-collar jobs comprised a mere six-tenths of a percent of the adult Choctaw workforce.[28]

The patronage economy employed more Choctaw women than men. Women worked as cooks and attendants in the PHS hospital and as housekeeping and kitchen aides at agency schools.[29] Clerical jobs went to the families of council members, which caused some resentment. At the council's request, the agency hired two female clerical workers in 1957, Miss Dorothy Bell (daughter of councilwoman Cleddie Bell), as stenographer and coordinator for the bookmobile program, and Miss

Josephine Ben (daughter of councilman Tom Ben of Standing Pine), as secretary for the Tribal Council. Miss Ben replaced Bonnie Kate Martin, wife of Councilman Phillip Martin.[30] Cornelia Issac, daughter of Councilman Jackson Issac of Pearl River, became assistant to the agency dentist.[31] Clerical salaries for agency work were $393.46 annually and openings were scarce.[32] Most Choctaw women needed employment beyond the BIA.

Damus Z. Rhodes, home management supervisor for the Muskogee Area Office, hoped to train Choctaw women as domestics. This plan represented a shift in the BIA's thinking about homemaking skills. In the early twentieth century, "outing programs" placed boarding school students as domestic workers among white families. BIA administrators had recognized that this constituted wage labor, but they always insisted that the ultimate goal of domestic employment was to transform Indian women into homemakers capable of establishing middle-class familial norms.[33] For the Mississippi Choctaws in the 1950s, however, officials no longer applied this gloss to domestic service but stated frankly their plans to train Indian women to be maids.

The tribal council also encouraged Indian women to become domestics but with different goals. They requested that the BIA hire more of them as housekeepers in Indian Service schools, not as an avenue to low-paid wage labor but as in-house training for home improvement and community leadership. This employment would help to interest "the Indian women in homemaking, club work, community development and the like."[34] This request was unusual, however, because council members feared that taking jobs associated with African Americans (such as domestic servants) would damage the Choctaws' standing as Indians. Generally, Choctaw women refused such employment, but there were a few exceptions in places where women had established relationships with the families prior to their employment as maids.[35] Even if Choctaw women had desired service sector jobs, however, other barriers remained.

As was the case with men, there were numerous African American women competing for such jobs, and these women understood English. One Choctaw woman hired to wash dishes at a café in Meridian was quickly fired because she spoke only Choctaw.[36] Learning to speak English was central to moving Choctaws into the labor market. Yet this caused some ambivalence because the use of Choctaw language was so crucial to Choctaw identity.

"Choctaw" is itself an English term—the word *Chata* being the indigenous expression. As a statement of ethnicity, the phrase *Chata hapi-a-kat, Chata il-anompoli hi-kat na-yuppa hapi-a* translates "We are Choctaw, and we speak Choctaw proudly." In their interactions with one another, Choctaws referred to themselves as *Chata*. They used the term Choctaw to refer to a public identity in association with non-*Chatas*. Each community had their own dialect of the Choctaw language that had evolved over years of isolation between communities. The more remote districts of Conehatta or Bogue Chitto held to older forms of language. By 1968, only 6 percent of Choctaw homes used English as their first language.[37] Thus, language served as a premier marker of Choctaw identity.

Choctaw leaders recognized the problems this posed in the labor market. Chairmen Chitto and York urged their colleagues to develop their English skills in council meetings to deal with "the controlling race in this country—whites." The rest of the council agreed and most meetings were held in English, which pleased agent Vance who always insisted on using English.[38]

Nonetheless, BIA personnel displayed a surprisingly tolerant attitude toward language assimilation in government schools. Supervisor Rhodes encouraged bilingualism.[39] Likewise, tribal relations officer Marie Hayes explained to the council that her frequent admonitions to speak English should not be taken to mean that she advocated "nonuse of the Choctaw language, which in itself was beautiful."[40] In a public relations piece for a magazine, Vance wrote that federal schools taught in English, but that Choctaw children "are not discouraged in the use of their native language at home. Thus, in the face of meager educational advantages, the Choctaws have mastered two vastly different languages."[41]

Even though administrators expressed admiration for the Choctaw language, oral histories recount that teachers in the schools could be harsh in their insistence that students speak English and conform as closely as possible to white middle-class norms.[42] They justified this because Choctaw ethnicity presented enormous problems for job placement, especially for women.[43] Area employers listed "Neat in appearance; if a woman, wears conventional dress" as one of four conditions for Choctaw employment.[44]

During the 1950s, however, the majority of Choctaw women still dressed in a distinctively ethnic manner reminiscent of the nineteenth century. They wore brightly colored ankle-length dresses and kept their hair long, gathering it up in beaded combs. Ethnic dressing was gendered, for Choctaw men generally wore more modern clothing. This difference might have been rooted in male roles as intermediaries or it may have been simply that women's clothing had changed more than men's since the nineteenth century.[45] Women's preference for traditional clothing was an expression of identity, but it is also possible that many women could not afford new clothes.[46] Whatever the reason for women's ethnic dressing, Supervisor Rhodes insisted that he could find women jobs if they could be convinced to don shirtwaist dresses and cut their hair.[47]

This task fell to the home extension agent hired in 1953, Mrs. Minnie Manny, "a full-blood Indian with considerable tact who could get her foot in the door where others failed," according to Rhodes.[48] Rather than demanding makeovers for Choctaw women, Manny took a generational approach, urging women to make more modern clothes for their children "who drop the costume as they advance in school."[49] Gender role training in Indian Service schools also encouraged Choctaw girls to "drop the costume."

In 1954 the Red Water Day School near Carthage reported that Choctaw schoolgirls had gotten haircuts and permanents, and had "attracted city-wide attention when they paraded the street with new permanent waves."[50] Although it is possible that these children were proud of their new haircuts, Choctaws tended to be reserved with outsiders.[51] More likely, agency personnel "paraded" the children to display the Choctaws' progress. Earlier in the century, straight hair had been a marker of Indian ethnicity invoked against insinuations of "Negro blood." Now, Choctaw children chemically curled their straight hair, and African American women sometimes straightened their curly tresses.[52] That both races underwent chemical processing of their hair to meet mainstream standards of beauty reinforced white hegemony.

The degree to which adopting the conventional norms of appearance contributed to women's employment is not documented. Examples of women working in service jobs in the private sector are scattered throughout agency records, and it is reasonable to assume that these women presented themselves in more modern dress. One woman held a job in the local laundry "for several years." Another worked in a nursing home.[53]

Yet whatever accommodations women made to obtain employment, segregation still constricted their options.[54] Two Choctaw women found jobs at a glove factory in Philadelphia in 1953 but were fired when the white women refused to work alongside them. The city hospital quickly dismissed a Choctaw nurse after white nurses protested her employment.[55] Segregation worked both ways, however, and Choctaws' self-selected isolation also impeded employment.[56] For example, in 1958 Vance reported that some women had accepted positions at the nursing home in Philadelphia, but "when the time came to leave their home, they declined"; he did not explain why.[57]

Even as they sought Choctaw assimilation in the labor market, BIA personnel launched an aggressive public relations campaign that stressed the Indians' exoticism. Marie Hayes informed the council that Choctaws suffered discrimination not because of their *actual* racial status but because of *how* they presented their ethnicity, something council members also acknowledged.[58] Hayes encouraged the council to take control of their image by promoting their "colorful Indian culture" for entertainment as a way to improve public relations.

Hayes arranged crafts sales and performances of Choctaw dances at meetings of white women's clubs. Mrs. Paul Vance, who chaired the Indian Affairs Committee for the Mississippi Federation of Women's Clubs from 1952 until 1959, worked alongside her.[59] As they had been

for decades, well-to-do-whites were interested in "quaint" Indian culture in the context of entertainment or collecting artifacts. When it
came time to hire Choctaws, however, Mississippians preferred more
assimilated Indians. Consequently, Choctaw allies made certain that
the Choctaws' neighbors saw both.

The 1955 issue of the *Mississippi Clubwoman* proved this point. The
magazine featured a picture of two ten-year-old Choctaw girls—their
hair stylishly bobbed and curled, their white dresses demurely ruffled—
who had recently played a piano recital "along with the white pupils,"
for the 20th Century Club of Philadelphia. The article praised Doris
Ann and Betty Lou Allen for their "talent and poise" and explained
that, since their parents could not afford music lessons, the 20th Century Club had established a scholarship program.[60] The subtext suggested that whites were willing to associate with Indians if they met
middle-class standards of appearance.

Yet the person who worked most closely with the Choctaws, agent
Paul Vance, was conflicted about the Indians' ethnicity. Vance's address
to a tourism convention in Jackson in 1958 highlighted this ambivalence.
He bemoaned the fact that the Choctaws clung to their language and traditional dress, because it made them "a museum piece and retards their
integration into the society about them." In the next moment, he promoted the Choctaws' "almost unlimited possibilities" to advance Mississippi tourism, suggesting a park at Nanih Waiya with an aboriginal village peopled by Choctaws performing an Indian drama of removal. This
idea was probably motivated by the success of the removal drama *Unto
These Hills* on the Eastern Cherokee reservation in North Carolina.[61]

Vance's 1957 promotional piece for *Mississippi Magic*, the journal
of the Mississippi Agricultural and Industrial Board, showed a similar incongruity. A picture on the front page featured an elderly Choctaw woman in traditional dress making cane baskets. Vance played
on his readers' nostalgia for the "vanishing Indian" by writing, "Visitors to Choctaw territory may be a bit disappointed to find so little of
the traditional Indian culture still in existence." Nonetheless, he continued, Indian women "carried the remnants" of this culture by keep-

ing "the age-old art of basket weaving alive."[62] Another photo featured two young women in traditional dress with the description "Colorful costumes are worn by the Choctaw women on special occasions."[63]

Another front-page picture showed four Choctaw teenagers at the Pearl River School. Two pretty young women wearing Christian Dior's New Look (full, mid-calf-length skirts), their hair bobbed and curled, stand near water fountains with two young men—their jeans carefully cuffed to break over the tops of their loafers and white socks, their sleeves rolled up, and their hair cut neatly in the current male fashion. The caption reads: "Younger Choctaws (right) dress in more modern fashion as they relax between classes at the Pearl River school in Neshoba."[64] In juxtaposing the picture of the modern teens with that of woman in traditional clothing, Vance assured Mississippians that the nostalgic Indian still lived in Mississippi and could deliver entertainment, but his younger charges were in step with the times and were employable.

The public framing of Choctaw ethnicity represented one of the most significant gulfs between the Choctaws and those who administered them. While government officials regarded Choctaw culture as an anachronism, Choctaws deployed their culture strategically, both in resistance to Jim Crow and as an assertion of indigeneity necessary for self-determination.[65] Recognizing the realities of the market in Indian authenticity, Choctaws promoted their crafts by appropriating stereotypes of Indians held by the dominant culture. They understood the political, social, and economic value of an Indian identity and they manipulated those values in service of Choctaw tribalism. The council's crafts program perfectly exemplified this approach.

Crafts and Tribal Fairs:
Ethnicity, Empowerment, and Economics

Although crafts failed to produce significant revenues, it provided small supplemental incomes that were important in poor communities. The agency promoted craftwork by offering weaving classes in agency schools. In 1944 and 1945 thirty-two schoolgirls and three Indian women studied weaving at the Pearl River, Conehatta, and Tucker schools.[66] Choctaw women also operated outside agency programs. For example, the M. G. Underwood Grocery and Market in Philadelphia began carrying Choctaw baskets in 1951, advertising them in the *Neshoba County Democrat* as "made by our own Choctaws, reasonable in price." Official BIA reports, however, never mentioned this sales venue.[67] Choctaw leaders sanctioned these individual efforts by seeking to raise production and expand marketing.

The council brought John A. Ketcher, a Cherokee Indian Service employee from Tahlequah, Oklahoma, to Mississippi to open a small workshop and sales room at the agency in 1952.[68] Ketcher supported Choctaw control of production by organizing craft associations of women artists. He encouraged the women to make tourist kitsch: "small crafts to be made in a hurry that sold well."[69] To sell these crafts, Marie Hayes enlisted the Business and Professional Woman's Club of Jackson, who sponsored a Choctaw Bazaar in 1952 as part of the State Federation of Women's Clubs' Small Businesses Services. It was designed to "promote the production and marketing of products originating in the homes as workshops of Mississippi people."[70]

Poverty limited entrepreneurship, however, for when Ketcher tried to collect the crafts consigned for the bazaar, the women had frequently already sold them, and he had to borrow crafts from Indians in other jurisdictions to complete his inventory. His instinct for the Mississippi market proved accurate: small inexpensive items sold out and the larger and more expensive ones did not. Ketcher sought a way to market leftover items outside the agency.[71]

The tribal council fulfilled Ketcher's goal in 1954 by leasing tribal land to the Carthage Chamber of Commerce in return for their agreement to construct a small shop.[72] That same year, the council opened a second craft outlet, the Tepee Craft Shop on Highway 80 between Jackson and Meridian. In both venues women produced the crafts and men ran the businesses.[73]

By 1955, Choctaw women's crafts were sold all over the United States and demand reportedly exceeded supply.[74] Unfortunately, this boom coincided with the termination of the Arts and Crafts Instructor in late 1954. Although the official Tribal program ended, Choctaw women continued to create crafts on their own.[75] Household production afforded women money to buy material for their children's clothing. The need for cloth meant that Choctaw women produced a huge volume of baskets—turning out seventeen hundred baskets in one nine-month period in 1959.[76]

The meager income was helpful, but Choctaw women may also have done craftwork for cultural reasons. Because it was an interruptible task, they could construct crafts around the demands of farm and family. Their handiwork also represented markers of Choctaw identity, especially when marketed with other public relations pageantry that played to tourist expectations of Indianness.[77] For example, the grand opening of the Tepee Craft Shop featured a stickball game, Indian songs and dances, and the "Choctaw Hillbilly Band." The council orchestrated press coverage in all mediums from print to television. Choctaw craft workers also promoted their merchandise in demonstrations for women's clubs and civic groups around the state. These exhibitions affirmed Choctaw artistry and ethnicity.[78]

Choctaw artists often deployed iconic images of Indianness that were far removed from their actual lives. They performed short skits at craft exhibits, such as the one based on the song "From the Land of Sky Blue Water," presented in 1954.[79] The play began with scenes of "early life in an Indian village," followed by "acting out of the lyrics of the song." For the second number, based on the song "Pale Moon: An Indian Love Song," the "chief beats the tom-tom; the brave sings, and the princess does the Indian sign language."[80]

The central character in these vignettes is the beautiful "Indian Princess" pursued by the forlorn lover, who likens her beauty to natural phenomena and bewails her aloofness and tragic end. The lovely "maiden" in both of these tunes is stoically silent and passive regarding her fate, which was to lose her way of life forever. The female actor's use of sign language underscored this message.[81]

This sketch capitalized on the classic romantic figure of the Indian Princess—one side of a dichotomous view of Indian women that helped to sanction colonialism: the princess/squaw. The silent princess personified indigenous destiny, tragically doomed to fall before the on-slaught of civilization.[82] These images appealed to the persistent rep-resentation of the Choctaws as a vanishing people, which stimulated purchases of Indian artifacts as a type of "salvage tourism."

A program staged by the Mississippi Federation of Women's Clubs in 1955 further illustrates this idea. In *Mississippi Memories* Choctaws appeared in act 1, "The Pioneer Period (1817–1840)," which had two scenes: "War Feast and Dance" and "Signing the Treaty." There was no mention of the injustice of removal or of Choctaws remaining in Mississippi. Instead, the play presented Choctaws as quaint primitives who had long since faded away.[83] It is not surprising that people who preferred stereotyped trinkets and toys to serious artistic works bought more craft items at exhibits invoking this trope. But what of the craft workers? Why did they participate in vignettes that portrayed their still vibrant culture as a relic of a faded past?

Aside from their practical value in helping to move products, the craft workers may have been distancing themselves from the tour-ists by marketing crafts in this way.[84] Princess iconography may have been a deliberate attempt to obscure the reality of hard agricultur-al labor which characterized most Choctaw women's lives. Depic-tion of Indian women as "squaw drudges" lay on the other side of the sexist colonial binary. The drudge engendered contempt because she represented a perceived failure of Indian initiative in assimilat-ing.[85] By deliberately offering the flip side of this duality, Choctaws could counter the stereotypes of impoverished Indians as degraded. By purchasing crafts, Mississippians sought to rescue the mythic In-dian princess, not the actual impoverished Choctaw woman behind the plow. The Choctaws' neighbors dissociated themselves from the damage that segregation promoted by interacting with Choctaws in highly stylized ventures.

The Choctaw Indian Fair represented one regular venue for mar-keting Choctaw ethnicity and promoting intercultural cooperation. The council staged the First Annual Choctaw Indian Fair in 1949 at the Pearl River School.[86] Choctaw fairs were well-publicized through-out Mississippi and attendance was always high. The *Neshoba County Democrat* furnished extensive daily coverage, and the Choctaws de-signed the advertising for radio and, beginning in 1956, television.[87] The fair featured dancers from reservations in the West and gendered representations of Choctaw culture.[88] Men demonstrated native athlet-ic skills with blowguns and played stickball. Women displayed baskets and beadwork, and competed for the title of "Best Dressed Choctaw Woman." The woman whose Indian-made outfit was the most authen-tic and aesthetically pleasing won the title.[89]

Capitalizing on the use of Indian women as cultural intermediaries (a popular image dating back to Pocahontas), beautiful Choctaw wom-en served public relations purposes for the tribe. The Neshoba County Chamber of Commerce began sponsoring Choctaw Princess contests at the fair beginning in 1956. The winner represented both the Choc-taws and the city of Philadelphia at civic events across the region.[90] The council also sent representatives to Miss Indian USA and the Miss In-dian America contest in hopes that this type of public relations work would eventually encourage admittance to public schools.[91]

The fair had a political venue with a similar public relations func-tion where Choctaw leaders invited policy makers and politicians to give speeches to fairgoers. The state superintendent of education spoke in 1951, and Representative Arthur Winstead made a speech in 1955.[92] Officials of the Neshoba County Fair repaid the Choctaws' outreach to white officials by including a Choctaw crafts booth at their fair be-ginning in the mid-1950s. The Neshoba County Fair was famous (or infamous, depending on one's perspective) throughout Mississippi for the oratories of Mississippi politicians such as James K. Vardaman and Theodore Bilbo, who often invoked racist rhetoric.[93]

Despite racial invectives, however, African Americans and Choc-taws mingled with whites at the Neshoba County Fair until after the *Brown* decision. In her reminiscences of the fair, Philadelphia doy-enne Florence Mars commented, "After the Supreme Court's school desegregation decision, blacks gradually ceased to attend the Fair ex-

Fig. 9. Choctaw Princess Loretta Steve, 1962–63. Photographer unknown.
Source: National Museum of the American Indian, Smithsonian Institution.

cept as workers."[94] Highlighting their status as acceptable nonwhites, the Choctaws opened their crafts booth on the Neshoba Fairgrounds around the same time.

The invitation to participate in the Neshoba County Fair underscored the Choctaws' position in the racial hierarchy as colorful exotics whose culture could generate revenues. In this context, their third racial status came to the forefront. A public relations piece in the *Memphis Commercial Appeal* in 1956 made this point most explicitly. The article proclaimed the Choctaw's racial purity under such headlines as "Miss. Indians Retain Racial Integrity" and "Choctaws Draw No Color Line but Seldom Marry Outside the Tribe." The spread featured numerous color pictures of Choctaws in traditional garb at the Neshoba Fair.[95] These images, and perhaps the assurance that Choctaws had preserved their racial integrity, prompted requests by civic groups for stickball games and dances, and Choctaws were happy to oblige.[96]

As automobile tourism increased in the postwar period, the Philadelphia Chamber of Commerce posted a sign at the Philadelphia city limits announcing a "Heap Big Welcome" to Philadelphia, "Capital of the Choctaw Nation."[97] They joined the Mississippi Federation of Women's Clubs to transform Nanih Waiya into a state park, which opened in 1960. The Choctaws requested permission to build a crafts shop on the site and urged park management to hire an Indian caretaker, but to no avail. The county alone benefited financially from the Choctaw's most sacred site.[98] The Choctaw Indian Fair remained the primary place where Choctaws had control of their public image.

The fair, however, was beset with internal tensions that highlighted the council's struggle to free itself from agency control. Most Choctaws appreciated the sociability of the occasion, but many also expressed frustration with the "thoroughly American way in which the fair was organized." Even though the tribal Agriculture Committee supervised an all-Choctaw Fair Board, the agency used the fair to promote acceptance of the BIA agenda.[99] In the youth division, for example, only students in good standing with their teachers could compete. Craft work-

Fig. 10. Choctaw dancers, 1962–63. Photographer unknown. Source: National Museum of the American Indian, Smithsonian Institution.

ers had to sell at designated times through the official crafts booth. The agency secured the judges for all categories of competition.[100] This kind of regulation was not unusual for county fairs in general, but some Choctaws preferred a more cooperative model.

In late 1958 the council finally convinced the BIA to grant them more control of their fair, and they staged the program themselves for the first time, paying most of their expenses out of gate receipts. The following year, they built a tribal fair ground at Pearl River, and have controlled the fair ever since.[101]

Although public performance showcased the Indians' continued presence in Mississippi (and thus buttressed their nonblack racial identity), there is no indication that it promoted integration in other public venues. Nonetheless, it may have reinforced interracial cooperation in economic development. Long before the successful completion of the Choctaw industrial park that transformed rural Mississippi in the 1970s, Choctaws and county officials worked together to try and bring industry to rural Mississippi.

Toward a Reservation Industrial Economy

The tribal council and the agency used public resources to attempt to lure private capital to the reservation.[102] In 1959 Sears, Roebuck, and Company considered opening a manufacturing plant in rural Mississippi. Officials from the Industrial Development Office of the BIA met with representatives from local chambers of commerce and examined potential sites.[103] Yet the one hundred thousand dollars the council had borrowed from the BIA Development Office to help construct the facility proved insufficient. The Philadelphia Chamber of Commerce stepped in and offered land, materials, and labor for infrastructure, and Congressman Winstead attempted to promote the plant. Nevertheless, Sears executives decided that the costs of shipping to major markets from rural Mississippi were prohibitive.[104]

Similar attempts to attract industries in 1961 and 1963 also fell through for the same reasons—Choctaw communities were just too isolated to be attractive.[105] In 1964 the Choctaws purchased an abandoned plant in Louisville, Mississippi, and contracted with the Spartus Corporation of Chicago to manufacture wooden cases for clocks. Although it was not strictly a tribal industry, this factory furnished some of the first manufacturing jobs for Choctaws.[106]

Other civic groups had greater success luring industry, and this brought about gradual changes in Choctaw employment. Industrial surveys of the reservation done in 1962 and 1968 indicated that "the percentage of Choctaw heads of households engaged in non-agricultural wage jobs increased from 23.8% in 1962 to 44.6% in 1968, and women's non-agricultural employment rose from 4.3% to 17.7%."[107] Although some of these figures reflected new jobs with the tribe, private-sector employment grew steadily after 1964 because of industrial expansion in east-central Mississippi.

From 1962 to 1965 manufacturing earnings for Neshoba County alone grew by nearly four thousand dollars.[108] In 1965 Superintendent Lonnie Hardin, who had replaced Vance in 1962, informed the council that fifty-two Choctaws had been hired by factories in Kosciusko,

Carthage, Philadelphia, Union, and Decatur.[109] The role of Title 7 of the 1964 Civil Rights Act (which forbade employment discrimination) in improving the Choctaws' place in this new labor market is a matter of some conjecture.[110]

The 1964 Civil Rights Act may have prompted some hiring, but Mississippi was not known for its compliance with civil rights legislation. For example, when the manager at the Wells Lamont glove factory requested that the Neshoba County Chamber of Commerce support anyone complying with Title 7 he was sharply rebuffed.[111] The well-publicized murder of three civil rights workers in Philadelphia in 1964 was only one act in a campaign of racial violence conducted by the Mississippi Klan from 1963 to 1969.[112] Neshoba County schools did not integrate until 1970, after the 1969 Supreme Court ruling in *Alexander v. Holmes County Board of Education*, which ordered compliance with *Brown*.[113] Federal civil rights legislation, then, was probably not responsible for expanded opportunities for Choctaws.

The gradual rise in factory employment for Choctaws probably reflected the outmigration of African Americans who fled rural Mississippi in these violent years. It may also have been a result of more Choctaws completing high school after 1964.[114] Yet the federal government played an important role in economic improvements; the concerted efforts of the Johnson administration to fight poverty changed the economic landscape of Choctaw country.

Public works programs marked the beginning of this shift. After intensive lobbying by tribal officials and the Mississippi congressional delegation, the BIA began a Public Works Program for Indians in 1963. The Choctaws received $210,000 to construct roads, pay for their forestry program, and improve farmlands in three counties declared "depressed" by the federal government—Neshoba, Leake, and Newton. Roughly seventy people signed up for work, and the program supplied temporary employment in unskilled and semiskilled jobs in 1963 and 1964.[115]

Tribal programs, including the Choctaw Housing Authority, created in 1965, also imparted jobs. The most significant changes to the Choctaw economy, however, came after the council voted unanimously to participate in the Economic Opportunity Act in 1964.[116] Shortly afterward, they formed the Choctaw Community Action Program, which became the vehicle for a massive rebuilding of the reservation economy. Out of this effort, the band created the "Choctaw Miracle," which started the long journey from poverty to prosperity over the next fifteen years.

In 1964, however, the Choctaws still had a 75 percent unemployment rate and 90 percent of Choctaws lived below the poverty line.[117] BIA officials argued that the only way for the Choctaws to obtain a decent standard of living was to relocate to urban areas. Once again the Choctaws faced removal and once again they resisted.

Conclusion

In the postwar years, both the tribal council and the Indian Service struggled to help the Choctaws improve their standard of living, although the two had different objectives in promoting development. The federal government wanted the Choctaws to be self-supporting so as to terminate their trust relationship with the tribe. The Choctaws desired self-sufficiency as a means of nation building.

Both groups recognized the challenges of holding Choctaw ethnicity in tension with accommodation to mainstream culture. BIA officials urged assimilation for the labor market, but, recognizing the value of Choctaw ethnicity for tourism, they also tried to market Indian identity in ceremonial contexts. Ironically, then, in Mississippi the BIA emphasized Indianness as a means of terminating an Indian nation. Gender played a significant role in this process. Choctaw women participated in the staging of Indian identity, both as actors and as the majority of craft workers, and were the specific targets of assimilation efforts.

Choctaws also promoted ethnicity in fairs and demonstrations, but for different purposes. They did not compartmentalize their Indianness as solely ceremonial. Instead they viewed their culture as central to self-identification and to their standing as an autonomous political entity. This identity was the centerpiece of their political resistance to those aspects of termination, particularly relocation, that they found abhorrent.

CHAPTER EIGHT

Relocation, Resistance, and Civil Rights, 1951–1964

Termination went hand in hand with the relocation program, an effort of the Indian Service to move Indians from isolated reservations to urban areas where employment opportunities were allegedly greater.[1] Government officials believed that relocation was the best solution to the Choctaws' chronic poverty. Most Choctaws, however, shunned relocation as reminiscent of removal. Determined to remain in their homelands, the Choctaw council pursued economic development. This led some councilmen to abandon the Choctaws' long-standing strategy of racial separatism and seek integration of public schools. For numerous reasons, the Choctaws' challenges to segregation operated independently of the broader civil rights movement in Mississippi.[2] Integration divided the council, for others were hesitant to expose Choctaw children to harassment, and everyone agreed that given the volatility of racial relations, they should proceed carefully. Consequently, Choctaws did not challenge segregation through direct action, but rather asserted their civil rights as Indians not subject to Jim Crow laws.

Choctaw leaders grounded this campaign in the band's unique political status as a domestic dependent nation. Their actions ultimately strengthened their sovereignty, for their civil rights activism exposed the role of Mississippi's racial politics in agency affairs and prompted substantial personnel changes. Choctaw leaders embraced pan-Indianism, which encouraged a new way of framing their political identity. Some councilmen deployed the rhetoric of the Cold War and avowed an

American identity based on their Indian citizenship. The Mississippi Choctaws' attempts to resist termination and relocation in the context of civil rights resulted in a revitalized nation building that is a crucial untold story of Mississippi's civil rights history.

Removal Revisited: Relocation

Even as they attempted to help Choctaws integrate the local workforce, government officials also concluded in 1952 that "a realistic approach to the economic reorganization of the Mississippi Choctaw Reservation area will require relocation of the majority of those now occupying reservation units."[3] In 1952 three World War II veterans and their families—Otis Stoliby, Willie McMillan, and Murphy Solomon—relocated to Chicago. McMillan found a job as a welder and lived at the YMCA. Stoliby secured employment in the International Harvester plant and rented a room with a kitchenette. Within four months, however, Solomon returned to Conehatta because the "Chicago pavement was too hard for his feet," and McMillan fell victim to alcoholism and returned to Mississippi. Stoliby remained, however, and became active in the Chicago Indian community, where he served on the advisory board of the relocation office.[4] By the end of 1954, forty-one more families had gone to Chicago and only nine had returned to Mississippi.[5]

Muskogee Area director W. O. Roberts attributed this success to stories that circulated among Choctaw communities about people like Stoliby. It was not because the council endorsed the program.[6] Although the councilman from Bogue Chitto, Prentiss Morris, moved to Chicago in 1953, most council members did not approve of relocation.[7] Officers of Relocation Services attended council meetings in 1955 and 1956 in hopes of convincing them otherwise. Several people asked about wages and housing, but were otherwise noncommittal.[8]

The BIA assigned Glenn Durham as relocation officer for the Choctaw Agency in 1957. Durham attended each council meeting and visited the community development clubs.[9] Thereafter, roughly seventy-five families relocated annually, and Choctaws started moving to St. Louis, San Francisco, San Jose, and Los Angeles as well as Chicago.

Most of those who relocated were younger. Often they were gradu-
ates of off-reservation schools and had some work experience beyond
farming and day labor.[10]

The council then sanctioned the program by creating a Relocation
Committee to interact with Durham and to address issues of tribal
membership that had arisen when Choctaws relocated.[11] The Choctaw
Constitution specified that tribal members must be residents of Mississippi. This had caused some women who conceived away from Mississippi to return home to give birth, resulting in families being separat-
ed for a long time because of the expense of relocating.[12] The council
unanimously approved a constitutional amendment to automatically
enroll children born to enrolled parents living in other states.[13]

BIA regulations required that the amendment be ratified through
election, but the agency staff usurped this procedure. Durham falsely
told agent Paul Vance that the Relocation Committee had delayed the
vote until they could educate their communities.[14] The chair of the Relocation Committee, Cleddie Bell, discovered Durham's deception in
1959 and angrily informed her colleagues. Chairman York then called
for an election that spring.[15] Despite efforts to encourage voting, only
177 voters turned out, and only five voted by absentee ballot. This fell
far short of the quorum needed to institute the change.[16]

The residence requirement remained until the constitution was
amended in 1969 to read: "Any child of one-half (1/2) or more Choctaw blood born to any enrolled member of the band after January 1,
1940, shall be entitled to membership."[17] The success of the second attempt to revise the constitution indicated greater involvement in tribal politics, perhaps because the Choctaw Community Action Agency
operating in the communities connected people more closely to the
council. Other than altering the constitution to accommodate relocated Choctaws the council did little to promote it.

Though several members expressed concern that the program could
hurt their claims case or their chances to open a high school, the Choctaws' love for their sacred homelands was the primary reason for resistance to relocation. "This is our home," one council member told soci-

ology doctoral student Charles Tolbert in 1957, "and we don't want to leave."[18] The general consensus was that the Choctaws should remain in their homelands by recruiting industry and resisting racial discrimination. The latter goal required challenging BIA personnel who upheld the racial status quo.

Segregation and Sovereignty:
Choctaw Civil Rights Strategies, 1955–1965

As they contended for their civil rights, the Choctaws did not embrace the civil rights movement. Even though the Choctaws' strategy of invoking the federal government was similar to the African American approach, the Choctaw campaign was distinctly Indian. The most outspoken leaders were Emmett York and Phillip Martin, who alternated in the chairmanship of the tribal council from 1955 to 1965. York and Martin asserted Choctaw sovereignty, grounded in indigeneity, and rejected alliances with anyone seeking civil rights for African Americans. This included the Civil Rights Commission, whose representative had called on the men while they were visiting Washington DC in 1960.[19]

Choctaw leaders feared that association with African Americans would hinder Choctaw advancement. They based this in part on the behavior of agency staff who conflated Indians and African Americans in order to discount both. For example, Vance had informed his staff that the delegate from the Civil Rights Commission had represented the NAACP. Recounting this to LaVerne Madigan, executive director of the advocacy group the Association on American Indian Affairs (AAIA), York explained that Vance hoped to "degrade the Choctaws as Negroes" by this remark.[20] Consequently, even though someone on the council told Madigan in 1962 that "if we wait long enough, we will have to face the fact that the Negroes won our rights for us," the majority of Choctaw leaders believed that Indian civil rights issues were different, and centered their campaign for integration on their Indian identity.[21]

Martin and several of his colleagues believed that the Choctaws suffered from discrimination less because of race than because of class. He argued that Choctaws needed only to "bring themselves up educationally and economically" to gain acceptance in the white community.[22] Martin's primary focus was therefore material rather than ideological. He believed that developing a reservation economy capable of creating regional prosperity would overcome prejudice. As he told interviewers in 2001, "given the choice between hating and eating, most will choose the latter."[23]

Choctaw indigeneity was central to Martin's civil rights vision. "The Choctaw Indians were here in Mississippi before anybody," he told the council in 1962. "When the white people came they brought with them the negroes as their slaves. So, in a nutshell, the white and negro [*sic*] problem is one of their own making. In my opinion, the basis of the Indian problem is entirely different." Their dilemma was not segregation but dispossession.[24] Martin argued that Indian tribes were domestic dependent nations whose sovereignty the federal government upheld against the power of the states.[25]

Choctaw political identity in the context of civil rights thus focused on their status as a sovereign Indian tribe, which they believed exempted them from Jim Crow laws. Emmett York put it most succinctly: "When will the people living around here and the government ever find out that we are not negroes [*sic*]. We know that this segregation is for negroes. Are we taken as [the] negro race of people by the United States?" After noting the common brotherhood of all humans "in the eyes of God," York asserted that "we are an Indian and we are always going to be Indians" and Congress had granted citizenship, hence equality, to all Indians.[26]

York associated Choctaw Americanism with the Indian Citizenship Act of 1924 and with Choctaws' unique relationship with the federal government. That African Americans were also guaranteed civil rights by the federal government was beside the point for York. York believed that African Americans came under state segregation statutes whereas Indians, wards of the federal government, did not.[27] Regarding segregation, York believed that federal recognition of Choctaws as full U.S. citizens rendered their status as nonwhite Mississippi citizens moot.

Three years after the federal government granted U.S. citizenship to Indians, however, the Supreme Court of Mississippi placed Choctaws under segregation laws. Racial discrimination against nonblack people of color in Mississippi had been customary rather than statutory until the 1927 case of *Gong Lum v. Rice*, when the justices held that the term "colored races" included everyone who was not white.[28] The case centered on a Chinese merchant living in the Delta, Gong Lum, who had enrolled his daughter Martha in Bolivar County's white public high school, which promptly expelled her. Lum filed suit on the grounds that Martha was not "a member of the colored race, nor is she mixed-blood, but that she is pure Chinese." The Mississippi High Court countered that the term "colored races" encompassed everyone who was not white.[29] The Mississippi legislature then passed a law in 1930 authorizing "schools for Indians and other races" that sanctioned separate schools for each race provided there were enough students to justify the expenditure.[30]

BIA officials in Washington and Oklahoma knew of this ruling but hoped to circumvent it through a careful strategy of selective integration.[31] Because Choctaw children went to white schools along the Gulf Coast, policy makers believed that segregation, rigid in statute, could be flexible in practice.[32] In 1951 special inspectors Evan L. Flory and T. W. Taylor met with the state superintendent of education to request integration of Choctaw children into white schools but were rebuffed.[33] The following year, tribal relations officer Marie Hayes suggested a gradualist path to school integration, changing hearts and minds one person at a time beginning with high school students.

Choctaw schools ended in the tenth grade, forcing Choctaw teens into government boarding schools for their last two years. Hayes called for expanding an existing program in which the children of sharecroppers boarded with families on tribal land to attend agency schools. She recommended paying white families a small stipend to board Choctaw students in their homes, beginning in Jackson and Meridian, "where there is less prejudice than in the local communities, and this should help pave the way for acceptance of Indian children in the public schools generally."[34]

The council declined this program. Instead, they voted to encourage integration through the Boy Scouts and designated funds to help defray the costs of attending scouting camps.[35] Tribal council minutes do not explain their choice, but a reluctance to send their children to live with other families and a general distrust of outsiders probably influenced their decision. A handful of Choctaw families, however, agreed to participate.

The boarding program was controversial, and Vance, who had praised the Lumbee Indians of North Carolina for not attempting integration, did not pursue it with much enthusiasm.[36] Vance placed students in Meridian—two in 1952 and seven in 1953—noting that there was "considerable hesitancy on the part of many schools to accept Indians for enrollment."[37] In 1955 Vance wrote that this reluctance "has been accelerated by the recent Supreme Court decision to complete refusal."[38]

The effect of the Supreme Court decision in *Brown v. Board of Education of Topeka* on the integration program was a matter of dispute. Vance claimed that it shut down enrollments, but Maude Lyons, the agency social worker, Victor Kaneubbe, an Oklahoma Choctaw Baptist missionary working in Philadelphia, and a local Methodist minister all placed seven more high school students in white homes in 1957. Kaneubbe wrote to Muskogee Area Director Paul Fickinger in 1960 informing him of several schools willing to admit Choctaws.[39] Vance, the person who would have placed the students, did not pursue Kaneubbe's lead.

The official position of the Indian Service gradually came to echo the southern critics of *Brown* who argued that the decision had abruptly ended a slow but steady progress in race relations following World War II.[40] In reality, *Brown* produced only a slight dip in the boarding program during the year 1954–55. By 1958, there were twenty-five children in public schools, seven in state colleges and universities, and seven in vocational schools. More Choctaw teenagers moved to homes in Meridian in 1960 and 1961.[41] Both before and after *Brown*, then, the boarding program had some success. Yet in 1964 the BIA abandoned this course, for the new Muskogee area director, Graham Holmes, had decided that the Choctaws needed more assimilation before integrating.[42]

This sudden concern with Choctaw levels of assimilation may have been a response to the increasingly explosive racial climate in Mississippi in the early 1960s. The violence surrounding the enrollment of

African American World War II veteran James Meredith at the University of Mississippi in 1962 and the murder of NAACP state field secretary Medgar Evers in Jackson that same year, the creation of the civil rights organization the Council of Federated Organizations, and Ku Klux Klan murders of three civil rights workers in Neshoba County during the 1964 Freedom Summer campaign all reflected racial tensions that encouraged the BIA to back away from integration.[43] Although white policy makers blamed the *Brown* decision, Kaneubbe, York, and Martin believed the failure was Vance's.[44] With the pressure for federal intervention in civil rights mounting in Washington, officials of the Kennedy and Johnson administrations moved cautiously on civil rights for Choctaws in Mississippi.[45]

Repercussions from the *Brown* decision probably played some part in keeping Choctaw teenagers out of white schools, but they did not halt an alleged gradual march of racial progress. In 1953 the Mississippi legislature had taken steps to forestall federal intervention by planning the "equalization" of Mississippi's segregated schools. They established the Legal Educational Advisory Committee in 1956 to "promote the interests of both races," which meant convincing African American leaders to accept voluntary segregation.[46] That same year, the Mississippi congressional delegation signed the "Southern Manifesto," a statement defying desegregation on the grounds of states' rights. Combined with Mississippi's participation in the 1948 Dixiecrat revolt, the legislature's behavior suggests that the state was not moving toward integration.[47]

Segregationists did grow relatively more militant after *Brown*, however, when they formed Citizen's Councils to intimidate anyone supporting integration. The councils pushed an amendment to the state constitution dissolving the public school system if integration appeared imminent.[48] Extralegal methods of upholding white supremacy in the aftermath of *Brown* included economic boycotts of black activists and their white supporters and ferocious lynchings, the most infamous being that of fourteen-year-old Emmett Till in Money, Mississippi, in 1955. Till's alleged murderers were acquitted by an all-white jury.[49]

This type of concerted backlash muted civil rights agitation in Mississippi in the late 1950s. The NAACP filed futile desegregation petitions with county school boards and attempted some low-key voter registration drives. Otherwise, most Mississippians who advocated civil rights in the late 1950s embraced the same type of unobtrusive route to integration favored by both the Choctaws and the BIA.[50] As integrationists pressed for compliance with the *Brown* decision, segregationists seized on the Choctaws to embellish their separatist rhetoric.

As in earlier political campaigns, the Choctaws served Mississippi politicians as symbols of southern viewpoints. In a 1953 Sunday school lesson, Philadelphia Baptist preacher Dr. Campbell asked his congregation to "compare the progress of the Southern Negro with that of the red man, wards of our government" and concluded that federal oversight of education had made the once self-sufficient Indians into slothful paupers. T. J. Scott (now retired from the Indian Service) wrote to Campbell to correct this erroneous impression.[51]

White Mississippians sometimes mentioned the Choctaws in their correspondence with their elected officials regarding segregation. R. C. Ervin of Crawford wrote Senator John Stennis in 1956 asking "where the Indian stood in all this integration question [*sic*]" and wondering if Choctaws were now free to integrate white schools. Stennis replied that this issue had not been tested before the courts.[52] The Biloxi Chamber of Commerce asked Stennis about the current state of Indian schools as part of their resolution condemning the use of federal troops in Little Rock that year.[53] In 1960 Mrs. N. Palmer wrote to Senator Eastland inquiring why no one posed the Choctaws' poverty as a civil rights issue. It was, she asserted, "a disgrace on the American Government." Eastland agreed and assured her that he raised the issue "time and time again in connection with the civil rights debate now in the Senate."[54] Mississippians once again used the Indians' poverty as evidence of federal incompetence. The value of this ploy may help account for their continued support of the Choctaws even after some Choctaws had moved toward integration.[55]

Segregated Indian schools supplied great public relations fodder for the defenders of Mississippi's status quo. When the agency opened a new junior high school in the Pearl River community in 1957 the *Jackson State Times* fired off an editorial titled "Somebody Forgot High Court Decision," sniffing that this new school, being "completely, rigidly segregated," was "inconsistent with federal policy." A second editorial a week later proclaimed, "Federal Cash Builds Segregated Schools," and lambasted the federal government for hypocrisy.[56] Vance sent clippings of these editorials to Fickinger, who instructed him to reply that whenever Mississippi integrated its schools they could take over BIA facilities.[57]

Similar editorials in the *Jackson Clarion Ledger* and the *Jackson Daily News* questioned why the Choctaws were so destitute when the federal government was educating them for success. "Even the most clever, liberal, tolerant, anti-South, poison-peddling propagandist of the Yankee Press" had surely noticed what a disappointment these schools were.[58] Since the federal government had failed the Choctaws, they had no business telling states how to run their schools.

In the midst of this debate, visits by African American college students to a Choctaw school fueled rumors that the BIA was going to enroll African American children in Indian Service schools. In 1959 Phillip Martin introduced a resolution resisting this action. It asserted that the U.S. Constitution did not discriminate "against any race of people," but the state of Mississippi did. Therefore, "until such time when the white population of this state accept [*sic*] the Negro socially," Choctaw schools would not welcome them. Martin and York both expressed regret at the necessity for the action and the resolution passed unanimously.[59] When the Choctaws pushed for integration, then, they meant integration with whites, at least until discrimination against blacks ceased.

Vance's response voiced regret that the Choctaws had to make such a statement, but he also called the resolution a good indicator of "how the Indian people feel on this issue" and of how southerners in general regarded race mixing. He admitted that he had permitted a group of African American college students to visit the Bogue Chitto and Tucker schools because he feared negative publicity if "some organization such as the NAACP" should hear that he had refused them. He requested a clear statement of policy "so that I will know what course to follow in the future."[60] The subtext of Vance's carefully worded letter is one of caution on a public relations issue and an intimation that the Choctaws, as southerners, were on his side in racial matters.

Roberts, on the other hand, condemned the resolution as inflammatory. Following the cue of many southerner segregationists, he called it a "bull in the china shop" strategy, like some "recommendations made by 'outsiders.'" He returned it unsigned "with the suggestion that it be permitted to be forgotten."[61] There is no further mention of the issue in the public record, so the council apparently followed Roberts's counsel.

School integration in the post-*Brown* years was entangled in several important issues: the Choctaws' need for education, their tribal sovereignty, and the segregationist leanings of agency personnel. All of these overlapping topics coalesced in 1958, when the Choctaws and their allies began a public relations campaign to improve the Indians' educational opportunities. The council now began demanding their children be admitted to local white high schools, and they pressured the agency staff to help them. Council minutes do not record the reasons for this change in attitude, but it is likely that the move was the result of several factors.

For one, Phillip Martin's election to the council in 1957 brought a new vision for economic advancement. Martin, a veteran of World War II, had witnessed how the Marshall Plan and the fortitude of Europeans had helped Europe rebound from wartime devastation. Martin was determined to see this same process occur in Mississippi. Along with other veterans, he had experienced life outside of the rigid boundaries of segregation and was more assertive interacting with the non-Choctaw world than some previous Choctaw leaders had been.[62]

Martin's entrance into politics also coincided with events that activated a nationwide network of allies in a campaign for Choctaw education. It began when University of Chicago anthropology graduate student Kirkland Osoinach, who had done fieldwork in Mississippi in 1957–58, drew the attention of a national Indian advocacy organization to Mississippi. Startled by the offhand self-deprecatory comments made by some Choctaw teenagers, Osoinach wrote a paper decrying the effects of segregation on the self-esteem of the segregated. Someone forwarded it to LaVerne Madigan at the AAIA requesting action.[63]

Madigan investigated the problem, interviewing a former agency employee who said of the Choctaw Agency staff that "they treat Niggers bad over there, but they treat Indians worse than Niggers, much worse."[64] Madigan then enlisted University of Chicago anthropology graduate student Pamela Coe, who had a good relationship with the Choctaws, to help. Coe met with Emmett York and the Reverend Benson Wallace, a Choctaw minister, and suggested that the Choctaws institute the "We Shake Hands" program, which had been used on the northern Great Plains to build constructive relationships between Indians and whites.[65]

Fearing a backlash, the men declined the program, but the relationship with the AAIA had been strengthened. The council now had to decide how to utilize the organization in a way consistent with their subdued approach to integration.[66] Simultaneously, the Choctaws came to the attention of the Highlander Folk School of Monteagle, Tennessee, an institution that trained community, labor, and civil rights organizers.[67] Highlander activist Alice Cobb, who had accompanied Highlander volunteers to Philadelphia in the summer of 1959, proposed that the Choctaws participate in a literacy project, which trained the disfranchised how to pass literacy tests for voting.[68]

Again Choctaw leaders declined with regrets, but they feared that connection with the Highlander Folk School would bring their own efforts to improve race relations to a "standstill" because of the controversy the integrated institution had generated. They explained that the white people who were slowly starting to accept them would turn on them, and that "the Choctaw people themselves would become frightened out of their own new initiative in seeking public school education." Tribal leaders wanted to work with Coe in a more moderate program.[69]

These examples further locate the Choctaws' conservatism on civil rights in the instability of their racial environment and their understandable unwillingness to face violence. Cognizant of the passionate national debate over civil rights, they probably also recognized the

frailty of their bonds with their white allies.[70] Even as activists in national Indian organizations such as the National Indian Youth Council (founded in 1961) were becoming confrontational, Choctaw leaders
remained reluctant to use direct action.[71]

Yet this did not preclude forceful political lobbying for better education, which led some Choctaws to insist more vociferously on BIA
support for integration. Like black civil rights activists, Choctaws depended on the federal government to help them obtain their goals; unlike black civil rights activists, Choctaws framed this demand by reference to their status as domestic dependent nations. Their relationship
with a national network of Indian activists facilitated this plan, which
began with education.

The Campaign for a Choctaw High School

When Victor Kaneubbe sparked a national debate over Indian education in Mississippi, Martin and York seized the moment. Kaneubbe was
working at a Baptist mission in Philadelphia when he discovered that
his daughter Vicky was caught between the seams of state and federal
school segregation statutes. Because Kaneubbe was an Oklahoma Choctaw and his wife, Eileen, was white, Vicky was unable to attend either
agency schools or white schools in Philadelphia. Kaneubbe first attempted to place Vicky in a Choctaw school, but school administrators advised
him that she would not fit in. He promptly filed an appeal with the Neshoba County School Board to admit his daughter to a public school.[72]

Kaneubbe called on the Muskogee Area Office for support, but the
interaction did not go well. Kaneubbe and Fickinger seemed to deliberately misunderstand one another. Fickinger accused Kaneubbe of "deliberate and intentional misrepresentations" of the BIA, while Kaneubbe charged Indian Service teachers of promoting "fear, mistrust, and
little real loving interest and concern."[73] The AAIA publicized this exchange in their newsletter and the situation escalated.[74]

Kaneubbe launched an all-out public relations assault on racism in
Philadelphia and began agitating for a Choctaw high school. He mimeographed a "fact sheet" detailing the Choctaws' problems with dis-

crimination, which he sent to his missionary network calling on them to petition Congress.[75] This generated a deluge of letters to Congress and the BIA from individuals and civic organizations all over the nation.[76] Unfortunately, the adverse publicity enraged the Philadelphia Baptist community, which immediately pressured the Board of Home Missions to remove Kaneubbe. His supervisor offered him a transfer to the Navajo reservation to avoid being terminated.[77] Madigan offered to pay Kaneubbe's legal bills if he went to court and then solicited the council for support.[78]

As with the Highlander issue, Chairman Martin was cautious, offering to help Kaneubbe with the agency but insisting that they could not back a lawsuit so damaging to race relations.[79] Tribal leaders explained that they preferred "to take quiet but definite steps" toward integration, which included getting rid of Vance. This would take time.[80] Kaneubbe was disappointed but agreed to cease agitation while he awaited the determination of the school board.[81] The board denied his appeal, but Kaneubbe decided to transfer rather than sue.[82]

Kaneubbe left the state, but Choctaws did not consider that an option. To remain in their homelands, however, they needed better educational opportunities. The furor Kaneubbe stirred up had activated supporters across the nation, and the tribal council joined them to lobby for a Choctaw high school. Even though this appeared to favor segregation, examination of the push for a Choctaw high school reveals a complex approach to civil rights grounded in Choctaw tribal sovereignty.

Choctaws had long desired their own high school. Cleddie Bell had first requested one in 1951 but was told that there were not enough students to justify the expense. Similar requests in 1952 and 1953 brought the same reply.[83] In 1955 Bell and Emeline Ben organized the Women's Council Club to advocate for a high school and dormitory.[84] The club sent letters to the Mississippi congressional delegation, and Representative William Arthur Winstead wrote commissioner of Indian affairs Glenn L. Emmons on their behalf.

Commissioner Emmons replied that the out-of-state boarding school experience would better prepare Choctaws for relocation.[85] Chairman

York countered that given a choice between boarding school and no education, Choctaws generally chose the latter.[86] Choctaws rejected the values of the dominant culture that emphasized economic advancement over family and community. As had been the case since 1830, connections to the Choctaw homeland were upheld at terrible cost to the Choctaws. If the BIA hoped to pressure the Choctaws into relocation by withholding educational opportunity in Mississippi, they would be disappointed. Meanwhile, the Choctaws' allies agitated on their behalf.

Kaneubbe's 1959 letter blitz had jump-started the high school campaign. National Congress of American Indians (NCAI) executive director Helen L. Peterson brought the Mississippi Federation of Women's Clubs on board, and Oklahoma Choctaw chief Harry Belvin joined the cause.[87] Phillip Martin asked his colleagues at the 1959 BIA Summer School Workshop in Brigham City, Utah, for support.[88] In response to the pressure, Vance finally requested a high school and dormitory for the Choctaws, and Mississippi's congressional delegation backed him.[89] The pressure had forced Vance to act on the Choctaws' behalf, but he had his own agenda.

Choctaws soon discovered that Vance's vision was at odds with their own. Rather than requesting a separate high school, Vance had asked the BIA to add high school curriculum and dormitories to existing schools in three locations. The Choctaws wanted one central school and dorm in the Pearl River community, which was closest to Philadelphia. Neither proposal proved viable, for there were still not enough students to approve the expense.[90] Nonetheless, Vance's blatant disrespect of Choctaw sovereignty coupled with his failures to actively help Choctaws gain admittance into public high schools prompted a sustained effort to remove him. Campaigning for their children's education had moved council members toward more militant action.

In a meeting with assistant secretary of the interior Roger Ernst in March 1960, Martin, York, J. C. Allen, and Madigan obtained a promise to transfer Vance.[91] The slowness of the process, however, finally nudged Martin to reverse his earlier reluctance to litigate. He informed secretary of the interior Fred Seaton that the Mississippi Choctaws were making one last plea to remove Vance "before we try to help ourselves in the courts." Martin complained that Vance wanted the Choctaws to "run away" from their problems in Mississippi, while the "Choctaw goal is to change the situation." Martin dismissed the idea that the *Brown* decision had derailed integration. Rather, he concluded, it had never really been attempted. He requested a new agency staff ready to implement "a long-range race-relations program." He ended his letter with "we want it on record that we spoke out as Choctaws." The council backed him.[92] This suggests that tribal leaders believed that, unlike Kaneubbe's challenge to the county school boards, a lawsuit against the federal government would probably not provoke repercussions in Mississippi. This action, however, alarmed the BIA.

In April 1961 Fickinger appeared before the council to advise against litigation. He attempted to co-opt the Choctaws by promising new dormitories for sharecroppers' children. "It means segregated schools, yes," he announced, but this was the Choctaws' regrettable reality "for some time to come." Chairman Martin disagreed. "I know," he replied, "that the United States Government is big enough and strong enough to do something about our situation here." Similarly, Emmett York retorted that segregation was based on fear, and that President Kennedy had once said never to "negotiate with fear, but don't fear to negotiate."[93] The Choctaws refused to back down, as the conflict over Vance's transfer had drawn attention to some politically sensitive issues.

In June 1962 Madigan informed Martin that Vance had not been transferred because he was married to the niece of the powerful Mississippi senator James Eastland.[94] Although he was an ally of the Choctaws, Interior Department officials nonetheless feared Eastland would block their funding if angered. Madigan suggested that the Choctaws should "leave [Vance] where he is and take away his power" by establishing a race-relations program administered by a special agent who would operate independent of the agency.[95] AAIA president Oliver la Farge suggested instead that they gather evidence of Vance's racism and again demand his transfer.[96] AAIA counsel Richard Schifter agreed, explaining that he was working with Commissioner Nash to move Vance.[97]

As the AAIA lobbied for Vance's removal, Choctaw leaders continued their attempts to procure a high school education for their children.

By 1962 the Choctaws finally had the requisite 198 eligible students, and the BIA agreed to construct a high school.[98] Once again Vance and the staff from the Muskogee Area Office began to plan the project without tribal input; it was Vance's last act as superintendent. In October 1962 the BIA transferred Vance and installed the Choctaws' choice for superintendent, former head of reservation schools Lonnie Hardin.[99] The Choctaws now had a superintendent sympathetic to their agenda. Martin called a special council meeting and introduced a resolution, drafted by himself and Emmett York, for a Choctaw high school. The plan highlighted their use of Choctaw tribalism to combat racial prejudice.

The resolution defended the Choctaws' sovereign right to control projects designed to benefit them. It listed Choctaw goals for education beginning with "eventual assimilation into the public school system under honorable conditions." This represented the council's first public challenge to school segregation. Yet Martin and York also reiterated their commitment to gradualism, noting that because this objective was far in the future, the Choctaws would use their Indian high school as a vehicle for integration, locating it in Philadelphia on land near the Choctaw agency or hospital.

Keeping with his emphasis on material changes as catalysts for altering racial attitudes, Martin proposed a segregated school to encourage integration. He suggested that "athletic and scholastic" interschool activities in Philadelphia would facilitate better race relations through "the joint cooperation of both the non-Indian and Indian people." A state-of-the-art high school in the middle of town would prove that the Choctaws were progressive enough to build the best schools and that Choctaw students were equal to whites.[100]

Other Choctaw leaders disagreed. Cleddie Bell and Houston Allen worried that Choctaws might be seen as trespassers—that townspeople "may not want us." Martin reminded them that "the white people came here as intruders" on what was Choctaw land. Consequently, whites could not tell Choctaws where to build a school. Councilwoman Nettie Jimmie feared the effects schooling among whites might have on the Choctaws' Indian identity. The "majority of our younger children will not carry on the old Choctaw customs," she said, "because they are already leaning toward the other way—non-Indian ways." Jim Gardner worried for the safety of young Choctaw women in town, and Houston Allen and Dean Wilson thought they had better ask the parents in their communities first.[101]

For Martin and York the high school was a matter of Choctaw self-determination, which they linked to their identity as Americans. Emmett York made a passionate speech that avowed their liberties as U.S. citizens "same as that Negro boy's case a while back. . . . The law is for all people," he proclaimed. The Choctaws needed to "think [of] ourselves as an American" and "work the white man's form of government" to their advantage. Martin concurred. The council had been empowered to govern by the federal government, and Choctaw communities had elected them to make these decisions—it was time for bold action. In the end, six voted in favor of the resolution and the motion carried. Bell, Allen, Gardner, Wilson, and Farmer registered their disagreement by abstaining.[102]

BIA officials shared the dissenters' skepticism. Eight years after the *Brown* decision, Neshoba County was still building segregated schools. Mississippians' hostile response to actions by the Congress of Racial Equality (CORE) and the Student Nonviolent Coordinating Committee (SNCC) may have prompted Superintendent Hardin to warn that an Indian school in the middle of town would alienate white citizens. A. B. Caldwell, the 1962 Muskogee Area director of schools, feared that the Mississippi congressional delegation would fight the appropriation if Indians "intruded" into Philadelphia, and 1963 Muskogee Area director Graham Holmes forwarded the resolution to Washington with everyone's recommendations against it.[103] Holmes met with the council in early 1963 to dissuade them from this action, ostensibly because of the disagreement it had generated between Choctaw leaders.[104]

York explained that the dispute was not between council members, but between the Choctaws and the BIA. He called on a Cold War analogy. "Let's look at it from this point of view as an American citizen," he began. "I hope it will never happen, but what if the communist organization took over this country? I wonder how many of you would turn over right quick and do what they say? I don't believe you would. I believe you would fight it a long time."[105] In framing the issue in the Cold War dichotomy of freedom versus tyranny, York was employing a common postwar activist tactic. The NCAI and the AAIA had both used this ploy in resisting termination.[106] Beyond finding this analogy rhetorically useful, York's invocation of Cold War language coupled an idea that was radical in Mississippi—integration—with a more conventional one—the U.S. fight against communist despotism.

Some on the council were unmoved by this speech and reiterated the gradualist agenda. Cleddie Bell countered York by explaining that the children of Pearl River feared attending school in Philadelphia because townspeople were hostile to them. She stressed that whites' attitudes must change for integration to occur.[107] Others feared provoking a backlash. The vote on the resolution reflected these deep divisions, with six out of the eleven present voting in favor and five abstaining. Council records did not record how individuals voted, but those who had opposed the 1962 measure—Bell, Allen, Gardner, Wilson, and Farmer—were most likely the abstainers.[108] The BIA agreed with the dissenters and built Choctaw Central High School at Pearl River.[109] Choctaw integration of white schools occurred gradually over the next few years. By 1970, the number of Choctaws attending white schools was roughly 16 percent of Choctaw students.[110]

Still, the drive for the high school and the matter of integration had produced national campaigns that brought the Choctaws into closer contact with pan-Indian organizations. This was the beginning of the band's foray into pan-Indianism, a strategy that served them well in the 1960s.

Choctaw Pan-Indian Activism

Working with national activists gave council members a broader perspective on Choctaw problems. In their battle against termination, both the AAIA and the NCAI expressed tribal sovereignty in the language of international politics. They likened conditions on Indian reservations to those in nations emerging from colonialism, and called for the equivalent of the Marshall Plan—a proposal called Point 5—to rebuild reservation economies. These activists proposed that the treatment of Native peoples in America provided propaganda for communist nations. They held that America's effort to hold the moral high ground in the Cold War was contingent on justice for Indians.[111]

It is likely that working with these people had encouraged Martin and York's use of Cold War analogies in council meetings and had shaped their views of Choctaws' American identity. Their connections to this activist network brought Martin and York to the American Indian Chicago Conference held at the University of Chicago, where Indian leaders from around the nation discussed tribal sovereignty.[112] Martin played a role in drafting the Declaration of Indian Purpose, which outlined Indian goals for self-determination, and was part of a delegation to Washington to present the document to the Kennedy administration and Congress.[113]

The Choctaws had interacted sporadically with the NCAI over the years. In a 1958 council meeting, Cleddie Bell had proposed they join, but the matter had dropped without a vote.[114] The council voted unanimously to join in 1963 and designated the tribal chairman as the official delegate to the NCAI annual conventions. The resolution declared that "it is essential that all Indian Tribes unite and dedicate themselves to the advancement of all Indian people."[115] Phillip Martin and Sally Ann Bell, the Choctaw Princess, attended the annual meeting in Bismarck, North Dakota, that year.[116] Martin's experience with pan-Indian networks convinced him that "all Indian problems are pretty much the same," and that a national organization could advance Choctaw sovereignty.[117] In working with the NCAI and the AAIA, some Choctaw leaders expanded their political identity to embrace pan-Indianism; the majority of Choctaws, however, did not.

A 1975 study of Choctaw identity by Bogue Chitto councilman Bobby Thompson and anthropologist John H. Peterson Jr. evaluated pan-Indianism. According to Thompson, older Choctaws had no word in their vocabulary for "Indian," although the word *mashkoki*, referring to Muskogean-language speakers, was occasionally used as shorthand for the term. More commonly, non-Choctaw Indians were called *Ehata holba*, translated "just-like-Chata." Older Choctaws made distinctions between Choctaws of different communities as well, anchoring their identities in the distinctive dialects of individual settlements. Younger Choctaws also identified with their communities but had more exposure to the world outside. Consequently, they were more likely to regard themselves as "Indian" in addition to being Chata.[118] Yet such personal notions of Indianness did not dissuade Choctaw leaders. By 1965, they were actively pursuing pan-Indianism with a regional focus—the United Southeastern Tribes, Inc. (USET).

Martin and York recognized that government seed money was crucial to developing a functioning reservation economy but worried that the BIA gave preferential treatment to western tribes. Seeking to increase their influence with the BIA, the Choctaws joined the Eastern Band of Cherokees and the Miccosukees and Seminoles of Florida, and with funds from the AAIA, founded USET in 1969.[119] As Emmett York noted, together the tribes had "at least 21 Congressmen" who could pressure BIA officials.[120] Choctaw leaders also successfully petitioned the BIA in 1970 to switch the band's administration from the Oklahoma field office to Washington DC, which oversaw the other USET members.[121] Mississippi Choctaws no longer had to compete with Oklahoma Choctaws for aid from the BIA, and they had potentially increased their political presence in Congress. The stage was set for the Choctaw Miracle.

Conclusion

The BIA viewed relocation as the best solution to racism and poverty in Mississippi, but the Choctaws disagreed. Rather than flee their homelands, they preferred to remain and improve their lives through political activism. Those efforts prompted some leaders to abandon their long-standing racial separatism and advocate integration of white high schools. Emmett York and Phillip Martin pushed this agenda even further when they proposed integrating the town of Philadelphia by building a model Choctaw high school there. Indian advocacy groups supported this goal, which pushed the council toward pan-Indianism. These actions support the conclusions of other scholars that attempts to extinguish Indian tribes during the late 1950s and early 1960s encouraged them to seek greater self-determination. This steady continual advocacy furnished a framework for the American Indian Movement, whose militant direct action has, until recently, dominated discussion of Indian activism in the postwar period.[122] The Choctaws' campaign for civil rights ultimately strengthened their sovereignty, as seen in their successful removal of agent Vance.

The actions of Martin and York also suggest that the Choctaws did not just sit out the civil rights movement, as some researchers have claimed.[123] Though they eschewed extralegal means, some Choctaw leaders nonetheless acted systematically to address discrimination. As they did so, they crafted a new Indian identity. By the end of the 1950s, assertions of full blood no longer appeared in Choctaw public declarations of their identity. Even though Indian blood still had relevance for enrollment, there was a subtle shift in activist tactics. Rather than focusing on their racial identity, Choctaw leaders such as Martin and York now adopted the language of the Cold War and avowed an American identity—one grounded in their Indian citizenship. The tactic fit the times, positioning the Choctaws as people who embraced their separate juridical and cultural status while also calling for inclusion in the benefits of American democracy.

Although the Choctaw's civil rights campaign did not integrate Mississippi's public schools, it nonetheless served as the catalyst for powerful nation building that ultimately transformed both the Choctaws and rural Mississippi. Over the next decade, Phillip Martin and his allies began the process of economic revitalization that came to be known as the Choctaw Miracle. True to Martin's strategy of seeking ideological and social change through enhanced material conditions, race relations improved as the reservation economy began to employ workers of all races.

Choctaw tribalism had played a starring role in the drama of civil rights in Mississippi. Recognizing this fact recasts historians' traditional understanding of civil rights activism as primarily a struggle between blacks and whites. In the South, Indians had brought about significant changes in race relations, in part because of their own unique relationship to the federal government.

Epilogue and Conclusions

Choctaw Juridical Status and Self-Determination, 1964–1977

Following the opening of the high school, the Mississippi Choctaws inaugurated a series of initiatives that ultimately brought about the Choctaw Miracle. Working within pan-Indian networks and with allies in the Mississippi congressional delegation, tribal leaders instituted dramatic changes. From 1964 to 1977, the band constructed its own judicial system and restructured the tribal government, eventually taking over most governmental operations from the Bureau of Indian Affairs. Tribal leaders also designed social service organizations and developed a successful economy.

Economic development depended on transforming rural Mississippi into a place where companies wanted to relocate, which meant addressing problems of poverty and crime. Choctaw leaders used the Choctaw Community Action Agency (CCAA) to renovate Choctaw communities. The tribal council initially founded the CCAA in 1964 to improve housing, but it soon became the framework for organizations that fundamentally altered Choctaw life. Phillip Martin stepped down from the council in 1964 to run the CCAA, where he instated community health initiatives, Head Start, and welfare services. The CCAA also created the Choctaw Housing Authority (CHA) in 1965 to build and repair houses and established a tribally owned construction business, the Chahta Development Company, in 1969.[1] As the tribal government expanded into economic ventures, Choctaw leaders recognized the need for an autonomous court system.

The Choctaws had a Tribal Court of Indian Offenses with one chief justice and two associate judges appointed by the secretary of the interior. The court had jurisdiction over misdemeanors in Choctaw communities. Major crimes such as rape, murder, and arson fell under the Major Crimes Act, an 1885 law that reserved prosecution of serious crimes committed on Indian lands for federal authorities.[2] In 1968 the Association on American Indian Affairs (AAIA) helped the council draft a comprehensive Choctaw criminal code. Martin then created an administrative structure for procuring and administering federal and state grants and began reaching out to businesses.[3]

These steps signaled the council's growing realization that the Choctaws would have to supply their own employment by enticing businesses to rural Mississippi. As an Indian reservation, Choctaw lands were exempt from state and federal taxes and regulations that some companies found burdensome. Once the band had its own legal system, Martin also marketed the reservation as a haven from lawsuits. Choctaws eager to obtain nonagricultural jobs supplied a cheap labor force. Senator John Stennis lobbied for state and federal matching funds at every step of Choctaw economic development.[4] The patronage economy was once again proving politically powerful.

In 1969 the Chahta Development Company secured funding from the Federal Economic Development Administration to construct an industrial park in the Pearl River community. It was completed in 1971 but remained empty until Packard Electric opened a plant to construct automotive wire harnesses for General Motors in 1979. Choctaws initially grappled with the discipline of factory work, but the band gradually gained a reputation for quality manufacturing, and the park began to fill.[5] These economic accomplishments prompted new political organization. Economic development meant the tribal government needed to be more centralized and focused on long-term planning. The council brought the CCAA under its authority and created the Strategic Planning Center for Choctaw Self-Determination in 1971. They streamlined governmental operations so that anyone desiring to open a business on the reservation followed one set of policies.[6]

This restructuring caused conflict with Superintendent John F. Gordon, who had replaced Hardin in 1968 and who recognized he was losing control of agency affairs. A skirmish ensued in which the council pressured the BIA to hire a Choctaw Indian agent and federal officials refused on the grounds that employing a Choctaw superintendent would result in a "conflict of interest." Officials finally relented and appointed Robert Benn as the first Choctaw Indian agent in 1972.[7]

Benn joined with the council to propose a new constitution, which shifted the office of tribal chief to a position elected at large, not from within the council, and clarified the separation of powers between the legislative and executive branches. Both the council and the chief would now serve for four years instead of two. The Choctaws ratified the constitution in 1975.[8] They had created a government aimed at maximizing their self-determination.

Choctaw nation building ultimately depended on the Choctaws' status as an Indian tribe, which had been debated since 1830. Interpretations of the Choctaws' legal standing turned on conflicting notions of what it meant to be an Indian polity. The criteria for evaluation fell into one of two rough categories—cultural and racial (or anthropological) Indianness and political and legal (or tribal) Indianness. The dispute over recognition raised the question: If Choctaws were culturally and racially Indian, what political and legal rights did they have in relationship to state and federal governments? A brief review of legal rulings from the 1836 trial of Little Leader in Mississippi to the U.S. Supreme Court decision in *United States v. John* in 1977 reveals how officials and allies assessed Choctaw identity over time.

When the State of Mississippi tried Choctaw mingo Little Leader for murder in 1836, he grounded his defense in his Indian identity, which he expressed both culturally and politically. As a Choctaw mingo, he believed that he was not under state jurisdiction. Although the lead prosecutor secured a conviction, he immediately united with the jury in winning a pardon because Little Leader lived as a Choctaw Indian. To Little Leader's neighbors, this meant that he was not fully subject to Mississippi laws. In the county court, Little Leader's anthropological Indianness protected him from the consequences of his legal status as a Mississippi citizen who had lost his tribal standing following removal.

Subsequent to this trial, however, other legal and administrative rulings reached different conclusions. The 1921 Supreme Court case of *Winton v. Amos* merged cultural and political Indianness and rejected the Choctaws' claims to Indian nationhood on both grounds. By discounting the Choctaws' fierce preservation of their culture and ignoring the administration of the Choctaws by the Office of Indian Affairs (OIA), the court concluded that the Choctaws were assimilated citizens of Mississippi, not Indians.[9] The BIA and various congressional committees took the same position when Choctaws pressed their land claims. Federal officials recognized only one Choctaw polity— the Choctaw Nation in Oklahoma. This precedent stood until the 1977 landmark Supreme Court case *United States v. John.*

The litigation began when the U.S. District Court for the Southern District of Mississippi indicted two Choctaws, Smith John and his son Harry Smith John, for attempted murder on Choctaw land in Leake County in 1976. The court convicted them of misdemeanor assault instead, and their lawyer appealed their conviction to the Fifth Circuit U.S. Court of Appeals.[10] Meanwhile, with the backing of the state supreme court, the Leake County Court indicted the Johns for aggravated assault and sentenced them to two years in the state penitentiary with credit for time served. Shortly thereafter, in 1977, the Fifth Circuit court issued a ruling.[11]

Even though the Fifth Circuit Court of Appeals recognized that "full-blooded Choctaw Indians" lived on the lands whose jurisdiction was in question, they held that Choctaw lands were not Indian Country in the legal definition of the term. The justices argued that the 1948 law defining Indian Country (18 USC §1151) specifically excluded "checkerboard" reservations in which Indian holdings were not contiguous, as was the case with the Choctaws. The justices also cited the Treaty of Dancing Rabbit Creek and *Winton v. Amos*, determining that the Mississippi Choctaws clearly had accepted termination of their tribal status when they elected to remain in Mississippi.[12]

The justices addressed the distinction between anthropological and political Indianness. They quoted *United States v. Antelope* (first argued in 1974) and *United States v. Heath* (1974) in which the Supreme Court had judged that, although an individual might be "anthropologically an Indian," the federal government recognized tribes, not individuals.[13] Therein lay the Mississippi Choctaws' dilemma. The Fifth Circuit court accepted the Mississippi Choctaws' anthropological Indianness but ruled that they were not a tribe, in part because their scattered lands were not a reservation.

The court interpreted the 1918 appropriation that opened the Choctaw agency as "a gratuity" given by Congress for the support of the Choctaws. They held that the appropriations bill never declared the Mississippi Choctaws to be a tribe, nor did it create a reservation or suspend the police powers of the state of Mississippi over Choctaw lands.[14] Likewise, the Act of 1939 declaring Choctaw lands to be held in trust functioned in a similar way. It "freed the lands from local, county, and state ad valorem taxation, like other federally owned land," but did not establish an actual Indian reservation.[15] The Choctaws remained a "remnant" of a tribe.

Accordingly, the Indian Reorganization Act (IRA) did not apply in Mississippi, for its purpose was to modify the government-to-government relationship with federally acknowledged tribes. The IRA "recognized that *the Choctaw Indian Tribe was located in the State of Oklahoma* (emphasis added)."[16] The justices concluded that federal assistance to the Mississippi Choctaws did not represent "the traditional 'federal guardian' 'Indian ward' relationship." OIA services were charity, much like aid to drought-stricken farmers, not acknowledgment of the Choctaws as a discrete political entity.[17] In 1977 the U.S. Supreme Court overturned these suppositions.

"Neither the fact that the Choctaws in Mississippi are merely a remnant of a larger group of Indians nor the fact that federal supervision over them has not been continuous affects the federal power to deal with them under these statutes," proclaimed the High Court in *Unit-*

ed States v. John. The court upheld the Major Crimes Act as appropriate to the Johns and denied state authority to try them. If the term "Indian Country" applied to "all land within the limits of any Indian reservation under the jurisdiction of the United States Government," then Choctaw lands were clearly Indian Country.[18]

Upholding the legality of the IRA in Mississippi, the court opined that designating trust lands in 1939 had created a reservation so that the Choctaws could organize politically. The 1945 Tribal Council was legitimate, for the Wheeler-Howard Act had defined eligible Indians not only by reservation status but also by racial categorization, as "all other persons of one-half or more Indian blood." This clearly included the Mississippi Choctaws.[19] Consequently, this "racial" group of Indians was also a polity.

The Supreme Court further maintained that anthropological Indianness was sufficient grounds for tribal recognition irrespective of the interruption in the government-to-government relationship. As legal scholar Charles F. Wilkinson has argued, the *John* decision meant that "tribalism is ultimately a matter of self-definition." Regardless of whether Indians have federal recognition or their political situation shifts dramatically, as in Indian Removal, "tribalism continues until the members themselves extinguish it. Tribalism depends on a tribe's own will."[20]

The Choctaws had always known this, and they waited over a century to hear those words from U.S. officials. Their tribal renaissance sheds light on several important topics in American history.[21] The first concerns the role of the state in mitigating poverty in the South. The Choctaws' Indian identity permitted them to claim resources that other marginalized poor people could not. While Progressivism initiated a handful of social service agencies in the South, most poor Mississippians had little aid from any level of government.[22] In the early twentieth century, however, the federal government gave Choctaws lands, vocational training, health care, and education. These assets were insufficient to free all Choctaws from peonage or to lift most Choctaws out of poverty, but they supported Choctaw communities, which in turn upheld their cultural identity. This was crucial to the Choctaws' collective well-being and to the Choctaw Miracle.

Choctaws transformed the commercial landscape of east-central Mississippi using two federal agencies—the Office of Economic Opportunity (OEO) and the BIA. OEO funds were available to everyone, but Choctaws could use them in conjunction with their political sovereignty, which provided a unique framework upon which to build a manufacturing economy. The agency represented the intrusion of the national state into the rural South, but it created a patronage economy that states' rights southerners nonetheless embraced.[23] Choctaws eventually gained control over BIA operations, and Choctaw nation building generated economic development. This, in turn, blunted racism, as white Mississippians decided that eating was, as Phillip Martin had predicted, indeed better than hating.

Consideration of the Choctaws' tribal rebirth also expands our understanding of the southern struggle for civil rights. Mississippi was the scene of many dramatic incidents in the civil rights movement, which historians have studied extensively without noting that Indians also contended for racial equality during those years. Proclaiming themselves the first Mississippians, Choctaws confronted segregation in their pursuit of self-determination as an Indian polity. This meant that their civil rights issues were, as Martin pointed out, different from African Americans, and the two did not unite to fight against Jim Crow. Nevertheless, the actions of both groups in the early 1960s represented a direct confrontation with racism and opposition to white supremacy. The Choctaws' battle against racial discrimination is the overlooked story of the civil rights movement. That racist politicians supported them during this time greatly complicates our construal of racial politics in the segregated South.

The Choctaws' alliances with white supremacists speak to the power of shared stories in forging political bonds between unlikely partners.[24] Choctaws had symbolic importance that synchronized with Mississippians' cherished values and regional identity. They were warriors, they were racial separatists, they were the worthy poor whose uplift demonstrated the charity of their benefactors. Their dispossession by federal officials buttressed the defense of states' rights. Perhaps most significantly, the Choctaws were a conduit for federal funds in an economically depressed region. Mississippi politicians did not regard the Choctaws as their racial equals, but their mostly constructive interactions with them reflect greater racial ambiguity than ideologies of white supremacy suggest.[25] Yet the Choctaws' story also has national implications for Indian history.

This analysis of Choctaw resurgence demonstrates the power of a dynamic and fluid tribalism to sustain and recreate Indian communities across several dramatic changes in Indian administration. The Choctaws' story augments interpretations of the consequences of Indian policy for Native peoples in four important areas: removal, allotment, the Indian Reorganization Act, and termination and relocation.

The history of the Mississippi Band of Choctaw Indians begins with removal. Although there is a voluminous literature on removal, scholars have paid far less attention to its aftermath in the South.[26] My research joins a growing body of work that reminds historians that removal did not extinguish the Indian presence. Indian peoples continued in their southern homelands by finding innovative ways to survive as a third racial group in a biracial region. Like other examinations of postremoval southern Indians, this work questions the Indian-white binary that has characterized much ethnohistorical scholarship and analyzes Indian experiences as part of a regional racial order that includes African Americans.[27] Placing Indians in this model further clarifies our comprehension of the role of race in Indian identity formation.[28] The Choctaw example underscores how Indians deployed race in complex ways to assert their treaty rights. Consideration of how Choctaws engaged federal blood quantum policies contributes to the flourishing scholarly dialogue on racial construction in the early twentieth century.

Numerous monographs explore federal efforts to assimilate Indians during the allotment era, 1889–1934. Contrasting the Mississippi Choctaw experiences with those of Indians in other regions, especially the West, challenges generalizations about this period. In the midst of massive dispossession and political disempowerment on reservations across the nation, the federal government purchased farms for the Choctaws, which freed some of them from tenancy, thereby strengthening community political leadership.[29] These closed communities reinforced Choctaw ethnicity, which also ran counter to the assimilationist goals of the Dawes Act.

Attempts to eradicate Indian culture characterized the administration of western Indians in the early twentieth century, but assimilationist efforts among the Choctaws were minimal in comparison. The relative absence of such pressures reflects the fact that the Dawes Act did not specifically apply to the Choctaws because they lacked tribal standing. Even so, Choctaws' early embrace of churches and schools convinced many policy makers that Choctaws had already assimilated. Choctaw men were farmers and eagerly sought government aid to make their marginal lands productive.

Officials' revulsion to the "hillbilly" environment of rural Mississippi also colored their vision for Choctaw country. In other jurisdictions, government officials believed that Anglo-Americans living among Indians would inspire a civilized way of life; indeed, it was one justification for opening Indian lands to white settlement. In rural Mississippi, however, agency personnel believed the Choctaws to be morally superior to many of their poor white neighbors and hoped that with government aid, the Indians would offer the beneficial example of how to live. This suggests that Office of Indian Affairs paternalism was more broadly constructed than many policy studies have indicated. While Indian Service personnel across the nation sought incorporation of Indians into the national state, OIA employees in the South added poor whites to this agenda. Class and regional prejudices thus figured prominently in the administration of the Choctaws.

As forced assimilation gave way to the IRA in 1934, the Mississippi Choctaws again afford a distinctive case study for comprehending Indian responses to federal agendas. In Mississippi, the promises of the IRA prompted a very politically sophisticated campaign to wrest control of the creation of tribal government from the Office of Indian Af-

fairs. My evaluation of the mixed results of this effort complements a broader assessment of the Indian New Deal that recognizes both costs and benefits to Indian peoples.[30]

Finally, Choctaws' responses to termination and relocation further elucidate historians' assessments of how Indians sought self-determination in the face of these initiatives. Both policies inflicted tremendous damage on some tribes but also served as a rallying point for resistance across Indian Country. The Choctaw tribal council devised strategies of self-termination by challenging racial discrimination and managing their own economic development through Great Society programs. These actions eventually produced the Choctaw Miracle.[31] The Choctaw situation also reveals gendered aspects of termination. Although historians of termination have noted the role of women activists in resistance, governmental efforts to "make over" Indian women for the labor market have not been analyzed in other studies.[32]

Beyond policy history, however, this investigation of the Choctaws' tribal rebirth is part of a new approach to ethnohistory that locates twentieth-century tribal politics along a continuum of Indian innovation in seeking self-determination. In their edited collection of articles on Indian activism, Daniel M. Cobb and Loretta Fowler posit a new paradigm for framing Indian political history as a series of continuing encounters. In this model, Indian activism is not centered on the "policy narrative [that] tells of dramatic shifts—first from assimilation to self-government and then from termination to self-determination." Instead, Cobb and Fowler suggest a methodology in which "continuity prevails as Native people consistently take steps within their communities and in outside relations with local, state, and federal governments to innovate, resist, and accommodate."[33] This study follows Cobb and Fowler's lead, tracing Choctaw activism and identity construction across the shifting sands of Indian policy from removal to the era of self-determination when the Choctaw Miracle occurred.

In the final analysis, the Choctaw Miracle is better understood not by reference to the miraculous, as if it were the result of a sudden burst of inexplicable brilliance, but rather as part of a broader Choctaw history. Choctaw economic and political recovery in Mississippi was ultimately the result of over a century of adroit political activism in which Choctaw leaders (with the support of their families and communities) successfully lobbied for their interests at all levels of government. Phillip Martin concludes his autobiography, *Chief*, by attributing the Choctaws' success to their "lobbying muscle."[34] It is my hope that this book honors those accomplishments by framing them as the culmination of his ancestor's enduring determination to live as Choctaws in their sacred homelands.

Abbreviations

AAIA	Association on American Indian Affairs
ADHA	Alabama Department of History and Archives, Montgomery, Alabama
BIA	Bureau of Indian Affairs
CCF	Central Classified Files, Choctaw
CIA	Commissioner of Indian Affairs
FCTA	Five Civilized Tribes Agency
MDAH	Mississippi Department of Archives and History, Jackson, Mississippi
NARA-DC	National Archives and Records Administration, Washington DC
NARA-SW	National Archives and Records Administration, Southwest Region, Fort Worth, Texas
OHS	Oklahoma Historical Society, Oklahoma City, Oklahoma
RG	Record Group
SAR	Superintendents' Annual Report to the Commissioner of Indian Affairs
WPA	Works Progress Administration

Notes

Introduction

1. For the Choctaw Miracle see, Mississippi Band of Choctaw Indians (MBCI), *Chahta Hapia Hoke*; Bordewich, *Killing the White Man's Indian*, 304–15; and Martin, Jeter, and Blanshard, *Chief*.

2. For the Choctaws' view of Martin's role in the Choctaw Miracle, see Denson, "The Passing of Chief," *Choctaw Community News*, http://www.choctaw.org/pdf /Mar2010cCN.pdf (accessed July 2, 2012).

3. *U.S. v. John*, 437 U.S. 634 (June 23, 1978), http://supreme.justia.com/us /437/634/case.html (accessed June 8, 2008).

4. The text of *Cherokee Nation v. Georgia* is widely available on the web. See http://www.law.cornell.edu/supct/html/historics/ussc_cr_0030_0001_zs.html (accessed November 10, 2011). For an astute analysis of how southeastern Indians have deployed nationalism in concert with other identities, see Lowery, *Lumbee Indians*.

5. Some historians have found Benedict Anderson's concept of "imagined communities" useful in discussing the development of nationalism in Indian country. The Mississippi Choctaws reflect Anderson's broader concept of a nation as "an imagined political community" founded on a shared sense of history and culture and a distinct territoriality. Anderson, *Imagined Communities*, 5–7; quotation on p.6.

6. For this perspective on Choctaw nationhood, see MBCI, *Chahta Hapia Hoke*, 4. Tribal chairman Phillip Martin expressed a similar interpretation of Choctaw identity in the years preceding government recognition. See Martin, Jeter, and Blanshard, *Chief*, 18–20, 41–43. Terminology for describing Indian polities can be problematic. Words like "band" and "tribe" harken back to old taxonomies that rank cultures along an evolutionary scale according to levels of cultural complexity. For this model see Service, *Primitive Social Organization*. An evolutionary classification implies that bands and tribes are characteristic of primitive peoples, which tends to confine Indians to the past. The Mississippi Choctaws, however, use all these terms interchangeably. They are the Mississippi Band of Choctaw Indians (to distinguish themselves from Choctaws in the West). Their website (http://www.choctaw.org) proclaims them to

be one of America's first Indian nations, and most of their own publications declare them to be a tribe. (The remark about being an Indian Nation was accessed on July 2, 2012.) I use the terms *nation* and *tribe* interchangeably because both denote the Choctaws as a polity existing apart from state and federal governments.

7. House Committee on Indian Affairs, "Land Claims &c. Under 14th Article Choctaw Treaty," May 11, 1836, H. Rep. 663, 24th Cong., 1st sess., 12; Crawford, "Report of the Secretary of War Communicating Information in Relation to the Contracts Made for the Removal and Subsistence of the Choctaw Indians," February 7, 1845, S. Doc. 86, 28th Cong., 2nd sess., 39.

8. Kidwell, *Choctaws and Missionaries*, 169; Peterson, "Mississippi Band of Choctaw Indians," 42–45.

9. For the decentralized nature of the Choctaw polity, see Peterson, "Mississippi Band of Choctaw Indians"; Tolbert, "Sociological Study"; Coe, "Lost in the Hills of Home." Thomas Mould, who worked in Choctaw communities from 1997 to 2000, argues that "Choctaw identity was negotiated most specifically and most vitally at the community level," but Choctaws also layered a collective identity over their community affiliations. Mould, *Choctaw Prophecy*, 197–205, quotation on p. 201.

10. My ideas about the construction of ethnic boundaries have been informed by Nagel, *American Indian Ethnic Renewal*; Knack, *Boundaries Between*; Barth, *Ethnic Groups and Boundaries*; Barth, "Enduring and Emerging Issues in the Analysis of Ethnicity"; and Harmon, *Indians in the Making*.

11. Although Mississippians revered Choctaw military service, Jeanette Keith's excellent study of draft resistance in the South complicates the standard narrative of the southern military tradition. She demonstrates that lower-class southerners frequently refused the call to arms while elite southerners were quick to call for military action because their loved ones were exempt. See Keith, *Rich Man's War, Poor Man's Fight*.

12. Theda Perdue's essay "Native Americans, African Americans, and Jim Crow" outlines the ways in which colonialism created and exploited tensions between African Americans and Indians.

13. For an overview of recent scholarship in southern history, see Seventy-Fifth Anniversary Issue of *Journal of Southern History* 75, no. 3 (2009).

14. For evaluation of how Chinese people fit into Mississippi's biracial model, see Loewen, *Mississippi Chinese*. For a historiographical essay that discusses recent scholarship on southern racial relations, see Jones, "Labor and the Idea of Race."

15. Colleen O'Neill and Brian Hosmer call for a more sophisticated exploration of the role of class in American Indian history. The articles in their edited collection, *Native Pathways*, take up that challenge admirably, as do four other exceptional works: Alexandra Harmon's book *Rich Indians*, David Chang's *Color of the Land*, Claudio Saunt's *New Order of Things*, and Colleen O'Neill's *Working the Navajo Way*.

16. Keith's *Rich Man's War* uncovers a similar pattern regarding states' rights. The essays in Elna C. Green's *New Deal and Beyond* also explore the ambivalent relationship between southern politicians and the federal government.

17. Donald Fixico notes, in "Federal and State Policies and American Indians," the relative lack of studies on Indians' relationship with state governments. Deborah E. Rosen's *American Indians and State Law* offers a superb review of this issue.

18. There are no scholarly studies of the Mississippi Choctaws for the period from 1918 to 1945. In the 1950s several graduate students explored Choctaws' levels of assimilation. These works provided an overview of the early twentieth century but little in the way of historical analysis from primary sources. See Farr, "Religious Assimilation"; Langford, "Study of the Educational Development of the Choctaw Indians in Mississippi"; Tolbert, "Sociological Study"; Coe, "Lost in the Hills of Home"; Peterson, "Mississippi Band of Choctaw Indians."

19. There are two versions of the sacred story that links the Choctaws to this mound. One centers on a primordial migration in which spiritual leaders carried a sacred pole that guided them to Nanih Waiya. Another posits that Choctaws emerged from within the mound. The tale of migration comes from Choctaw historian Donna L. Akers, *Living in the Land of Death*, 1–2. Choctaw anthropologist Valerie Lambert, in *Choctaw Nation*, 19–20, also prefers this story. A second account tells how the Choctaws emerged from beneath the mound. Clara Sue Kidwell, who is of Choctaw descent, discusses both in *Choctaws and Missionaries*, 3.

20. For how some American Indians came to view people by reference to skin color, see Shoemaker, *Strange Likeness*, 125–40. For the complexity of indigenous ideologies regarding Indian blood, see Meyer, "American Indian Blood Quantum Requirements," 231–51, and Strong and Van Winkle, "'Indian Blood,'" 547–76.

21. The degree to which joining USET suggests a self-conscious southern identity for Choctaws is difficult to determine. Chief Phillip Martin referred to Choctaws as "we southerners." Martin, Jeter, and Blanshard, *Chief*, 15. Choctaw Bobby Thompson lists many cultural traits that mark Choctaws as southerners but concludes, "One's identity as a Choctaw in Mississippi is not so much southern as shaped by the experience of existing for the past 140 years in the rigidly stratified society of the rural south." Thompson and Peterson, "Mississippi Choctaw Identity," 179–80, quotation on p. 180. A southern identity was not part of their campaign for tribal rebirth, however, and it is therefore not analyzed in this work.

22. Historians have concluded that the Great Society allowed Indians access to resources for community development free from Bureau of Indian Affairs paternalism. Even though they had their own bureaucratic problems, Great Society programs served Native self-determination in new ways. Clarkin, *Federal Indian Policy*; Cobb, "'Us Indians Understand the Basics,'" "Philosophy of an Indian War," and *Native Activism in Cold War America*; Hoikkala, "Mothers and Community Builders"; Kersey, *Assumption of Sovereignty*.

1. From the First Removal

1. In "Obituary of Nations," James Taylor Carson correctly argues that the word "removal" sanitizes what was essentially ethnic cleansing in the South.

2. Mississippi statute quoted in Carson, *Searching for the Bright Path*, 115; Stuart, *Sketch of the Cherokee and Choctaw Indians*, 24–25; Commission to the Five Civilized Tribes, *Sixth Annual Report of the Dawes Commission for 1899*, 77–80.

3. Carson, *Searching for the Bright Path*, 116–18.

4. This description of the Choctaw polity is taken from Carson, *Searching for the Bright Path*, 96–99. For LeFlore's leadership, see Carson, "Greenwood LeFlore."

5. Halbert, "Story of the Treaty of Dancing Rabbit Creek," 376. The commissioners stripped Choctaw words from the records, but Halbert reconstructed the essence of their speeches from interviews with Choctaws who were present. For the disagreements over removal, see Carson, *Searching for the Bright Path*, 112–26.

6. Carson, *Searching for the Bright Path*, 118–23. The figure of six thousand Choctaws is from Halbert, "Story of the Treaty of Dancing Rabbit Creek," 375, 385–90.

7. For Choctaw removal, see DeRosier, *Removal of the Choctaw Indians*, and Debo, *Rise and Fall*. Rev. Henry C. Benson describes removal and resettlement in Indian Territory in *Life among the Choctaw Indians*, 21–25.

8. "The Treaty of Dancing Rabbit Creek, Article 14," in Kappler, *Indian Affairs*, 222.

9. For policy makers' assumptions on which Choctaws would remain in Mississippi, see *Journal of the Proceedings at the Treaty of Dancing Rabbit Creek*, S. Doc. 512, 21st Cong., 1st sess., 256–61. The terms "mixed blood" and "full blood" imply that race is a meaningful predictor of behavior, an idea that is now discredited. Similarly, the racial term "white" is a social construction designed to differentiate people of European descent from people of color and has little meaning as a fixed category of race. Nonetheless, numerous people in the nineteenth and twentieth centuries invested great meaning in ideologies of "blood." This study uses the terms solely to reflect this historical construction. For the views of southeastern Indians in the antebellum period regarding intermarriage with white settlers, see Perdue, *"Mixed Blood" Indians*.

10. Perdue, *"Mixed Blood" Indians*, 73. There is a broad literature on racist thinking in Indian affairs. Claudio Saunt provides a succinct summary of these ideas in *Black, White, and Indian*, 55–61. For an overview of ideologies of Indian-white marriages, see Maillard, "The Pocahontas Exception."

11. Carson's book *Searching for the Bright Path* briefly discusses preremoval slavery as does O'Brien in *Choctaws in a Revolutionary Age*.

12. Wells, "Role of Mixed-Bloods in Mississippi Choctaw History," 44; Perdue, *"Mixed Blood" Indians*, ch. 1.

13. Wells, "Role of Mixed-Bloods," 47–49, 50–52. Over the years, the testimony of Choctaws who applied for Article 14 lands noted this motivation repeatedly. I do not mean to imply that those Choctaws who removed were less spiritual than those who stayed, only to note the reasons given by Article 14 claimants for staying.

14. For the migration story, see Akers, *Living in the Land of Death*, 1–2, and Lambert, *Choctaw Nation*, 19–20. For the emergence story see Kidwell, *Choctaws and Missionaries*, 3, and Carson, *Searching for the Bright Path*, 8.

15. Estimates of remaining Choctaws vary across the secondary sources. Major F. W. Armstrong's census, taken shortly after removal, estimated 4,554, which was probably low given the reticence of many Choctaws to come forward. See House Committee on Indian Affairs, "Land Claims &c. Under 14th Article Choctaw Treaty," May 11, 1836, H. Rep. 663, 24th Cong., 1st sess., 12–13. T. Hartley Crawford (CIA) claimed that perhaps seven thousand Choctaws remained as late as 1843. Crawford, "Report of the Secretary of War Communicating Information in Relation to the Contracts Made for the Removal and Subsistence of the Choctaw Indians," February 7, 1845, S. Doc. 86, 28th Cong., 2nd sess., 39.

16. U.S. House, "Memorial of the Choctaw Indians," February 1, 1836, H. Doc. 119, 24th Cong., 1st sess.; House Committee, "Land Claims &c.," H. Rep. 663, 4.

17. Ward's register is found in House Committee, "Land Claims &c.," H. Rep. 663, 32–33.

18. U.S. House, "Petition of the Citizens of the State of Mississippi Remonstrating against Indian Claims," February 1, 1836, H. Doc. 89, 24th Cong., 1st sess. House Committee, "Land Claims &c.," H. Rep. 663, 1–54, contains extensive testimony detailing Ward's incompetence and the abuses of Mississippi settlers. For the role of speculators, see Young, *Redskins, Ruffleshirts, and Rednecks*, 47–72.

19. The 1832 state constitution gave the Mississippi legislature the power to grant "all the rights and privileges of free white citizens" to remaining Choctaws and Chickasaws, subject to terms the legislature might impose. Mississippi Historical Society, "The Mississippi Constitution of 1832," Article VII, Section 18, http://mshistory.k12. ms.us/articles/101/the-mississippi-constitution-of-1832 (accessed August 31, 2011).

20. U.S. Senate, "Message of the President of the United States Transmitting the Correspondence in Relation to the Proceedings and Conduct of the Choctaw Commission under the Treaty of Dancing Rabbit Creek," January 30, 1844, S. Doc. 168, 28th Cong., 1st sess., Exhibit A, "Copy of Power of Attorney from Indians to Gwinn . . . Left with Col. Cobb." Hereafter cited as "President's Report on the Choctaw Commission."

21. This was certainly the view of the Mississippi legislature at the time. See U.S. House, "Memorial of the Legislature of the State of Mississippi upon the Subject of Lands Acquired by Treaty from the Choctaw Nation of Indians.," H.R. Doc. 75, 22nd Cong., 1st sess. Young, *Redskins, Ruffleshirts, and Rednecks*, 53–72, also portrays the Choctaws as victims of speculators, as does Satz, "Mississippi Choctaw," 3–32.

22. "Copy of Power of Attorney from Indians to Gwinn," in "President's Report on the Choctaw Commission," S. Doc. 168, 118–21. For Choctaw ethnic communities, see Kidwell, *Choctaws and Missionaries*, and "Choctaw Struggle for Land and Identity."

23. Cobb had a settlement of followers in Leake County. "Testimony of Col. Samuel Cobb, September 12, 1843," in "President's Report on the Choctaw Commission," S. Doc. 168, 144.

24. Testimony of William E. Richardson in House Committee on Indian Affairs, *Hearings on Enrollment in the Five Civilized Tribes*, April–August 1913, 63rd Cong, 2nd sess., 29–30, 36.

25. Halbert, "Introduction of Christianity and Education among the Choctaws," ch. 12 of "History of the Choctaw Indians East of the Mississippi," n.d., 213, unpublished manuscript in Halbert Papers, box 4, folder 2, ADHA.

26. Halbert, "History of the Choctaw Indians," 214, Halbert Papers.

27. A commission investigating the failures of Article 14 recognized Little Leader's position when they took testimony at his home in 1835. House Committee, "Land Claims &c.," H. Rep. 663, 59.

28. Halbert, "Life of Little Leader or Hopaii Iskitimi," unpaginated notebook, Halbert Papers. There are two notebooks on this topic, one in box 4, folder 4, and the other in folder 5 of the same box. The one in folder 5 is more complete and is the one cited in this book.

29. Halbert, "Life of Little Leader."

30. Davis, *Recollections of Mississippi*, 60; Halbert, "Life of Little Leader."

31. Davis, *Recollections of Mississippi*, 62.

32. Unfortunately, records of this trial were destroyed when the Kemper County courthouse burned in 1912. Kemper County did not have a newspaper at the time of the trial, and perusal of the state's other newspapers, the *Mississippian* and the *Natchez Courier and Journal*, yielded no reports of the proceedings. Halbert, "Life of Little Leader"; Davis, *Recollections of Mississippi*, 61–62.

33. "Petition Sent to the Governor of the State of Mississippi, Dec. 1, 1837," typescript in the Works Progress Administration (WPA) Files, interviews for Kemper County, box 10731, folder: History, MDAH. For the Mississippi military tradition in the antebellum period, see Olsen, *Political Culture*.

34. Davis, *Recollections of Mississippi*, 61–62.

35. Halbert, "Life of Little Leader"; Davis, *Recollections of Mississippi*, 61–62.

36. U.S. House, "Memorial of the Legislature," H. Doc. 75. The best analysis of the legal conflicts over Choctaw lands and the role that national and local party politics played in this battle is Young, *Redskins, Ruffleshirts, and Rednecks*.

37. Novak, "Legal Transformation of Citizenship."

38. For an excellent analysis of how this ideology affected Indians' rights to state citizenship, see Rosen, *American Indians and State Law*, 33–36.

39. Halbert, "Life of Little Leader."

40. U.S. House, "Application for Indemnity, For Being Deprived by Settlers of Reservations of the Choctaw Indians," February 1, 1836, H. Doc. 1415, 24th Cong., 2nd sess., 1.

41. Choctaws' fluid conceptions of power are skillfully analyzed in O'Brien, *Choctaws in a Revolutionary Age*.

42. U.S. House, "Petition of the Citizens," H. Doc. 89, 1–2.

43. "Records of the Proceedings of the Choctaw Commission," Entry 268: Journal, 1837–1838, folder: RG 75, and "Records of Commissioners Publius Pray, P. D. Vroom, and James R. Murray," Entry 270: Evidence, 1837–1838, Depositions, folder 270, both in Choctaw Removal Records, Atkinson/Elliot Indian Agency,

box 4, Special Collections, Mitchell Memorial Library, Mississippi State University, Starkville.

44. Senator Bell summarized this report on behalf of the House Committee on Indian Affairs, "Land Claims &c.," H. Rep. 663, 1–12.

45. U.S. Senate, "Petition of a Number of Citizens of Mississippi Praying Congress to Institute into the Claims of Choctaw Indians to Reservations under the Treaty of Dancing Rabbit Creek.," January 21, 1837, S. Doc. 91, 24th Cong., 2nd sess., 2.

46. Usner, *Indian Work*, ch. 1.

47. "Official Documents Containing Brief Summary of Facts Relative to Choctaw Claims," April 25, 1846, appendix to Riley, "Choctaw Land Claims," 393; House Committee, "Land Claims &c.," H. Rep. 663, 295, and passim.

48. Kidwell, *Choctaws and Missionaries*, 171–73.

49. "President's Report on the Choctaw Commission," S. Doc. 168, 142–46.

50. T. Hartley Crawford to Hon. John F. H. Claiborne, Ralph Graves, Esq., and Roger Barton, Esq., October 24, 1842, in "President's Report on the Choctaw Commission," S. Doc. 168; E. B. Merritt, Assistant Commissioner of Indian Affairs, to Hon. Claude Weaver, House of Representatives, February 19, 1914, in Records of the Indian Claims Commission, RG 279, box 618, NARA-DC.

51. J. F. H. Claiborne, "Statement of Protest, 1843," Claiborne Papers, microfilm reel 1, vol. 2: 1841–54, LOC. Claiborne himself was a speculator. Kidwell, *Choctaws and Missionaries*, 168.

52. Claiborne to Crawford, May 8, 1843, in "President's Report on the Choctaw Commission," S. Doc. 168, 38–40.

53. Claiborne, *Mississippi as a Province, Territory, and State*, 1:512. Choctaw historian Bob Ferguson notes that the use of the pipe indicates "sincere intentions." See http://www.choctaw.org/about MBCI/history/treaties1830.html (accessed July 1, 2009).

54. For Indian diplomacy and treaty language, see Williams, *Linking Arms Together*.

55. Samuel Cobb quoted in Claiborne, *Mississippi as a Province*, 512–13. The original speech is in *Niles Weekly Register* 64 (April 29, 1843): 131–32. Even though Claiborne may have embellished Cobb's oratory, I believe he captured the intent of the speech, which is consistent with the findings of other research on Indian treaty language and protocol.

56. Samuel Cobb quoted in Claiborne, *Mississippi as a Province*, 513. For Pushmataha's hagiography, see Lincecum, *Pushmataha*.

57. Williams, *Linking Arms Together*.

58. Hoxie, "Missing the Point," 30.

59. Halbert, "History of the Choctaw Indians," 214–15, Halbert Papers.

60. "Testimony of Samuel Cobb," in "President's Report on the Choctaw Commission," S. Doc. 168, 144–46. Claiborne also discusses these charges: Claiborne to Hon. T. Hartley Crawford, CIA, November 21, 1843, and "Statement to the Proceedings of the Board of Choctaw Commissioners, November 30, 1843," both in Claiborne Papers, microfilm reel 1, vol. 2: 1841–54, pp. 11–12.

61. Letter of T. Hartley Crawford, September 5, 1844, in "Report of the Secretary of War," S. Doc. 86, 28th Cong., 2nd sess., 36–39.

62. "Brief Summary of Facts Relative to Choctaw Claims," appendix to Riley, "Choctaw Land Claims," 393.

63. Swanton, *Source Material*, 392.

64. Frances E. Leupp to President Theodore Roosevelt, March 16, 1908, in House Committee on Indian Affairs, *Hearings on Enrollment*, 118. Both Kidwell, in *Choctaws and Missionaries*, and Peterson, in "Mississippi Band of Choctaw Indians," document this view of African Americans. For data on African American lives in this period, see Scarborough, "Heartland of the Cotton Kingdom," 323–45.

65. Stickball games (*ishtaboli*) involved two teams whose object was to strike a small ball either against or through the opposing team's goal posts using a stick with a small basket attached. Historically these games acted to mediate political relations between villages, sometimes substituting for warfare. Swanton, *Source Material*, 140–60.

66. Swanton, *Source Material*, 140–60.

67. Kidwell, *Choctaws and Missionaries*, 169, and "Choctaw Struggle for Land and Identity," 78–79; Peterson, "Mississippi Band of Choctaw Indians," 42–45; The Cooper roll is available online at http://www.accessgenealogy.com/native/cooper/index.htm (accessed February 2, 2006). Clan names and locations are found on the Cooper roll.

68. Bolton, *Poor Whites*, ch. 5; Watkins, "Some Social and Economic Aspects," 44–50; Peterson, "Mississippi Band of Choctaw Indians," 40–47. Peterson argued that sharecropping was a post–Civil War pattern, but Bolton, *Poor Whites*, 37–38, documents it in antebellum times.

69. Testimony of William E. Richardson, in House Committee on Indian Affairs, *Hearings on Enrollment*, 29; Peterson, "Mississippi Band of Choctaw Indians" 28–29, 34–50.

70. U.S. Senate, "Memorial of the Delegates and Representatives of the Choctaw Nation of Indians," March 18, 1856, S. Misc. Doc. 31, 34th Cong., 1st sess., 1–5; Statement of Clarence Miller, Representative from Missouri, in "Report and Statement on H. R. 19213," in U.S. House, "Report and Statement of the Subcommittee on Indian Affairs," January 10, 1913, 62nd Cong., 3rd sess., 15–17.

71. This settlement was known as the Net Proceeds Case. For a comprehensive discussion of this issue, see Kidwell, *Choctaws in Oklahoma*, ch. 9.

72. Testimony of P. J. Hurley, in House Committee on Indian Affairs, *Hearings on Enrollment*, 12. In 1915 the Choctaw Nation documented this distribution. U.S. House, "Memorial of the Choctaw and Chickasaw Nations Relative to the Rights of the Mississippi Choctaws," 6–7.

73. Crawford, "Report of the Secretary of War . . . Removal and Subsistence of the Choctaw Indians," February 7, 1845, S. Doc. 86, 32.

74. Cobb, *Mississippi Scenes*, 158–59 and 177–78; Olmsted, *Journey in the Back Country*, 177–78.

75. Olsen, *Political Culture*, 17–37; Fulkerson, *Random Recollections*, 12.

76. Rev. N. L. Clarke, "The Baptist Choctaw Mission," Halbert Papers, box 2, folder 11; Amis, *Recollections of Social Customs*, 1–11; Farr, *Religious Assimilation*, 27; Kidwell, *Choctaws and Missionaries*, 175.

77. Bolton, *Poor Whites*, 4–5.

78. Cobb, *Mississippi Scenes*, 158–59 and 177–78.

79. For the proslavery argument, see Fitzhugh, *Cannibals All!*

80. Simms also extolled Anglo-American conquest of Indians in *The Yemassee*.

81. Simms, "Oakatibbe, or the Choctaw Sampson," 192–93. Electronic version at http://docsouth.unc.edu/southlit/simmscabin1/simmscabin1.html. For ideologies regarding the so-called remnant Indians following removal, see Usner, "Images of Lower Mississippi Valley Indians," 128–37. Usner in *Indian Work* has made this same point with reference to Simms's work on Oakatibbe. See also Martin, "My Grandmother Was a Cherokee Princess," 120–47.

82. Simms, "Oakatibbe," 194–95, 208.

83. Spann, "Choctaw Indians as Confederate Soldiers," 560–61; Brown, *History of Newton County*, 96. Kidwell claims that several captured Choctaws died in Union prison camps (*Choctaws and Missionaries*, 170); Major Spann argued that they were paraded around New York City parks as "curiosities for the sport of sight seers" (560). A WPA informant also noted that the Choctaws were sent north. Minnie Nichols, "Historical Research Project for the WPA, Assignment No. 18," folder: War, Civil and Spanish American, WPA Files, Newton County, box 10776, MDAH. Brown suggested that they went to Indian Territory (*History of Newton County*, 97).

84. Spann, "Choctaw Indians as Confederate Soldiers," 560–61; Brown, *History of Newton County*, 96.

85. Spann, "Choctaw Indians as Confederate Soldiers," 560.

86. Spann, "Choctaw Indians as Confederate Soldiers," 560.

87. Spann, "Choctaw Indians as Confederate Soldiers," 561.

88. By 1915 Mississippi was the third largest producer of lumber in the nation. Yates and Rideout, *Red Clay Hills of Neshoba*, 68.

89. Kirwan, *Revolt of the Rednecks*, 54–55.

90. Kirwan, *Revolt of the Rednecks*, 44–46.

91. Yates and Rideout, *Red Clay Hills*, 101.

92. Harris, *Day of the Carpetbagger*, 328, 371–405. For analysis of Mississippi communities that openly defied segregation, see Bynum, *Free State of Jones*.

93. Harris, *Day of the Carpetbagger*, 692–97.

94. For Mississippi miscegenation laws, see Browning, "Anti-Miscegenation Laws in the United States," 28. Twelve states regulated Indian marriages. See Roundtree, "Indians of Virginia," 41–43; Lovett, "African and Cherokee by Choice," 207; Maillard, "Pocahontas Exception," 351–86; Pascoe, "Miscegenation Law," 44–69.

95. Coleman, "Mississippi Constitution of 1890," 12–14. Customary discrimination is mentioned throughout the government documents and secondary literature on the Mississippi Choctaws.

96. Peterson, "Mississippi Band of Choctaw Indians," 62–63; Watkins, "Some Social and Economic Aspects," 71.

97. Harris, *Day of the Carpetbagger*, 575–78; Farr, "Religious Assimilation," 28.

98. Kidwell, *Choctaws and Missionaries*. Statistical data on mission schools is on pp. 144–45; postremoval missionary activity is found in ch. 9.

99. Clarke, "The Baptist Choctaw Mission," box 2, folder 11, Halbert Papers; Kidwell, *Choctaws and Missionaries*, 178–79.

100. Augustine Breek, "The Catholic Choctaw Indian Mission in Neshoba County, 1883–1904," box 2, folder 11, Halbert Papers.

101. Data on church membership from Kidwell, *Choctaws and Missionaries*, 176–83. See also Langford, "Holy Rosary Indian Mission."

102. For primary source accounts of Choctaw Church services during this period, see Sawyer, "Choctaw Indians of Mississippi," pt. 2, 209, and Brown, *History of Newton County*, 20–27. For the Choctaw perspective on the importance of their language for Christian liturgy, see Locke, "Choctaw Catholic Catechism," 21–22. For continuation of traditional rituals, see Halbert, "Courtship and Marriage among the Choctaws," 222–24; Halbert, "Funeral Customs of the Mississippi Choctaws," 353–66; Watkins, "Choctaws in Mississippi," 69–77; Sawyer, "Choctaw Indians of Mississippi," pt. 1, 160–64.

103. Brown, *History of Newton County*, 21.

104. "Questionnaire on Tribal Organization," Summer 1934, CCF: 068-9544A-1936, BIA, NARA-DC.

105. Baptist preachers at the turn of the century included Scott York, Isham Johnson, Charley Thomas, Thompson Baker, Billie Gibson, Seaborn Smith (who also taught school in Neshoba County), Alen Willis, Jeff Jackson, and Willie Jimmie. Farr, *Religious Assimilation*, 35. Methodists educated Choctaw convert Simpson Tubby at Milsaps College in Jackson, Mississippi. He became an influential preacher and community leader. Brown, *History of Newton County*, 22.

106. Simpson Tubby, in Swanton, *Source Material*, 100–102.

107. Watkins, "Choctaws in Mississippi," 71.

108. Brown, *History of Newton County*, 8.

109. This work is reprinted in Lincecum, *Pushmataha*.

110. Claiborne, *Mississippi as a Province*, 510.

111. Claiborne, *Mississippi as a Province*, 522.

112. Halbert, "Indian Schools in Mississippi," 576.

113. Rowland, *History of Mississippi*, 2:235–39.

114. Spann, "Choctaw Indians as Confederate Soldiers," 561.

115. Typescript of article from the *New Orleans Times-Democrat*, May 28, 1903, in WPA Files, interviews for Newton County, box 10776, folder: History, MDAH.

116. Spann, "Choctaw Indians as Confederate Soldiers," 561.

117. Spann, "Choctaw Indians as Confederate Soldiers," 561.

118. Spann, "Choctaw Indians as Confederate Soldiers," 561.

119. Brown, *History of Newton County*, 9. For the vanishing Indian, see Philip Deloria, *Playing Indian*, and Joel Martin, "My Grandmother Was a Cherokee Princess," 120–47.

120. Claiborne, *Mississippi as a Province*, ch. 33; Halbert, "Courtship and Marriage among the Choctaws of Mississippi," 222–24.

121. On February 4, 1882, House Bill 486, *An Act to Establish Public Schools for the Indians in East Mississippi*, was read twice and referred to the Education Committee. It passed on February 27, 1882. *Journal of the House of the State of Mississippi*, 1882, 267, 482. The *Journal of the Senate of the State of Mississippi*, 1882 also noted the bill's progress on pp. 419 and 459. There are no records of the deliberations, and newspaper sources also neglected discussion of why the legislature opened Indian schools. Most likely, the bill was part of a broader push for education that occurred that year. See Rowland, *History of Mississippi*, 2:223–24. Report of John T. Reeves, Special Superintendent of the Indian Service, "On Need of Additional Land and School Facilities for the Indians living in the State of Mississippi," December 7, 1916, H. Doc. 1464, 64th Cong, 2nd sess., 2. Kidwell, *Choctaws and Missionaries*, 182–83; Halbert, "Indian Schools in Mississippi," 574–75; Langford, "Study of Educational Development," 33–35.

122. Reeves Report; Kidwell, *Choctaws and Missionaries*, 182–83; Halbert, "Indian Schools in Mississippi," 574–75; Langford, "Study of the Educational Development," 33–35.

123. Halbert, "Mississippi Choctaws," 35–38.

124. Halbert, "Mississippi Choctaws," 37.

125. Halbert, "Indian Schools in Mississippi," 576.

126. Halbert, "Indian Schools in Mississippi," 576.

127. Anthropologist Tom Mould discusses prophecies of removal in *Choctaw Prophecy*.

2. From the Second Removal

1. Berkhofer analyzed this discrepancy in *White Man's Indian*, 3–4. Philip Deloria expands this idea in *Playing Indian*.

2. Davis, "Mississippi Choctaws." For Williams's career, see Osborn, *John Sharp Williams*, and Dickson, *An Old-Fashioned Senator*.

3. Kidwell, *Choctaws and Missionaries*, 184–85; Carter, *Dawes Commission*, 69–103; Coker, "Pat Harrison's Efforts."

4. Carter, *Dawes Commission*. Recent studies of racial categories in allotment include Sturm, *Blood Politics*; Garroutte, *Real Indians*; Naylor, *African Cherokees*; and Yarbrough, *Race and the Cherokee Nation*.

5. Jaimes, "Federal Indian Policy," 116; Sturm, *Blood Politics*, 78–81; Garroutte, *Real Indians*, 57–58.

6. For the alleged inferiority of full-blood Indians, see Hoxie, *Final Promise*, and Meyer, *White Earth Tragedy*. Government officials considered Choctaws with

black ancestry to be more competent than full-bloods. See Debo, *And Still the Waters Run*, 134–36.

7. The literature on racism in this period is vast. A succinct analysis of national trends is found in Rebecca Edwards's perceptive synthesis, *New Spirits*, 213–24, 239–42. See also Williamson, *Crucible of Race*. For racial thinking in anthropology, see Stocking, *Race, Culture, and Evolution*.

8. For how the Choctaw Nation dealt with this issue, see Kidwell, *Choctaws in Oklahoma*, ch. 12.

9. Unlike their ancestors at the time of the 1830 treaty, most Choctaws in the late nineteenth century had English names. Commission to the Five Civilized Tribes, *Sixth Annual Report of the Dawes Commission for* 1899, 17. Choctaws also switched Christian and surnames over generations. Reeves Report, December 7, 1916, H. Doc. 1464, 64th Cong., 2nd sess., 25.

10. Archibald McKennon, "Mississippi Choctaws, Report of the Problems of Identifying Them, 1900," 305, Oklahoma Historical Society (OHS), microfilm roll 11, housed at NARA-SW.

11. For ubiquitous references to racial phenotypes in allotment, see Commission to the Five Civilized Tribes, *Annual Reports of the Commission to the Five Civilized Tribes in the Indian Territory to the Secretary of the Interior*.

12. John Sharp Williams to Tams Bixby, August 23, 1901, OHS, microfilm roll 61, NARA-SW.

13. Willis Van Devanter, Assistant Attorney General to the Secretary of the Interior, December 3, 1901, OHS, microfilm roll 61, NARA-SW.

14. Commission to the Five Civilized Tribes, *Sixth Annual Report of the Dawes Commission for* 1899, 77–80.

15. McKennon, "Mississippi Choctaws," 303–31. How one presented oneself was a common method of determining their social capital and thus one's place in the racial hierarchy. See Johnson, "The Slave Trade," and Hodes, "The Mercurial Nature."

16. Commission to the Five Civilized Tribes, *Sixth Annual Report of the Dawes Commission for* 1899, 77–80; Ruling of the Supreme Court in *Winton v. Amos*, 255 U.S. 373 (1921), found in *Case Findings on the McKennon Roll*, http://www .accessgenealogy.com/native/mckennon/casefindingsmckennonroll.htm (accessed February 5, 2008).

17. Commission to the Five Civilized Tribes, *Sixth Annual Report of the Dawes Commission for* 1899, 92.

18. "Testimony before the Dawes Commission in Carthage, Philadelphia, and Decatur," Entry 105—Records of Testimony, FCTA, NARA-SW. For a more detailed analysis of the process in Mississippi, see Osburn, "'Any Sane Person.'"

19. Johnson quoted in Sawyer, "Choctaw Indians of Mississippi," pt. 1, 163.

20. McKennon, "Mississippi Choctaws," OHS, 303–30; Sawyer, "Choctaw Indians of Mississippi," pt. 1, 163; Supplemental Brief of Harry J. Cantwell and William E. Richardson, Attorneys for the Mississippi Choctaws, in House Committee on In-

dian Affairs, *Hearings on Enrollment*, April–August 1913, 63rd Cong, 2nd sess., 132–34. For information on the attorneys who worked with the Choctaws, see "Testimony before the Dawes Commission in Carthage, Philadelphia, and Decatur," 96–99.

21. Coker, "Pat Harrison's Efforts."

22. "Petition of the Mississippi Choctaws," February 13, 1900, H. Doc. 426, 56th Cong., 1st sess., 1.

23. Although lawyers drafted the petitions and memorials sent to Congress, I believe that these documents represented the viewpoints of Choctaw leaders.

24. Kidwell, *Choctaws and Missionaries*, and Peterson, "Mississippi Band of Choctaw Indians," both document this position with respect to African Americans.

25. "Petition of the Mississippi Choctaws," February 13, 1900, H. Doc. 426, 56th Cong., 1st sess., 1.

26. House Committee on Indian Affairs, "Treaty Rights of Mississippi Choctaws," January 29, 1901, H. Rep. 2522, 59th Cong., 2nd sess., 0.

27. Jack Amos was a Mississippi Choctaw who believed that the government's failure to fulfill Article 14 entitled him to an allotment in Mississippi. The Federal Court of the Central District of Indian Territory disagreed. See Newton County, Mississippi, Historical and Genealogical Society, http://nchgs.org/native/jackamos/ (accessed June 19, 2008).

28. U.S. House, "An Agreement with the Choctaw and Chickasaw Tribes of Indians, March 27, 1902," H. Doc. 512, 57th Cong., 1st sess., section 41; "Ruling of the Supreme Court in *Winton v. Amos*," 255 U.S. 373 (1921), in *Case Findings on the McKennon Roll*, http://www.accessgenealogy.com/native/mckennon/casefindings mckennonroll.htm (accessed January 5, 2008).

29. Carter, *Dawes Commission*, 85. These numbers were not surprising given that P. J. Hurley, national attorney for the Choctaw Nation, estimated that Choctaw citizenship was worth "from $5,000.00 to $8,000.00." *Report of P. J. Hurley to the Honorable Cato Sells for* 1915, 4, Hurley Papers, box 12, folder 7, University of Oklahoma Libraries.

30. U.S. Senate, "Rights of the Mississippi Choctaws in the Choctaw Nation, Memorial of the Full-Blood Mississippi Choctaws Relative to Their Rights in the Choctaw Nation," April 21, 1902, S. Doc. 319, 57th Cong., 1st sess., 2, 34.

31. For disposition of the memorial, see *Case Findings on the McKennon Roll*, http://www.accessgenealogy.com/native/mckennon/casefindingsmckennonroll.htm (accessed February 5, 2008).

32. Supplemental Brief of Harry J. Cantwell and William E. Richardson, Attorneys for the Mississippi Choctaw and "Disposition of Pat Chitto," in House Committee on Indian Affairs, *Hearings on Enrollment*, 63rd Cong., 2nd sess., 3 and 134, respectively.

33. Carter, *Dawes Commission*, 86.

34. "A List of Mississippi Choctaws who Petitioned Congress and the President of the United States in 1906 and 1907," in House Committee on Indian Affairs, *Hearings on Enrollment*, 63rd Cong, 2nd sess., 2, 87.

35. *Report of P. J. Hurley to the Honorable Cato Sells for 1915*, 4–5, Hurley Papers, box 12, folder 7.

36. Census calculations by Peterson, "Mississippi Band of Choctaw Indians," 97.

37. Reeves Report; for information on the New Choctaw Baptist Association, see p. 25. Langford, "Holy Rosary Indian Mission," 115–17.

38. Attorneys Robert L. Owen and Charles Winton led the efforts to get Mississippi Choctaws on the tribal rolls. Kidwell, *Choctaws in Oklahoma*, 166–69.

39. This bill was H.R. 4536. "Testimony of Pat Harrison," in House Committee on Indian Affairs, *Hearings on Enrollment*, 827–29.

40. One of the attorneys for Cantwell and Crews, Luke Connerly (who was an unsuccessful applicant for enrollment) helped found the Society of Mississippi Choctaws. Its purpose was to "recover the rights to which we are justly entitled in law and in equity under the 14th article of the Treaty of 1830." "Preamble to the Constitution of the Society of the Mississippi Choctaws," Hurley Papers, box 5, folder 1.

41. Connerly documented the poverty of the group: "We are all poor people with very limited means." Members of the society paid one dollar to join and ten cents monthly dues. Luke Connerly to P. J. Hurley, n.d., Hurley Papers, box 5, folder 1. Comments on the lack of Choctaw language among the society are found in "Testimony of Luke Connerly," in House Committee on Indian Affairs, *Hearings on Enrollment*, 426.

42. "Testimony of Luke Connerly," in *Hearings on Enrollment*, 415–17, quotation on p. 417.

43. Applicants had to convince fourth-fifths of the Membership Committee of the Chief Council or any Local Council of their ancestry. Article 3, *Constitution of the Society of the Mississippi Choctaws*, Hurley Papers, box 5, folder 1.

44. References to Negro blood are found in *Amendment to the Constitution of the Society of the Mississippi Choctaws*, Hurley Papers, box 5, folder 1.

45. "Report of Inspector James McLaughlin re Contracts with Mississippi Choctaws," in House Committee on Indian Affairs, *Hearings on Enrollment*, 845.

46. Because it is difficult to establish Indian identity in the historical record with complete certainty, some of these individuals may possibly have had Indian ancestors. Yet they did not live as Indians in any manner recognized by established Indian communities.

47. "Testimony of Luke Connerly," in House Committee on Indian Affairs, *Hearings on Enrollment*, 396–97, 406.

48. The sheriff's remark is found in the Reeves Report, 26. Reeves also observed that "many of these 'claimants' are fair haired, with blue eyes, and bear no more physical resemblance to real Indians than do the present descendants of Pocahontas." Reeves Report, 25–26. My own perusal of the Harrison County census failed to discern any Indians, but it may have been that the census recorders simply classified Indians as African Americans.

49. Membership Rolls of the Society of Mississippi Choctaws, http://www.nanations.com/mschoctaw/index.htm (accessed June 26, 2005). The 1853 census

taken by special agent Douglas Cooper listed some Choctaws along the coast. Cooper's final numbers must be taken with caution, however, as he mentioned that Indians in several locations refused to talk to him. See "Cooper Rolls," http://www. accessgenealogy.com/native/cooper/index.htm (accessed June 26, 2005). Choctaw educator Henry S. Halbert, in *Biennial Report of the State Superintendent of Public Education to the Legislature of Mississippi for Scholastic years* 1893–1894 *and* 1894–1895, 535–36, and "Okla Hannali," also noted Choctaws along the Gulf Coast. I thank Dan Usner for urging me to recognize that there were indeed Choctaws along the Mississippi coast regardless of the legitimacy of the Society of Mississippi Choctaw.

50. The Mississippi, Alabama, and Louisiana Choctaw Council's bill, H.R. 8007, was filed with the Committee on Indian Affairs in 1913. U.S. House, *Congressional Record*, 63rd Cong., 1st sess. (1913), 4633.

51. For the actions of the council and their bill, see "Proposed Legislation for the Full-Blood and Identified Choctaws of Mississippi, Louisiana, and Alabama, with Memorial, Evidence, and Brief," in House Committee on Indian Affairs, *Hearings on Enrollment*, 122–23; Testimony of James Arnold, in House Committee, *Hearings on Enrollment*, 119.

52. "Proposed Legislation," in House Committee, *Hearings on Enrollment*, 122–23.

53. Arnold had claimed Choctaw ancestry but failed to win enrollment. The court records on this process are found in the Ross Collins Papers, boxes 2–4, Manuscript Division, Library of Congress.

54. Testimony of James Arnold, in House Committee, *Hearings on Enrollment*, 119.

55. "Proposed Legislation," 120.

56. "Proposed Legislation," 122–25.

57. "The Mississippi Choctaw Claim, January 21, 1914" (Judd and Detweiler, 1914), 7, in Choctaw Indians, Clippings Files, MDAH.

58. "Mississippi Choctaw Claim," 1–7. The right of the tribe to determine its own membership is central to tribal sovereignty. For an incisive review of opinions on how this determination should be undertaken, see TallBear, "DNA, Blood, and Racializing the Tribe," and Garroutte, *Real Indians*.

59. "Mississippi Choctaw Claim," 2–3.

60. "Mississippi Choctaw Claim," 1, 9, 12.

61. A. A. Jones, First Assistant Secretary of the Interior, to J. E. Arnold, March 12, 1914, in Records of the Indian Claims Commission, RG 279, Docket 52, box 618, NARA-DC.

62. "Report of the Honorable Franklin K. Lane, Secretary of the Interior, on the Harrison Bill (H.R. 12586)," Hurley Papers, box 15, folder 17.

63. Partial listing of people who petitioned the federal government on behalf of the Mississippi Choctaws: J. D. Rogers, W. W. Coursey, J. T. McCune, L. M. Adams, Eugene Carleton, and T. T. Wells, of Newton County, to J. E. Arnold, March 13, 1914; C. C. Davis, Union Drug Store, Union MS, to Whom It May Concern, March 14, 1914; Floyd Loper, Scott County, March 27, 1914; A. J. Brown and A. G.

Petty, Newton County, March 17, 1914; Z. C. Hagan MD to Congress and Senate of the United States of America, March 14, 1914; Williams Brooke Company, Union, to Members of the United States Senate and Congress, March 14, 1914; Merchants of Sandersville MS to House Committee on Indian Affairs, March 16, 1914; and T. B. Sullivan, Attorney at Law for Mississippi Choctaws Phillip Dixon, Ellis Sam, Green Sam, Surry Bollie, George Barney, Allen Willis, Dixon Willis, Pat Chitto, Jim Willis, Wesley Johnson, Jack Camel, and Irvin Sockey, June 16, 1909, all in House Committee on Indian Affairs, *Hearings on Enrollment*, 86–88.

64. Williams Brooke Company, Union MS, to Members of the United States Senate and Congress, March 14, 1914, House Committee on Indian Affairs, *Hearings on Enrollment*, 86.

65. J. E. Arnold, *Indian's Friend*, September 1915, clipping in Hurley Papers, box 4, folder, 18.

66. Over his eight years in Congress, Pat Harrison spent more time attempting to win resources for the Mississippi Choctaws than he did on any other piece of legislation. Coker, "Pat Harrison, the Formative Years, 1911–1919," 92. Despite his passion for the Choctaws, there is virtually nothing in his papers relating to this topic beyond official speeches and newspaper clippings. Pat Harrison Papers, Williams Library, University of Mississippi, Oxford.

67. Morgan, *Redneck Liberal*, 47; Coker, *Pat Harrison*, 6, 31–32; Kirwan, *Revolt of the Rednecks*, 81–182, 273–74. For racial conditions in the Mississippi Delta, see Woodruff, *American Congo*.

68. Kirwan notes that Vardaman's actions sometimes belied his bellicose speeches. *Revolt of the Rednecks*, 145–52, 163, quotation on pp. 146–47. Vardaman's biographer, William F. Holmes, in *White Chief,* likewise paints him as a more complex figure than his screeds might suggest.

69. For the filing of the bill see U.S. House, *Congressional Record*, 63rd Cong., 1st sess. (1913), 4633. The reasons Powers filed the bill have not survived in the public record. For Powers's biography, see *Biographical Directory of the United States Congress*, http://bioguide.congress.gov/scripts/biodisplay.pl?index=p000487.

70. For a perceptive analysis of notions of Indian authenticity, see Raibmon, *Authentic Indians*. Dan Usner also develops this theme in *Indian Work*. For analysis of how numerous popular writers portrayed Indian culture in the late nineteenth and early twentieth centuries, see Smith, *Reimagining Indians*.

71. Coker, "Pat Harrison's Efforts," 42.

72. Some of Harrison's constituents criticized him for selling out state's rights for patronage. See "On Betraying Dixie's Trust," *Norfolk Virginian-Pilot*, January 13, 1938, Harrison Papers, box 54, folder: Clippings, 1938.

73. W. P. Williams to Members of the United States Senate and Congress, March 14, 1914, House Committee on Indian Affairs, *Hearings on Enrollment*, 86.

74. Numerous histories of the South discuss the boll weevil. See Daniel, *Breaking the Land*.

75. Comments of Senator Williams, *Congressional Record*, vol. 51, pt. 2, 63rd Cong., 2nd sess., (1913–14), 10716; Harrison, "The Mississippi Choctaw: Speech by the Hon. Pat Harrison of Mississippi in the House of Representatives, December 12, 1912," 13–14, Hurley Papers, box 4, folder 2, quotation on 13; Comments of Senator Williams, *Congressional Record*, vol. 53, pt. 5, 64th Cong., 1st sess. (1915–16), 4922; Comments of Senator Vardaman, *Congressional Record*, vol. 53, pt. 5, 64th Cong., 2nd sess. (1916), 2122.

76. Comments of Senator Vardaman, *Congressional Record*, vol. 53, pt. 5, 64th Cong., 1st sess. (1915–16), 4930, and 2nd sess. (1916), 2121.

77. On two separate occasions Senator Williams informed his colleagues that when he hired laborers, he had to verify the work done by poor whites and "dark-eys," but not that done by the Indians. Comments of Senator Williams, *Congressional Record*, vol. 51, pt. 2, 63rd Cong., 2nd sess. (1913–14), 10713–17; and vol. 53, pt. 5, 64th Cong., 1st sess. (1915–16), 4922.

78. Comments of Congressman Harrison, *Congressional Record*, vol. 53, pt. 3, 64th Cong., 1st sess. (1915–16), 2172.

79. For analysis of the language of pity in describing Indian adaptation to economic challenges of colonialism, see Usner, *Indian Work*.

80. Comments of Senator Williams, *Congressional Record*, vol. 53, pt. 5, 64th Cong., 1st sess. (1915–16), 4924.

81. For numerous references to Choctaw poverty, see Harrison, "Mississippi Choctaw: Speech," 6; Comments of Representative Harrison, *Congressional Record*, vol. 53, pt. 3, 64th Cong., 1st sess., (1915–16), 2163; Comments of Senator Williams, *Congressional Record*, vol. 51, pt. 2, 63rd Cong., 2nd sess. (1913–14), 10949; Comments of Senator Vardaman, *Congressional Record*, vol. 51, pt. 2, 63rd Cong., 2nd sess. (1913–14), 11013.

82. Rand, *Ink on My Hands*, 51.

83. Testimony of Pat Harrison, in House Committee on Indian Affairs, *Hearings on Enrollment*, 727, 735, 746–60; Comments of Congressman Harrison, *Congressional Record*, vol. 51, pt. 2, 63rd Cong., 2nd sess. (1913–14), 2172.

84. Comments of Senator Williams, *Congressional Record*, vol. 53, pt. 5, 64th Cong., 1st sess. (1915–16), 4923–24, and *Congressional Record*, 63rd Cong., 2nd sess. (1913–14), 11016; Comments of Senator Vardaman, *Congressional Record*, 63rd Cong., 2nd sess. (1913–14), 5155, 5152.

85. Harrison "Mississippi Choctaw: Speech," 5–7; Comments of Representative Harrison, *Congressional Record*, vol. 53, pt. 5, 64th Cong., 1st sess. (1915–16), 2172; Comments of Senator Williams, *Congressional Record*, vol. 51, pt. 2, 63rd Cong., 2nd sess. (1913–14), 10715; Quin, "Speech of Percy E. Quin of Mississippi in the House of Representatives, February 5, 1916," 15–16; Comments of Senator Vardaman, *Congressional Record*, vol. 51, pt. 2, 63rd Cong., 2nd sess. (1913–14), 11013, and 3rd sess. (1914), 5154–56; and *Congressional Record*, vol. 53, pt. 5, 64th Cong., 1st sess., 4929, and 2nd sess., 2122.

86. Deloria, *Playing Indian*, ch. 1.

87. In the decade following the Spanish-American War, many white southerners emotionally reentered the Union even as they simultaneously celebrated their regional identity. Wilson, *Baptized in Blood*, and Cox, *Dixie's Daughters*. For a study of Reconstruction that documents dissenters from the sanctification of the Lost Cause and Jim Crow, see Bynum, *Long Shadow of the Civil War*.

88. Quin, "Speech," 8.

89. Harrison, "Mississippi Choctaw: Speech," 15–16.

90. Judging the motives of historical actors is always difficult. In his exploration of the glorification of Indians as vanishing noble savages in literature, performance, and art between 1880 and 1930, Alan Trachtenberg writes, "Partly this suggests a wish to exonerate guilt, but evidence of confessed guilt was rare." He argues that such efforts nonetheless functioned as a means of catharsis and self-justification regardless of whether or not that was their intended goal. Trachtenberg, *Shades of Hiawatha*, xxiv.

91. Coker, "Pat Harrison's Efforts," 59; On Venable, see Rowland, *History of Mississippi*, 2:436.

92. Hurley to Richardson, House Committee on Indian Affairs, *Hearings on Enrollment*, 94.

93. Kidwell, *Choctaws and Missionaries*, 193; Coker, "Pat Harrison's Efforts," 57–59.

94. William Webb Venable, notice in the *Neshoba County Democrat*, March 15, 1917, 5.

95. "The Choctaws," *Neshoba County Democrat*, March 22, 1917, 3.

96. U.S. House, "Condition of the Mississippi Choctaws, Union MS, March 16, 1917," in *Hearings Before the Committee on Investigation of the Indian Service*, 1:125, 131, 141, 146, 147, 162, 172.

97. U.S. House, "Condition of the Mississippi Choctaws," quotation on p. 125; remarks on council on p. 123.

98. Jaimes, "Federal Indian Policy," 123–38; Edmunds, "Native Americans, New Voices," 733–34.

99. Harmon, "Tribal Enrollment Councils," 179. For American Indians and skin color, see Shoemaker, *Strange Likeness*. For indigenous ideologies of blood, see Meyer, "American Indian Blood Quantum Requirements," and Strong and Van Winkle, "'Indian Blood.'"

100. Sturm, *Blood Politics*, 136–41.

101. For debates over Indians' notions of race, see TallBear, "DNA, Blood, and Racializing the Tribe."

102. For a sharp critique of the difficulties in sorting out competing variables of identity in historical studies of race and ethnicity, see Kolchin, "Whiteness Studies."

103. Although there is certainly political disagreement among Mississippi Choctaws, my study of Choctaw leadership has not uncovered any divisions based on blood. For conflicts that employ these divisions, see Meyer, *White Earth Tragedy*; Lambert, *Choctaw Nation*; and Rosier, *Rebirth of the Blackfoot Nation*.

104. U.S. House, "Memorial of the Choctaw and Chickasaw Nations Relative to the Rights of the Mississippi Choctaws," Hurley Papers, box 17, folder 3.

105. "Petition of the Mississippi Choctaws," February 13, 1900, H. Doc. 426, 56th Cong., 1st sess., 1.

3. Establishment of the Agency

1. *Winton v. Amos*, 255 U.S. 373 (1921), in *Case Findings on the McKennon Roll*, http://caselaw.lp.findlaw.com/scripts/getcase.pl?court=us&vol=255&invol=373 (accessed June 18, 2008).

2. Raibmon, *Authentic Indians*, 183.

3. Cato Sells, CIA, to Mrs. J. E. Arnold, September 10, 1917, CCF–Choctaw: 806-81856, BIA, NARA-DC.

4. The estimate of "several hundred" came from Choctaw superintendent Archie H. McMullen's report, "A Brief History of the Mississippi Choctaw Prepared in 1954," typescript in Entry 327, box 43, file: Mississippi Choctaw History, FCTA, NARA-SW. Statistical analysis is from Peterson, "Mississippi Band of Choctaw Indians," 111–12; Simpson Tubby to Secretary of the Interior, April 27, 1918, CCF: 100-36832, BIA, NARA-DC.

5. Interview with Baxter York, April 8, 1974, Southeastern Indian Oral History Project, Neshoba County Library, Philadelphia MS. See also Peterson, "Mississippi Band of Choctaw Indians," 109.

6. Reverend William Ketcham to A. J. Ahern, August 12, 1918, Records of the Bureau of Catholic Indian Missions (BCIM), microfilm reel 88.

7. Culbertson Davis, Stratton MS, to Ketcham, August 5, 1918; Ketcham to Ahern, August 12, 1918; Willie Solomon to Ketcham, September 25, 1918; John Williams to Ketcham, September 28, 1918, BCIM Records, reel 88.

8. Ahern to Davis, August [?], 1918, BCIM Records, reel 88.

9. Interview with Baxter York, April 8, 1974. Choctaw informants told anthropologist John Peterson Jr. a similar story of draft resistance. Peterson, "Mississippi Band of Choctaw Indians," 109; S. Adams, Major General, the Adjutant General's Office, to CIA, November 17, 1939, RG 279, Records of the Indian Claims Commission, Closed Docketed Case Files, 1947–82, box 620, NARA-DC.

10. Keith, *Rich Man's War*. For Mississippi's leading role in draft resistance, see p. 108.

11. For Indian reactions to conscription, see Britten, *American Indians in World War I*, 51–72. Data on Choctaw veterans in World War I was gathered from genealogy websites, accessed September 30, 2007, that are no longer active.

12. J. A. Charley to Ketcham, April 17, 1918, BCIM Records, reel 88.

13. For information on all Choctaw veterans, see http://www.choctaw.org/aboutMBCI/veterans/index.html (accessed November 1, 2013).

14. Historical Census Browser, University of Virginia, Geospatial and Statistical Data Center: http://fisher.lib.virginia.edu/collections/stats/histcensus/index.html (accessed February 10, 2007).

15. Keith, *Rich Man's War*, 138–42. For the relative isolation of Kemper, Newton, and Scott Counties, see Reeves Report, 12–14.

16. Keith, *Rich Man's War*, 141.

17. The veterans from the band's principal families are too numerous to list. For Indian motives for enlistment, see Britten, *American Indians in World War I*, and Krouse, *North American Indians in the Great War*.

18. See Keith, *Rich Man's War*, for Vardaman, Williams, and the war.

19. The use of Choctaw language as military code is mentioned on the website of the Choctaw Nation of Oklahoma, http://www.choctawnation.com/history/people /code-talkers/code-talkers-of-wwi/ (accessed November 1, 2013). Records of the Office of the Commissioner of Indian Affairs, Cato Sells Scrapbook, entry 177B, box 1, stack 11E2, row 30, compartment 9, shelf 1, RG 75, BIA, NARA-DC. The scrapbook contains numerous clippings of Sells's enlistment speeches urging Indians to sign up for the armed forces.

20. "Indian Commissioner Sells Will Visit the Seminoles in Florida," clipping from the *Miami Herald*, February 1, 1918, in Sells Scrapbook.

21. Sells to J. Hardin Mallard, Chairman, Presbyterian Missions, Meridian MS, May 1, 1918, CCF: 800-37509, BIA, NARA-DC.

22. Frank J. McKinley, Special Agent, to Commissioner Sells, November 23, 1922, CCF: 100-98178-1922, BIA, NARA-DC.

23. Reeves Report, 23–24; "Lost Tribes of the South," clipping from the *Fort Worth Record*, February 25, 1918, in Sells Scrapbook. Peterson notes that Dr. McKinley had previous ties to the Choctaw ("Mississippi Band of Choctaw Indians," 113).

24. Robert L. Newberne, Chief Medical Supervisor, "A General Report on the Mississippi Choctaw Agency," 1921, CCF: 150-28854-1921, BIA, NARA-DC. Newberne mentions only the boarding house—it may have been the Mary Cooper Boarding House, as noted on a map in Yates and Rideout, *Red Clay Hills of Neshoba*, 86.

25. Yates and Rideout, *Red Clay Hills of Neshoba*, 202–13; Ruth P. Rush, "Assignment Twenty," folder: Industry, WPA Files, Neshoba County, box 10773, MDAH; Kirwan *Revolt of the Rednecks*, 40–41.

26. Reeves Report, 23–24. U.S. House, "Condition of the Mississippi Choctaws, Union MS," 1:117–78.

27. Reeves Report, 24. At these hearings, Simpson Tubby mentioned the Choctaws' reluctance to work in sawmills, an observation confirmed by J. D. Pace, Mayor of Union MS, in U.S. House, "Condition of the Mississippi Choctaws," 121–22 and 167, respectively; Comby testimony, 134–35.

28. Testimony regarding women is found in the statements of Phillip Dixon, 158; Simpson Tubby, 122–23; and J. D. Pace, 161, U.S. House, "Condition of the Mississippi Choctaws." Information on Choctaw women shunning work as maids comes from the 1950s, but there is no reason to believe that this attitude did not hold for the earlier period. See Damus Z. Rhodes, Home Management Supervisor, to W. O. Roberts, Area Director of the Muskogee District, November 30, 1953, Entry 327, box 42, file: Miscellaneous, FCTA, NARA-SW; Report of Peyton Carter, Supervisor, No-

vember 13, 1924, CCF: 150-86815-1924, BIA, NARA-DC. Information on Ms. Jim was found in a caption under the picture of her new house in Rhodes's report. Peterson, "Mississippi Band of Choctaw Indians," 206.

29. U.S. House, "Condition of the Mississippi Choctaws," 122–23, 158; Sidney B. Schamber, "Points of Interest: The Indian Agency," WPA Files, Neshoba County, box 10773, folder: Philadelphia, MDAH; Federal Writers' Project, *Mississippi: A Guide to the Magnolia State* (New York: Viking Press, 1938), 466–67.

30. Yates and Rideout, *Red Clay Hills of Neshoba*, 202–13; Ruth P. Rush, "Assignment Twenty," WPA Files, Neshoba County, box 10773, MDAH.

31. Langford, "A Study of the Educational Development of the Choctaw Indians in Mississippi," 33–35; Reeves Report, 2, 11.

32. Reeves Report, 2; U.S. House, "Condition of the Mississippi Choctaws," 121–22.

33. U.S. Senate, "Survey of Conditions," 7674–77, 7681–90.

34. Yates and Rideout, *Red Clay Hills of Neshoba*, 202–13; Ruth P. Rush, "Assignment Twenty," folder: Industry, WPA Files, Neshoba County, box 10773, MDAH.

35. McKinley to Sells, December 14, 1919, CCF: 032-14730, BIA, NARA-DC. For information on Choctaw employment in sawmills prior to McKinley's arrival, see U.S. House, "Condition of the Mississippi Choctaws," 121–22, 167, and Reeves Report, 24.

36. Quotation is from Reeves Report, 23–24; U.S. House, "Condition of the Mississippi Choctaws," 117–18.

37. U.S. House, "Condition of the Mississippi Choctaws."

38. Reeves Report, 24.

39. U.S. House, "Condition of the Mississippi Choctaws," testimony of Jessie Ben, 150–52.

40. Reeves Report, 24–25. For the Arnold's church and farmlands, see Farr, *Religious Assimilation*, 36–37, and Mrs. J. E. Arnold to Mr. McLemore, Union MS, July 9, 1920; W. W. Venable to Cato Sells, July 16, 1920, CCF: 800-60719, BIA, NARA-DC.

41. Reeves Report, 2–3, 11.

42. Reeves Report, 2, 13. Within five years, however, Scott County had constructed an Indian school at "Indiantown"; it had fifteen pupils. Newberne Report, 30.

43. On efforts to make all American citizens conform to white middle-class norms, see Trachtenburg, *Incorporation of America*; Painter, *Standing at Armageddon*; Cashman, *America in the Gilded Age*; Edwards, *New Spirits*.

44. For assimilation policy, see Hoxie, *Final Promise*. Hoxie argues that by the early twentieth century, policy makers had shifted their focus from transforming Indians into middle-class citizens to vocational education and training in manual labor (see pp. 147–210).

45. Inspection of Peyton Carter, April 4, 1922, 16, CCF: 150-32247, BIA, NARA-DC.

46. Carter Inspection, April 4, 1922, 16; Newberne Report, 5.

47. Newberne Report, 4.

48. For a superb overview of the discourse of poverty and Indians, see Usner, *Indian Work*, especially ch. 3.

49. For similar efforts to uplift poor rural whites, see Hoffschwelle, *Rebuilding the Rural Southern Community*. For how the OIA negotiated class within its ranks and in its mission, see Cahill, *Federal Fathers and Mothers*, 152–60, 223–27.

50. Rand, *Ink on My Hands*, 48–49. Yates and Rideout, *Red Clay Hills of Neshoba*, 203–12, 214.

51. Newberne Report, 5; Carter Inspection, April 4, 1922, 6.

52. Rand, *Ink*, 239.

53. As a child, Mars saw two men gunned down in the streets, and Rand witnessed a murder in his own office doorway. Mars, *Witness in Philadelphia*, 17; Rand, *Ink*, 247.

54. Carter Inspection, April 4, 1922, "Introduction."

55. Summary of dates for schools in Peterson, "Mississippi Band of Choctaw Indians," 129. For details on the actual schools, see Newberne Report, 26–27.

56. Virtually every school inspection remarked that Mississippi's schools were segregated, and some commented on segregation of public conveyances and facilities. See especially "Mississippi Choctaws: Final Report of Jess L. Ballard, United States Probate Attorney, February 27–June 12, 1919," in U.S. Senate, "Survey of Conditions," 7731; Report of Walter S. Stevens on the Choctaw Reservation, July 5–8, 1923, CCF: 150-60774-1923, BIA, NARA-DC; McKinley to CIA, December 31, 1924, CCF: 150-86815-1924, BIA, NARA-DC; and Newberne Report, 20.

57. "Final Report of Jess L. Ballard," in U.S. Senate, "Survey of Conditions," 7731.

58. To the Commissioner of Indian Affairs, n.d., filed January 12, 1923, in Inspection of Peyton Carter, January 1923, CCF: 150-20899, BIA, NARA-DC.

59. W. J. Weir to Commissioner of Indian Affairs, n.d., filed January 12, 1923, in Carter Inspection, January 1923.

60. McKinley to CIA, n.d., filed January 12, 1923, in Carter Inspection, January 1923.

61. Virtually every OIA document dealing with Indian education in Mississippi commented on the Choctaws' desire for education. The literature on Indian education is voluminous. See Adams, *Education for Extinction*, and Ellis, *To Change Them Forever*. Recent reappraisals of government boarding schools by Indian scholars emphasize how Indian children endured and sometimes turned the experience to their benefit. Lomawaima, *They Called It Prairie Light*; Child, *Boarding School Seasons*; and Archuleta, Child, and Lomawaima, *Away from Home*.

62. Report of Earl Henderson, Assistant Secretary of the Board of Indian Commissioners, May 25, 1927, unpaginated, CCF: 150-31344-1927, BIA, NARA-DC; Robert J. Enochs, Choctaw Superintendent, to CIA, May 14, 1927, CCF: 100-98178-1922, BIA, NARA-DC.

63. Enochs to CIA, May 14, 1927, CCF: 100-98178-1922, BIA, NARA-DC; Henderson Report, May 25, 1927.

64. McKinley estimated that roughly 90 percent of the Choctaw population were sharecroppers at the time the agency opened. McKinley to Sells, November 23, 1922, CCF: 100-98178-1922, BIA, NARA-DC. The figure was also logged in "Report of G. E. E. Lindquist, March 1929," CCF: 150-9490-1929, BIA, NARA-DC. Even though the 1916

Reeves Report said the majority of Choctaws were laborers or farmhands, all subsequent agency documents reported them as sharecroppers. There could have a major shift in employment practices in the intervening years, but it is more likely that Reeves's assessment was an anomaly. He hinted as much when he observed that the boll weevil infestation had reduced the number of farmers in all demographic groups. It is also highly possible that most Choctaw men farmed for subsistence and supplemented this with wage work.

65. McKinley to Sells, November 23, 1922, CCF: 100-98178-1922, BIA, NARA-DC.

66. McKinley to Sells, December 27, 1918, CCF: 800-102544-1918, BIA, NARA-DC.

67. "Final Report of Jess L. Ballard," quoted in Newberne Report, 5–6.

68. McKinley to Sells, May 16, 1919, CCF: 140-42814, BIA, NARA-DC.

69. McKinley to Sells, November 11, 1920, CCF: 134-104702-1920, BIA, NARA-DC.

70. For peonage, see Daniel, *In the Shadow of Slavery*, and Woodruff, *American Congo*. McKinley to Sells, May 16, 1919, CCF: 140-42814, BIA, NARA-DC; Newberne Report, 6.

71. Henderson Report, May 25, 1927.

72. McKinley to Sells, May 16, 1919, CCF: 140-42814, BIA, NARA-DC, and McKinley to Sells, November 23, 1922, CCF: 100-98178-1922, BIA, NARA-DC.

73. Testimony of Henry L. Rodger, Attorney at Law, in U.S. Senate, "Survey of Conditions of the Indians in the United States," in *Hearings Before the Subcommittee on Indian Affairs*, 7763.

74. Report of Earl Henderson, Assistant Secretary of the Board of Indian Commissioners, June 28, 1924, unpaginated, CCF: 130-47964-24, BIA, NARA-DC; Report of R. L. Spalsbury, District Superintendent, to CIA, October 25, 1926, unpaginated, Section: Home Building, CCF: 150-52093-1926, BIA, NARA-DC.

75. Inspectors' reports almost never provided names of those who approached them and pressed the claims agenda. See Spalsbury Report, October 25, 1926, and the Henderson Report, June 28, 1924. For the names of Indians who pressed claims, see the testimony of Olmon Comby and Pat Chitto in U.S. Senate, "Survey of Conditions," 7674 and 7698.

76. McKinley to Charles E. Burke, CIA, February 29, 1924; Burke to McKinley, April 3, 1924; McKinley to Burke, April 21 and 24, 1924, in U.S. Senate, "Survey of Conditions," 7723 and 7733, respectively. In 1926 OIA Inspector Robert Spalsbury requested an attorney to settle the allotment issue. He suggested working through the agency so as to circumvent rapacious lawyers who periodically offered to expedite claims in return for half the settlement. Robert Spalsbury to CIA, October 25, 1926, in Spalsbury Report, 1926.

77. Testimony of Harry M. Carter, in U.S. Senate, "Survey of Conditions," 7707–12; Enoch's reply is on 7708; E. B. Merritt, Assistant Commissioner of Indian Affairs, to Enochs, December 15, 1925, in "Survey of Conditions," 7738.

78. Testimony of Harry M. Carter, in "Survey of Conditions," 7707–12; Enoch's testimony is on 7708.

79. Testimony of Senator Frazier and Representative Collins, in "Survey of Conditions," 7686–87.

80. Testimony of Harry M. Carter, in "Survey of Conditions," 7707–12.

81. Choctaw testimony is found on the following pages: Olmon Comby, 7670–74 (Comby's name was spelled Olmarr in the transcripts); Ed Willis, 7674–77; Willie Jimmie, 7681–90, quotation on 7685 and remarks of Collins on 7686; Willie Solomon, 7690–94; Simpson Tubby, 7814–15, Tom Jackson, 7782–86; Ike Jimmie, 7794–95.

82. Testimony of Pat Chitto, 7694–99, quotation on 7698, in "Survey of Conditions."

83. Henderson Report, May 25, 1927.

84. Peterson, "Mississippi Band of Choctaw Indians," 124; Evan L. Flory, Chief, Branch of Soil Conservation, and T. W. Taylor, Chief, Branch of Management Planning, "Choctaw Study, 1951," Entry 327, box 37, file: Special Problems among the Choctaw, FCTA, NARA-SW. Economic data is found on pp. 5–15. See also Thompson and Peterson, "Mississippi Choctaw Identity: Genesis and Change," 188.

85. For a description of Indian farming methods, see Newberne Report.

86. McKinley to CIA, November 23, 1922, CCF: 100-98178-1922, BIA, NARA-DC; Peterson, "Mississippi Band of Choctaw Indians," 118.

87. Peterson, "Mississippi Band of Choctaw Indians," 120–25. Concerns over cotton prices, boll weevils, and weather are found throughout the reports and correspondence of virtually everyone who worked with the Choctaws.

88. The Act of June 21, 1939, shifting the status of the reimbursable farms to trust lands, is documented in "Proclamation," Oscar Chapman, Assistant Secretary, Department of the Interior, December 4, 1944, CCF: 931-1-10154-1948, BIA, NARA-DC.

89. Peterson, "Mississippi Band of Choctaw Indians," 120, 122, 127–28.

90. Peterson, "Mississippi Band of Choctaw Indians," 195; Henderson Report, June 28, 1924.

91. Burke to McKinley, August 13, 1923, CCF: 916-000-1923, BIA, NARA-DC; Enochs to CIA, April 15, 1927, CCF: 910-1927, BIA, NARA-DC; Annual Statistical Report, Choctaw Agency, 1934, Section One, 2, CCF: 919-70945, BIA, NARA-DC.

92. Enochs to CIA, March 15, 1929, in "Report of G. E. E. Lindquist," March 1929, CCF: 150-9490-1929, BIA, NARA-DC.

93. Peterson notes the preference of some for working on private rather than government lands: "Mississippi Band of Choctaw Indians," 128. OIA inspector Henry Roe Cloud, investigating problems in Mississippi in 1931, found otherwise: "The few who have escaped from this enslavement can not [*sic*] express adequately their heartfelt gratitude and their intense desire to cooperate for their own independence in the constructive efforts laid down by the Government." See "Report of Henry Roe Cloud on the MI Choctaw Situation, September 22, 1931, Re Farmer T. J. Scott," 4, CCF: 150-29352-1931, BIA, NARA-DC (hereafter cited as the Roe Cloud Report). It is possible that the Choctaws were telling Roe Cloud what they believed he wanted to hear, yet it is also not unreasonable to view this sentiment as sincere.

94. Testimony of Olmon Comby, in U.S. Senate, "Survey of Conditions," 7670.

95. Henderson Report, June 28, 1924.

96. Henderson Report, June 28, 1924. The historical record is not sufficient to ascertain the amount of influence the PTA exerted.

97. Enochs to CIA, May 14, 1927, CCF: 100-98178-1922, BIA, NARA-DC; Henderson Report, May 25, 1927.

98. Henderson Report, May 25, 1927.

99. Henderson Report, May 25, 1927; Enochs to CIA, May 14, 1927, CCF: 100-98178-1922, BIA, NARA-DC.

100. *Winton v. Amos*, 255 U.S. 373 (1921), http://caselaw.lp.findlaw.com/scripts /getcase.pl?court=us&vol=255&invol=373 (accessed June 18, 2008)

101. *Winton v. Amos*.

102. "School Inspection of Samuel H. Thompson, Superintendent of Schools," March 22, 1932, 7–8, CCF: 806–6507-1932, BIA, NARA-DC.

103. Testimony of E. T. Winston, in "Survey of Conditions," 7699.

104. Winston, in "Survey of Conditions," 7699.

105. Winston, in "Survey of Conditions," 7699.

106. Winston, in "Survey of Conditions," 7700–7701, quotation on 7700.

107. Winston, in "Survey of Conditions," 7699, 7703.

4. Agency and Patronage Economy

1. Frank J. McKinley, Choctaw Agent, to Cato Sells, CIA, May 16, 1922, in Carter Inspection, April 4, 1922, CCF: 150-32247, BIA, NARA-DC

2. Rand, *Ink on My Hands*, 153. OIA inspector R. L. Spalsbury also commented that when the government began constructing schools for Indians, "local poor whites also spruced up their schools." Spalsbury Report, October 25, 1926, CCF: 150-52093-1926, BIA, NARA-DC.

3. Rand, *Ink*, 154–61.

4. *Union (MS) Appeal*, October 27, 1921, box 3, folder 3, Ross Collins Papers, Manuscript Division, Library of Congress, Washington DC.

5. Name illegible, to Ross Collins, October 22, 1921; J. D. Taylor to Ross Collins, October 31, 1921, box 3, folder 3, Ross Collins Papers.

6. Because the 1918 influenza epidemic had drawn attention to the Choctaws, the legislation establishing the agency specified that the superintendent (also known as the agent) must be a physician. Sells to J. Hardin Mallard, Chairman, Presbyterian Missions, Meridian MS, May 1, 1918, CCF: 800-37509, BIA, NARA-DC.

7. McKinley to CIA, January 10, 1924; E. B. Merritt, Assistant CIA, to McKinley, October 6, 1924, CCF: 150-60774-1923, BIA, NARA-DC. McKinley to Hon. Charles H. Burke, CIA, December 31, 1924, in Carter Inspection, April 4, 1922; "Report of Elinor D. Gregg, Supervisor of Field Nurses and Field Matrons, 12-23-27," 2, CCF: 150-5302-1928, BIA, NARA-DC.

8. "A Hospital," *Neshoba County Democrat*, September 27, 1923, 1.

9. Joe Jennings, Superintendent of Indian Schools, Eastern Area, Vernon L. Beggs, Supervisor of Indian Education, and A.B. Caldwell, Superintendent of Indian Educa-

tion, Lake States Area, "A Study of the Social and Economic Condition of the Choctaw Indians in Mississippi in Relation to the Educational Programs," May 1935, CCF: 806-38014-1935, BIA, NARA-DC. A list of agents is found on p. 5.

10. Henderson Report, May 25, 1927; Neshoba County Chamber of Commerce to CIA, June 7, 1929, CCF: 806-26636-1929, BIA, NARA-DC; "Boarding School Planned," *Neshoba County Democrat*, June 6, 1929, 1.

11. "Indian Hospital to Rise," *Neshoba County Democrat*, July 21, 1921, 1.

12. "Report of Walter S. Stevens, Medical Director, 4th District, March 4, 1929," CCF: 150-11434-1929, BIA, NARA-DC; "Indian Hospital Opens Monday," *Neshoba County Democrat*, April 5, 1928, 1.

13. "Philadelphia Hospital Opens Doors," *Neshoba County Democrat*, April 7, 1927, 1. Dr. Yates provided contract medical services to the Pearl River and Tucker communities, which he continued after his hospital opened. Yates and Rideout, *Red Clay Hills of Neshoba*, 42, 104, 116, 187, 120–21, 133, 208; Robert J. Enochs, Choctaw Superintendent, to CIA, January 11, 1929, CCF: 731-1833-29, BIA, NARA-DC; Inspection of John H. Holt, Supervisor of Indian Education, September 25, 1930, 6, CCF: 150-51947-1931, BIA, NARA-DC.

14. "Citizens Plan Boarding School," *Neshoba County Democrat*, June 6, 1929, 1.

15. Neshoba County Chamber of Commerce to CIA, June 7, 1929, CCF: 806-26636-1929, BIA, NARA-DC.

16. Enochs to CIA, June 7, 1929, CCF: 806-26636-1929, BIA, NARA-DC.

17. Emmett York to CIA, September 7, 1928; Merritt to York, September 24, 1928, CCF: 806-45059-1928, BIA, NARA-DC; "Indian Hospital Equipment Purchased, Dr. Enochs Was Accompanied by Two High School Boys Entering School," *Neshoba County Democrat*, September 29, 1927, 2; Burke to Enochs, June 20, 1929, CCF: 806-26636-1929, BIA, NARA-DC.

18. Citing every item on the Choctaw and the agency in the *Neshoba County Democrat* would be spatially prohibitive.

19. "Govt. Officials Pleased," *Neshoba County Democrat*, April 6, 1922, 1.

20. *Neshoba County Democrat*, "20th Century Edition," October 9, 1931: Father J. T. McKenna, "History of the Holy Rosary Catholic Mission"; no author listed, "The Choctaw Indian Hospital"; Mrs. R. J. Enochs, "History of the Choctaw Indians"; R. L. Breland continued this narrative the following year in "The Story of Neshoba." *Neshoba County Democrat*, February 19, 1932.

21. *Neshoba County Democrat*: "New Organization at Indian Agency," January 15, 1932, 1; "Indian Service Employees Union Formed in City," April 8, 1932, 1.

22. *Neshoba County Democrat*: "Society Notes," September 20, 1928, 4; "Society Notes," March 1, 1929, 1; "Society Notes," September 11, 1931, 1; "Neshoba Library Receives Books for the Enochs," June 17, 1932; "Dr. R. J. Enochs Gets Transfer to Kayenta, Ariz.," July 1, 1932, 1; "Farewell Party of Mrs. Enochs," and "Enochs Honored Tuesday Evening," June 17, 1932, 1.

23. *Neshoba County Democrat*: "Mrs. H. G. King Congratulated on Indian Work," October 2, 1931, 1; "Local Women Named as District Chairmen," December 11, 1931,

1; "Local Talent to Broadcast Tuesday: Indian Program," December 14, 1934, 1. The women's social status is mentioned in Yates and Rideout, *Red Clay Hills*, 115, 186, 209.

24. "Indians Have Pleasant Gathering at Pearl River School," *Neshoba County Democrat*, October 6, 1921, 1.

25. "Tucker Indian School Opens," *Neshoba County Democrat*, November 18, 1920, 2.

26. *Neshoba County Democrat*: "Pearl River Indian School," November 6, 1928, 7; January 31, 1929, 5; and March 7, 1929, 5; "Choctaw Indian Agency Notes," February 14, 1930, 1.

27. This was the title of Rand's chapter that discussed Choctaws in his autobiography.

28. *Neshoba County Democrat*: "Court Room Crowded," February 24, 1921, 1; "Choctaw Caught with Liquor," June 23, 1921, 1; "Thomas Bell Shot by Negro," March 22, 1921, 1; "Morris Indians Sentenced in Tubby Death," and "Indian Dance Results in Cutting Scrape," October 2, 1932, 1; "Choctaw Fatally Stabbed Saturday Night at Tucker," October 14, 1933, 1; "Indian Knocked in Head, Dead, Found in Car Sun. Morning," November 27, 1936, 1.

29. "Young Choctaw Student Writes Mississippi Choctaw History," *Neshoba County Democrat*, May 2, 1931, and May 29, 1931, 1.

30. Rand, *Ink*, 139.

31. Rand, *Ink*, 139–51, quotation on p. 150.

32. "Govt. Officials Pleased," *Neshoba County Democrat*, April 6, 1922, 1.

33. Carter Inspection, January 1923, 2.

34. Rand, *Ink*, 45–47. Rand does not explain that the school was part of the Methodist mission. That information came from the Newberne Report, 1921, CCF: 150-28854-1921, BIA, NARA-DC.

35. Enochs to CIA, April 14, 1927, CCF: 100-98178-1922, BIA, NARA-DC.

36. Clipping from *Neshoba County Democrat*, November 3, 1927, filed with Enochs to CIA, November 6, 1927, CCF: 100-98178-1922, BIA, NARA-DC.

37. Two recent works analyze how many non-Indians define Indians by reference to notions of primitivism. See Usner, *Indian Work*, and Raibmon, *Authentic Indians*.

38. This historical trajectory is analyzed in Morgan, *Redneck Liberal*, and Kirwan, *Revolt of the Rednecks*.

39. Rand, *Ink*, 207–17.

40. For more on the role of class in shaping ideologies of race, see Fields, "Ideology of Race in American History."

41. Morgan, *Redneck Liberal*, 1–23.

42. Coleman, "Mississippi Constitution of 1890," 12–14. Both Kirwan and Morgan note that Mississippi's oligarchy held poor whites in contempt and frequently attempted to shut poor whites out of politics. See Morgan, *Redneck Liberal*, ch. 1, and Kirwan, *Revolt of the Rednecks*.

43. Rand, *Ink*, chs. 8, 12, 14, 22, and 27–31 discuss local politics. Analysis of the understanding clause is found on p. 229, where Rand recorded the disenfranchisement of African Americans.

44. Choctaws never pushed for voting rights until the mid-twentieth century.

45. The quotation is from Mars, *Witness in Philadelphia*, 39. For her pedigree, see pp. 7–8, and Yates and Rideout, *Red Clay Hills*, 128, 171–75.

46. Mars, *Witness*, 38–39. I thank Jeanette Keith for explaining that these accusations of sullenness meant insufficiently obsequious to their "betters."

47. Rand, *Ink*, 50, 172–79.

48. For gradations in the social hierarchy of whites, see Fields, "Ideology of Race," 143–78, and Keith, *Rich Man's War*, 118.

49. Mars, *Witness*, 3, 29–30; Rand, *Ink*, ch. 15.

50. Carter Inspection, April 4, 1922, 1; Henderson Report, June 28, 1924, CCF: 130-47964-24, BIA, NARA-DC; "Report of G. E. E. Lindquist," March 1929, CCF: 150-9490-1929, BIA, NARA-DC. See also Newberne Report, 5, 8, 4.

51. For references to Choctaws and African Americans, see U.S. Senate, "Survey of Conditions," 125–26, 146, 156, 159, 161. Tubby's remarks are on pp. 125–26.

52. As Lucy Maddox argued in *Citizen Indians*, Indian intellectuals in the Society of American Indians, a pan-Indian group in the early decades of the twentieth century, commented extensively on racism.

53. "Report of the Hon. Clement S. Ucker, Board of Indian Commissioners, August 17, 1922," 8, CCF: 150-74704-1922, BIA, NARA-DC.

54. Henderson Report, May 25, 1927.

55. Newberne Report, 5, 14.

56. Interview with Mr. Barry Davis Jim Sr., Mississippi Oral History Project, http://www.usm.edu/oralhistory/lodi.html (accessed April 21, 2006). Phillip Martin emphasized this approach to race relations in his autobiography. Martin, Jeter, and Blanshard, *Chief*, 41–45.

57. Only one OIA inspector ranked blacks above Choctaws—R. L. Spalsbury, in 1926. Those who viewed Choctaws as higher in the social order were Earl Henderson (1924) and agent Archie C. Hector (1935). In 1921 inspector Robert L. Newberne opined that "the colored people of Neshoba have progressed out of proportion to the white race," and Florence Mars argued that "poor white trash" were the lowest forms of life in Neshoba County. Henderson Report, June 28, 1924; Spalsbury Report, October 25, 1926; Newberne Report, "Narrative Section," 2; Mars, *Witness*, 38–39.

58. Stevens Report, July 5–8, 1923, "Health Section," 3. The authors of the WPA Guidebook observed the poor conditions for sharecroppers and concluded that race was not a factor in their degradation. Rather, they blamed the "banker-merchants" for driving the entire "pernicious system." Federal Writers' Project, *Mississippi: A Guide to the Magnolia State*, 104–5.

59. McKinley estimated approximately 10 percent of the total tribal population in 1922 owned their farms; however, he did not have accurate records and probably overestimated. By 1936 twenty-four out of 405 Choctaw families—approximately 6 percent—owned their own land. In 1962, however, anthropologist John Peterson estimated the Choctaw yeomanry at slightly more than 2 percent. It is possible that

more than half the Indians who owned farms had lost them, or perhaps the population grew faster than the yeomanry. McKinley to Sells, November 23, 1922, CCF: 100-98178-1922, BIA, NARA-DC; Report of Edna Graves, Supervisor of Home Economics, February 20–March 20, 1936, 6, CCF: 800-4313-1951, BIA, NARA-DC. Information comparing black and Choctaw farm ownership is found in Peterson, "Mississippi Band of Choctaw Indians," 126–27.

60. Mars, *Witness*, 3; Rand, *Ink*, 318.

61. Mars, *Witness*, 1; Rand, *Ink*, 317; "Assignment Ten: Races and Nationalities in Neshoba County," WPA Files, Neshoba County, box 10773, MDAH; Henderson Report, May 25, 1927; Historical Census Browser, University of Virginia, Geospatial and Statistical Data Center, http://fisher.lib.virginia.edu/collections/stats/histcensus /index.html (accessed October 2, 2007).

62. Mars, *Witness*, 40.

63. Roe Cloud Report, 15, CCF: 150-29352-1931, BIA, NARA-DC.

64. Rand, *Ink*, 323–24.

65. Rand, *Ink*, 82–83, 172–85, quotation on p. 185.

66. Rand, *Ink*, 318, 326; Mars, *Witness*, 16.

67. Yates and Rideout, *Red Clay Hills*, 204–6. Cotton prices fluctuated wildly over the 1920s, from $28.69 in 1923 to $12.47 in 1926. Data on prices from McCain, "Triumph of Democracy," 94.

68. Rand explained that these actions were meant "to frighten away the workers," presumably to free the jobs for white men. Rand, *Ink*, 326.

69. Roe Cloud Report, 15. Scott's popularity among the Choctaws was also noticed by a scholar who worked among them in the 1950s. Tolbert, "Sociological Study," 134.

70. MacLean, *Behind the Mask of Chivalry*, ch. 3; Feldman, *Politics, Society, and the Klan in Alabama*, 7, 27–28; Percy, *Lanterns on the Levee*, 234. For the Neshoba County Klan in the 1920s, see Mars, *Witness*, 15, and Rand, *Ink*, ch. 32. Also see press coverage in the *Neshoba County Democrat*: Andrew Gibson, "To My Fellow Citizens of Neshoba County," January 18, 1923, 4; "A. DeWeese Writes Letter on Klan Speech," January 18, 1923, 1; "Unfortunate Sermon," reprint of an editorial in the *Jackson Daily News*, March 29, 1923, 1; "Many Visitors Attend Klan Celebration on Tuesday Evening," October 30, 1924, 1; ad for KKK rally, October 27, 1925, 4.

71. Roe Cloud Report, 15. Scott's salary appears in C. L. Trowbridge, Field Representative, "Report on Thomas Scott, Farmer, Choctaw Jurisdiction, State of Mississippi," May 9, 1931, CCF: 150-29352-1931, BIA, NARA-DC, hereafter cited as Trowbridge Report.

72. Montgomery and Elmore, *Register to the Papers of Henry Bascom Collins*, 3. Thanks to Dan Usner for calling these to my attention.

73. Hoxie, *Final Promise*, 163–69.

74. In 1916 the loss of Anishinaabe forest allotments to corporations had prompted an investigation into the blood quantum of Indians selling their allotments to timber companies. Meyer, *White Earth Tragedy*, 170.

75. Henry Bascom Collins Papers, box 53: Archeological Expeditions, 1922–27; folder: Field Notes, Mississippi and Louisiana, 1926, National Anthropological Archives, Suitland MD.

76. Collins, "Anthropometric Observations on the Choctaw."

77. Swanton, *Source Material*, 4.

78. Swanton, *Source Material*, 4, 47, 49–50, 54–55, 100–103, 110, 126–27, 134–36, 139, 153–54, 158, 169, 186–87, 198–99, 217–18, 224–26, 238–39.

79. There are few reports of Klan interactions with American Indians in the Southeast. The most infamous occurred in 1958 when the Lumbee Indians of Roberson County, North Carolina, routed a Klan rally outside the town of Maxton. See Oakley, *Keeping the Circle*, 76–77. Oakley skillfully unpacks simplistic and racist coverage of the event in "'When Carolina Indians Went on the Warpath.'"

80. "What We Think of the Ku Klux Klan," *Neshoba County Democrat*, January 4, 1923, 1. References to the attacks on Rand for the editorial are found in Andrew Gibson, "To My Fellow Citizens of Neshoba County," January 18, 1923, 4; "A. DeWeese Writes Letter on Klan Speech," January 18, 1923, 1; and "Unfortunate Sermon," also in *Jackson Daily News*, March 29, 1923, 1. Refusing to be intimidated, Rand continued criticizing the Klan: "The Weakening of the K.K.K.," September 4, 1924, 1; "The Kamelia," September 16, 1923, 1; "Many Visitors Attend Klan Celebration on Tuesday Evening," October 30, 1924, 1, all in *Neshoba County Democrat*.

81. Rand remarked that preachers played a very prominent role in the KKK. Rand, *Ink*, 325. Nancy MacLean's study of the Klan in Athens, Georgia, found a similar situation. MacLean, *Behind the Mask of Chivalry*, 15.

82. In the Mississippi Delta, the Klan saw to it that Catholics were fired, their businesses embargoed, and their election to public office blocked. Percy, *Lanterns on the Levee*, 234.

83. Interview with Baxter York, April 8, 1974, Southeastern Indian Oral History Project, Neshoba County Library, Philadelphia MS.

84. York paraphrased McKinley's comments in his interview. Interview with Baxter York, April 8, 1974, 4.

85. McKinley to Sells, September 22, 1920, CCF: 134-104702-1920, BIA, NARA-DC.

86. Mallard to Sells, April 24, 1918, CCF: 800-37509-1918, BIA, NARA-DC.

87. Langford, "Holy Rosary Indian Mission," 117.

88. Sells to McKinley, February 9, 1920, CCF: 816.1-11382-1920, BIA, NARA-DC.

89. Father Ahern to Rev. John E. Gunn, Bishop of Natchez, July 17, 1919; Father Ketchum to Gunn, July 29, 1919, BCIM Records, reel 92.

90. Ahern to Gunn, July 17, 1919; Ketchum to Gunn, July 29, 1919, BCIM Records, reel 92.

91. J. D. Taylor to Ross Collins, October 31, 1921, box 3, folder 3, Ross Collins Papers; Mallard to Cato Sells, April 24, 1918, CCF: 800-37509, BIA, NARA-DC.

92. MacLean, *Behind the Mask*, 15, and Feldman, *Politics, Society, and the Klan*, ch. 7, argue that opposition to the Klan in other locations came from the upper class-

es. For Neshoba County, see Mars, *Witness*, 15; Rand, *Ink*, 322; "A. DeWeese Writes Letter on Klan Speech," *Neshoba County Democrat*, January 18, 1923, 1.

93. Mars, *Witness*, 8–9, 15, 35.

94. Testimony of Mr. J. H. Hester and Mr. J. C. Garrett, in Roe Cloud Report, 30–31.

95. "A. DeWeese Writes Letter on Klan Speech," January 18, 1923, *Neshoba County Democrat*, 1. Information on his business is found in Yates and Rideout, *Red Clay Hills*, 203–4.

96. *Neshoba County Democrat*: "A. DeWeese Writes Letter on Klan Speech," January 18, 1923, 1; Andrew Gibson, "To My Fellow Citizens of Neshoba County," January 18, 1923, 4.

97. Gibson, "To My Fellow Citizens of Neshoba County."

98. Rand, *Ink*, 178–79, 269.

99. Rand, *Ink*, 112–13, 264–65; Yates and Rideout, *Red Clay Hills*, 211.

100. Rand, *Ink*, 264–79. Mars described the Neshoba County she grew up in as "controlled by the leading citizens—doctors, merchants, large landowners, and the directors in the two banks." Mars, *Witness*, 40.

101. *Neshoba County Democrat*: Gibson, "To My Fellow Citizens"; "A. DeWeese Writes Letter on Klan"; "Unfortunate Sermon," March 29, 1923, 1.

102. "Neshoba County Mississippi," ccf: 806-29982-1929, bia, nara-dc.

103. This concern was similar to anti-Klan campaigns elsewhere in the South. MacLean, *Behind the Mask*, 15; Feldman, *Politics, Society, and the Klan*, ch. 7.

104. Needing African American laborers, Delta planters such as Percy and Williams preferred to maintain racial control with the unspoken threat of violence rather than actual violence. Chalmers, *Hooded Americanism*, 68–69. Williams's papers contain no references to his work with Indians, but Dickson, in *An Old-Fashioned Senator*, discusses his patrician attitudes toward his constituents.

105. Rice, *Ku Klux Klan*, 48–49; Rand, *Ink*, 331.

106. The Klan continued to operate but at a much lower profile. Rice, *Ku Klux Klan*, 13, 48–49; Rand, *Ink*, 331; "The Weakening of the Klan," *Neshoba County Democrat*, December 8, 1927, 1.

107. Mars, *Witness*, 29–30; "DeWeese Picnic Great Event," July 12, 1923, *Neshoba County Democrat*.

108. Fields, "Ideology and Race," 143–78.

109. Roe Cloud Report, 15.

110. Stevens Report, July 5–8, 1923.

111. McKinley to cia, September 5, 1923, in Stevens Report, July 5–8, 1923.

112. E. B. Merritt to McKinley, October 6, 1924, in Stevens Report, July 5–8, 1923.

113. James E. Arnold to Hon. Secretary of the Interior, April 17, 1918; Merritt to Arnold, May 8, 1918; Arnold to Hon. Secretary of the Interior, April 17, 1918, ccf: 800-35654-1918, bia, nara-dc; Mrs. J. E. Arnold to Mrs. Woodrow Wilson, August 25, 1917, ccf: 806-81856-1917, bia, nara-dc.

114. The Home Mission Board of the Southern Baptist Convention helped the Arnolds establish a mission in 1920, but the couple's practice of letting Choctaws live on their small farm appeared to some to encourage "indolence," and they lost their funding. Farr, *Religious Assimilation*, 36–37; Mrs. Arnold to Mr. McLemore, Union MS, July 9, 1920; W. W. Venable to Cato Sells, July 16, 1920, CCF: 800-60719-1920, BIA, NARA-DC. For the McLemore family, see the Federal Writer's Project, *Mississippi: A Guide to the Magnolia State*, 228–31. Merritt to W. W. Venable, July 28, 1920, CCF: 800-60719-1920, BIA, NARA-DC.

115. McKinley to Sells, April 28, 1918, CCF: 806-27538-1918, BIA, NARA-DC; McKinley to Sells, September 21, 1919, CCF: 816.1-81570-1919, BIA, NARA-DC.

116. McLemore to Carter, n.d.; Carter to Harvey B. Peairs, Chief Supervisor in Charge of Education, n.d., Carter Inspection, January 1923.

117. For Collins's early career, see Kirwan, *Revolt of the Rednecks*. Ross Collins's campaign literature from the 1940s, on file in the MDAH, contains summaries of his accomplishments in public office. See "Ross Collins Is the People's Candidate for U.S. Senator," http://mdah.state.ms.us/arrec/digital_archives/series/broadsides /detail/116980-broadside-01.jpg and 116980-broadside-02.jpg.

118. The papers of the lawsuit are found in several boxes in the Ross Collins Papers. For the ad and letters, see box 3, folder 3.

119. For the Arnolds' accusations, see box 2, folder 4, Ross Collins Papers.

120. Plea of the Defendant, James Arnold v. Ross A. Collins, Thomas J. Scott, and F. J. McKinley, box 3, folder 3, Ross Collins Papers.

121. Merritt to McKinley, April 12, 1923, box 3, folder 3, Ross Collins Papers.

122. The debate over Arnold's ancestry centered on phenotypical markers of race. During a campaign debate in Neshoba County, for example, Mrs. Arnold asked James's sister to take down her hair and show everyone how straight it was. She obliged but there is no record of what her hair looked like. Rand to Collins, July 10, 1940; Collins to Rand, July 16, 1940, box 3, folder 5, Ross Collins Papers.

123. Exhibit A: Last Will and Testament of James Arnold, May 11, 1870, box 2, folder 1, Ross Collins Papers.

124. Collins to McKinley, April 4, 1923, box 3, folder 3, Ross Collins Papers.

125. Collins to Dr. H. B. Watkins, Noxapater MS, January 17, 1924, box 3, folder 1, Ross Collins Papers.

126. For Arnold's appeal, see John Spurgeon, Managing Editor, *Washington Post*, to Collins, April 1, 1924, box 3, folder 3, Ross Collins Papers. For his departure from Union, see Farr, *Religious Assimilation*, 37.

127. Gaston Cooper, Sebastopol MS, to Brother Arnold, September 1, 1935; Arnold to Collier, September 3, 1935; Collier to Arnold, September 23, 1935, CCF: 916-48942-1935, BIA, NARA-DC.

128. Arnold to the Honorable Secretary of the Interior, October 15, 1940, CCF: 723-69166-1940, BIA, NARA-DC.

129. Arnold to Secretary of the Interior, October 15, 1940; D. E. Murphy to Arnold, October 28, 1940, CCF: 723-69166-1940, BIA, NARA-DC.

130. Lindquist Report, March 1929, Section 2, CCF: 150-9490-1929, BIA, NARA-DC.

131. Harry M. Carter, Agency Clerk, to Enochs, October 9, 1931, in Roe Cloud Report, 15.

132. Trowbridge Report, 7–10, May 9, 1931, CCF: 150-29352-1931, BIA, NARA-DC.

5. Depression and Indian New Deal

1. Boll weevils and drought sunk cotton prices in the early 1930s. Emmerich, "Collapse and Recovery," 94, 115–19.

2. Federal Writers' Project, *Mississippi: A Guide to the Magnolia State*, 225; SAR, 1935, Section 2, Agricultural Development, CCF: 919-70945-1938, BIA, NARA-DC.

3. Yates and Rideout, *Red Clay Hills of Neshoba*, 203–7.

4. Most of these projects benefited community leaders. Willie Allen, Robert Henry, John Mingo, Tom Stoliby, Jim Henry, Cephus Thompson, Bob Anderson, Williston and Will Billy, Pat Chitto, Paul Farve, Irving and Mike Sockey, Simpson Tubby, Necie York, and Willie Solomon all got home improvements. Robert J. Enochs, Choctaw Superintendent, SAR, 1930, 11, M101, roll 20, BIA, NARA-DC.

5. Roy McLeed, "Indians in Jones County, Sandersville Reservation," WPA Files, Jones County, box 10727, folder: Indians, Mississippi, MDAH.

6. McCain, "Triumph of Democracy," and Emmerich, "Collapse and Recovery," in McLemore, *History of Mississippi*, 2:94 and 104–8.

7. Earl Given, Agency Farmer, "Farm Agent Annual Report, Carthage District, 1933," 3. Photographs accompanying T. J. Scott's "Annual Report of Division of Extension and Industry" showed the Indians on this project. CCF: 031-00-1933, BIA, NARA-DC.

8. Archie C. Hector, Choctaw Superintendent, to John Collier, CIA, November 18, 1935, Collier to Hector, November 22, 1935 RG 75, CCC—Indian Division, Entry 1000, General Records files, box 57, Choctaw, BIA, NARA-DC; Hector to CIA, November 23, 1934; Harvey K. Meyer, Choctaw Superintendent, to CIA, February 14, 1939; Meyer to CIA, February 17, 1939; Meyer to CIA, May 4, 1939; D. E. Murphy, Director, Indian Division, CCC, to H. K. Meyer, May 24, 1939, CCC—Indian Division, Entry 1001, Records Concerning Enrollee Programs, 1937–42, box 7-PI-163, Choctaw, file 10646-1939, BIA, NARA-DC; Hector to Collier, March 14, 1934, CCF: 150-54948-1933, BIA, NARA-DC.

9. McMullen to CIA, November 4, 1941, CCF: 720-50405-1941, BIA, NARA-DC.

10. McMullen to CIA, August 17, 1940, April 17, 1941, October 21, 1941, and January 12, 1942, CCC—Indian Division, Entry 1001.

11. McMullen to CIA, June 23, 1942, CCC—Indian Division, Entry 1001.

12. See the "Industries" sections of the Superintendents' Annual Reports for the decade of the 1930s, M101, roll 20, Records of the Office of the Commissioner of Indian Affairs, BIA, NARA-DC. For specific reports of women in adult education classes, see "Memorandum Left With Supt. A.C. Hector, Choctaw Agency, 1934," CCF: 917-11708-1934, BIA, NARA-DC; "Report of the Department of Home Economics, Choctaw Agency, 1935," CCF: 031-422-88-1935; "Annual Report of the Community Teacher, 1939–1940," 1, CCF: 031-52861-1940, BIA, NARA-DC.

13. "Mississippi Choctaw Indian Agency, Farm Report, Carthage District, 1932," 4, CCF: 031-00-1932, BIA, NARA-DC; "Home Economics Report of the Standing Pine School for 1939–1940," 1, CCF: 031-52861-1940, BIA, NARA-DC.

14. "Report of the Nutrition Institute, by Misses Brewer and O'Quinn" (field nurse and home economist respectively), Home Economics Conference, Choctaw Agency, August 30–September 1, 1939, 3, CCF: 031-52861-1940, BIA, NARA-DC.

15. Scott to Collier, February 8, 1935, CCF: 919-70945-1938, BIA, NARA-DC.

16. Home Extension Report, 1943, CCF: 031-3657-1944, BIA, NARA-DC.

17. "Annual Report of the Community Teacher, 1939–1940," n.d., 2–3; "Home Economics Report of the Bogue Homa School for 1939–1940," 3, CCF: 031-52861-1940, BIA, NARA-DC.

18. "Annual Report of the Community Teacher, 1939–1940," n.d., 3, CCF: 031-52861-1940, BIA, NARA-DC. Preparation of items for fairs was noted in virtually every report in this large folder.

19. "Home Economics Report of the Bogue Homa School for 1939–1940," 1; "Home Economics Report of the Conehatta School for 1939–1940," 1; "Home Economics Report of the Standing Pine School for 1939–1940," 2, CCF: 031-52861-1940, BIA, NARA-DC.

20. Jennings, Beggs, and Caldwell, "A Study of the Social and Economic Conditions of Choctaw Indians in MS in Relation to the Educational Programs," May 1945, 17, CCF: 806-38014-1932, BIA, NARA-DC. It could be that women were producing baskets without agency help or that women were teaching each other basket weaving.

21. Meyer to CIA, September 6, 1939; McMullen to CIA, August 7, 1940; McMullen to CIA, October 21, 1940, CCC—Indian Division; Entry 1001; interview with B. F. McIntosh, Agency Farmer, "Exhibit X," Roe Cloud Report, September 22, 1931, 4, CCF: 150-29352-1931, BIA, NARA-DC.

22. Money from the Public Works Administration and a state gasoline tax financed the roads. Emmerich, "Collapse and Recovery," 114–16.

23. *Mississippi: A Guide to the Magnolia State*, 466–67.

24. *Mississippi: A Guide to the Magnolia State*, first quotation on p. 49, second quotation on p. 59.

25. *Mississippi: A Guide to the Magnolia State*, 45–59, 70–71, 227, 464–68.

26. For the WPA Folklore Project, see http://lcweb2.loc.gov/wpaintro/wpahome .html (accessed July 17, 2006). The Mississippi Folklore Project is found in Series 447: Historical Research Material, Mississippi Department of Archives and History (MDAH), Jackson MS. Like African Americans, Indians have a separate box, 10538, indicating their segregated status.

27. WPA Files, Neshoba County: box 10773, Newton and Noxubee Counties: box 10776, Jones County: box 10727, folder: Assignment Nine: Indians, MDAH.

28. WPA Files, Leake County: box 10744, Winston County: box 10788, Jones County: box 10727, Kemper County: box 10731, Newton and Noxubee Counties: box 10776, Neshoba County: box 10773, Pearl River: box 10788, Harrison County: box 10699, Hancock County: box 10697, folder: Assignment Nine: Indians, MDAH.

29. Dunbar Rowland, Director of MDAH, to Brown Williams, Department of Highways, September 30, 1935; Williams to Munch Luke, October 2, 1935, in Fabian Fraser Papers (z789f), MDAH. This entire collection is contained in one folder.

30. Hector to CIA, October 11, 1935; H. W. Dorsey, Administrative Assistant to the Secretary, Smithsonian Institution, November 1935, Fraser Papers.

31. Moreau B. Chambers, Curator of the State Archives, to Fabian Fraser, November 25, 1935; Chambers to Fraser, March 5, 1936, Fraser Papers.

32. Chambers to Fraser, December 20, 1935, February 7, 1936, and May 16, 1936, Fraser Papers.

33. Chambers to Fraser, July 2, 1936, Fraser Papers.

34. Chambers to Mr. T. J. Bolster, Director, District No. 2, WPA, Meridian MS, August 10, 1936, Fraser Papers.

35. In 1939 the Greenville chamber of commerce in nearby Washington County wrote the commissioner of Indian affairs for permission to place some Choctaws on the mounds in their county as a tourist exhibit. The commissioner replied that in order to prevent the "exploitation" of the Choctaws, they had to draw up a contract with specific instructions for the treatment of Indians. The project then fell through. Willard L. McIlwain, Greenville MS, to Collier, September 28, 1939; William Zimmerman Jr., Assistant Commissioner of Indian Affairs, to McIlwain, November 2, 1939, CCF: 042-63719-1939, BIA, NARA-DC.

36. Enochs, SAR, 1931, Industry, unpaginated, M101, roll 20; Hector to Collier, September 12, 1934, on the need for direct relief funds, CCF: 919-70945-38, BIA, NARA-DC.

37. Given, "Farm Agent Annual Report 1933, Carthage District," CCF: 031-00-1933, BIA, NARA-DC.

38. Hector to Superintendent of Indian Affairs, July 30, 1937, CCC—Indian Division, Entry 1000; McMullen to CIA, November 4, 1941, and April 22, 1942, Advance Estimate for Direct Relief Funds for Fiscal Year 1944, CCF: 720-50405-1941, BIA, NARA-DC.

39. Roe Cloud Report, 2–4.

40. W. H. Hodge to Senator Pat Harrison, May 5, 1930, in Trowbridge Report, May 9, 1931, CCF: 150-29352-1931, BIA, NARA-DC.

41. Trowbridge to Charles J. Rhodes, CIA, May 8, 1931, Trowbridge Report.

42. "T. J. Scott, Interview, October 6, 1931," Roe Cloud Report, 2.

43. Enochs, SAR, 1932, Agriculture, unpaginated, M 1011, roll 20.

44. For Luckett Anderson and Willie Sam, Scott coordinated timber sales and paid taxes and funeral expenses. For Lonnie Scott, who inherited a large estate in Oklahoma from her father, he acted as co-guardian, along with attorney E. S. Richardson, and administered her estate. Roe Cloud Report, 6–9.

45. "Report on Thomas Scott," Trowbridge Report, 9–11; "T. J. Scott, Interview," Roe Cloud Report, 7–9.

46. "Report on Thomas Scott," Trowbridge Report, 9–11; "T. J. Scott, Interview," Roe Cloud Report, 7–9.

47. "Report on Thomas Scott," Trowbridge Report, 9–11; "T. J. Scott, Interview," Roe Cloud Report, 7–9.

48. "T. J. Scott, Interview," Roe Cloud Report, 2.

49. "T. J. Scott, Interview," Roe Cloud Report, 8.

50. "T. J. Scott, Interview," Roe Cloud Report, 8.

51. Enochs, "Reply to the Report of C.R. Trowbridge, Field Representative, on the Choctaw Indian Agency—Mississippi," March 7, 1932, Roe Cloud Report.

52. Testimony of J. H. Hester, Exhibit "BB," Testimony of J. C. Garrett, Exhibit "L," Testimony of George Mars, Exhibit "U," Roe Cloud Report.

53. R. L. Callahan, Neshoba County Agent, to CIA, June 27, 1931; J. H. Lynch, Administrative Officer, Farmers' Seed Loan Office, Memphis TN, to CIA, April 7, 1931; W. McArthur, Philadelphia Drought Relief Committee, to J. H. Lynch, April 6, 1931. Mr. Cadenhead's letter was not filed, but an undated note written by Lynch acknowledged it. McKinley to Trowbridge, May 7, 1931, letters filed with Roe Cloud Report.

54. W. W. Kyzar to CIA, June 30, 1931, Roe Cloud Report.

55. Lamont Rowlands, Chairman, Mississippi Finance Committee, Republican National Committee, to Mr. Henry Roe Cloud, October 27, 1931, Exhibit "DD"; F. E. Leach, Mayor of Carthage, June 27, 1931, Roe Cloud Report.

56. Willie Jim and Billy Nicky testified that they preferred Enochs. For their and other Choctaws' testimony, see Exhibit "O": Edgar Tubby, Bob Henry, Cefus Thompson, Mrs. Necie York, Dick Tubby, John Anderson, Mrs. Simpson Tubby, Pat Chitto, Jim Henry, Robert Henry, Minnie Waiter, and Olmon Cumby, Roe Cloud Report.

57. Enochs to CIA, May 26, 1931; Testimony of Olmon Cumby, Exhibit "O," Roe Cloud Report.

58. C. R. Trowbridge to CIA, December 1, 1931, Roe Cloud Report," 18.

59. Roe Cloud castigated him for not conferring with state and county agricultural authorities, as Scott had done. Roe Cloud Report, 18; Trowbridge Report, 15.

60. Roe Cloud Report, 13, 2.

61. Roe Cloud Report, 13, 2.

62. The IRA has gotten mixed reviews from historians and Indian communities. Though it represented a noteworthy departure from forced assimilation, it was still carried out in a paternalistic manner that many Indians found insensitive to their indigenous political traditions. Indians accepted or rejected the IRA depending on their own political agendas. See Cobb and Fowler's summary of reaction to the IRA across tribes in *Beyond Red Power*, 109. For the Indian New Deal, see Philp, *Collier's Crusade*; Taylor, *New Deal and American Indian Tribalism*; Deloria and Lytle, *Nations Within*; Kelly, *Assault on Assimilation* and *Navajo Indians and Federal Indian Policy*; Parman, *Navajos and the New Deal*; Hauptman, *Iroquois and the New Deal*; Fowler, *Tribal Sovereignty*; and Biolsi, *Organizing the Lakota*.

63. For the text of the IRA, see http://www.cskt.org/gov/file/reorganizationact.pdf. Collier wrote articles for the popular press explaining his policy; these are also available on the web. See Collier, "A New Deal for the American Indian," *Literary Digest*,

April 7, 1938, 21, online: "A Bill of Rights for the Indians," http://historymatters.gmu
.edu/d/5059/ and "We Took Away Their Best Lands, Broke Treaties," in *Annual Report of the Secretary of the Interior for the Fiscal Year Ended June 30, 1938* (Washington DC, 1938), 209–11: http://historymatters.gmu.edu/d/5058.

64. Enochs to CIA, May 14, 1927, CCF: 100-98178-1922, BIA, NARA-DC.

65. Hector to Collier, March 14, 1934, CCF: 150-54948-1933. Ironically, when the majority of the TBC decided to do exactly that by forming a rival organization, Mrs. Starr did not join them in this organization. Hector to Collier, June 10, 1934, CCF: 150-54948-1933. BIA, NARA-DC.

66. Joe Chitto to Collier, April 30, 1934, CCF: 150-54948-1933, BIA, NARA-DC.

67. Collier to Joe Chitto, June 7, 1934, CCF: 150-54948-1933, BIA, NARA-DC.

68. E. T. Winston, Vice President of the Mississippi Choctaw Indian Welfare Association, to Collier, July 24, 1936, CCF: 150-54948-1933, BIA, NARA-DC.

69. Winston had become friends with Bilbo when as governor, Bilbo made Pontotoc the summer capital of the state and established his office there in the summer of 1930. Winston, *Story of Pontotoc*, pt. 2, 321. For the MCWA, see Winston to CIA, July 31, 1934, CCF:150-54948-1933, BIA, NARA-DC; Mississippi Choctaw Indian Federation (MCIF) to Honorable Senators Pat Harrison and Hubert D. Stevens and Congressmen Ross Collins, Wall Doxey, W. M. Whittington, John E. Rankin, Jeff Busby, William M. Colmer, and Russell Elizey, May 19, 1934, CCF: 068-9544A-1936, BIA, NARA-DC; Hector to CIA, August 21, 1934, CCF: 150-54948-1933, BIA, NARA-DC. Quotation from E. T. Winston, "Choctaws Turn to Friends Among Pale Faces in Effort to Recapture Old Glories," *Memphis Commercial Appeal*, August 21, 1934.

70. MCIF to Senators Harrison and Stevens and Congressmen Collins, Doxey, Whittington, Rankin, Busby, Colmer, and Elizey, May 19, 1934, CCF: 068-9544A-1936, BIA, NARA-DC.

71. Hector to Collier, June 10, 1934; Collier to Scott, July 30, 1934, CCF: 150-54948-1933, BIA, NARA-DC.

72. Collier to Tribal Business Committee, July 30, 1934, CCF: 150-54948-1933, BIA, NARA-DC.

73. Collier to Joe Chitto, July 30, 1934, CCF: 150-54948-1933, BIA, NARA-DC. The petition of July 14, 1934 was filed with the letter to Joe Chitto.

74. Collier to Tribal Business Committee, Collier to Hector, and Collier to Joe Chitto, all July 30, 1934, CCF: 150-54948-1933, BIA, NARA-DC.

75. Joe Chitto to Collier, August 16, 1934, CCF: 150-54948-1933, BIA, NARA-DC.

76. Joe Chitto to Collier, August 16, 1934, CCF: 150-54948-1933, BIA, NARA-DC.

77. Joe Chitto to Hector, August 14, 1934, CCF: 150-54948-1933, BIA, NARA-DC.

78. The Choctaws' fluid conceptions of power and government are skillfully analyzed in O'Brien's *Choctaws in a Revolutionary Age*.

79. Joe Chitto to Collier, August 16, 1934, CCF: 150-54948-1933, BIA, NARA-DC.

80. Joe Chitto to Collier, August 16, 1934, CCF: 150-54948-1933, BIA, NARA-DC.

81. Earl Richardson to Collier, September 11, 1934, CCF: 150-54948-1933, BIA, NARA-DC.

82. Report of Edna Groves, Supervisor of Home Economics, February 20–March 20, 1936, CCF: 800-4313-1951, BIA, NARA-DC.

83. Swanton, *Source Material*, 96–102; Debo, *Rise and Fall*, 21. For Choctaw political ranking, see O'Brien, *Choctaws in a Revolutionary Age*.

84. Constitution of the Mississippi Choctaw Indian Federation (MCIF), 1934, Article II, Section 2, CCF: 068-9544A-36, BIA, NARA-DC.

85. Constitution of the MCIF, 1934, Article V, Sections 1 and 2, CCF: 068-9544A-36, BIA, NARA-DC.

86. Lambert, *Choctaw Nation*, 30.

87. Constitution of the MCIF, 1934, Article VII, CCF: 068-9544A-36, BIA, NARA-DC.

88. Joe Chitto to Collier, August 20, 1934, CCF: 150-54948-1933, BIA, NARA-DC.

89. Joe Chitto to Collier, August 20, 1934, CCF: 150-54948-1933, BIA, NARA-DC.

90. Winston was a collector of Indian artifacts, historian of the Chickasaws, and tireless champion of the Choctaws. See the biographical sketch of him in the WPA's "History of Pontotoc County," pt. 2, 266–70, and pt. 3, 142–46, in the Pontotoc County Library, Pontotoc MS.

91. Winston to Collier, July 31, 1934, CCF: 150-54948-1933, BIA, NARA-DC.

92. Collier to Winston, August 17, 1934, CCF: 150-54948-1933, BIA, NARA-DC.

93. Hector to Collier, August 21, 1934; see Hector to Shippe, Director of Extension Services, December 1, 1934, for the mention of the congressman who attended the ceremony. All in CCF: 150-54948-1933, BIA, NARA-DC.

94. Hector to Collier, August 21, 1934, CCF: 150-54948-1933, BIA, NARA-DC.

95. Clipping, "Choctaw Lovers of Land: Legend Surrounds Start," *Daily Jackson News*, September 10, 1934, CCF: 150-54948-1933, BIA, NARA-DC. For the economic aspects of the Indian New Deal, see Philp's introduction to *Indian Self-Rule*, 17.

96. R. L. Breland, "The Story of Neshoba," *Neshoba County Democrat*, February 1, 1935, Vertical Files: Indians, Neshoba County Library, Philadelphia MS.

97. Clipping, "Choctaws Turn to Friends among Pale Faces in Effort to Recapture Old Glories," unidentified newspaper, n.d., CCF: 150-54948-1933, BIA, NARA-DC.

98. Clipping, "Choctaws Turn to Friends among Pale Faces," CCF: 150-54948-1933, BIA, NARA-DC.

99. Clippings, "Choctaws Turn to Friends among Pale Faces," and "Mississippi Association Tries to Restore Rights of Choctaw Nation," unidentified newspaper, n.d., CCF: 150-54948-1933, BIA, NARA-DC.

100. Winston quoted in "Heap Big Injuns," *Jackson Daily News*, n.d., clipping in box 997, folder 3, Theodore G. Bilbo Papers, McCain Library and Archives, University of Southern Mississippi, Hattiesburg.

101. Clipping, "Choctaw Lovers of Land," *Daily Jackson News*, September 10, 1934, CCF: 150-54948-1933, BIA, NARA-DC.

102. Clipping, "State Indian Nation Forms," *Meridian Star*, n.d., CCF: 150-54948-1933, BIA, NARA-DC.

103. Winston to Collier, July 31, 1934, CCF: 150-54948-1933, BIA, NARA-DC.

104. Constitution of the Mississippi Choctaw Welfare Association, Article 3, CCF: 150-54948-1934, BIA, NARA-DC.

105. Peterson, "Mississippi Band of Choctaw Indians," 13–14.

106. Winston to Collier, August 20, 1934, CCF: 150-54948-1933, BIA, NARA-DC.

107. "Choctaw Lovers of Land," *Daily Jackson News*, September 10, 1934, CCF: 150-54948-1933, BIA, NARA-DC.

108. E. T. Winston to Collier, November 13, 1935, and February 24, 1936, CCF: 150-54948-1933, BIA, NARA-DC.

109. For an analysis of the impact of the New Deal in the South, see Cobb and Namorato, *New Deal and the South*, and Green, *New Deal and Beyond*.

110. For problems with tenants, see Daniel, "Federal Farm Policy and the End of an Agrarian Way of Life," 397–406. For the ways in which the New Deal hastened the growth of agribusiness, see Fite, *Cotton Fields No More*, and Cobb, *Industrialization and Southern Society*. For information on the New Deal and social welfare policy across the South, see the essays in Green, *New Deal and Beyond*.

111. Winston to Collier, July 31, 1934, CCF: 150-54948-1933, BIA, NARA-DC.

112. Memorandum to Extension, August 29, 1934, unsigned, CCF: 150-54948-1933, BIA, NARA-DC.

113. Hector to Collier, August 7, 1934, CCF: 150-54948-1933, BIA, NARA-DC.

114. Hector to Collier, August 20, 1934, CCF: 150-54948-1933, BIA, NARA-DC.

115. Joe Chitto to Hector, August 14, 1934, Hector to Collier, August 20, 1934, CCF: 150-54948-1933, BIA, NARA-DC.

116. Hector to Collier, June 10, 7, 20, and August 21, September 21 and 25, 1934; Hector to Mr. Shippe, Director of Extension Work, December 1, 1934, CCF: 150-54948-1933, BIA, NARA-DC.

117. Hector to Collier, April 1, 1935, CCF: 150-54948-1933, BIA, NARA-DC.

118. Collier to E. T. Winston, February 21, 1936, CCF: 150-54948-1933, BIA, NARA-DC.

119. Hector to CIA, April 1, 1935, CCF: 150-54948-1933, BIA, NARA-DC. If Joe Chitto was indeed behind this, he was unaware that abstaining from voting registered as a yes vote.

120. Rev. Ed W. Willis, Chief, MCIF, to Winston, September 30, 1935, Jennings to Collier, June 26, 1936, CCF: 150-54948-1933, BIA, NARA-DC.

121. Hector to Collier, December 29, 1934, CCF: 150-54948-1933, BIA, NARA-DC.

122. Hector to Collier, December 29, 1934, CCF: 150-54948-1933, BIA, NARA-DC.

123. On the continued activities of the MCIF, see Winston to CIA, November 13, 1935, and February 24, 1936; Collier to Winston, February 21, 1936, CCF: 150-54948-1933, BIA, NARA-DC.

124. Memo of Byrd Issac, Secretary, Tribal Business Council (TBC), April 15, 1934, CCF: 057-21159-1936, BIA, NARA-DC.

125. For the gradual diminishment of the Pearl River strike, see Hector to Collier, June 18, 1935, CCF: 134-48712-33, BIA, NARA-DC.

126. Henry Jim et al. to Senators Theodore Bilbo and Pat Harrison and Congressmen Bill Colmer and Albert Dunn, June 4, 1935, CCF: 134-48712-33, BIA, NARA-DC. For the Bogue Homa school strike, see S. Keyzer, teacher at Bogue Homa Day School, to Hector, June 11, 1935, CCF: 134-48712-33, BIA, NARA-DC.

127. Henry Jim et al. to Senators Bilbo and Harrison and Congressmen Colmer and Dunn, June 4, 1935; Colmer to Collier, June 8, 1935; Colmer to Collier, June 8, 1935, CCF: 134-48712-33, BIA, NARA-DC. Winston frequently carbon-copied his correspondence with the OIA to all these individuals.

128. Hector to Shippe, December 1, 1934, CCF: 150-54948-1933, BIA, NARA-DC. These Choctaws told WPA interviewer Frances Griffith that their strike had forced the Indian Service to act on this matter. WPA Files, Jones County: box 19727, folder: Assignment Nine: Indians, MDAH.

129. Jennings to Collier, June 26, 1936, CCF: 150-54948-1933, BIA, NARA-DC.

130. Jennings to Collier, September 21, 1936, CCF: 150-54948-1933, BIA, NARA-DC.

131. For an analysis of this policy, see Spruhan, "Indian as Race/Indian as Political Status."

132. Jennings to Collier, September 21, 1936, CCF: 150-54948-1933, BIA, NARA-DC.

133. Jennings and Westwood to Collier, September 21, 1936, CCF: 150-54948-1933, BIA, NARA-DC.

134. Willis to Bilbo, May 3, 1940, box 967, folder, 20, Bilbo Papers.

135. Nathan Margold, Solicitor, Department of the Interior, Memorandum for the Office of Indian Affairs, August 31, 1936, Records of the Indian Claims Commission, RG 279, box 620 NARA-DC.

136. The Act of June 21, 1939, shifting the status of the reimbursable farms to trust lands, is mentioned in "Proclamation," Oscar Chapman, Assistant Secretary, Department of the Interior, December 4, 1944, CCF: 931-1-10154-1948, BIA, NARA-DC.

137. Chapman, "Proclamation," CCF: 931-1-10154-1948, BIA, NARA-DC. On oil interests, see Walter V. Woehlke to Joe Jennings, April 18, 1944; Reeves to Jennings, April 24, 1944; Jennings to McMullen, August 21, 1944; McMullen to CIA, May 4, 1945; Chapman to McMullen, May 22, 1945, CCF: 066-9545-1936, BIA, NARA-DC; Interview with Baxter York, July 5, 1973, Southeastern Indian Oral History Project, Neshoba County Library, Philadelphia MS.

138. McMullen to CIA, February 15, 1944, CCF: 066-9545-1936, BIA, NARA-DC; McMullen to CIA, May 4, 1945, 068-9544A-1936, BIA, NARA-DC.

139. *Constitution and By-Laws of the Mississippi Band of Choctaw Indians*, Article III, Entry 327, box 43, file: Mississippi Band of Choctaw Indians, FCTA, NARA-SW.

140. Five of the nine had opposed Hector. Choctaw Tribal Council to CIA, January 5, 1945, CCF: 066-9544-1936, BIA, NARA-DC.

141. Jackson, Issac, et al., to Honorable Secretary of the Interior, Secretary of the Treasury, and Treasurer of the United States, October 10, 1933, RG 279, box 620, Records of the Indian Claims Commission, NARA-DC.

142. Jackson, Issac et al. to Honorable Secretary of the Interior, Secretary of the Treasury, and Treasurer of the United States, October 10, 1933, 7–9.

143. Jackson, Issac et al. to Honorable Secretary of the Interior, Secretary of the Treasury, and Treasurer of the United States, October 10, 1933, 14–15.

144. Collier to Thomas Moore and Odie Moore, September 18, 1934, RG 279, box 620, Records of the Indian Claims Commission, NARA-DC.

145. Correspondence on the claim, Senate Bill 1939, box 997, folder, 4, Bilbo Papers.

146. Pat Chitto to Collier, March 18 and March 23, 1935; Collier to Pat Chitto, April 12, 1935, CCF: 059-16319-1935, BIA, NARA-DC.

147. Collier to Pat Chitto, April 12, 1935, CCF: 059-16319-1935. BIA, NARA-DC.

148. Collier to Pat Chitto, April 12, 1935, CCF: 059-16319-1935, BIA, NARA-DC; U.S. Senate, "Claims of the Choctaw Indians of Mississippi, May 13, 1935," S. Rep. 781, 74th Cong., 1st sess.; U.S. House, "Choctaw Indians of Mississippi, April 15, 1936," H. Rep. 2415, 74th Cong, 2nd sess.

149. "An Act Conferring Jurisdiction on the Court of Claims to Hear and Determine the Claims of the Choctaws of the State of Mississippi," S. 1478, box 997, folder, 3, Bilbo Papers; Memorandum for the Assistant to the Attorney General Joseph B. Keenan, February 17, 1938, 6, RG 279, box 620, Records of the Indian Claims Commission, NARA-DC.

150. "Speech of Theodore Bilbo to the Committee on Indian Affairs, May 11, 1939," 3, typescript, box 997, folder, 4, Bilbo Papers.

151. "Testimony of Ross A. Collins Before the Subcommittee on Indian Affairs, March 21, 1939," 5–7; "Testimony of William E. Richardson Before the Subcommittee on Indian Affairs, March 21, 1939," 8–39; "Testimony of Thomas E. Rhodes, Before the Subcommittee on Indian Affairs, March 28, 1939," 41–54, box 997, folder, 3, Bilbo Papers.

152. "Opinion of the Committee," 67, copy of the *Congressional Record*, box 997, folder 3, Bilbo Papers.

153. Memorandum for the Assistant to the Attorney General Joseph B. Keenan, February 17, 1938, RG 279, box 620, Records of the Indian Claims Commission, NARA-DC.

154. This decision is recorded in two documents, S. Rep. 997, 75th Cong., 1st sess., July 22, 1937, and H. Rep. 2233, 75th Cong., 3rd sess., April 26, 1938, box 997, folder, 1, Bilbo Papers; Typescript of the president's veto message copied from the *Congressional Record*, vol. 83, no. 130, July 5, 1938, p. 13371, box 997, folder 1, Bilbo Papers.

155. "Resolution of the Choctaw Indians of the State [*sic*] of Mississippi, Alabama, and Louisiana," RG 279, box 618, Records of the Indian Claims Commission, NARA-DC.

156. Greek L. Rice, Attorney General of Mississippi, to Bilbo, n.d., 14, box 997, folder 3, Bilbo Papers. The Central Classified Files (CCF)–Choctaw, BIA, NARA-DC, contain many letters lobbying for these bills in Entry 121: 030-040, Statistics.

157. For passage of the bill in both committees in 1942, see Bilbo to Mrs. Armand Srinson, Greenwood MS, June 30, 1942, box 977, folder 1, Bilbo Papers. For its failure to move after the committee approved it, see the letters of J. M. Stewart, Director of Lands, BIA, to numerous constituents over 1940, CCF: 013-53104-1940, BIA, NARA-DC.

158. McMullen to CIA, December 4, 1950, RG 279, Docket 52, box 620, Records of the Indian Claims Commission, NARA-DC. Nate Williamson, Attorney at Law, Meridian, to Theodore Bilbo, June 11, 1943, references the Club in this lobbying effort, box 997, folder 1; Willis to Bilbo, June 10, 1940, box 996, folder, 1, Bilbo Papers.

159. Bilbo to Williamson, June 14, 1943, box 997, folder 1, Bilbo Papers.

160. Oscar Chapman, Assistant Secretary of the Interior, Memorandum to the Commissioner of Indian Affairs, May 22, 1944, CCF: 068-9544A-1936, BIA, NARA-DC.

161. The state archives in Jackson have no records of the MCWA, nor does the Pontotoc County Library or Pontotoc County Historical Society. E. T. Winston's grandson Toby Winston had not heard of the MCWA. Interview with Toby Winston, February 14, 2008, in Winston's home, Pontotoc MS.

162. Quotation from "Choctaw Lovers of Land," *Daily Jackson News*, September 10, 1934, CCF: 150-54948-1933, BIA, NARA-DC.

6. Choctaw Tribal Council

1. The terms "bureau" and "office" were used interchangeably in reference to the Indian Service throughout the nineteenth and twentieth centuries. The official letterhead of the Indian Service read "Office of Indian Affairs" until 1947, when the name was changed to Bureau of Indian Affairs. Prucha, *Great Father*, 1227–29.

2. In "Building toward Self-Determination," Peter Iverson suggested that the threat of termination sometimes strengthened Indian institutions and built alliances with state and local officials. The best full-length studies of tribal councils in the mid-twentieth century certainly make this point. See Parman, *Navajos and the New Deal*; Hauptman, *Iroquois and the New Deal*; Fowler, *Arapahoe Politics*; Biolsi, *Organizing the Lakota*; Rosier, *Rebirth of the Blackfoot Nation*.

3. On termination, see Fixico, *Termination and Relocation*, and Philp, *Termination Revisited*.

4. For World War II and Indians, see Bernstein, *American Indians and World War II*.

5. MBCI, *Chahta Hapia Hoke*, 50–51; Archie H. McMullen, Choctaw Superintendent, to CIA, March 22, 1946, CCF: 891-23048-1946, BIA, NARA-DC; McMullen, "A Brief History of the Mississippi Band of Choctaw Indians, Prepared in 1954," 10, Entry 327, box 43, file: Mississippi Choctaw History, FCTA, NARA-SW.

6. This trend was seen across the United States. Extension Report, January 1–December 31, 1943, 9, CCF: 031-3657-1944, BIA, NARA-DC.

7. The Choctaws were not alone in needing this type of assistance. In rural Mississippi most small farmers borrowed money to make their crops.

8. The other agencies were the Farm Security Administration and the Farm Credit Administrations. Extension Reports, January 1–December 31, 1940, CCF: 031-1733-1940; 1941, CCF: 031-3682-1942; 1943, CCF: 031-3657-1944; 1945, CCF: 031-5544-1946; 1946, CCF: 031-2436-1947, all in BIA, NARA-DC.

9. Extension Report, January 1–December 31, 1945, 1, CCF: 031-5544-1946, BIA, NARA-DC.

10. Jennings, Beggs, and Caldwell, "Study of the Social and Economic Condition of the Choctaw Indians in Mississippi," May 1945, 11–12, 17, CCF: 806-38014-1937, BIA, NARA-DC.

11. Jennings, Beggs, and Caldwell, "Study of Social and Economic Conditions," 15, 10, 52.

12. The lease returned an annual rental fee of $5.00 per acre the first year and $1.25 per acre thereafter. Jennings, Beggs, and Caldwell, "Study of Social and Economic Conditions," 21–22.

13. Jennings, Beggs, and Caldwell, "Study of Social and Economic Conditions," 15.

14. Jennings, Beggs, and Caldwell, "Study of Social and Economic Conditions," 10.

15. The hospital lacked an isolation unit and skilled X-ray technicians to identify the disease. Jennings, Beggs, and Caldwell, "Study of Social and Economic Conditions," 55–60.

16. Tolbert, "Sociological Study," 135–38; Coe, "Lost in the Hills of Home," 30–42. Coe notes the beginnings of economic development under the council, but she does not offer a systematic analysis of those efforts. Paul Vance, Choctaw Superintendent, to Honorable A. L. Miller, Chairman of Committee on Interior and Insular Affairs, June 17, 1953, Entry 327, box 42, file: Mississippi Choctaw Band, re: Tribal Organization, FCTA, NARA-SW.

17. Peterson, "Mississippi Band of Choctaw Indians," 140–41.

18. Tolbert's 1958 sociology dissertation noted that none of the council members had completed high school. The first representative to have completed some college course work was Prentice Morris, elected in 1953 from Bogue Chitto; Phillip Martin had a high school education and ten years' service in the air force. Tolbert, "Sociological Study," 138.

19. In 1953 agent Vance remarked that there was competition for expenditures of funds among the communities. These conflicts, however, do not appear in the minutes of the tribal council. Vance to Miller, June 17, 1953, Entry 327, box 42, file: Mississippi Choctaw Band, re: Tribal Organization, FCTA, NARA-SW.

20. For conflicts between "full bloods" and "mixed bloods" in the postwar era, see Rosier, *Rebirth of the Blackfoot Nation*; Lambert, *Choctaw Nation*; Sturm, *Blood Politics*. In each of these examples, designations of blood are not predicated solely on phenotypes but are based on culture and place of residence as well.

21. The retiring and humble nature of the Choctaws is a theme that resonates throughout the historical documentation. Coe, who did fieldwork in Philadelphia in 1960, discussed this at length in "Lost in the Hills of Home," 45–50. See also Moore and Steve, "Dropout Study, 1964," 4, Entry 327, box 37, file: Miscellaneous Correspondence, 1962–66, FCTA, NARA-SW.

22. For a list of Choctaw veterans, see MBCI, *Chahta Hapia Hoke*, 50–51.

23. Vance to Miller, June 17, 1953, Entry 327, box 42, file: Mississippi Choctaw Band, re: Tribal Organization, FCTA, NARA-SW.

24. List of council members compiled from Minutes of the Tribal Council, 1945–1965, Choctaw Tribal Archives, Pearl River High School, Choctaw MS.

25. Thanks to Mike Tsosie of the Colorado River Reservation for this interpretation of the importance of food preparation to the political processes of Native Americans. Activities of the Women's Council Club are reported throughout the Minutes of the Tribal Council. For the creation of the club, see Minutes of the Choctaw Tribal Council, October 12, 1954. For their lobbying for a high school, see April 12, 1955, 9–10, Tribal Archives.

26. For women serving on election committees, see "Community Election Committees, 1955," Entry 327, box 40, file: Tribal Minutes, 1955, Minutes of the Choctaw Tribal Council, July 14, 1953, Tribal Archives. Information on their economic activities is scattered throughout the BIA files.

27. Choctaws' political fragmentation was nothing new, for the Choctaw Nation of the nineteenth century was only loosely consolidated and local independence was esteemed. See Carson, *Searching for the Bright Path*, and O'Brien, *Choctaws in a Revolutionary Age*.

28. *Constitution and By-Laws of the Mississippi Band of Choctaw Indians*, ratified April 20, 1945, Article IV, Section 1, Article V, Section 1, Article VI, Section 1, Entry 326, box 43, file: Mississippi Band of Choctaw Indians, FCTA, NARA-SW.

29. Jennings, Beggs, and Caldwell, "Study of Social and Economic Conditions," 24; Minutes of the Choctaw Tribal Council, July 10, 1945, unpaginated.

30. Minutes of the Choctaw Tribal Council, July 10, 1945, unpaginated.

31. Tribal Council Minutes for the 1940s are incomplete but available at the Tribal Archives.

32. James Arenston, Supervisor of Indian Education, to McMullen, June 11, 1946, CCF: 819.1: 23048-1946, BIA, NARA-DC; Home Extension Reports for 1946–1949, CCF: 031-2436-1947, 031-3967-1948, 031-1516-1949, BIA, NARA-DC.

33. McMullen to CIA, February 4, 1947, CCF: 819.1: 23048-1946, BIA, NARA-DC; Home Extension Report, 1949, CCF: 031-2609-1950, BIA, NARA-DC.

34. Home Extension Report for 1948, CCF: 031-1516-1947, BIA, NARA-DC. For assessment of the loan program, see "Memo to Area Director from Area Credit Officer, Mrs. Ada C. Burdeau, finance specialist," October 22, 1951, 2, Area Director's Report for 1951, Entry 327, box 37, file: Special Problems among the Choctaws, FCTA, NARA-SW, hereafter cited as Burdeau Memo.

35. Home Extension Report for 1948, CCF: 031-1516-1947, BIA, NARA-DC. The council voted in 1949 to raise the interest rates from 3 to 4 percent to generate additional revenues. In 1950 they decided to use forty thousand dollars of tribal funds for an industrial assistance program. Home Extension Report for 1948, CCF: 031-1516-1947, and Home Extension Report for 1950, CCF: 031-1569-1951, BIA, NARA-DC.

36. Burdeau Memo.

37. Area Director's Report for 1951, 5. Medical inspector Martha E. Keaton likewise lamented the Choctaws' "complete lack of self-confidence." "Report of Visit to Choctaw Indian Agency, Philadelphia, Mississippi, August 1–9, 1951," in the Area Director's Report for 1951.

38. Evan L. Flory, Chief, Branch of Soil Conservation, and T. W. Taylor, Chief, Branch of Management Planning, "Choctaw Study, 1951," 26–27, Entry 327, box 37, file: Special Problems among the Choctaw, FCTA, NARA-SW.

39. Joe Chitto to Honorable John R. Nickols [*sic*], June 17, 1949, box 249, folder 10, Choctaw 1949–1960, Documents of the Association on American Indian Affairs (AAIA Papers), Seeley G. Mudd Manuscript Library, Princeton University, Princeton NJ. Thirty-nine members of the Standing Pine community also signed this letter.

40. John Province, Assistant Commissioner of Indian Affairs, to Alexander Lesser, Executive Director, AAIA, July 15, 1949, box 249, folder 10, Choctaw 1949–1960, AAIA Papers.

41. "Choctaw Study, 1951," 3.

42. Joe Chitto to W. O. Roberts, Area Director, November 14, 1951, Entry 327, box 42, file: Tribal Minutes, 1951; W. O. Roberts to the Commissioner of Indian Affairs, November 20, 1951, Entry 327, box 42, file: Tribal Minutes, 1951, FCTA, NARA-SW; "Choctaw Study, 1951," 4.

43. Minutes of the Choctaw Tribal Council, December 10, 1952, 10, Tribal Archives.

44. Charlie Ben to the CIA, October 15, 1952, Entry 327, box 42, file: 1951–54, FCTA, NARA-SW. Council member Cleddie Bell also contacted area director Roberts to support Chitto's statements about Vance. Cleddie Bell to Roberts, January 7, 1952, Entry 327, box 42, file: 1951–54, FCTA, NARA-SW.

45. Roberts to CIA, July 17 and August 8, 1952, Entry 327, box 42, file: 1951–54, FCTA, NARA-SW.

46. John Jay Skates Jr., "World War II and Its Effects," 125.

47. Florence Mars, *Witness in Philadelphia*, 42–45.

48. McMillen, "Development of Civil Rights, 1956–1970," in *History of Mississippi*, 157.

49. "Choctaw Study, 1951," 3.

50. Vance to W. O. Roberts, December 3, 1951; Ethelyn Saloli to Joe Jennings, November 16, 1951; W. O. Roberts to CIA, December 5, 1951, Entry 327, box 42, file: Mississippi Band of Choctaw Indians, 1951–53, FCTA, NARA-SW.

51. Oliver La Farge, President, AAIA, to Philo Nash, CIA, June 26, 1962, box 242, folder 11, Choctaw 1949–1960, AAIA Papers.

52. Minutes of the Choctaw Tribal Council, July 10, 1945, unpaginated, Tribal Archives.

53. Minutes of the Choctaw Tribal Council, July 10, 1945, unpaginated; October 8, 1946, 1, Tribal Archives.

54. By 1955, agent Vance reported that three Sun Oil Company leases had netted $3,701.30. Minutes of the Choctaw Tribal Council, April 12, 1955, 1, Tribal Archives. For the resolution for new leases in 1956, see Minutes of the Choctaw Tribal Council, April 10, 1956, 12, Tribal Archives.

55. Temporary Council to the Commissioner of Indian Affairs, January 5, 1945, CCF: 066-9544-1936, BIA, NARA-DC.

56. Minutes of the Choctaw Tribal Council, July 10, 1945, and July 17, 1947, unpaginated, Tribal Archives.

57. Minutes of the Special Called Meeting of the Mississippi Band of Choctaw Indians, December 23, 1952, 1–10, Tribal Archives.

58. Minutes of the Special Called Meeting of the Mississippi Band of Choctaw Indians, December 23, 1952, 1–5, Tribal Archives.

59. Minutes of the Special Called Meeting of the Mississippi Band of Choctaw Indians, December 23, 1952, 6–10, Tribal Archives.

60. Speaking from her experience as owner of a general merchandise store, Bell lectured Vance that the proprietor of a store must consult with all the managers before advertising a sale. Minutes of the Choctaw Tribal Council, January 10, 1956, unpaginated, Tribal Archives.

61. Minutes of the Choctaw Tribal Council, April 10, 1956, unpaginated, Tribal Archives.

62. Minutes of the Choctaw Tribal Council, October 9, 1956, 20, 23, and 22, respectively, Tribal Archives.

63. *Constitution and By-Laws of the Mississippi Band of Choctaw Indians*, Article VII, Section I, G, and C, quoted by Chitto in the Minutes of the Choctaw Tribal Council, October 9, 1956, 23, Tribal Archives.

64. Minutes of the Choctaw Tribal Council, October 9, 1956, 26–28, Tribal Archives.

65. Minutes of the Choctaw Tribal Council, October 9, 1956, 22, Tribal Archives.

66. Minutes of the Special Called Meeting of the Mississippi Band of Choctaw Indians, October 23, 1956, 7, Tribal Archives.

67. Minutes of the Special Called Meeting of the Mississippi Band of Choctaw Indians, October 23, 1956, 9, Tribal Archives.

68. Minutes of the Special Called Meeting of the Mississippi Band of Choctaw Indians, October 23, 1956, 10, Tribal Archives. By invoking the rhetoric of the Cold War, Billie was using a rhetorical device that many Indians had adopted during these years. See Cobb, "Talking the Language of the Larger World."

69. Minutes of the Special Called Meeting of the Mississippi Band of Choctaw Indians, October 23, 1956, 11, Tribal Archives.

70. The yea votes were Bobbie Hickman, Dolphus Henry, Mary Lou Farmer, Frank Johnson, Mack Jimmie, and Ellis Sam. Burton Bell, Hudson Tubby, Sam Wilson, Bilbo John, and Woodrow Billie cast the nay votes.

71. See Cobb, *Native Activism in Cold War America*.

72. Minutes of the Choctaw Tribal Council, May 13, 1958, 6–9, Tribal Archives.

73. Minutes of the Choctaw Tribal Council, April 12, 8–9, and July 12, 1960, 6, Tribal Archives.

74. Minutes of the Choctaw Tribal Council, January 9, 1962, 5–6, Tribal Archives. Cho-17-62 authorizing these small sales was against regulations but was nonetheless approved by the Area Office. Marie Hayes, Tribal Affairs Officer, to Paul Fickinger, Area Director, Muskogee Office, January 18, 1962, Entry 327, box 41, file: Mississip-

pi Choctaw Resolutions, 1961; Minutes of the Choctaw Tribal Council, January 9, 1962, 5–6, Tribal Archives; Vance to Holmes, Area Director, Muskogee Office, April 20, 1962, Entry 326, box 12, file: Resolutions, FCTA, NARA-SW.

75. Paul C. Rosier coined this term in his book *Rebirth of the Blackfoot Nation*, 3.

76. "Choctaw Study, 1952." Economic data is found on pp. 5–15; Peterson, "Mississippi Band of Choctaw Indians," 120, 122, 127–28.

77. Although this sentiment was not recorded in the minutes of the council meetings, Choctaw informants expressed it to anthropologists—Coe in the late 1950s and again a decade later to Peterson. Council minutes do record that numerous Choctaws articulated their opposition to paying for their land to their representatives on the council. For data on Choctaw houses, see "Comprehensive Environmental Sanitation Report," Entry 327, box 44, file: Comprehensive Environmental Sanitation Report, FCTA, NARA-SW.

78. SAR, 1951, 7, Entry 327, box 42, file: Annual Reports, FCTA, NARA-SW.

79. "Choctaw Study, 1951," Entry 327, box 37, file: Special Problems among the Choctaw. Economic data is found on pp. 5–15.

80. "Interpretation of the Powers of the Tribal Council According to the Constitution and By-laws of the Mississippi Band of Choctaw Indians, presented to the Tribal Council, February 7, 1952," Tribal Archives.

81. Minutes of the Choctaw Tribal Council, December 6, 1951, 8, Tribal Archives.

82. Minutes of the Choctaw Tribal Council, December 6, 1951, 8–10, Tribal Archives.

83. Minutes of the Choctaw Tribal Council, March 11, 1952, 4–10, Tribal Archives.

84. Minutes of the Choctaw Tribal Council, March 11, 1952, 4–10, Tribal Archives. Because the council minutes are inconsistent in delineating people's votes, conclusions about why this vote went as it did must be cautiously drawn. It may have been, however, that some council members feared to record this vote because the issue was so contentious. This interpretation is supported by the fact that some members actually voted no instead of merely abstaining. This was unusual.

85. Minutes of the Choctaw Tribal Council, April 8, 1952, 2–3, Tribal Archives.

86. Roberts to CIA, August 15, 1952, Entry 327, box 40, Mississippi Choctaw Minutes and Resolutions (1953–59); file: 1950–52.

87. Minutes of the Choctaw Tribal Council, January 11, 1953, 10–11, Tribal Archives.

88. Minutes of the Choctaw Tribal Council, January 13, 1953, 2, (quotation) 5–6, Tribal Archives.

89. Minutes of the Choctaw Tribal Council, April 14, 1953, 2, Tribal Archives.

90. See the comments of Councilman Berkley York and J. C. Allen in the Minutes of the Tribal Council, April 10, 1951, 1–2; Joe Chitto's and Cleddie Bell's remarks in the Minutes of the Choctaw Tribal Council, April 14, 1953, 4, and the letter from Standing Pine community leader Charlie Ben in the same minutes, 20, Tribal Archives. For all practical purposes, the superintendent *was* the agency, but the Choctaws preferred to distinguish the two for reasons that were not recorded.

91. Minutes of the Choctaw Tribal Council, April 14, 1953, 6–9, and October 13, 1953, 10–11, 16–17, Tribal Archives.

92. Vance to Roberts, March 26, 1953, Entry 327, box 40, file: 1950–52, FCTA, NARA-SW.

93. Minutes of the Choctaw Tribal Council, January 12, 1954, 9, Tribal Archives.

94. "Summary of Conference, Mississippi Choctaw Delegation, Area Director's Office, February 17, 1954," quotation on p. 4, Entry 327, box 43, file: Mississippi Band of Choctaw Indians, FCTA, NARA-SW.

95. Minutes of the Choctaw Tribal Council, April 13, 1954, 9–14, Tribal Archives.

96. Minutes of the Choctaw Tribal Council, January 10, 1956, 4, Tribal Archives.

97. Minutes of a Special Called Meeting of the Choctaw Tribal Council, January 19, 1956, 5, Tribal Archives.

98. Minutes of a Special Called Meeting of the Choctaw Tribal Council, January 19, 1956, 7–10, Tribal Archives. Frank Johnson of Conehatta was the lone voice of dissent, telling the council that his community leaders had met and approved the rental program ten to one.

99. Minutes of the Choctaw Tribal Council, April 10, 1956, 12, Tribal Archives.

100. Minutes of the Choctaw Tribal Council, November 6, 1957, 3–4, 6–9, Tribal Archives.

101. Minutes of the Choctaw Tribal Council, January 13, 1959, 21, Tribal Archives.

102. Minutes of the Choctaw Tribal Council, February 23, 18, and April 12, 1960, 5–7, Tribal Archives.

103. Minutes of a Special Called Meeting, October 19, 1960, 10–19, Tribal Archives.

104. Minutes of the Choctaw Tribal Council, April 10, 1962, 12–17, Tribal Archives.

105. Minutes of the Choctaw Tribal Council, July 10, 1962, 6–11, and October 9, 1956, 6–9, Tribal Archives.

106. Minutes of the Choctaw Tribal Council, January 12, 1965, 7, and January 12, 1965, 5–7, Tribal Archives.

107. Minutes of the Choctaw Tribal Council, January 14, 1964, 9–10, and January 14, 1965, 4–7, Tribal Archives.

108. Ferguson, "Re-Establishment of Tribal Government"; Minutes of the Tribal Council, April 13, 1965, 8–9, Tribal Archives.

109. Martin to Eastland, March 26, 1965, Series 4, box: Constituents, file: Mississippi Band of Choctaw Indians, James O. Eastland Papers.

110. Marie C. McGuire, Commissioner of Public Housing, to Senator Eastland, April 12, 1965, Series 4, box: Constituents, file: Mississippi Band of Choctaw Indians, Eastland Papers.

111. "Public Notice," Phillip Martin and Emmett York, "Report on the General Council Meeting, Mississippi Band of Choctaw Indians, June 11, 1965," Entry 327, box 37, file: General Council Meeting, NARA-DC.

112. Minutes of the Choctaw Tribal Council, April 13, 1965, 8–9, and October 12, 1965, 2–3, Tribal Archives.

113. Minutes of the Choctaw Tribal Council, April 8, 1947, and July 17, 1947, unpaginated, Tribal Archives; D. S. Myer, CIA, to Mr. J. B. Myers, Secretary-General of

the Better Business Bureau of Baton Rouge LA; October 5, 1951, Entry 327, box 43, file: Mississippi Choctaw Claims, NARA-DC.

114. The papers of Congressman William M. Colmer contain two folders of such letters, and Senator Bilbo's papers contain four. The Papers of Representative Arthur Winstead contain scrapbooks and no correspondence. All collections in the McCain Library and Archives, University of Southern Mississippi, Hattiesburg. Numerous letters are also found in the Eastland Papers and the John C. Stennis Papers, Congressional and Political Research Center of Mississippi State University, Starkville MS.

115. McMullen to J. A. Riddell, November 27, 1950, Riddell to McMullen, November 30, 1950, McMullen to CIA, December 4, 1950, Entry 327, box 43, file: Mississippi Choctaw Claims, FCTA, NARA-SW.

116. W. E. Moore to Eastland, February 20, 1959, Series 4, Constituents files, file: Mississippi Band of Choctaw Indians, Eastland Papers; Minutes of the Choctaw Tribal Council, February 7, 1952, 6, Tribal Archives.

117. H. M. Crutchfield, Chief, Branch of Land, to Roberts, April 8, 1952, Entry 327, box 43, file: Mississippi Choctaw Claims, 1951–62, FCTA, NARA-SW.

118. "Brief of the Mississippi Choctaws before the Indian Claims Commission, February 4, 1954," 1–11, Records of the Indian Claims Commission, box 617, RG 279, NARA-DC.

119. "Answer before the Indian Claims Commission," 1–3, Records of the Indian Claims Commission, RG 279, NARA-DC.

120. Public Law 726, August 13, 1946 (H.R. 4497), 60 Stat. 1049, "AN ACT to create an Indian Claims Commission, to provide for the powers, duties, and functions thereof, and for other purposes," is online at http://arts-sciences.und.edu/native -media-center/_files/docs/1933-1950/1946indianclaimscommissionact.pdf.

121. Philp, *Termination Revisited*, 30–31.

122. "Answer before the Indian Claims Commission," 1–3, Records of the Indian Claims Commission, RG 279, NARA-DC.

123. "Opinion of the Commission," Records of the Indian Claims Commission, RG 279, NARA-DC. This ruling is also available online at "Indian Claims Commission Decisions," http://digital.library.okstate.edu/icc/vo3/vo3toc.html.

124. The exact condition of the Choctaws' tribal status in Oklahoma in the early twentieth century is a matter of some dispute. In *Choctaw Nation* political anthropologist Valarie Lambert reviews literature arguing that the Choctaw tribe ceased to exist following allotment and Oklahoma statehood. Lambert then counters that the Choctaws in fact continued to "occupy the politico-legal category of 'American Indian tribe'" during the early twentieth century. She maintains that the period between 1907 and 1970 was one in which Choctaw corporate identity waned, but their tribalism continued in their collective resources and the office of chief (see pp. 59–60). The fact that the Choctaws of Oklahoma were allowed to file a motion to intervene in this case as the Choctaw Nation supports Lambert's thesis. Kidwell, *Choctaws in Oklahoma*, also discusses this issue.

125. "Answer of the Choctaw Nation to Appellee's Motion to Dismiss," 11–15, Docket No. 52. For *Winton v. Amos* see, http://caselaw.lp.findlaw.com/scripts /getcase.pl?court=US&vol=255&invol=373.

126. "Answer of the Choctaw Nation to Appellee's Motion to Dismiss," 15–17, Docket No. 52.

127. "Answer of the Choctaw Nation to Appellee's Motion to Dismiss," 24, 31, Docket No. 52.

128. "In the United States Court of Claims, Appeals," Docket no. 2-55, decided January 31, 1956, 14, 17, 18, Docket No. 52.

129. CIA to Mrs. Betty Jo Ledbetter, Memphis TN, n.d., Entry 326, box 43, file: Mississippi Choctaw Claims, FCTA, NARA-SW.

130. Minutes of the Choctaw Tribal Council, February 7, 1958, 12–14, Tribal Archives.

131. "Plan of Sydney Reagan Sr. and Sydney Reagan Jr.," Entry 327, box 43, file: Mississippi Choctaw Claims, FCTA, NARA-SW; Minutes of the Choctaw Tribal Council, January 13, 1959, 12, and October 14, 1959, 37–41, Tribal Archives.

132. Minutes of the Choctaw Tribal Council, October 11, 1960, 5–6, 19–21, Tribal Archives.

133. Minutes of the Choctaw Tribal Council, April 9, 1963, 4–7, Tribal Archives.

134. Transcript from WHOC radio program of October 28, 1954, 4, Entry 327, box 43, file, Mississippi Band of Choctaw Indians, FCTA, NARA-SW; Minutes of the Choctaw Tribal Council, October 13, 1953, 14, Tribal Archives.

135. Transcript from WHOC radio program of October 28, 1954, 4–8; Minutes of the Choctaw Tribal Council, October 13, 1953, 14, Tribal Archives; Roberts to CIA, November 23, 1951, Entry 327, box 42, file: Mississippi Band of Choctaw Indians, 1951–53. Hayes drafted the "Outline, Social and Economic Needs, Mississippi Band of Choctaw, May 1, 1952," a detailed plan for economic development. The minutes of the July 8, 1952, Tribal Council note that they had read her plan and approved of it. The tribe implemented various aspects of the plan over the decade of the 1950s. Minutes of the Tribal Council, July 8, 1952, Tribal Archives.

136. "Annual Report of the Home Extension Council Club, July 1956," Entry 326, CCF, box 34, file: Community Development Association 5th Annual Meeting, FCTA, NARA-SW.

137. SAR, 1959, 31, FCTA, NARA-SW.

138. "Choctaw Community Development Program," "Handbook of Rules and Interpretation of the Score Sheet for 1955 Choctaw Community Development Program," Vance to Fickinger, December 17, 1954, Entry 327, box 43, file: Mississippi Band of Choctaw Indians, FCTA, NARA-SW; Minutes of the Choctaw Tribal Council, January 11, 1955, unpaginated, Tribal Archives.

139. Peterson, "Mississippi Band of Choctaw Indians," 267.

140. Minutes of the Choctaw Community Development Clubs for 1954, 1955, 1956, SAR, 1958, 31, Entry 327, box 43, file: Mississippi Band of Choctaw Indians, FCTA, NARA-SW.

141. Minutes of the Choctaw Community Development Clubs for 1954, 1955, 1956.

142. Directory of Community Development Clubs, Entry 327, box 43, file: Mississippi Band of Choctaw Indians, FCTA, NARA-SW.

143. SAR, 1955–1965, Entry 327, box 36, FCTA, NARA-SW.

144. Minutes of the Choctaw Tribal Council, April 9, 1957, 10, Tribal Archives.

145. Report of Marie Hayes, Tribal Relations Officer, June 23, 1958, Entry 327, box 43, file: Mississippi Choctaw History, FCTA, NARA-SW.

146. SAR, 1957, 6; SAR 1958, 61, Entry 327, box 36, FCTA, NARA-SW.

147. Minutes of the Choctaw Tribal Council, November 6, 1958, 6, Tribal Archives; SAR 1957, 9, Entry 327, box 36, FCTA, NARA-SW.

148. Minutes of the Choctaw Tribal Council, October 8, 1963, 2, Tribal Archives.

149. Minutes of the Choctaw Tribal Council, April 8, 1958, 8–9, Tribal Archives.

150. SAR, 1952 and 1953, Entry 327, box 36; "Annual Report of the Home Extension Club Council," Entry 326, box 34; SAR, 1958, 37, all FCTA, NARA-SW.

151. Herbert Kinnard, Extension Worker, "1952 Annual Report of Extension Work," n.p., Entry 570, box 6, FCTA, NARA-SW.

152. Damus Z. Rhodes, Home Management Supervisor, to W. O. Roberts, Area Director of Muskogee District, November 30, 1953, Entry 327, box 42, file: Miscellaneous. Anthropologist John Peterson remarked in 1970 that changes in the status of African Americans appeared to have had major effects on the Choctaw but that more research was needed. Peterson, "Assimilation, Separation and Out-Migration," 1293–94. For analysis of the lives of female African American sharecroppers, see Jones, *Labor of Love, Labor of Sorrow.*

153. SAR, 1959, 30, FCTA, NARA-SW.

154. For Mississippi's Home Demonstration Program, see Moore, "'Window to the World,'" and Jolly, "Selected Leaders in Mississippi Home Economics." Moore and Jolly argue that these programs offered rural women important training in leadership. For some white families, and a handful of African American ones, the home extension service also raised the standard of living.

7. Termination, Segregation

1. On postwar policy see Fixico, *Termination and Relocation*; Philp, *Termination Revisited* and *Indian Self Rule*; Cowger, *National Congress*; Drinnon, *Keepers of Concentration Camps*; Vine Deloria Jr., *American Indian Policy*; and Hosmer, *Native Americans and the Legacy of Harry S. Truman*. Dan Cobb's *Native Activism in Cold War America* provides a fresh analysis of this period that locates Indian activism in the context of international politics and the Cold War.

2. W. O. Roberts, Director, Muskogee Area Office, introduction to "Outline of Needs for the Social and Economic Development of the Mississippi Band of Choctaw Indians," by Marie Hayes, Tribal Relations Officer, Entry 326, box 43, file: Outline, Social and Economic Need, Mississippi Band of Choctaw, May 1, 1952, FCTA, NARA-SW.

3. Minutes of the Choctaw Tribal Council, October 17, 1952, 1–3, Tribal Archives, Pearl River High School, Choctaw MS; Paul Vance, Choctaw Superintendent, to Honorable A. L. Miller, Chairman of the Committee on Interior and Insular Affairs, June 17, 1953, Entry 327, box 42, file: Mississippi Choctaw Band, re: Tribal Organization, FCTA, NARA-SW.

4. Management Improvement Schedule, 1953, Field Health Section, Entry 327, box 44, file: Management Improvement Schedule, FCTA, NARA-SW.

5. Cleddie Bell to Roberts, January 4, 1954, Entry 327, box 43, file: Mississippi Band of Choctaw Indians, 1954–55, FCTA, NARA-SW; Minutes of the Choctaw Tribal Council, January 12, 1954, 5–9, Tribal Archives.

6. T. J. Scott to Senator James O. Eastland, January 18, 1954; Eastland to Scott, January 21, 1954, Series 4: Constituents' Files, Eastland Papers; Representative Arthur Winstead to CIA, January 22, 1945, Glenn Emmons, CIA, to Hon. Arthur Winstead, February 26, 1945, Entry 327, box 36, file: Choctaw Hospital, FCTA, NARA-SW; Emmons to Senator John Stennis, January 21, 1954, Stennis to Emmons, January 26, 1954, Stennis Papers.

7. Memo from Roberts to Vance, March 4, 1954, Entry 327, box 36, file: Choctaw Hospital, quotation on p. 7, FCTA, NARA-SW.

8. Vance to Roberts, Memorandum of Understanding Between the Leake County Hospital Carthage MS and the Choctaw Area Field Office, Bureau of Indian Affairs, March 4, 1954, Entry 326, box 36, file: Choctaw Indian Hospital, FCTA, NARA-SW.

9. Fixico, *Termination and Relocation*, 92; Ferguson, "Re-Establishment of Tribal Government," 15.

10. Minutes of the Choctaw Tribal Council, October 8, 1957, 7, Tribal Archives.

11. This quotation is from the speech of Dr. Emery Johnson, Director of the Indian Health Services, at the dedication of the new hospital. MBCI, *Chahta Hapia Hoke*, 23.

12. Minutes of the Choctaw Tribal Council, April 12, 1960, 11A–14, Tribal Archives.

13. Minutes of the Choctaw Tribal Council, January 31, 1963, 6–7, Tribal Archives.

14. Minutes of the Choctaw Tribal Council, January 14, 1964, 1–2; April 14, 1964, 7–9; October 13, 1964, 2, Tribal Archives; MBCI, *Chahta Hapia Hoke*, 23–25.

15. MBCI, *Chahta Hapia Hoke*, 25.

16. These jobs included, a sign-painting establishment, a dry cleaners, the Philadelphia hospital, an International Harvester dealership, and the A&P store. Robert Cullum, Placement and Relocation Officer, to Roberts, November 13, 1951, Entry 326, box 34, file: Relocation, FCTA, NARA-SW.

17. "Choctaw Study, 1951," 5–15; Tolbert, "Sociological Study," 234; Minutes of the Tribal Council, December 6, 1951, 3–4, Tribal Archives.

18. Tolbert, "Sociological Study," 235.

19. Peterson, "Mississippi Band of Choctaw Indians," 197–99; Moore and Steve, "Dropout Study, 1964," 4, Entry 327, box 37, file: Miscellaneous Correspondence, 1962–66, FCTA, NARA-SW.

20. The federal government has a long history of training racial minorities for low-wage, low-status jobs. Goldfield, *Black, White, and Southern,* 28–31; Cullum to Roberts, re: Visit, July 25–31, 1951, Entry 326, box 37, file: Special Problems among the Choctaw, FCTA, NARA-SW.

21. Cullum to Roberts, re: Visit, July 25–31, 1951.

22. Cullum to Roberts, re: Visit, July 25–31, 1951.

23. Cullum to Roberts, November 13, 1951, Entry 326, box 34, file: Relocation, FCTA, NARA-SW.

24. Cullum to Roberts, January 15, 1952, December 15, 1952, and January 31, 1953, Entry 326, box 42, file: Mississippi Band of Choctaw Indians, 1951–53; Cullum to Lane Hart, Chief Programs and Methods Department, Mississippi Employment Security Commission; Cullum to J. S. Bliss, Florida State Employment Service, Cullum to Mrs. Ruth Andreu, Florida State Employment Service, January 19, 1952, Entry 326, box 34, file: Relocation, FCTA, NARA-SW.

25. Scott to Eastland, July 1, 1955, Series 4, Eastland Papers.

26. Emmons to Hon. Arthur Winstead, May 23, 1955, Entry 327, box 43, file: Mississippi Band of Choctaw Indians, FCTA, NARA-SW; Tolbert, "Sociological Study," 234–35.

27. Special Called Meeting of the Tribal Council, October 31, 1951, 7; Minutes of the Tribal Council, December 6, 1951; Minutes of the Tribal Council for April 9, 1957, Tribal Archives.

28. Tolbert, "Sociological Study," 234–35.

29. "Choctaw Study, 1951," 5–15, Tolbert, "Sociological Study," 234; Emmons to Winstead, May 23, 1955, filed with the Minutes of the Tribal Council for 1955, Entry 327, boxes 40 and 43, respectively, FCTA, NARA-SW; Tolbert, "Sociological Study," 126.

30. SAR, 1957, 25, Entry 327, box 36, file: Annual Reports: 1953–58, FCTA, NARA-SW; Scott to Eastland, July 1, 1955, Series 4, Eastland Papers.

31. Minutes of the Tribal Council, April 12, 1955, 1–3, Tribal Archives.

32. Sanitation Report for 1957–58, Entry 327, box 44, file: "Comprehensive Environmental Sanitation Report," FCTA, NARA-SW; "Financial Report: October 11, 1955, through October 7, 1957," Minutes of the Tribal Council, November 6, 1957, Tribal Archives.

33. For how Indian women used outing programs for their own ends, see ch. 4 of Osburn, *Southern Ute Women.* In the early twentieth century, OIA administrators gradually lowered their expectations for Indians from prosperous yeoman farmers to low-paid wage workers. Hoxie, *Final Promise,* 237–38. Nonetheless, Indian women were still expected to follow white gender roles and become homemakers. Ironically, the Indian Service itself hired numerous Indian women to work outside their homes. Cahill, *Federal Fathers and Mothers,* 85, 112–13, 123–29, 260–61. For a multinational approach to the study of indigenous women in the labor force, see the excellent essays in *Indigenous Women and Work,* edited by Carol Williams. For a sensitive and astute analysis of Indian domestics under the outing program in Tucson, Arizona, see Hastings, *Matrons and Maids.*

34. Minutes of the Choctaw Council, October 31, 1951, 10–12, Tribal Archives.

35. Peterson, "Mississippi Band of Choctaw Indians," 205–6; "Choctaw Study, 1951," 11; SAR, 1958, 40, and 1957, 9, Entry 327, box 36, FCTA, NARA-SW.

36. Damus Z. Rhodes, Home Management Supervisor, Muskogee Area Office, to Roberts, November 30, 1953, Entry 327, box 42, file: Miscellaneous, FCTA, NARA-SW.

37. Thompson and Peterson, "Mississippi Choctaw Identity," 186–90.

38. Quotation by Emmett York, Minutes of the Tribal Council, July 14, 1953. Chitto also called for the use of English. Minutes of the Tribal Council, January 10, 1956, 2. For Choctaw language as passive resistance in council meetings, see Minutes of a Special Called Meeting of the Tribal Council, January 19, 1955, 5, all in Tribal Archives.

39. Rhodes to Roberts, November 30, 1953, Entry 327, box 42, file: Miscellaneous, FCTA, NARA-SW.

40. Minutes of the Tribal Council, November 13, 1952, 8–9, Tribal Archives.

41. Vance, "Mississippi's Choctaw Indians," *Mississippi Magic*, Mississippi Agricultural and Industrial Board, 1957, 9–11, quotation from p. 9, Entry 327, box 43, file: Mississippi Choctaw History, FCTA, NARA-SW.

42. Author's personal communication with Choctaw friend who requested anonymity, Nashville TN, August 9, 2008; "Indian Segregation in Mississippi," box 249, folder 10, Choctaw 1949–1960, AAIA Papers. There is no author named, but it is accompanied by a letter from Mrs. John Osoinach. It is likely a report from Kirk Osoinach, a graduate student from the University of Chicago who did fieldwork in Mississippi in 1957.

43. Vance to Miller, June 17, 1953, Entry 327, box 42, file: Mississippi Choctaw Band, re: Tribal Organization; Marie Hayes, "Outline of Needs for the Social and Economic Development of the Mississippi Band of Choctaw Indians," Entry 326, box 43, file: Outline, Social and Economic Need, Mississippi Band of Choctaw, May 1, 1952, FCTA, NARA-SW.

44. Rhodes to Roberts, November 30, 1953, and Robert M. Cullum to Roberts, August 10, 1923, both in Entry 327, box 37, file: Special Problems among the Choctaw, FCTA, NARA-SW. Home Economics teacher Juanita Nofflett suggested that Choctaw women organize personal grooming clubs to "raise themselves to a level of acceptance of the people around us." Tribal Council Minutes, October 31, 1951, Tribal Archives. Other observers noted Choctaw traditional dress as an economic liability and a barrier to "progress." See M. L. Hayes, "The Mississippi Band of Choctaw Indians," June 23, 1958, file: Miscellaneous, Entry 327, box 42, and SAR, 1958, 40, Entry 327, box 36, FCTA, NARA-SW.

45. One observer of Choctaw culture in the 1950s, Etha M. Langford, observed that the only change in men's clothing from the nineteenth to the twentieth centuries was in the location of the buttons—shirts that buttoned down the back were replaced by shirts that buttoned in the front. See Langford, "Study of the Educational Development of the Choctaw Indians in Mississippi," 61.

46. Economic data on possessions is scattered throughout the agency records. For one example, see SAR, 1958, "Report of the Branch of Welfare," 34–37, Entry 327, box 36, FCTA, NARA-SW.

47. "A Brief History of the Mississippi Band of Choctaw Indians, Prepared in 1954," no author, Entry 327, box 43, file: Mississippi Choctaw History, FCTA, NARA-SW.

48. Rhodes to Roberts, November 30, 1953, Entry 327, box 37, file: Special Problems among the Choctaw, FCTA, NARA-SW.

49. SAR, 1959, 32, Entry 327, box 36, FCTA, NARA-SW.

50. SAR, 1954, "Annual Report of the Red Water School, June 30, 1954," 51–52, Entry 327, box 36, FCTA, NARA-SW.

51. Numerous observers commented on the shyness of Choctaw children. Some specific references include SAR, 1956, 14, and the 1953 "Resolution of the Choctaw Tribal Council" on closing the hospital. Minutes of the Tribal Council for January 12, 1953, Tribal Archives.

52. In the postwar popular press, women's hairstyles figured prominently in assessments of women in the public eye. Joanne Meyerowitz argues that evaluations stressing women's beautiful hair in discussions of women's accomplishments may have "cloaked a submerged fear of lesbian, mannish, or man-hating women." Meyerowitz, "Beyond the Feminine Mystique," 233. For social constructions of beauty and race, see Peiss, *Hope in a Jar*. In his "Sociological Study," Tolbert interpreted girls' hairstyles as an indication of their parents' conservatism, noting that parents who wanted their children to "advance" allowed girls to cut their hair and "native families did not" (130).

53. "Choctaw Study, 1951," 11; SAR, 1958, 40 and 1957, 9, Entry 327, box 36, FCTA, NARA-SW.

54. "Choctaw Study, 1951," 11; SAR, 1958, 40 and 1957, 9, Entry 327, box 36, FCTA, NARA-SW.

55. Tolbert, "Sociological Study," 126–27, 236.

56. See Peterson, "Assimilation, Separation, and Out-Migration."

57. SAR, 1958, 40, Entry 327, box 36, FCTA, NARA-SW.

58. Minutes of the Choctaw Tribal Council, November 15, 1952, January 10, 1956, April 9, 1957, and October 14, 1959, Tribal Archives.

59. Mrs. A. H. McMullen was a member of the Philadelphia Women's Club from 1943 to 1951, but unlike the previous wives of superintendents, she did not chair the Indian Affairs Committee. Mrs. Paul Vance joined the Women's Club in 1946 and began chairing the Indian Affairs Committee after her husband took over as superintendent in 1952, presiding until 1958 or 1959. Yearbooks of the Philadelphia Women's Clubs, Miscellaneous Files, Records of the Mississippi Federation of Women's Clubs (MFWC); Clippings from the *Mississippi Clubwomen*, 1954–55, Entry 327, box 43, file: Mississippi Band of Choctaw, FCTA, NARA-SW; Mrs. Lamar Tripp, President MFWC, to Vance, April 25, 1955; Mrs. R. F. Stiles, President, 2nd District, MFWC, to Vance, April 23, 1955; Fickinger to Mrs. Edward Breland, State Chair of Indian

Affairs for GFWC, May 9, 1955; Mrs. H. T. Key, Indian Welfare Committee Chairman, District 2, to Club Friends, January 21, 1955, Entry 327, box 43, file: untitled, FCTA, NARA-SW.

60. Clipping from the *Mississippi Clubwoman*, 1954–55, Entry 327, box 43, file: Mississippi Band of Choctaw, FCTA, NARA-SW.

61. See Vance, "Address to Tourism Convention, May 23, 1958," Entry 327, box 42, file: Miscellaneous, FCTA, NARA-SW. For the Eastern Band of Cherokee's drama *Unto These Hills*, see Finger, *Cherokee Americans*.

62. Vance, "Mississippi's Choctaw Indians," 10, and "Address to Tourism Convention," clippings in Entry 327, box 42, file: Miscellaneous, FCTA, NARA-SW.

63. Vance, "Mississippi's Choctaw Indians," 11.

64. Vance, "Mississippi's Choctaw Indians," 9.

65. By this I do not mean to imply that Choctaws did not deploy their culture primarily because it constituted who they were, but only to note how they performed their ethnicity with respect to their neighbors and allies.

66. Flora Dee Goforth, Supervisor of Indian Education, to Archie H. McMullen, Choctaw Superintendent, April 3, 1944, April 14, 1944; McMullen to CIA, June 12, 1945; Willard W. Beatty, Director of Education, to McMullen, June 18, 1945, Goforth to Joe Jennings and McMullen, July 10, 1945, all in CCF: 812-78443-1940, BIA, NARA-DC.

67. Quotations are from ads that ran in the *Neshoba County Democrat*, February 15, 1951, 18, and August 21, 1952, 20. The ads ran sporadically throughout 1951 and 1952.

68. Vance to Roberts, November 21, 1951, Entry 327, box 42, file: Mississippi Band of Choctaw Indians, 1951–53, FCTA, NARA-SW; Minutes of the Choctaw Council, October 31, 1951, Tribal Archives.

69. John A. Ketcher, Instructor of Arts and Crafts, "General Report of Activities, October 5, to December 31, 1953," in "Management Improvement Schedule," Entry 327, box 44, file: Mississippi Band of Choctaw Indians, 1951–53, FCTA, NARA-SW.

70. Hayes, "Outline of Needs for the Social and Economic Development of the Mississippi Band of Choctaw Indians, FCTA, NARA-SW.

71. Ketcher, "General Report of Activities, October 5 to December 31, 1953," Entry 327, box 44, file: Mississippi Band of Choctaw Indians, 1951–53. Ketcher borrowed weavings from women in Tahlequah, Oklahoma.

72. Minutes of the Choctaw Council, October 12, 1954, Tribal Archives.

73. SAR, 1954, 10–11, Entry 327, box 36; Ketcher, "Management Improvement Schedule," Entry 327, box 44, file: Mississippi Band of Choctaw Indians, 1951–53, FCTA, NARA-SW.

74. Information on demand for Choctaw crafts is found in "Brief History of the Mississippi Band of Choctaw Indians," 7, Entry 327, box 43, file: Mississippi Choctaw History, FCTA, NARA-SW.

75. Management Improvement Schedule, 1954–1955, Entry 327, box 44, file: Mississippi Band of Choctaw Indians, 1951–53, FCTA, NARA-SW.

76. SAR, 1959, 65, Entry 327, box 36, FCTA, NARA-SW. Anthropologist Jessica R. Cattelino also notes the importance of small-scale crafts production to family survival. Cattelino, "Casino Roots."

77. For Indian basketry as a strategy of both economic and cultural survival, see Usner, *Indian Work*, ch. 4.

78. SAR, 1954, 10–11, Entry 327, box 36; Ketcher to William A. Amos, Area Supervisor for Education, January 8, 1953, "Management Improvement Schedule," Entry 327, box 44, both FCTA, NARA-SW.

79. The song, composed by ethnomusicologist Charles Wakefield Cadman and published in 1909, was supposedly "Founded Upon a Tribal Melody" that had inspired a poem by Nellie Richmond Eberhart. It is a tale of an Indian man's unrequited love for a "captive maid" brought to his village. For a sympathetic biography of Cadman, see PBS, "I Hear America Singing," Composer Profiles, http://www.pbs .org/wnet/ihas/composer/cadman.html.

80. SAR, 1954, 10, Entry 327, box 36, FCTA, NARA-SW.

81. SAR, 1954, 10, Entry 327, box 36, FCTA, NARA-SW.

82. Green, "The Pocahontas Perplex," and Albers and James, "Illusion and Illumination."

83. *Mississippi Memories: A Pageant Written and Produced by Members of the Mississippi Federation of Women's Clubs*, April 15, 1955, Entry 327, box 43, file: Mississippi Band of Choctaw Indians, FCTA, NARA-SW.

84. Michael Harkin comments on ways in which indigenous people interact with tourists seeking an "authentic" Indian experience: "Misinformation, psychological distancing, and above all, satire are common techniques for achieving a separation from the touristic arena." Harkin, "Staged Encounters," 578. There is a substantial literature on Indians' engagement with public performance. Deloria, *Playing Indian*; McBride, "Lucy Nicolar," and Hafen, "Gertrude Simmons Bonnin," discuss women's performance. For a broader overview of the topic, see Maddox, *Citizen Indians*.

85. The best discussion of how condescending views of Indian labor shape these negative images is Usner's *Indian Work*.

86. Ferguson, "Reestablishment of Tribal Government," 15; SAR, 1951, 12, Entry 327, box 36, FCTA, NARA-SW.

87. SAR, 1958, 3, Entry 327, box 36, FCTA, NARA-SW. From 1951 to 1965 the *Neshoba County Democrat* featured a pictorial review of the Choctaw Indian Annual Fair each September.

88. Press release for the Choctaw Indian Fair, 1952, Entry 327, box 40; file: Minutes (1958–59), Mississippi Band of Choctaw Indians, Fairs; Pictorial Review of the Choctaw Indian Annual Fair, *Neshoba County Democrat*, September 20, 1951.

89. The fair programs and press releases for 1952, 1954, 1956, and 1960 are in the file "Mississippi Band of Choctaw Indians, Fairs," Entry 326, box 42, FCTA, NARA-SW. Instructions for the Best Dressed Choctaw Woman are found in the 1952 program, p. 13.

90. SAR, 1956, Entry 327, box 36, FCTA, NARA-SW. For the importance of the Choctaw princess, see MBCI, http://www.choctaw.org/ and *Chahta Hapia Hoke*, 42.

91. Minutes of the Choctaw Tribal Council, April 9, 1957, 17, 23, Tribal Archives; Vance to Fickinger, July 24, 1957, Entry 327, box 40, file: Minutes—Mississippi Band of Choctaw Indians (1957), FCTA, NARA-SW.

92. Schedule of the Choctaw Indian Fair, August 31–September 2, 1955, Entry 327, box 40; file: Minutes (1958–59), Mississippi Band of Choctaw Indians, Fairs, FCTA, NARA-SW.

93. For a warm nostalgic look at the Neshoba County Fair, see Mars, *Witness in Philadelphia*, 31–35.

94. Mars, *Witness*, 25.

95. William Sorrels, "Mississippi's Forgotten Indians," *Memphis Commercial Appeal*, Sunday morning edition, April 29, 1956, sec. 5, 1 and 5, CCF: 041-00-1955, BIA, NARA-DC.

96. SAR for 1954–1962, "Public Relations" section, Entry 327, box 36, FCTA, NARA-SW.

97. A picture of this sign is attached to a memo by Vance to Fickinger, November 16, 1960, Entry 327, box 42, file: Mississippi Band of Choctaw Indians, 1960–62, FCTA, NARA-SW. There is no mention of when the sign was first displayed.

98. SAR 1956–1960, 3, Entry 327, box 36, FCTA, NARA-SW; MBCI, *Chata Hapia Hoke*, 5–6. The state operated the park until 2006, when the legislature turned it over to the Choctaws. Mississippi Legislature, 2006 Regular Session, Senate Bill 2803, "An Act to Return the Nanih Waiya State Park and Mound to the Mississippi Band of Choctaw Indians, to Amend Sections 29-1-1 and 55-3-47, Mississippi Code of 1972, to Conform, and for Related Purposes," http://billstatus.ls.state.ms.us/documents/2006/html/SB/2800-2899/SB2803IN.html (accessed May 25, 2009).

99. Pam Coe, "More Agency Than They Bargained for and Less Land," Paper for Anthropology 192, Spring 1958, 19, box 249, file 10, AAIA Papers. For the Agriculture Committee and the fair, see "Rules and Regulations," Entry 327, box 42, file: Mississippi Band of Choctaw Indians, 1951–52, FCTA, NARA-SW.

100. "Rules and Regulations," Entry 327, FCTA, NARA-SW.

101. SAR 1958, 3, Entry 327, box 36, FCTA, NARA-SW; Minutes of the Choctaw Tribal Council, October 13, 1959, 24–26, Tribal Archives.

102. Minutes of the Choctaw Tribal Council, April 9, 1957, 14–15, Tribal Archives. For the improved rural manufacturing economy, see Peterson, "Assimilation, Separation, and Out-Migration," 197–99, and Moore and Steve, "Dropout Study, 1964," 4.

103. Minutes of the Choctaw Tribal Council, October 14, 1959, 35–37, Tribal Archives.

104. Minutes of the Choctaw Tribal Council, October 11, 1960, 1–6, Tribal Archives.

105. Minutes of the Choctaw Tribal Council, July 11, 1961, 1–8, and October 8, 1963, 13–14; Minutes of a Special Called Meeting of the Choctaw Tribal Council, August 26, 1963, 1–4, Tribal Archives.

106. Minutes of the Choctaw Tribal Council, October 13, 1964, 12; Minutes of a Special Called Meeting of the Choctaw Tribal Council, November 27, 1964, 1–5, Tribal Archives; Moore and Steve, "Dropout Study, 1964," 4.

107. Peterson, "Assimilation, Separation, and Out-Migration," 1290. For analysis of employment by community, see Peterson's 1970 study, *Socio-Economic Characteristics of the Mississippi Choctaw Indians.*

108. Data on Neshoba County from surveys by the College of Business, Mississippi State University, Starkville, quoted in Mars, *Witness,* 273.

109. Minutes of the Choctaw Tribal Council, July 13, 1965, 5, Tribal Archives.

110. Peterson credited Title 7 of the 1964 Civil Rights Act with improving the Choctaws' place in the labor market. Peterson, "Assimilation, Separation, and Out-Migration," 1289.

111. Bowers complied anyway, hiring both Choctaws and African Americans, but his fears of being bombed did not materialize. Mars, *Witness,* 273–74.

112. For a detailed discussion of the KKK in Neshoba County in the 1960s, see Whitehead, *Attack on Terror,* and Cagin and Dray, *We Are Not Afraid.* A Choctaw man found the slain workers' burned-out car and reported it to the agency, who then called the FBI. Minutes of the Choctaw Tribal Council, October 25, 1951, Tribal Archives.

113. Mars, *Witness,* 276–77.

114. Mars, *Witness,* 274.

115. Minutes of the Choctaw Tribal Council, January 8, 1963, 7, and January 23, 1964, 3; Minutes of a Special Called Meeting of the Choctaw Tribal Council, January 31, 1963, 1–6, Tribal Archives.

116. Minutes of the Choctaw Tribal Council, October 13, 1963, 11–12, Tribal Archives.

117. Minutes of the Choctaw Tribal Council, October 13, 1963, 11–12, Tribal Archives.

8. Relocation, Resistance

1. For termination, see note 1 of chapter 7. For relocation, see Fixico, *Urban Indian Experience;* Carpio, *Indigenous Albuquerque;* Thrush, *Native Seattle;* Ramirez, *Native Hubs;* and Rosenthal, *Reimagining Indian Country.* First-hand analyses of these policies are found in Philp, *Indian Self Rule.*

2. For analysis of the politics of state and federal recognition for tribes in Alabama and Louisiana from the late 1960s to the 1990s, see Bates, *The Other Movement.*

3. Robert Cullum, Area Placement and Relocation Officer, to W. O. Roberts, Area Director of the Muskogee Area Office, May 8, 1952, Entry 326—Office of Tribal Operations, CCF, 1947–65, box 37, file: Special Problems, 1952–53, FCTA, NARA-SW.

4. Tolbert, "Sociological Study," 243–45; Cullum to Roberts, May 1, 1952; Willie McMillan to Paul Vance, Choctaw Superintendent, April 20, 1952; Otis Stoliby to Vance, April 21, 1952; Roberts to Charles F. Miller, Chief of Placement Branch, September 18, 1953, Entry 326, box 34, file: Relocation. For the Indian community in Chicago, see Straus, *Native Chicago,* 159–230. When I visited in 2004, the flag of the Mississippi Band was prominently displayed in the Chicago American Indian Center.

5. SAR, 1953, 25, Entry 3271947–65, box 36, file: Annual Reports: 1953–58, FCTA, NARA-SW.

6. Roberts to Miller, September 18, 1953, Entry 326, box 34, file: Relocation; SAR, 1954, 26–28, Entry 327, box 36, both FCTA, NARA-SW.

7. SAR 1954, 27, Entry 327, box 36, FCTA, NARA-SW.

8. Kent Fitzgerald, Relocation Officer from the Central Office, Kurt Dreifus, Relocation Officer from the Chicago Office, and Robert Cullum spoke. Minutes of the Choctaw Tribal Council, January 11, 1955, 1–4; Minutes of the Choctaw Tribal Council, October 9, 1956, 17–19, Tribal Archives, Pearl River High School, Choctaw MS.

9. SAR 1957, 9–11, FCTA, NARA-SW; Peterson, "Mississippi Band of Choctaw Indians," 242.

10. Peterson, "Assimilation, Separation, and Out-Migration," 1289.

11. Tolbert, "Sociological Study," 245–47; Peterson, "Mississippi Band of Choctaw Indians," 207. Mrs. Cleddie Bell, Mrs. Mary Lou Farmer, and John Mingo served on this committee. Minutes of the Choctaw Tribal Council, October 8, 1957, 12, Tribal Archives.

12. SAR 1960, 16, and 1961, 12, FCTA, NARA-SW.

13. Minutes of the Choctaw Tribal Council, April 9, 1957, 2–3, July 9, 1957, 11–12, Tribal Archives.

14. Vance to Fickinger, June 23, 1958, Minutes of the Choctaw Tribal Council, January 14, 1959, Tribal Archives.

15. Minutes of the Choctaw Tribal Council, January 13, 1959, 3–8, Tribal Archives.

16. Vance to Fickinger, May 14, 1959, Fickinger to CIA, May 20, 1959, box 36, file: Amendment to Constitution By-Laws. The amendments were to do away with residency requirements for membership. Academics who worked with the Choctaws in the 1950s and early 1960s all noted the lack of connection between the council and most Choctaws.

17. Virgil Harrington, Area Director, Muskogee Area Office, to Paul Billie, Chicago, March 27, 1970. For the revised constitution, see MBCI, http://www.choctaw .org/government/court/constitution.html (accessed February 7, 2012).

18. Tolbert, "Sociological Study," 247.

19. Minutes of the Choctaw Tribal Council, April 12, 1960, 17, Tribal Archives.

20. Emmett York to LaVerne Madigan, March 24, 1960, box 249, folder 10, Choctaw 1949–1960, AAIA Papers.

21. "Report on the Mississippi Choctaws," n.d., filed with LaVerne Madigan's papers from 1962. Internal clues in the document indicate that it is probably a report that she made as AAIA executive director. See box 245, folder 11, Choctaw 1949–1960, AAIA Papers. Oral histories of Choctaws Barry Davis Jim Sr., Jason York, and Kenneth York stress that the Choctaws felt that they were on the peripheries of the civil rights movement because of their separate status as Indians. Mississippi Oral History Program, Mississippi Band of Choctaw Indians, volume 727, Center for Oral History and Culture, University of Southern Mississippi, Hat-

tiesburg. For analysis of this divide on the national level, see Cobb, *Native Activism in Cold War America*.

22. Minutes of a Special Called Meeting of the Choctaw Tribal Council, December 11, 1962, 19, Tribal Archives.

23. White and White, "Phillip Martin: Mississippi Choctaw," 202.

24. Minutes of a Special Called Meeting of the Choctaw Tribal Council, December 11, 1962, 10–18, Tribal Archives. Martin expressed the same sentiments about civil rights as Vine Deloria Jr. In Deloria's 1969 "Indian manifesto," *Custer Died for Your Sins*, he chastised African American civil rights leaders for missing the Indians' main focus: "tribal existence within the homeland reservation" (183). Yet African American activists sometimes enunciated a similar conception of dispossession, feeling that they were being driven from their homelands by racist backlash. See James C. Cobb, "Searching for Southernness," in *Redefining Southern Culture*, 125–49.

25. Minutes of the Choctaw Tribal Council, July 9, 1963, 1, Tribal Archives.

26. Minutes of the Choctaw Tribal Council, January 11, 1961, 17, Tribal Archives.

27. Minutes of the Choctaw Tribal Council, January 11, 1961, 17, Tribal Archives. For the Indian Citizenship Act of 1924, see http://digital.library.okstate.edu/kappler /vol4/html_files/v4p1165.html (accessed March 10, 2010).

28. *Gong Lum v. Rice*, http://www.brownat50.org/brownCases/PreBrownCases /GongLumvRice1927.html (accessed August 6, 2008). Loewen discusses this case in *Mississippi Chinese*, 61–69.

29. *Gong Lum v. Rice*, http://www.brownat50.org/brownCases/PreBrownCases /GongLumvRice1927.html (accessed August 6, 2008).

30. For Mississippi's racial laws, see Murray, *States' Laws on Race and Color*, 238; J. P. Coleman, Attorney General of Mississippi, to Burdette Richardson, Circuit Clerk, Philadelphia MS, October 18, 1950, Entry 327, box 42, file: Special Problems, FCTA, NARA-SW.

31. Roberts to CIA, August 17, 1953, Entry 327, box 37, file: Special Problems, FCTA, NARA-SW.

32. Report of Joe Jennings, June 26, 1935, CCF: 150-54948-1933, BIA, NARA-DC.

33. Memo, T. H. Heard, Reservation Principle, to Vance, December 29, 1951, Entry 327, box 42, file: Special Problems among the Mississippi Choctaws, FCTA, NARA-SW.

34. Minutes of the Choctaw Tribal Council, September 11, 1947, unpaginated, Tribal Archives; Marie Hayes, "Outline of Needs for the Social and Economic Development of the Mississippi Band of Choctaw Indians," Section 2, Education, and notes for Section 7, Welfare, unpaginated, Entry 326, box 43, file: Outline, Social and Economic Need, Mississippi Band of Choctaws, May 1, 1952, FCTA, NARA-SW.

35. Commissioner Dillon Myer attended a council meeting to push this plan, but the council remained noncommittal. Minutes of the Choctaw Tribal Council, De-

cember 6, 1951, 3. For the Boy Scout alternative, see Minutes of the Choctaw Tribal Council, July 8, 1952, 2–3, Tribal Archives.

36. Richard Schifter, General Council, AAIA, to LaVerne Madigan, Executive Director, AAIA, December 28, 1959; Victor Kaneubbe to Fickinger, January 8, 1960; box 249, folder 10. Oliver La Farge, AAIA *Newsletter*, June 1960, Entry 327, box 42, file: 1960–62, FCTA, NARA-SW.

37. Management Improvement Schedule for 1952–1953, Entry 327, box 44, file: Management Improvement Schedule, 1952–56, FCTA, NARA-SW.

38. Management Improvement Schedule for 1955, Entry 327, box 44, file: Management Improvement Schedule, 1952–56, FCTA, NARA-SW.

39. Schifter to Madigan, December 28, 1960; Victor Kaneubbe to Fickinger, January 8, 1960, box 249, folder 10, AAIA Papers.

40. James C. Cobb skillfully debunks this argument in *Brown Decision*.

41. SAR 1958, 30, SAR 1960, 26, SAR 1961, 26, Entry 327 box 36, FCTA, NARA-SW.

42. Management Improvement Schedule for 1954–55; SAR 1956 has data from 1951 to 1956 on placements in white homes—see p. 41. For later failed attempts, see Minutes of the Choctaw Tribal Council, April 11, 1961, 3–19. For the BIA's gradualist approach, see Minutes of the Choctaw Tribal Council, April 11, 1961, 13–19; Martin noted the program's demise in the council meeting of January 8, 1963, see p. 6, all in Tribal Archives. For the help of "outside agitators" in moving the program forward, see Victor Kaneubbe to Fickinger, January 8, 1960, box 249, folder 10, AAIA Papers. For the ending of the campaign to place Choctaw students in white homes, see Minutes of the Choctaw Tribal Council, January 8, 1963, 5, Tribal Archives.

43. Cobb, *Most Southern Place on Earth*, 230–52; Mars, *Witness in Philadelphia*, 84–119.

44. Notes by LaVerne Madigan on phone conversations with Cullum, August 18, 1960, box 249, folder 11; York to Madigan, March 24, 1960; Martin to Madigan, March 31, 1960, box 249, folder 10, AAIA Papers.

45. In 1961 the Subcommittee on Constitutional Rights of the Senate Judiciary Committee began hearings to determine if Indians' civil rights were being violated. Like many southern legislators, the chair of the committee was an ardent segregationist who nonetheless showed an interest in Indian problems. The committee concluded that Indians were suffering from racial discrimination. This process led to the passage of the Indian Civil Rights Act, which, ironically, focused on protecting Indians from civil rights violations by tribal governments. Clarkin, *Federal Indian Policy in the Kennedy and Johnson Administrations*, 262–69. For more on Indian activism in the civil rights years, see Daniel M. Cobb, "Philosophy of an Indian War," and "'Us Indians Understand the Basics'"; and Hoikkala, "Mothers and Community Builders."

46. McMillen, "Development of Civil Rights," 154–59. McMillen notes that Mississippi's business leaders dreaded bad publicity about racial issues and backed such initiatives with great zeal. John Dittmer makes a similar case in *Local People*.

47. For the "Southern Manifesto," see Cobb, *Brown Decision*, 49. For the Dixiecrats, see Winter, "New Directions," 142–44.

48. For the Mississippi State Sovereignty Commission, see http://www.mdah .state.ms.us/arlib/contents/er/sovcom/scagencycasehistory.php (accessed June 2, 2009); Mars, *Witness in Philadelphia*, 56–59.

49. Cobb, *Most Southern Place on Earth*, 209–29. In Neshoba County, Florence Mars describes how the Klan destroyed her family's business because they were insufficiently hostile to civil rights. Mars, *Witness in Philadelphia*, 137–40.

50. Cobb, *Most Southern Place on Earth*, 232; McMillen, "Development of Civil Rights," 166. For grassroots civil rights organizing in Mississippi during these years, see Dittmer, *Local People*, and Payne, *I've Got the Light of Freedom*.

51. T. J. Scott to Dr. L. Bracey Campbell, December 10, 1953, Series 4: Constituents' Files, Eastland Papers.

52. R. C. Ewing to Senator John Stennis, May 7, 1956; Stennis to Ewing, May 18, 1956, folder: 1957, Stennis Papers.

53. Carrol Frazier Landrum, Biloxi MS, to Senator John Stennis, October 3, 1957, folder: 1957, Stennis Papers.

54. Mrs. N. Palmer to Senator Eastland, March 28, 1960, Series 4: Constituents' Files, Eastland Papers. Eastland may have spoken with his Senate colleagues about the Choctaws, but the issue does not appear in the debates over civil rights in the *Congressional Record* from 1953 through 1964. The specific page citations for this entire discussion are too numerous to list, but there is an index to every volume with page citations for each member's remarks on various issues.

55. Patronage continued to play a role as well. The papers of all Mississippi politicians contain numerous letters from constituents hoping to win contracts at the Choctaw Agency. A couple of examples are W. H. White to Senator Stennis, August 13, 1953; Stennis to Rex Lee, Associate Commissioner of Indian Affairs, August 19, 1953, folder: 1957, Stennis Papers.

56. Clippings from *Jackson State Times*, September 10 and 16, 1957, in Entry 327, box 42, file: Miscellaneous, FCTA, NARA-SW.

57. Fickinger to Vance, October 10, 1957, in Entry 327, box 42, file: Miscellaneous, FCTA, NARA-SW.

58. *Jackson Clarion Ledger* and *Daily News*, February 1, 1959, box 249, file 10, AAIA Papers.

59. Minutes of the Choctaw Tribal Council, April 14, 1959, 16–20, Tribal Archives.

60. Vance to Roberts, April 17, 1959, Entry 327, box 41, file: Mississippi Choctaw Resolutions, 1960.

61. Roberts to Vance, November 9, 1960, Entry 327, box 41, file: Mississippi Choctaw Resolutions, 1960.

62. White and White, "Phillip Martin," 197–98; Martin, Jeter, and Blanchard, *Chief*, 63–68. This process was also at work among African American veterans. For a succinct statement of how one Choctaw World War II veteran described his duty to his

country, see "Indians Fight America's Wars Because 'This is Our Country, Too,'" Choctaw Says," Department of Defense, Internal News, http://www.defense.gov/specials /nativeam02/fight.html (accessed August 3, 2012).

63. "Indian Segregation in Mississippi," Mrs. John A. Osoinach, to Dear Sirs, February 10, 1958, box 249, folder 10, AAIA Papers.

64. Madigan to Oliver La Farge, April 7, 1959, AAIA, box 249, folder 10, AAIA Papers.

65. Pam Coe to LaVerne Madigan, July 20, 1959, box 249, folder 10, AAIA Papers. LaVerne Madigan and the Midwestern Intertribal Council planned this program of outreach to communities near reservations on the northern Great Plains. It included establishing a League of Women Voters in reservation communities, creating a speakers' bureau of tribal elders, distributing educational materials on Indians, "promoting understanding and responsibility in youth groups," and hiring an employment officer to help Indians get jobs. See the *Lewiston Evening Journal*, September 11, 1957, p. 6, for a press release on the program, http://news.google.com/newspapers?nid=19 13&dat=19570911&id=TcdGAAAAIBAJ&sjid=8vMMAAAAIBAJ&pg=1029,847798 (accessed June 25, 2012).

66. Madigan to Coe, October 5, 1959; Coe to Madigan, October 15, 1959, box 249, folder 10, AAIA Papers.

67. The Highlander Folk School was founded in 1932 by Myles Horton and Don West in Grundy County, Tennessee. Their work with Dr. Martin Luther King Jr. and Rosa Parks did not endear them to white Tennesseans, and they became the targets of Klan intimidation, police harassment, and finally, legal actions for violating Tennessee's segregation statures. For information on the Highlander Folk School, see their website at http://www.highlandercenter.org (accessed June 2, 2009).

68. For Osoinach's interactions with Highlander, see Coe to Madigan, n.d., but Madigan replied on June 9, 1959; Samuel Birnkrant to Madigan, February 9, 1960, Helen McMillan Meyers to Madigan, February 12, 1960, box 249, folder 10, AAIA Papers.

69. Madigan to Alice Cobb, March 14, 1960, box 249, folder 10, AAIA Papers.

70. For an analysis of the relationship between the Choctaws and their white allies, see Osburn, "Mississippi Choctaws and Racial Politics."

71. For the direct action tactics of the National Indian Youth Council, see Shreve, *Red Power Rising*.

72. Fickinger to Kaneubbe, December 31, 1959; Kaneubbe to Madigan, January 18, 1960, box 249, folder 10, AAIA Papers.

73. Fickinger to Kaneubbe, December 31, 1959; Kaneubbe to Madigan, January 18, 1960, box 249, folder 10, AAIA Papers.

74. "Mississippi Discrimination Against First Grade Pupil," clipping from the AAIA Newsletter, Entry 327, box 42, file: 1960–61, FCTA, NARA-SW.

75. Victor Kaneubbe, "Our Experiences in Race Relations as Your Missionary in this Field," box 249, folder 10, AAIA Papers.

76. Victor Kaneubbe, "The Condition of the Choctaw Indian," mimeographed handout, box 2, folder 10, BIA 1964, Stennis Papers. This document appeared with

letters requesting a high school in all the papers of the Mississippi congressional delegation. The Stennis Papers had forty letters on this topic. Senator James O. Eastland's files contained twenty letters. William Colmer received ten. These numbers may not appear significant, but even as few as two or three letters can sometimes influence legislation. Complete citations and content analysis for these letters would be prohibitive, but the bulk of them listed the need to train Indian leaders in their communities and their desire to preserve Choctaw families as reasons for their support of the high school.

77. Fickinger to Kaneubbe, December 31, 1959, box 249, folder 10; Kaneubbe to Madigan, May 3, 1960, box 249, folder 11, AAIA Papers.

78. Madigan to Kaneubbe, March 17, 1960; Madigan to Martin, March 14, 1960, box 249, folder 10, AAIA Papers.

79. Martin to Madigan, March 31, 1960, box 249, folder 10; Kaneubbe to Madigan, April 6, 1960, box 249, folder 11, AAIA Papers.

80. Madigan to Kaneubbe, March 14, 1960, box 249, folder 10, AAIA Papers.

81. Madigan to Kaneubbe, April 6, 1960, box 249, folder 11, AAIA Papers.

82. He based this on a scripture admonishing Christians not to go to court (1 Corinthians 6:7), and his discussion with former Mississippi governor J. P. Coleman, who warned that the state would shut down the entire public school system should a school desegregation case make it to court. Madigan to Kaneubbe, July 4, 1960, box 249, folder 11, AAIA Papers. For the decision to close Mississippi's schools, see McMillen, "Development of Civil Rights, 1956–1970," 154–59.

83. Minutes of the Choctaw Tribal Council, October 31, 1951, 4; October 17, 1952, 1; November 13, 1952, 3; July 14, 1953, 8–9, Tribal Archives.

84. Minutes of the Choctaw Tribal Council, April 12, 1955, 9–10, Tribal Archives.

85. Winstead to Emmons, April 27, 1955; Emmons to Winstead, May 23, 1955, Entry 327, box 43, file: Mississippi Band of Choctaw Indians, FCTA, NARA-SW.

86. Minutes of the Choctaw Tribal Council, October 18, 1957, 8–9, Tribal Archives.

87. Hilda Cragun, Secretary, to Helen L. Peterson, Executive Director, National Congress of American Indians, to Mississippi Choctaw Tribal Council, June 1, 1959, box 249, folder 10; Harry J. Belvin to AAIA, July 23, 1959, box 249, folder 10, AAIA Papers.

88. Minutes of the Choctaw Tribal Council, July 14, 1959, 6–7, Tribal Archives.

89. Minutes of the Choctaw Tribal Council, October 14, 1959, 29, Tribal Archives.

90. Minutes of the Choctaw Tribal Council, October 14, 1959, 29–35, Tribal Archives.

91. Madigan to J. C. Allen, March 14, 1960, box 249, folder 10, AAIA Papers.

92. Martin to Fred A. Seaton, Secretary of the Interior, September 27, 1960, box 249, folder 11, AAIA Papers. Madigan also wrote Undersecretary Elmer Bennett reminding him of the promise to move Vance. Madigan to Elmer Bennett, Undersecretary of the Interior, November 29, 1960, AAIA, box 249, folder 11, AAIA Papers.

93. Minutes of the Choctaw Tribal Council, April 11, 1961, 15–18, Tribal Archives.

94. Madigan to Martin, June 8, 1962, box 249, folder 11, AAIA Papers.

95. Madigan to Martin, June 8, 1962, box 249, folder 11, AAIA Papers.

96. La Farge to Madigan and Schifter, June 12, 1962, box 249, folder 11, AAIA Papers.

97. Schifter to La Farge and Madigan, June 15, 1962, box 249, folder 11, AAIA Papers.

98. Minutes of the Choctaw Tribal Council, April 12, 10–11, July 10, 1960, 9–11, April 10, 1962, 5–6, Tribal Archives.

99. Madigan to La Farge and Schifter, June 25, 1962; La Farge to Nash, June 26, 1962; Schifter to La Farge, July 13, 1962; La Farge to Madigan, July 17, 1962, box 249, folder 11, AAIA Papers, Minutes of the Choctaw Tribal Council, October 9, 1962, 1, Tribal Archives.

100. Minutes of a Special Called Meeting of the Choctaw Tribal Council, December 11, 1962, 9–10, Tribal Archives.

101. Minutes of a Special Called Meeting of the Choctaw Tribal Council, December 11, 1962, 10–18, Tribal Archives.

102. Minutes of a Special Called Meeting of the Choctaw Tribal Council, December 11, 1962, 9–18, Tribal Archives. York was not clear regarding which "Negro boy's case" he meant, but since the context was education, it might have been James Meredith.

103. Lonnie Hardin, Choctaw Superintendent, to Commissioner of Indian Affairs, December 17, 1962; A. B. Caldwell, Area Director of Schools, to CIA, December 31, 1962; Area Director Graham Holmes to CIA, January 15, 1963, Tribal Archives. For increased direct action in Mississippi, see Cobb, *Most Southern Place on Earth*, 232.

104. Minutes of the Choctaw Tribal Council, January 8, 1963, 5–8, Tribal Archives.

105. Minutes of the Choctaw Tribal Council, January 8, 1963, 6–7, Tribal Archives.

106. For an astute analysis of this process, see Cobb, *Native Activism*.

107. Minutes of the Choctaw Tribal Council, January 8, 1963, 1–6, Tribal Archives.

108. Holmes to the Honorable Commissioner of Indian Affairs, January 15, 1963, Entry 326, box 12, folder 064, Resolutions, FCTA, NARA-SW.

109. Telegram from Arthur Winstead to Philip Martin, April 9, 1963, Tribal Archives.

110. Peterson, "Mississippi Band of Choctaw Indians," 250–51.

111. Cobb, *Native Activism*, 8–29.

112. For Osoinach's role in the conference, see "Indian Segregation in Mississippi," box 249, folder 10, Choctaw 1949–1960, AAIA Papers.

113. Minutes of the Choctaw Tribal Council, July 11, 1961, 18–20, Tribal Archives.

114. Minutes of the Choctaw Tribal Council, July 18, 1958, 4, Tribal Archives.

115. Minutes of the Choctaw Tribal Council, April 9, 1963, 9–10, Tribal Archives.

116. Minutes of the Choctaw Tribal Council, October 8, 1963, 7–12, Tribal Archives.

117. Minutes of the Choctaw Tribal Council, January 12, 1965, 15, Tribal Archives.

118. Thompson and Peterson, "Mississippi Choctaw Identity," 189–92.

119. Minutes of the Organization Meeting of the Board of Directors, USET, June 27, 1969. For York's remarks, see Minutes of the Meeting of USET, November 14–15, 1968," both in Entry 326, box 18, file: United Southeastern Tribes, FCTA, NARA-SW.

120. United Southeastern Tribes Meeting, November 14–15, 1968, CCF: 076, box 18, file: United Southeastern Tribes, FCTA, NARA-SW.

121. "Resolution to Have the Mississippi Band of Choctaw Indians Directly Under the Bureau of Indian Affairs Office in Washington DC"; "Commissioner Bruce Decides in Favor of Choctaw BIA Change to Washington Office," clipping from *Choctaw Community News*, June 15, 1970, 1, Entry 326, box 99, file: Choctaw, 1967–1970, FCTA, NARA-SW.

122. For Native American voices on self-determination and federal policy, see Philp, *Indian Self Rule*; Cobb and Fowler, *Beyond Red Power*; and Cobb, *Native Activism*.

123. White and White, "Phillip Martin," 202; Peterson, "Mississippi Band of Choctaw Indians," 235.

Epilogue and Conclusions

1. Peterson, "Choctaw Self-Determination," 144.

2. AAIA, "Exclusive Federal Jurisdiction Over Crimes Committed by Indians in Indian Country, Memorandum to Indian Tribes," n.d.; data on enforcement of this act in S. Bobo Dean, "Law and Order on the Mississippi Choctaw Reservation," November 5, 1970, 12–17, both in box 249, folder 12: Choctaw 1967–70, AAIA Papers.

3. Peterson, "Choctaw Self-Determination," 239–44; "Resolution Establishing a Community Action Program Legal Service Advisory Board," April 12, 1967, CCF: 054-064, Entry 326: Office of Tribal Operations, box 13, file: Resolutions, 1967, FCTA, NARA-SW; Dean, "Law and Order on the Mississippi Choctaw Reservation," 15; White and White, "Phillip Martin," 198.

4. The Stennis Papers include eight folders of correspondence addressing Choctaw economic development.

5. White and White, "Phillip Martin," 199; Peterson, "Choctaw Self-Determination," 156–57; Peter Michelmore, "Uprising in Indian Country," *Reader's Digest*, November 1984, 69–76, Stennis Papers.

6. Peterson, "Choctaw Self-Determination," 144; Bryant Rogers, Program Development Officer, to William Myler, Director, Association on American Indian Affairs, August 11, 1971, box 249, folder 12, Choctaw 1967–1970, AAIA Papers.

7. See Peterson, "Choctaw Self-Determination," 144–45; Ferguson, "Reestablishment of Tribal Government," Annotated Chronological Outline.

8. Peterson, "Choctaw Self-Determination," 147; See also *Revised Constitution and Bylaws of the Mississippi Band of Choctaw Indians* on their tribal website, http://www.choctaw.org/government/court/constitution.html (accessed February 7, 2012).

9. "School Inspection of Samuel H. Thompson, Superintendent of Schools, March 22, 1932," 7–8, CCF: 806-6507-1932, BIA, NARA-DC.

10. *U.S. v. John*, United States Court of Appeals, Fifth Circuit, October 11, 1977, http://bulk.resource.org/courts.gov/c/f2/560/560.f2d.1202.76-1518.html (accessed June 18, 2008). This link no longer works, but a copy of this summary of the case is in the author's possession.

11. *U.S. v. John*, 5–6.

12. *U.S. v. John*, 11–22, 35–40.

13. *U.S. v. John*, 49.

14. *U.S. v. John*, 58–62.

15. *U.S. v. John*, 64.

16. *U.S. v. John*, 57.

17. *U.S. v. John*, 81–86.

18. *U.S. v. John*, 437 U.S. 634, June 23, 1978, http://supreme.justia.com/us/437/634 /case.html (accessed June 8, 2008).

19. *U.S. v. John*, 437 U.S. 635.

20. Wilkinson, *American Indians*, 77.

21. In "Beyond the New Indian History," Nicholas Rosenthal surveys recent ethnohistorical scholarship that incorporates Indian history into the broader context of American history. The best works have always done this, yet most historians frustratingly sideline Indian history as irrelevant to the main narratives of American history. This study contextualizes Indian history in the larger historical narrative of southern history.

22. Green, *New Deal*, ix–x.

23. Indian agencies represented a significant federal presence in the West but were less prevalent in the South, where there are only nine federally recognized tribes. For the federal government in the West, see Richard White, *"It's Your Misfortune,"* 57–60; Cahill, *Federal Fathers and Mothers*; and Jacobs, *White Mother*. For a listing of federally recognized tribes in the South, see Cramer, *Cash, Color, and Colonialism*, 41; Roth, "Overview," 184–85; Bureau of Indian Affairs, Tribal Directory, http:// www.bia.gov/WhoWeAre/bia/ois/TribalGovernmentServices/TribalDirectory/index.htm (accessed August 4, 2012). For the wide range of responses to federal intervention in rural America, see the essays in Stock and Johnston, *Countryside in the Age of the Modern State*.

24. Saunt, "Telling Stories: The Political Uses of Myth," makes an analogous argument regarding stories for Cherokees and Creeks.

25. In recent years, historians of the South have acknowledged that the boundaries between African Americans and whites were frequently blurred, redrawn, and crossed. The seventy-fifth anniversary issue of the *Journal of Southern History* has several historiographic articles noting this trend. Only two of them, however, include Indians in their analysis of race relations: Jones, "Labor and the Idea of Race," and Hornsby-Gutting, "Manning the Region."

26. For an incisive critique of how historians of the South have neglected to include postremoval Indians in their work, see Perdue, "Legacy of Indian Removal."

27. Scholars of southwestern Indians also employ a tri-racial model that includes Hispanics.

28. I am defining studies of postremoval southern Indians broadly to include the Five Tribes in Indian Territory and Oklahoma. Studies of other so-called remnant tribes in the Southeast present similar evidence of how southerners in different states dealt with racial groups that did not fit their binary white-black model. Blu, *Lumbee*

Problem; Finger, *Eastern Band of Cherokees*; Finger, *Cherokee Americans*; Kersey, *Pelts, Plumes, and Hides*; Kersey, *Florida Seminoles and the New Deal*; Kersey, *Assumption of Sovereignty*; Lerch, *Waccamaw Legacy*; Oakley, *Keeping the Circle*; Kramer, *Cash, Color, and Colonialism*; Lowery, *Lumbee Indians*; Sturm, *Blood Politics*; Saunt, *Black, White, and Indian*; Miles, *Ties that Bind*; Chang, *Color of the Land*. Two collections of essays also make this point: Williams, *Southeastern Indians since the Removal Era*, and Paredes, *Indians of the Southeastern United States*.

29. Another exception to the general pattern of land loss occurred in New Mexico, where President Theodore Roosevelt by executive order declared the lands of the Pueblo Indians to be reservations. See Lawrence, *Lessons from an Indian Day School*, 17–64.

30. For an overview of the literature on the Indian New Deal, see note 2 in chapter 6 of this book.

31. For an overview of the literature on termination and relocation, see the first note in chapters 7 and 8 of this book.

32. The most famous women in that fight were Ada Deer and LaDonna Harris. See Harris's autobiography, *LaDonna Harris*, and Lurie, "Ada Deer." Colleen O'Neill's excellent study of Navajo workers uncovered a very different view of gender roles in termination. Officials implementing the policy discounted women's labor as insignificant to Navajo self-sufficiency. Navajos did not regard it as such, of course. O'Neill, *Working*, 89–90.

33. Cobb, "Continuing Encounters," 58.

34. Martin, Jeter, and Blanshard, *Chief*, 235–47.

Bibliography

Archival Sources

Association on American Indian Affairs (AAIA). Records. Seeley G. Mudd Manuscript Library, Princeton University, Princeton NJ.

Bilbo, Theodore G., Papers. M2. McCain Library and Archives, Special Collections, University of Southern Mississippi, Hattiesburg MS.

Bureau of Catholic Indian Missions (BCIM). Records. General Correspondence, 1853–ongoing, n.d., Series 1-1. Department of Special Collections, Raynor Memorial Libraries, Marquette University, Milwaukee WI.

Bureau of Indian Affairs, Department of the Interior, Record Group 75. National Archives and Records Administration, Washington DC (NARA-DC).

    CCC—Indian Division, Entry 1000, General Records, box 57, Choctaw.

    Central Classified Files (CCF)—Choctaw.

    Records of the Office of the Commissioner of Indian Affairs. Superintendent's Annual Reports (SAR), 1920–1935, Choctaw Agency, M101, roll 20.

Claiborne, J. F. H., Papers. Manuscripts Division, Library of Congress, Washington DC.

Choctaw Indians. Clippings Files. Mississippi Department of Archives and History (MDAH), Jackson MS.

Choctaw Removal Records, Atkinson/Elliot Indian Agency, box 4, Special Collections, Mitchell Memorial Library, Mississippi State University, Starkville MS.

    "Records of Commissioners Publius Pray, P. D. Vroom, and James R. Murray." Entry 270: Evidence, 1837–1838, Dispositions, folder 270.

    "Records of the Proceedings of the Choctaw Commission." Entry 268: Journal, 1837–1838, folder RG 75.

Choctaw Tribal Council. Minutes. Mississippi Band of Choctaw Indians Tribal Archives, Pearl River High School, Choctaw MS.

Collins, Henry Bascom. Papers. National Anthropological Archives, Suitland MD.

Collins, Ross. Papers. Manuscripts Division, Library of Congress, Washington DC.

Colmer, William M., Papers. M24. McCain Library and Archives, Special Collections, University of Southern Mississippi, Hattiesburg MS.

Eastland, James O., Papers. Department of Archives and Special Collections, J. D. Williams Library, University of Mississippi, Oxford MS.

Five Civilized Tribes Agency (FCTA). Bureau of Indian Affairs, Record Group 75. National Archives and Records Administration, Southwest Region (NARA-SW), Fort Worth TX.

    Entry 105—Records of Testimony (006).

    Entry 326—Central Classified Files, 1943–71. Records of the Office of Tribal Operations.

    Entry 327—Office Files of Tribal Affairs Officer, 1947–65. Records of the Office of Tribal Operations.

    Entry 570—Extension and Relief—Narrative and Statistical Reports. Records Relating to Extension and Relief Programs.

Fraser, Fabian. Papers. Mississippi Department of Archives and History (MDAH), Jackson MS.

Halbert, Henry S., Papers. Alabama Department of History and Archives, Montgomery AL.

Harrison, Pat. Papers. Department of Archives and Special Collections, J. D. Williams Library, University of Mississippi, Oxford MS.

Hurley, Patrick Jay. Papers. Western History Collections, University of Oklahoma Libraries, Norman OK.

Indian Claims Commission, Records of. Docket No. 52, boxes 617, 618, 620, Entry IIUD, Files 71–80. RG 279. National Archives and Records Administration, Washington DC (NARA-DC).

McLemore, Richard Aubrey. Papers, 1915–1969. Mississippi Department of Archives and History (MDAH), Jackson MS.

Mississippi Federation of Women's Clubs. Records. Mississippi Department of Archives and History (MDAH), Jackson MS.

Mississippi Oral History Project. Center for Oral History, McCain Library, University of Southern Mississippi, Hattiesburg MS.

Oklahoma Historical Society (OHS), National Archives and Records Administration, Southwest Region (NARA-SW), Fort Worth TX.

Southeastern Indian Oral History Project, University of Florida. Interviewer: Staff of *Nanih Waiyah*. Vertical File: Choctaw Indians, Neshoba County Library, Philadelphia MS.

Stennis, John C., Papers. Series 7: Interior Department. Subseries: Interior—General. BIA, 1953–1977, box 2. Congressional and Political Research Center of Mississippi State University, Starkville MS.

Williams, John Sharp. Collection. Department of Archives and Special Collections, J. D. Williams Library, University of Mississippi, Oxford MS.

Works Progress Administration (WPA) Files. Histories of Jones, Newton, Neshoba, Noxubee, Kemper, Leake, Scott, Lauderdale, Pearl River, and Winston Counties. Series 447: Historical Research Material. Mississippi Department of Archives and History (MDAH), Jackson MS.

Published Sources

Adams, David Wallace. *Education for Extinction: American Indians and the Boarding School Experience, 1875–1928.* Lawrence: University Press of Kansas, 1995.

Akers, Donna L. *Living in the Land of Death: The Choctaw Nation, 1830–1860.* East Lansing: Michigan State University Press, 2004.

Albers, Patricia C., and William R. James. "Illusion and Illumination: Visual Images of American Indian Women in the West." In *The Women's West,* edited by Susan Armitage and Elizabeth Jameson, 35–50. Norman: University of Oklahoma Press, 1987.

Alexander, Charles. *The Ku Klux Klan in the Southwest.* Norman: University of Oklahoma Press, 1995.

Amis, A. B., Sr. *Recollections of Social Customs in Newton and Scott Counties, Mississippi, Fifty Years Ago.* Meridian MS: self-published, 1934.

Anderson, Benedict. *Imagined Communities: Reflections on the Origin and Spread of Nationalism,* rev. ed. New York: Verso Press, 2006.

Archuleta, Margaret L., Brenda J. Child, and K. Tsianina Lomawaima, eds., *Away from Home: American Indian Boarding School Experiences.* Lincoln: University of Nebraska Press, 2006.

Barth, Fredrik. "Enduring and Emerging Issues in the Analysis of Ethnicity." In *The Anthropology of Ethnicity: Beyond Ethnic Groups and Boundaries,* edited by Hans Vermeulen and Cora Govers, 11–32. Amsterdam: Het Spinhuis, 1994.

———. *Ethnic Groups and Boundaries.* Boston: Little, Brown, 1969.

Bates, Denise E. *The Other Movement: Indian Rights and Civil Rights in the Deep South.* Tuscaloosa: University of Alabama Press, 2012.

Benson, Henry C. *Life among the Choctaw Indians and Sketches of the South-West.* Cincinnati: L. Swormstedt and A. Poe, 1860.

Berkhofer, Robert K., Jr. *The White Man's Indian: Images of the American Indian from Columbus to the Present.* New York: Vintage Books, 1979.

Bernstein, Alison. *American Indians and World War II: Toward a New Era in Indian Affairs.* Norman: University of Oklahoma Press, 1990.

Biolsi, Thomas. *Organizing the Lakota: The Political Economy of the New Deal on the Pine Ridge and Rosebud Reservations.* Tucson: University of Arizona Press, 1992.

Blu, Karen I. *The Lumbee Problem: The Making of an American Indian People.* Lincoln: University of Nebraska, 2001.

Bolton, Charles C. *Poor Whites of the Antebellum South: Tenants and Laborers in Central North Carolina and Northeast Mississippi.* Durham NC: Duke University Press, 1994.

Bordewich, Fergus M. *Killing the White Man's Indian: Reinventing Native Americans at the End of the Twentieth Century*. New York: Anchor Books, 1996.

Britten, Thomas A. *American Indians in World War I: At War and At Home*. Albuquerque: University of New Mexico Press, 1997.

Brown, A. J. *History of Newton County, Mississippi, from 1834–1894*. Jackson MS: Clarion-Ledger Company, 1894.

Browning, James R. "Anti-Miscegenation Laws in the United States." *Duke Bar Journal* 1, no. 1 (March 1951): 26–41.

Bynum, Victoria. *The Free State of Jones: Mississippi's Longest Civil War*. Chapel Hill: University of North Carolina Press, 2002.

———. *The Long Shadow of the Civil War: Southern Dissent and Its Legacies*. Chapel Hill: University of North Carolina Press, 2010.

Cagin, Seth, and Philip Dray. *We Are Not Afraid: The Story of Goodman, Schwerener, and Chaney and the Civil Rights Campaign for Mississippi*. New York: Bantam, 1998.

Cahill, Cathleen. *Federal Fathers and Mothers: A Social History of the United States Indian Service, 1869–1933*. Chapel Hill: University of North Carolina Press, 2011.

Carpio, Myla Vicenti. *Indigenous Albuquerque*. Lubbock: Texas Tech University Press, 2011.

Carson, James Taylor. "Greenwood LeFlore: Southern Creole, Choctaw Chief," 221–236. In *Pre-removal Choctaw History: Exploring New Paths*. Edited by Greg O'Brien. Norman: University of Oklahoma Press, 2008.

———. "The Obituary of Nations: Ethnic Cleansing, Memory, and the Origins of the Old South." *Southern Cultures* 14, no. 4 (2008): 6–31.

———. *Searching for the Bright Path: The Mississippi Choctaw from Prehistory to Removal*. Lincoln: University of Nebraska Press, 1999.

Carter, Kent. *The Dawes Commission and the Allotment of the Five Civilized Tribes, 1893–1914*. Orem UT: Ancestry.com, 1999.

Cashman, Dennis Sean. *America in the Gilded Age*. New York: New York University Press, 1984.

Cattelino, Jessica R. "Casino Roots: The Cultural Production of Twentieth-Century Seminole Economic Development." In Hosmer and O'Neill, *Native Pathways*, 66–90.

Chalmers, David M. *Hooded Americanism: The History of the Ku Klux Klan*. New York: New Viewpoints, 1965; 5th printing, 1981.

Chang, David. *The Color of the Land: Race, Nation, and the Politics of Landownership in Oklahoma, 1832–1929*. Chapel Hill: University of North Carolina Press, 2010.

Child, Brenda J. *Boarding School Seasons: American Indian Families, 1900–1940*. Lincoln: University of Nebraska Press, 1995.

Claiborne, J. F. H. *Mississippi as a Province, Territory, and State*. Jackson MS: Power and Barksdale, 1880.

Clarkin, Thomas. *Federal Indian Policy in the Kennedy and Johnson Administrations, 1961–1969*. Albuquerque: University of New Mexico Press, 2001.

Cobb, Daniel M. "Continuing Encounters." In Cobb and Fowler, *Beyond Red Power*, 57–69.

———. *Native Activism in Cold War America: The Struggle for Sovereignty*. Lawrence: University Press of Kansas, 2008.

———. "Philosophy of an Indian War: Indian Community Action in the Johnson Administration's War on Indian Poverty, 1964–68." *American Indian Culture and Research Journal* 22, no. 2 (1998): 71–103.

———. "Talking the Language of the Larger World: Politics in Cold War (Native) America." In Cobb and Fowler, *Beyond Red Power*, 161–71.

———. "'Us Indians Understand the Basics': Oklahoma Indians and the Politics of Community Action, 1964–1970." *Western Historical Quarterly* 33, no. 1 (2002): 41–66.

Cobb, Daniel M., and Loretta Fowler, eds. *Beyond Red Power: American Indian Politics and Activism since 1900*. Santa Fe: School for Advanced Research Press, 2007.

Cobb, James C. *The Brown Decision, Jim Crow, and Southern Identity*. Athens: University of Georgia Press, 2005.

———. *Industrialization and Southern Society, 1877–1984*. Lexington: University Press of Kentucky, 1984.

———. *The Most Southern Place on Earth: The Mississippi Delta and the Roots of Regional Identity*. New York: Oxford University Press, 1992.

———. *Redefining Southern Culture: Mind and Identity in the Modern South*. Athens: University of Georgia Press, 1999.

Cobb, James C., and Michael Namorato, eds. *The New Deal and the South*. Jackson: University Press of Mississippi, 1984.

Cobb, Joseph B. *Mississippi Scenes, or Sketches of Southern and Western Life and Adventure, Humorous Satirical, and Descriptive, Including the Legend of Black Creek*. Philadelphia MS: A. Hart, 1851.

Coe, Pamela. "Lost in the Hills of Home: Outline of Mississippi Choctaw Social Organization." Master's thesis, Columbia University, 1960.

Coker, William Sidney. "Pat Harrison: The Formative Years, 1911–1919." Master's thesis, University of Southern Mississippi, 1962.

———. "Pat Harrison's Efforts to Reopen the Choctaw Citizenship Rolls." *Southern Quarterly* 3 (1965): 36–61.

Collier, John. "A New Deal for the American Indian." *Literary Digest*, April 7, 1938, 21.

———. "We Took Away Their Best Lands, Broke Treaties." In *Annual Report of the Secretary of the Interior for the Fiscal Year Ended June 30, 1938*, 209–11. Washington DC: Government Printing Office, 1938.

Coleman, James P. "The Mississippi Constitution of 1890 and the Final Decade of the Nineteenth Century." In McLemore, *A History of Mississippi*, 2:3–28.

Collins, Henry Bascom. "Anthropometric Observations on the Choctaw." *American Journal of Physical Anthropology* 8 (October–December 1925): 425–36; 9 (January–March 1928): 353–55.

Commission to the Five Civilized Tribes. *Sixth Annual Report of the Commission to the Five Civilized Tribes in the Indian Territory to the Secretary of the Interior.* Washington DC: Government Printing Office, 1899.

Cowger, Thomas W. *The National Congress of American Indians: The Founding Years.* Lincoln: University of Nebraska Press, 1999.

Cox, Karen L. *Dixie's Daughters: The United Daughters of the Confederacy and the Preservation of Confederate Culture.* Gainesville: University of Florida Press, 2003.

Crawford, T. Hartley, Commissioner of Indian Affairs. "Report of the Secretary of War Communicating Information in Relation to the Contracts Made for the Removal and Subsistence of the Choctaw Indians," February 7, 1845. S. Doc. 86, 28th Cong., 2nd sess. (1845), microfiche 451.

Cushman, Horatio B. *History of the Choctaw, Chickasaw, and Natchez Indians.* Greenville TX: Highlight Printing House, 1899.

Daniel, Pete. *Breaking the Land: The Transformation of Cotton, Tobacco, and Rice Cultures since 1880.* Urbana: University of Illinois Press, 1985.

———. "Federal Farm Policy and the End of an Agrarian Way of Life." In *Major Problems in the History of the American South*, vol. 2: *The New South*, edited by Paul D. Escott and David R. Goldfield, 397–405. Lexington MA: D. C. Health and Company, 1990.

———. *The Shadow of Slavery: Peonage in the South, 1901–1969.* Urbana: University of Illinois Press, 1961.

Davis, Edward. "The Mississippi Choctaws." *Chronicles of Oklahoma* 10, no. 11 (1932): 257–66.

Davis, Reuben. *Recollections of Mississippi and Mississippians*, rev. ed. Jackson: University and College Press of Mississippi, 1972.

Debo, Angie. *And Still the Waters Run: The Betrayal of the Five Civilized Tribes.* Norman: University of Oklahoma Press, 1989.

———. *The Rise and Fall of the Choctaw Republic.* Norman: University of Oklahoma Press, 1961.

Deloria, Philip. *Playing Indian.* New Haven CT: Yale University Press, 1999.

Deloria, Vine, Jr. *American Indian Policy in the Twentieth Century.* Norman: University of Oklahoma Press, 1985.

———. *Custer Died for Your Sins: An Indian Manifesto.* Norman: University of Oklahoma Press, 1988.

Deloria, Vine, Jr., and Clifford Lytle. *The Nations Within: The Past and Future of American Indian Sovereignty.* New York: Pantheon Books, 1984.

Denson, Beasley. "The Passing of Chief." *Choctaw Community News* 40, no. 3 (2010): 1.

DeRosier, Arthur H., Jr. *The Removal of the Choctaw Indians.* Knoxville: University of Tennessee Press, 1970.

Dickson, Harris. *An Old-Fashioned Senator: A Story Biography of John Sharp Williams.* New York: Frederick Stokes Co., 1925.

Dittmer, John. *Local People: The Struggle for Civil Rights in Mississippi*. Urbana: University of Illinois Press, 1994.

Drinnon, Richard. *Keepers of Concentration Camps: Dillon S. Meyer and American Racism*. Berkeley: University of California Press, 1987.

Edmunds, David R. "Native Americans, New Voices: American Indian History, 1895–1995." *American Historical Review* 100 (1995): 717–40.

Edwards, Rebecca. *New Spirits: Americans in the Gilded Age, 1865–1905*. New York: Oxford University Press, 2006.

Ellis, Clyde. *To Change Them Forever: Indian Education at the Rainy Mountain Boarding School, 1893–1920*. Norman: University of Oklahoma Press, 1996.

Emmerich, J. Oliver. "Collapse and Recovery." In McLemore, *A History of Mississippi*, 2:97–119.

Farr, Eugene James. "Religious Assimilation, a Case Study: The Adoption of Christianity by the Choctaw Indians of Mississippi." ThD diss., New Orleans Baptist Theological Seminary, 1948.

Federal Writers' Project of the Works Progress Administration. *Mississippi: A Guide to the Magnolia State*, 2nd ed. New York: Viking Press, 1938, 1943.

Fields, Barbara J. "Ideology of Race in American History." In *Region, Race, and Reconstruction: Essays in Honor of C. Vann Woodward*, edited by J. Morgan Kousser and James McPherson, 143–78. New York: Oxford University Press, 1982.

Feldman, Glenn. *Politics, Society, and the Klan in Alabama, 1915–1949*. Tuscaloosa: University of Alabama Press, 1999.

Ferguson, Bob. "The Re-Establishment of Tribal Government: 50th Anniversary Ceremonies." Choctaw MS: Mississippi Band of Choctaw Indians, 1995.

Finger, John R. *Cherokee Americans: The Eastern Band of Cherokees in the Twentieth Century*. Lincoln: University of Nebraska, 1993.

———. *The Eastern Band of Cherokees, 1819–1900*. Knoxville: University of Tennessee Press, 1984.

Fite, Gilbert C. *Cotton Fields No More: Southern Agriculture, 1865–1980*. Lexington: University Press of Kentucky, 1984.

Fitzhugh, George. *Cannibals All! Or Slaves without Masters*. Richmond VA: A. Morris Publisher, 1857.

Fixico, Donald. "Federal and State Policies and American Indians." In *A Companion to American Indian History*, edited by Philip Deloria and Neal Salisbury, 379–96. Malden MA: Blackwell Publishing, 2004.

———. *Termination and Relocation: Federal Indian Policy, 1945–1960*. Albuquerque: University of New Mexico Press, 1986.

———. *The Urban Indian Experience in America*. Albuquerque: University of New Mexico Press, 2000.

Fowler, Loretta. *Arapahoe Politics, 1851–1978: Symbols in Crisis and Authority*. Lincoln: University of Nebraska Press, 1982.

————. *Tribal Sovereignty and the Historical Imagination: Cheyenne-Arapaho Politics.* Lincoln: University of Nebraska Press, 2002.

Fulkerson, Horace S. *Random Recollections of Early Days in Mississippi.* Vicksburg, 1885; reprint, Baton Rouge: Louisiana State University Press, 1937.

Garroutte, Eva Marie. *Real Indians: Identity and the Survival of Native America.* Berkeley: University of California Press, 2003.

Goldfield, David R. *Black, White, and Southern: Race Relations and Southern Culture, 1940 to the Present.* Baton Rouge: Louisiana State University Press, 1990.

Green, Elna C., ed. *The New Deal and Beyond: Social Welfare in the South since 1930.* Athens: University of Georgia Press, 2003.

Green, Rayna. "The Pocahontas Perplex: The Image of Indian Women in American Culture." *Massachusetts Historical Review* 16, no. 4 (1976): 698–714.

Hafen, Jane. "Gertrude Simmons Bonnin: For the Indian Cause." In Perdue, *Sifters: Native American Women's Lives,* 127–40.

Halbert, Henry S. "The Choctaw Creation Legend." *Publications of the Alabama Historical Society* 4 (1900b): 267–70.

————. "A Choctaw Migration Legend." *American Antiquarian and Oriental Journal* 16, no. 4 (1894): 215–16.

————. "The Choctaw Robin Goodfellow." *American Antiquarian and Oriental Journal* 17 (1895): 157.

————. "Courtship and Marriage among the Choctaws of Mississippi." *American Naturalist* 16 (1882): 222–24.

————. "Funeral Customs of the Mississippi Choctaws." *Publications of the Mississippi Historical Society* 3 (1900): 353–66.

————. "The Indians in Mississippi and Their Schools." In *Biennial Report of the State Superintendent of Public Education to the Legislature of Mississippi for Scholastic Years 1893–94 and 1894–95,* 534–45. Jackson MS: Clarion-Ledger Print, 1895.

————. "Indian Schools." In *Biennial Report of the State Superintendent of Public Education to the Legislature of Mississippi for Scholastic Years 1895–96 and 1897–98,* 23–30. Jackson MS: Clarion-Ledger Print, 1896.

————. "Indian Schools in Mississippi." In *Biennial Report of the State Superintendent of Public Education to the Legislature of Mississippi for Scholastic Years 1891–92 and 1892–93,* 574–75. Jackson MS: Clarion-Ledger Print, 1894.

————. "The Mississippi Choctaws." In *Biennial Report of the State Superintendent of Public Education to the Legislature of Mississippi for Scholastic Years 1897–98 and 1898–99,* 35–38. Jackson MS: Clarion-Ledger Print, 1896.

————. "Nanih Waiya, the Sacred Mound of the Choctaws." *Publications of the Mississippi Historical Society* 2 (1899): 223–34.

————. "Okla Hannali, or the Six Towns District of the Choctaws." *American Antiquarian and Oriental Journal* 15, no. 3 (1893): 146–49.

————. "Story of the Treaty of Dancing Rabbit Creek." *Publications of the Mississippi Historical Society* 6 (1902a): 373–402.

Harmon, Alexandra. *Indians in the Making: Ethnic Relations and Indian Identities around Puget Sound*. Berkeley: University of California Press, 1998.

———. *Rich Indians: Native People and the Problem of Wealth in American History*. Chapel Hill: University of North Carolina Press, 2010.

———. "Tribal Enrollment Councils: Lessons on Law and Indian Identity." *Western Historical Quarterly* 32 (2001): 175–200.

Harkin, Michael. "Staged Encounters: Postmodern Tourism and Aboriginal Peoples." *Ethnohistory* 50, no. 3 (2003): 575–85.

Harris, LaDonna. *LaDonna Harris: A Comanche Life*. Lincoln: University of Nebraska Press, 2006.

Harris, William C. *The Day of the Carpetbagger: Republican Reconstruction in Mississippi*. Baton Rouge: Louisiana State University Press, 1979.

Harrison, Pat. "The Mississippi Choctaw: Speech by the Hon. Pat Harrison of Mississippi in the House of Representatives, December 12, 1912." Washington DC: Government Printing Office, 1912.

Hastings, Victoria K. *Matrons and Maid: Regulating Indian Domestic Service in Tucson, 1914–1934*. Tucson: University of Arizona Press, 2012.

Hauptman, Lawrence. *The Iroquois and the New Deal*. Syracuse NY: Syracuse University Press, 1981.

Hodes, Martha. "The Mercurial Nature and Abiding Power of Race: A Transnational Story." *American Historical Review* 108, no. 1 (2003): 84–118.

Hoffschwelle, Mary. *Rebuilding the Rural Southern Community: Reformers, Schools, and Homes in Tennessee, 1900–1930*. Knoxville: University of Tennessee Press, 1998.

Hoikkala, Paivi. "Mothers and Community Builders: Salt River Pima and Maricopa Women in Community Action." In *Negotiators of Change: Historical Perspective on Native American Women*, edited by Nancy Shoemaker, 213–34. New York: Routledge, 1995.

Holmes, William F. *The White Chief: James Kimble Vardaman*. Baton Rouge: Louisiana State University Press, 1970.

Hornsby-Gutting, Angela M. "Manning the Region: New Approaches to Gender in the South." *Journal of Southern History* 75, no. 3 (2009): 663–76.

Hosmer, Brian, ed. *Native Americans and the Legacy of Harry S. Truman*. Kirksville MO: Truman State University Press, 2010.

Hosmer, Brian, and Colleen O'Neill, eds. *Native Pathways: American Indian Culture and Economic Development in the Twentieth Century*. Boulder: University Press of Colorado, 2004.

Hoxie, Frederick E. *A Final Promise: The Campaign to Assimilate the Indians, 1880–1920*. Lincoln: University of Nebraska Press, 1984.

———. "Missing the Point: Academic Experts and American Indian Politics." In Cobb and Fowler, *Beyond Red Power*, 16–32.

Iverson, Peter. "Building toward Self-Determination: Plains and Southwestern Indians in the 1940s and 1950s." *Western Historical Quarterly* 16, no. 2 (1985): 163–73.

Jacobs, Margaret D. *White Mother to a Dark Race: Settler Colonialism, Maternalism, and the Removal of Indigenous Children in the American West and Australia, 1880–1940.* Lincoln: University of Nebraska Press, 2009.

Jaimes, M. Annette. "Federal Indian Policy: A Usurpation of Indigenous Sovereignty in North America." In *The State of Native America: Genocide, Colonization, and Resistance,* edited by M. Annette Jaimes, 123–38. Boston: South End Press, 1992.

Johnson, Walter. "The Slave Trade, the White Slave, and the Politics of Racial Determination in the 1850s." *Journal of American History* 87, no. 1 (2000): 13–38.

Jolly, Helen Sue. "Selected Leaders in Mississippi Home Economics: An Historical Inquiry." PhD diss., Mississippi State University, 1995.

Jones, Jacqueline. "Labor and the Idea of Race in the American South." *Journal of Southern History* 75, no. 3 (2009): 613–26.

———. *Labor of Love, Labor of Sorrow: Black Women, Work, and the Family from Slavery to the Present.* New York: Basic Books, 1985.

Kappler, Charles J., ed. *Indian Affairs: Laws and Treaties,* vol. 2. Washington DC: Government Printing Office, 1982.

Keith, Jeanette. *Rich Man's War, Poor Man's Fight.* Chapel Hill: University of North Carolina Press, 2004.

Kelly, Lawrence C. *The Assault on Assimilation: John Collier and the Origins of Indian Policy Reform.* Albuquerque: University of New Mexico Press, 1983.

———. *The Navajo Indians and Federal Indian Policy, 1900–1935.* Tucson: University of Arizona Press, 1968.

Kersey, Harry Jr. *An Assumption of Sovereignty: Social and Political Transformation among the Florida Seminoles, 1953–1979.* Lincoln: University of Nebraska Press, 1996.

———. *The Florida Seminole and the New Deal, 1932–1945.* Gainesville: University Press of Florida, 1998.

———. *Pelts, Plumes and Hides: White Traders among the Seminole Indians, 1870–1930.* Gainesville: University Press of Florida, 1975.

Kidwell, Clara Sue. *Choctaws and Missionaries in Mississippi, 1818–1819.* Norman: University of Oklahoma Press, 1995.

———. *The Choctaws in Oklahoma: From Tribe to Nation, 1855–1970.* Norman: University of Oklahoma Press, 2007.

———. "The Choctaw Struggle for Land and Identity in Mississippi, 1830–1918." In Wells and Tubby, *After Removal: The Choctaw in Mississippi,* 64–93.

Kirwan, Albert D. *Revolt of the Rednecks: Mississippi Politics: 1876–1925.* Gloucester MA: Peter Smith, 1964.

Kolchin, Peter. "Whiteness Studies: The New History of Race in America." *Journal of American History* 89, no. 1 (2002): 154–73.

Knack, Martha C. *Boundaries Between: The Southern Paiutes, 1775–1995.* Lincoln: University of Nebraska Press, 2001.

Kramer, Rene Ann. *Cash, Color, and Colonialism: The Politics of Tribal Acknowledgement.* Norman: University of Oklahoma Press, 2005.

Krouse, Susan Applegate. *North American Indians in the Great War*. Lincoln: University of Nebraska Press, 2007.

Lambert, Valerie. *Choctaw Nation: A Story of American Indian Resurgence*. Lincoln: University of Nebraska Press, 2007.

Langford, Etha M. "A Study of the Educational Development of the Choctaw Indians in Mississippi." Master's thesis, University of Southern Mississippi, 1953.

Langford, Sister John Christopher, MSBT. "Holy Rosary Indian Mission: The Mississippi Choctaw and the Catholic Church." In Wells and Tubby, *After Removal: The Choctaw in Mississippi* 112–21.

Lawrence, Adrea. *Lessons from an Indian Day School: Negotiating Colonization in Northern New Mexico, 1902–1907*. Lawrence: University Press of Kansas, 2011.

Lerch, Patricia. *Waccamaw Legacy: Contemporary Indians Fight for Survival*. Tuscaloosa: University of Alabama Press, 2004.

Lincecum, Gideon. *Pushmataha: A Choctaw Leader and His People*. Tuscaloosa: University of Alabama Press, 2004.

Loewen, James. *Mississippi Chinese: Between Black and White*. Cambridge MA: Harvard University Press, 1971.

Locke, Victor Mural. "The Choctaw Catholic Catechism." *Indian Sentinel Quarterly* 1, no. 1 (1916): 21–22.

Lovett, Laura. "African and Cherokee by Choice: Race and Resistance under Legalized Segregation." In *Confounding the Color Line: The Indian-Black Experience in North America*, edited by James F. Brooks, 192–222. Lincoln: University of Nebraska Press, 2002.

Lowery, Malinda Maynor. *Lumbee Indians in the Jim Crow South: Race, Identity, and the Making of a Nation*. Chapel Hill: University of North Carolina Press, 2010.

Lomawaima, Tsianina K. *They Called It Prairie Light: The Story of Chilocco Indian School*. Lincoln: University of Nebraska Press, 1994.

Lurie, Nancy Oestreich. "Ada Deer: Champion of Tribal Sovereignty." In Perdue, *Sifters: Native American Women's Lives*, 223–41.

Maddox, Lucy. *Citizen Indians: Native American Intellectuals, Race, and Reform*. Ithaca NY: Cornell University Press, 2006.

Maillard, Kevin Noble. "The Pocahontas Exception: The Exemption of American Indian Ancestry from Racial Purity Law." *Michigan Journal of Race and Law* 12, no. 2 (2007): 351–86.

Mars, Florence. *Witness in Philadelphia*. Baton Rouge: Louisiana State University Press, 1977.

Martin, Joel. "My Grandmother Was a Cherokee Princess: Representations of Indians in Southern History." In *Dressing in Feathers: The Construction of the Indian in American Popular Culture*, edited by S. Elizabeth Bird, 120–47. Boulder CO: Westview Press, 1996.

Martin, Phillip, Lynne Jeter, and Kendall Blanshard. *Chief: The Autobiography of Chief Phillip Martin, Longtime Tribal Leader, Mississippi Band of Choctaw Indians*. Branson MS: Quail Ridge Press, 2009.

MacLean, Nancy. *Behind the Mask of Chivalry: The Making of the Second Ku Klux Klan*. New York: Oxford University Press, 1994.

McBride, Bunny. "Lucy Nicolar: The Artful Activism of a Penobscot Performer." In Perdue, *Sifters: Native American Women's Lives*, 141–59.

McCain, William D. "The Triumph of Democracy." In McLemore, *A History of Mississippi*, 2:59–96.

McLemore, Richard Aubrey, ed. *A History of Mississippi*. 2 vols. Hattiesburg: University and College Press of Mississippi, 1973.

McMillen, Neil. "Development of Civil Rights, 1956–1970." In McLemore, *A History of Mississippi*, 154–76.

Meyer, Melissa L. *The White Earth Tragedy: Ethnicity and Dispossession at a Minnesota Anishinaabe Reservation*. Lincoln: University of Nebraska Press, 1994.

———. "American Indian Blood Quantum Requirements: Blood Is Thicker than Family." In *Over the Edge: Remapping the American West*, edited by Valerie J. Matsumoto and Blake Allmendinger, 231–51. Berkeley: University of California Press, 1998.

Meyerowitz, Joanne. "Beyond the Feminine Mystique." In *Not June Cleaver: Women and Gender in Postwar America, 1945–1960*, edited by Joanne Meyerowitz, 233–63. Philadelphia: Temple University Press, 1994.

Miles, Tiya. *Ties that Bind: The Story of an Afro-Cherokee Family in Slavery and Freedom*. Berkeley: University of California Press, 2005.

Mississippi, State of. House. *Journal of the House of the State of Mississippi, 1882*. Jackson MS: J. L. Power State Printer, 1882.

Mississippi, State of. Senate. *Journal of the Senate of the State of Mississippi, 1882*. Jackson MS: J. L. Power State Printer, 1882.

Mississippi Band of Choctaw Indians (MBCI). *Chahta Hapia Hoke: We Are Choctaw*. Philadelphia MS: Mississippi Band of Choctaw Indians, 1981.

"The Mississippi Claim, January 21, 1914." Judd and Detweiler Inc. Printers, 1914.

Mississippi Federation of Women's Clubs. *The Mississippi Federation of Women's Clubs*. Jackson MS: Mississippi Federation of Women's Clubs, 1950.

Mississippi Historical Society. "The Mississippi Constitution of 1832." In *Mississippi History Now*, http://mshistory.k12.ms.us/articles/101/the-mississippi-constitution-of-1832.

Morgan, Chester M. *Redneck Liberal: Theodore G. Bilbo and the New Deal*. Baton Rouge: Louisiana State University Press, 1985.

Montgomery, Robert Lynn, and Nigel Elmore. *Register to the Papers of Henry Bascom Collins*. Smithsonian Institution: National Anthropological Archives, 1992.

Moore, Danny Blair. "'Window to the World': Educating Rural Women in Mississippi, 1911–1965." PhD diss., Mississippi State University, 1991.

Mould, Tom. *Choctaw Prophecy: A Legacy of the Future.* Tuscaloosa: University of Alabama Press, 2003.

Murray, Pauli. *States' Laws on Race and Color.* Athens: University of Georgia Press, 1997.

Nagel, Joanne. *American Indian Ethnic Renewal: Red Power and the Resurgence of Identity and Culture.* New York: Oxford University Press, 1996.

Naylor, Celia E. *African Cherokees in Indian Territory: From Chattel to Citizens.* John Hope Franklin Series in African American History and Culture. Chapel Hill: University of North Carolina Press, 2008.

Novak, William J. "The Legal Transformation of Citizenship in Nineteenth-Century America." In *The Democratic Experiment: New Directions in American Political History,* edited by Meg Jacobs, William Novak, and Julian E. Zelizer, 84–119. Princeton NJ: Princeton University Press, 2003.

Oakley, Christopher Arris. *Keeping the Circle: American Indian Identity in Eastern North Carolina, 1885–2004.* Lincoln: University of Nebraska Press, 2005.

———. "'When Carolina Indians Went on the Warpath': The Media, the Klan, and the Lumbees of North Carolina." *Southern Cultures* 14, no. 4 (2008): 55–84.

O'Brien, Greg. *Choctaws in a Revolutionary Age, 1750–1830.* Lincoln: University of Nebraska Press, 2002.

Olmsted, Frederick Law. *A Journey in the Back Country.* New York: Schocken Books, 1970.

Olsen, Christopher J. *Political Culture and Secession in Mississippi: Masculinity, Honor, and the Antiparty Tradition, 1830–1860.* New York: Oxford University Press, 2000.

O'Neill, Colleen. *Working the Navajo Way: Labor and Culture in the Twentieth Century.* Lawrence: University Press of Kansas, 2005.

Osborn, George C. *John Sharp Williams: Planter-Statesman of the Deep South.* Gloucester MA: P. Smith, 1964.

Osburn, Katherine M. B. "'Any Sane Person': Race, Rights, and Tribal Sovereignty in the Construction of the Dawes Rolls for the Choctaw Nation." *Journal of the Gilded Age and Progressive Era* 9, no. 4 (2010): 451–71.

———. "Mississippi Choctaws and Racial Politics." *Southern Cultures* 14, no. 4 (2008): 32–54.

———. *Southern Ute Women: Autonomy and Assimilation on the Reservation, 1887–1934.* 2nd ed. Lincoln: University of Nebraska Press, 2008.

Painter, Nell Irvin. *Standing at Armageddon: The United States, 1877–1919.* New York: W. W. Norton, 1988.

Paredes, J. Anthony, ed. *Indians of the Southeastern United States in the Late 20th Century.* Tuscaloosa: University of Alabama Press, 1992.

Parman, Donald. *The Navajos and the New Deal.* New Haven CT: Yale University Press, 1976.

Pascoe, Peggy. "Miscegenation Law, Court Cases, and Ideologies of 'Race' in Twentieth-Century America." *Journal of American History* 83, no. 1 (1996): 44–69.

Payne, Charles. *I've Got the Light of Freedom: The Organizing Tradition and the Mississippi Freedom Struggle*. Berkeley: University of California Press, 1995.

Peiss, Kathy. *Hope in a Jar: The Making of America's Beauty Culture*. New York: Holt Paperbacks, 1999.

Percy, William Alexander. *Lanterns on the Levee*. New York: Alfred A. Knopf, 1950.

Peterson, John H., Jr. "Assimilation, Separation, and Out-Migration in an American Indian Group." *American Anthropologist* 74 (October 1972): 1286–95.

———."Choctaw Self-Determination in the 1980s." In *Indians of the Southeastern United States in the Late 20th Century*, 140–61. Tuscaloosa: University of Alabama Press, 1992.

———. "The Mississippi Band of Choctaw Indians: Their Recent History and Current Relations." PhD diss., University of Georgia, 1970.

———. *Socio-Economic Characteristics of the Mississippi Choctaw Indians*, Report 34, Education Series 9. Starkville MS: Social Science Research Center of Mississippi State University, 1970.

Perdue, Theda. "The Legacy of Indian Removal." *Journal of Southern History* 78, no. 1 (2012): 3–36.

———. *"Mixed Blood" Indians: Racial Construction in the Early South*. Athens: University of Georgia Press, 2005.

———. "Native Americans, African Americans, and Jim Crow." In *indiVisible: African-Native American Lives in the Americas*, edited by Gabrielle Tayac, 21–33. Washington DC: Smithsonian Institution, National Museum of the American Indian, 2009.

———, ed. *Sifters: Native American Women's Lives*. New York: Oxford University Press, 2001.

Philp, Kenneth R. *Indian Self Rule: First-Hand Accounts of Indian-White Relations from Roosevelt to Reagan*. Salt Lake City UT: Howe Brothers, 1986.

———. *John Collier's Crusade for Indian Reform, 1920–1954*. Tucson: University of Arizona Press, 1977.

———. *Termination Revisited: American Indians on the Trail to Self-Determination, 1933–1953*. Lincoln: University of Nebraska Press, 1999.

Prucha, Francis Paul. *The Great Father: The United States Government and the American Indians*, vols. 1 and 2. Unabridged. Lincoln: University of Nebraska Press, 1995.

Quin, Percy. "Speech of Percy E. Quin of Mississippi in the House of Representatives, February 5, 1916." Washington DC: Government Printing Office, 1916.

Raibmon, Paige. *Authentic Indians: Episodes of Encounter from the Late-Nineteenth-Century Northwest Coast*. Durham NC: Duke University Press: 2005.

Ramirez, Renya K. *Native Hubs: Culture, Community, and Belonging in Silicon Valley and Beyond*. Durham NC: Duke University Press, 2007.

Rand, Clayton. *Ink on My Hands*. New York: Carrick and Evans, 1940.

Reeves, John T., Special Superintendent of the Indian Service. "On Need of Additional Land and School Facilities for the Indians Living in the State of Mississippi," presented to the Committee on Indian Affairs, December 7, 1916, H. Doc. 1464, 64th Cong., 2nd sess. (1916–17).

Rice, Arnold S. *The Ku Klux Klan in American Politics*. Washington DC: Public Affairs Press, 1962.

Riley, Franklin L. "Choctaw Land Claims." *Publications of the Mississippi Historical Society* 8 (1904): 345–95.

Rosen, Deborah E. *American Indians and State Law: Sovereignty, Race, and Citizenship, 1790–1880*. Lincoln: University of Nebraska Press, 2007.

Rosenthal, Nicolas G. "Beyond the New Indian History: Recent Trends in the Historiography on Native Peoples of North America." *History Compass* 4/5 (2006): 962–74.

———. *Reimagining Indian Country: Native American Migration and Identity in Twentieth-Century Los Angeles*. Seattle: University of Washington Press, 2007.

Rosier, Paul C. *Rebirth of the Blackfoot Nation, 1912–1954*. Lincoln: University of Nebraska Press, 2004.

Roth, George. "Overview of Southeastern Tribes Today." In Paredes, *Indians of the Southeastern United States in the Late 20th Century*, 183–202.

Rowland, Dunbar. *History of Mississippi: The Heart of the South*, vol. 2. Chicago: S. J. Clarke Publishing Company, 1925.

Roundtree, Helen. "The Indians of Virginia: A Third Race in a Biracial State." In Williams, *Southeastern Indians since the Removal Era*, 27–48.

Satz, Ronald N. "The Mississippi Choctaw: From the Removal Treaty to the Federal Agency." In Wells and Tubby, *After Removal: The Choctaw in Mississippi* 3–32.

Saunt, Claudio. *A New Order of Things: Property, Power, and the Transformation of the Creek Indians, 1733–1816*. Cambridge: Cambridge University Press, 1999.

———. *Black, White, and Indian: Race and the Unmaking of an American Family*. New York: Oxford University Press, 2005.

———. "Telling Stories: The Political Uses of Myth and History in the Cherokee and Creek Nations." *Journal of American History* 93, no. 3 (2006): 673–697.

Sawyer, Charles A. "The Choctaw Indians of Mississippi, Parts One and Two." *Twin Territories* 4, no. 6 (1902): 160–64; and 4, no. 7 (1902): 205–11.

Scarborough, William K. "Heartland of the Cotton Kingdom." In McLemore, *A History of Mississippi*, 1:310–51.

Service, Elman R. *Primitive Social Organization: An Evolutionary Perspective*. New York: Random House, 1962.

Shoemaker, Nancy. *A Strange Likeness: Becoming Red and White in Eighteenth-Century North America*. Oxford: Oxford University Press, 2004.

Shreve, Bradley G. *Red Power Rising: The National Indian Youth Council and the Origins of Native Activism*. Norman: University of Oklahoma Press, 2011.

Simms, William Gilmore. "Oakatibbe, or the Choctaw Sampson." In Simms, *The Wigwam and the Cabin*, 176–208. New York: Wiley and Putnam, 1845.

————. *The Yemassee: A Romance of Carolina*. New York: Harper and Brothers, 1844.

Skates, John Jay, Jr. "World War II and Its Effects." In McLemore, *A History of Mississippi*, 2:120–39.

Smith, Sherry L. *Reimagining Indians: Native Americans through Anglo Eyes, 1880–1940*. New York: Oxford University Press, 2000.

Spann, Major S. G. "Choctaw Indians as Confederate Soldiers." *Confederate Magazine* 13, no. 12 (1905): 560–61.

Spruhan, Paul. "Indian as Race/Indian as Political Status: Implementation of the Half Blood Requirement under the Indian Reorganization Act, 1934–1945." *Rutgers Race and the Law Review* 8 (2006): 27–49.

Stock, Catherine McNicol, and Robert D. Johnston, eds. *The Countryside in the Age of the Modern State: Political Histories of Rural America*. Ithaca NY: Cornell University Press, 2001.

Stocking, George W. *Race, Culture, and Evolution: Essays in the History of Anthropology*. Chicago: University of Chicago Press. 1982.

Straus, Terry, ed. *Native Chicago*. 2nd ed. Chicago: American Indian Center of Chicago, 2002.

Strong, Pauline Turner, and Barrik Van Winkle. "'Indian Blood': Reflections on the Reckoning and Refiguring of Native North American Identity." *Cultural Anthropology* 11, no. 4 (1996): 547–76.

Stuart, John. *A Sketch of the Cherokee and Choctaw Indians*. Little Rock: Woodruff and Few, 1837.

Sturm, Circe. *Blood Politics: Race, Culture, and Identity in the Cherokee Nation of Oklahoma*. Berkeley: University of California Press, 2002.

Swanton, John R. *Source Material for the Social and Ceremonial Life of the Choctaw Indians*. Bulletin No. 103. Washington DC: Government Printing Office, 1931.

TallBear, Kim. "DNA, Blood, and Racializing the Tribe." *Wicazo Sa Review* (Spring 2003): 81–107.

Taylor, Graham D. *The New Deal and American Indian Tribalism: The Administration of the Indian Reorganization Act, 1934–1945*. Lincoln: University of Nebraska Press, 1980.

Thompson, Bobby, and John H. Peterson Jr. "Mississippi Choctaw Identity: Genesis and Change." In *The New Ethnicity: Perspectives from Ethnology*, edited by John W. Bennett, 189–92. Minneapolis: West Publishing Company, 1975.

Thrush, Coll. *Native Seattle: Histories from the Crossing Over Place*. Chapel Hill: University of North Carolina Press, 2012.

Tolbert, Charles M. "A Sociological Study of the Choctaws in Mississippi." PhD diss., Louisiana State University, 1958.

Trachtenberg, Alan. *The Incorporation of America: Culture and Society in the Gilded Age*. New York: Hill and Wang, 1982.

————. *Shades of Hiawatha: Staging Indians, Making Americans, 1880–1930*. New York: Hill and Wang, 2004.

U.S. Congress. House. "An Agreement with the Choctaw and Chickasaw Tribes of Indians, March 27, 1902." H. Doc. 512, 57th Cong., 1st sess. (1902).

———. "Application for Indemnity, For Being Deprived by Settlers of Reservations of the Choctaw Indians," February 1, 1836. H. Doc. 1415, 24th Cong., 2nd sess. (1836).

———. "Choctaw Indians of Mississippi, April 15, 1936." H. Rep. 2415, 74th Cong., 2nd sess. (1936).

———. "Condition of the MS Choctaws, Union MS, March 16, 1917." In *Hearings Before the Committee on Investigation of the Indian Service, March 12–14, 1917*, vol. 1. Washington DC: Government Printing Office, 1917.

———. "Petition of the Citizens of the State of Mississippi Remonstrating against Indian Claims," February 1, 1836. H. Doc. 89, 24th Cong., 1st sess. (1837).

———. "Petition of the Mississippi Choctaws," February 13, 1900. H. Doc. 426, 56th Cong., 1st sess. (1900).

———. "Memorial of the Choctaw and Chickasaw Nations Relative to the Rights of the Mississippi Choctaws, Submitted for Consideration in Connection with H.R. 19213." Washington DC: Government Printing Office, 1913.

———. "Memorial of the Choctaw Indians," February 1, 1836. H.R. Doc. 119, 24th Cong., 1st sess. (1836).

———. "Memorial of the Legislature of the State of Mississippi upon the Subject of Lands Acquired by Treaty from the Choctaw Nation of Indians." H.R. Doc. 75, 22nd Cong., 1st sess. (1832), microfiche 217.

———. "Report and Statement of the Subcommittee on Indian Affairs," January 10, 1913. 62nd Cong., 3rd sess. (1913), microfiche group 2, SUDOC: Y4In2/1:D19/2.

U.S. Congress. House Committee on Indian Affairs. *Hearings on Enrollment in the Five Civilized Tribes*, April–August 1913. 63rd Cong., 2nd sess. (1913), microfiche group 1A, SUDOC: Y4.In2/1:F58/3.

———. "Land Claims &c. Under 14th Article Choctaw Treaty," May 11, 1836. H. Rep. 663, 24th Cong., 1st sess. (1836), microfiche 295.

———. "Treaty Rights of Mississippi Choctaws," January 29, 1901. H. Rep. 2522, 59th Cong., 2nd sess. (1907).

U.S. Congress. Senate. "Claims of the Choctaw Indians of Mississippi, May 13, 1935," S. Rep. 781, 74th Cong., 1st sess. (1935).

———. *Journal of the Proceedings at the Treaty of Dancing Rabbit Creek*. S. Doc. 512, 21st Cong., 1st sess. (1830).

———. "Memorial of the Delegates and Representatives of the Choctaw Nation of Indians," March 18, 1856. S. Misc. Doc. 31, 34th Cong., 1st sess. (1856), microfiche 835.

———. "Message of the President of the United States Transmitting the Correspondence in Relation to the Proceedings and Conduct of the Choctaw Commission under the Treaty of Dancing Rabbit Creek," January 30, 1844. S. Doc. 168, 28th Cong., 1st sess. (1844), microfiche 433.

———. "Petition of a Number of Citizens of Mississippi Praying Congress to Institute into the Claims of Choctaw Indians to Reservations under the Treaty of

Dancing Rabbit Creek," January 21, 1837. S. Doc. 91, 24th Cong., 2nd sess. (1837).

———. "Rights of the Mississippi Choctaws in the Choctaw Nation, Memorial of the Full-Blood Mississippi Choctaws Relative to their Rights in the Choctaw Nation," April 21, 1902. S. Doc. 319, 57th Cong., 1st sess. (1901–2).

———. "Survey of Conditions of the Indians in the United States." In *Hearings before the Subcommittee on Indian Affairs*, 71st Cong., 3rd sess., pt. 16 (1930–31). Washington DC: Government Printing Office, 1931.

Usner, Daniel H., Jr. "Images of Lower Mississippi Valley Indians." In Usner, *American Indians in the Lower Mississippi Valley: Social and Economic Histories*, 128–37. Lincoln: University of Nebraska Press, 1998.

———. *Indian Work: Language and Livelihood in Native American History.* Cambridge MA: Harvard University Press, 2009.

Watkins, Esther Belle. "Some Social and Economic Aspects of Antebellum Neshoba County." Master's thesis, University of Alabama, 1942.

Watkins, John A. "The Choctaws in Mississippi." *American Antiquarian and Oriental Journal* 16, no. 2 (1894): 69–77.

Wells, Samuel J. "The Role of Mixed-Bloods in Mississippi Choctaw History." In Wells and Tubby, *After Removal: The Choctaw in Mississippi*, 42–55.

Wells, Samuel J., and Roseanna Tubby, eds. *After Removal: The Choctaw in Mississippi.* Jackson: University Press of Mississippi, 1986.

White, Benton R., and Christine Schultz White. "Phillip Martin: Mississippi Choctaw." In *The New Warriors: Native American Leaders Since 1900*, edited by R. David Edmunds, 195–209. Lincoln: University of Nebraska Press, 2001.

White, Richard. *"It's Your Misfortune and None of My Own": A New History of the American West.* Norman: University of Oklahoma Press, 1991.

Whitehead, Don. *Attack on Terror: The FBI against the Ku Klux Klan in Mississippi.* New York: Funk and Wagnalls, 1970.

Wilkinson, Charles F. *American Indians, Time, and the Law: Native Societies in a Modern Constitutional Democracy.* New Haven CT: Yale University Press, 1987.

Williams, Carol, ed. *Indigenous Women and Work: From Labor to Activism.* Urbana: University of Illinois Press, 2012.

Williams, Robert A., Jr. *Linking Arms Together: American Indian Treaty Visions of Law and Peace, 1600–1800.* New York: Routledge, 1999.

Williams, Walter L., ed. *Southeastern Indians since the Removal Era.* Athens: University of Georgia Press, 1979.

Williamson, Joel. *The Crucible of Race: Black-White Relations in the American South since Emancipation.* New York: Oxford University Press, 1984.

Wilson, Charles Reagan. *Baptized in Blood: The Religion of the Lost Cause, 1865–1920.* Athens: University of Georgia Press, 1980.

Winston, E. T. *The Story of Pontotoc*, pt. 2. Pontotoc MS: Pontotoc Progress Print, 1931.

Winter, William F. "New Directions in Politics, 1948–1956." In McLemore, *A History of Mississippi*, 2:140–54.

Woodruff, Nan. *American Congo: The African American Freedom Struggle in the Delta*. Cambridge MA: Harvard University Press, 2003.

Yarbrough, Fay A. *Race and the Cherokee Nation: Sovereignty in the Nineteenth Century*. Philadelphia: University of Pennsylvania Press, 2007.

Yates, Jenelle, B., and Theresa T. Rideout, eds. *Red Clay Hills of Neshoba: Roots, Reflections, Ramblings*. Philadelphia MS: Neshoba County Library, 1992.

Young, Mary Elizabeth. *Redskins, Ruffleshirts, and Rednecks: Indian Allotments in Alabama and Mississippi, 1830–1860*. Norman: University of Oklahoma Press, 1961.

Index

Page numbers of illustrations are in italic.

Choctaw Resurgence in Mississippi:
Race, Class, and Nation Building
in the Jim Crow South, 1830–1977
By Katherine M. B. Osburn

Cherokee Women:
Gender and Culture Change, 1700–1835
By Theda Perdue

The Brainerd Journal:
A Mission to the Cherokees, 1817–1823
Edited and introduced by Joyce B. Phillips
and Paul Gary Phillips

Seminole Voices: Reflections on
Their Changing Society, 1970–2000
By Julian M. Pleasants
and Harry A. Kersey Jr.

The Yamasee War: A Study of Culture,
Economy, and Conflict in the Colonial South
By William L. Ramsey

The Cherokees: A Population History
By Russell Thornton

Buffalo Tiger: A Life in the Everglades
By Buffalo Tiger and Harry A. Kersey Jr.

American Indians in the Lower Mississippi
Valley: Social and Economic Histories
By Daniel H. Usner Jr.

William Bartram on the Southeastern Indians
Edited and annotated
by Gregory A. Waselkov
and Kathryn E. Holland Braund

Powhatan's Mantle:
Indians in the Colonial Southeast
Edited by Peter H. Wood, Gregory A.
Waselkov, and M. Thomas Hatley

Creeks and Seminoles: The Destruction
and Regeneration of the Muscogulge People
By J. Leitch Wright Jr.

To order or obtain more information on these or other
University of Nebraska Press titles, visit www.nebraskapress.unl.edu.

CPSIA information can be obtained
at www.ICGtesting.com
Printed in the USA
LVHW040022290720
661757LV00002B/167